# OPC Unified Architecture

Wolfgang Mahnke • Stefan-Helmut Leitner •
Matthias Damm

# OPC Unified Architecture

Wolfgang Mahnke
Stefan-Helmut Leitner
ABB Forschungszentrum
Ladenburg
Wallstadter Str. 59
68526 Ladenburg
Germany
wolfgang.mahnke@de.abb.com
stefan.leitner@de.abb.com

Matthias Damm
ascolab GmbH
Automation Systems
Communication Lab.
Am Weichselgarten 7
91058 Erlangen
Germany

ISBN 978-3-642-08842-1        e-ISBN 978-3-540-68899-0

DOI 10.1007/978-3-540-68899-0

*Cover design*: KüenkelLopka GmbH

Printed on acid-free paper

9 8 7 6 5 4 3 2 1

springer.com

# Foreword by Tom Burke

The OPC Foundation is very honored to endorse this superior book and the excellent work that the authors have put together. This book provides a solid framework of understanding about the OPC Foundation specifications and technology from the beginning of OPC up through and including the most important OPC inter-operability standard, that being the OPC Unified Architecture.

The authors of this book, I have been pleased to know for many years, clearly are the architectural and development leaders who have enabled OPC to be so widely successful. The readers of this book are fortunate to be able to learn from the experts who actually developed the OPC Foundation Unified Architecture specifications and technology.

The OPC Unified Architecture was developed by over 30 companies over approximately 5 years. Complete reference implementations and technology were developed to validate the specifications and prove the technical feasibility. The purpose of the OPC Unified Architecture was to enable a platform-independent interoperability standard for moving data/information between the factory floor and the enterprise. During the course of the development it was obvious that the OPC Unified Architecture was well positioned to expand beyond industrial auto-mation. OPC has expanded into areas of building automation, security, home automation, power generation, packaging, and petrochemicals. Because of the highly scalable architecture of OPC UA, it is also well-positioned for deployment in intelligent embedded devices.

OPC UA is a collaborative effort with other standards organizations as well. OPC UA is also built on the premise of do not reinvent technology that already exists. OPC pulls all the pieces together as necessary for true secure reliable inter-operability.

This book provides you a solid foundation to learn everything you could ever want to know about developing world-class products for multi-vendor interopera-bility based on OPC UA.

The OPC Foundation is proud to recognize the achievements and quality work that the authors have put together in developing and assembling this book. I encourage you to read this book multiple times and use it as a constant preference as you develop or use OPC-based products in your respective domain. You as a reader are very fortunate to have obtained this book.

I encourage you to constantly refer and take advantage of this book for all your OPC needs.

Tom Burke
President and Executive Director OPC Foundation

# Foreword by Jim Luth

More than 5 years in the making, OPC Unified Architecture represents a revolutionary step forward for vendors wishing to write software that interoperates with others. A group of dedicated volunteer members of the OPC Foundation contributed countless hours to complete this ambitious endeavor. By combining the tried and true functionality of the previous generation of OPC Interfaces along with the latest advances in computer science (e.g., Object Oriented Programming, Service Oriented Architecture, the Semantic Web, Network Model Databases), OPC UA represents a generic framework for exposing and consuming data and metadata of any complexity.

In the mid-nineties, the OPC Foundation published its first Microsoft COM specification for Data Access (DA) that specified how a server would expose a simple hierarchical organization of items (tags) that could be read, written, and subscribed to by conformant clients. The Foundation quickly followed up with additional popular specifications for different types of data, in particular, Alarms & Events and Historical Data. With the invention of XML Web Services and the promise of vendor neutral communication, the Foundation created XML-DA, a platform independent Web Service interface for Data Access with similar functionality as the original COM version. Unfortunately, the performance of the Web Service version was orders of magnitude slower than the COM version, so XML-DA could not be viewed as a newer and better replacement for the platform specific COM version. The OPC Unified Architecture was born out of the desire to create a true replacement for all of the existing COM-based specifications without losing any features (or performance) in the process. Here are some of the design goals of OPC UA:

- Support a wider range of applications that use complex instead of simple data (MES, ERP, Asset Management...).
- Allow Data Access, Alarms & Events, and Historical data to be exposed using a single set of generic, data-agnostic Services.
- Allow the nodes in the address space to be connected in hierarchies and non-hierarchical "meshes."
- Future-proof the specifications by making them abstract and not dependent on existing communication technologies.
- Specify concrete data serializations and protocol mappings using accepted internet standards (Web Services, XML, HTTP, TCP ...)
- Allow rich metadata to be exposed (the same way the data itself is), so that generic clients can interpret data without a priori knowledge.

All these goals and more have been realized in OPC UA. We now have implementable specifications, communication stacks, and SDKs in multiple programming languages and higher level third-party toolkits. We now invite the rest of the world to go forth and create software applications that interoperate at the highest possible semantic levels using OPC UA.

With the reach-for-the-stars design goals and the huge scope of OPC UA, the specifications, currently comprised of 13 Parts and climbing, while terse, dense, and exact, are not the easiest way for developers and architects to approach OPC UA. I like to use the corollary to SQL. There are thousands of software developers skilled at developing SQL applications, yet most have never read the SQL specifications. They learned SQL by reading books, studying vendor documentation, taking classes, etc. This book, written by key authors and contributors to the OPC UA specification and coding effort, represents the best way to learn and use OPC UA in your programming and design tasks.

Jim Luth
Technical Director OPC Foundation

# Preface

## Motivation for This Book

The OPC Foundation provides specifications for data exchange in industrial automation. There is a long history of COM/DCOM-based specifications, most prominent OPC Data Access (DA), OPC Alarms and Events (A&E), and OPC Historical Data Access (HDA), which are widely accepted in the industry and implemented by almost every system targeting industrial automation.

Now the OPC Foundation has released a new generation of OPC specifications called OPC Unified Architecture (OPC UA). With OPC UA, the OPC Foundation fulfills a technology shift from the retiring COM/DCOM technology to a service-oriented architecture providing data in a platform-independent manner via Web Services or its own optimized TCP-based protocol. OPC UA unifies the previous specifications into one single address space capable of dealing with current data, alarms and events and the history of current data as well as the event history. A remarkable enhancement of OPC UA is the Address Space Model by which vendors can expose a rich and extensible information model using object-oriented techniques. OPC UA scales well from intelligent devices, controllers, DCS, and SCADA systems up to MES and ERP systems. It also scales well in its ability to provide information; on the lower end, a model similar to Classic OPC can be used, providing only base information, while at the upper end, highly sophisticated models can be described, providing a large amount of metadata including complex type hierarchies.

There is a high interest in the advanced modeling capabilities in many domains and there are already initiatives to standardize information models based on OPC UA. Examples of these activities are FDI where a common field device description is targeted and common activities with MIMOSA (Maintenance Information – ERP and above), S95 (Production Information – MES), and PLCopen (Industrial Control).

The OPC UA specification currently consists of 13 parts and therefore 13 documents, some specifying the base technology and others defining specific information models. An example is a model describing how to provide process automation-specific alarm information. All in all, there are over 700 pages of specification, written to be accurate and complete. The specification primarily defines how to do things and to a lesser extent explains why it was designed that way. This is the way specifications have to be written to be widely applied by many developers and to guarantee interoperability between different applications. As a result, the OPC UA specification is hard to read for someone new to OPC UA. This is also true of other specifications such as SQL or UML.

With this book, we want to fill this gap and provide an easy to understand introduction to OPC UA. We will not provide the same level of detail as the specification, but rather introduce and explain the main concepts of OPC UA. We will give guidelines that help you in determining the best alternative among different concepts for your use cases and requirements. We will also target relevant topics that are not directly addressed in the specification but are needed to apply OPC UA.

## Who Should Read This Book?

If you are interested in the OPC Unified Architecture – and that is probably the reason why you are reading this text – you should read this book. It is written by the editors of the key parts of the OPC UA specification, and they will explain to you what is behind the acronym OPC UA.

We had a broad audience in mind when writing this book, including people with the following tasks:

- Judging whether OPC UA should be applied in their applications (decision makers)
- Applying OPC UA in their client or server applications (software architects, engineers, and developers)
- Using applications based on OPC UA (administrators and engineers, e.g., responsible for configuring a process control system; not end users such as operators of a process control system).

This book will introduce the communication and information modeling concepts of OPC UA. It will explain how to define your model and how to access the data. You will learn how redundancy, security, and more are addressed in OPC UA and how well it performs compared to Classic OPC. However, you will not find any code examples. When you implement your OPC UA application, it is expected that you will use an SDK and you should look into the documentation of such an SDK for coding examples. This book explains how the mechanisms behind any OPC UA SDK – the OPC UA Services – work and how to model your information in OPC UA. It also explains the information you can expect when accessing an OPC UA server.

You do not have to be familiar with Classic OPC to read this book. You should have a basic understanding of object-oriented concepts in order to understand the information modeling. Some basic knowledge of software architecture is needed to understand the underlying architecture of OPC UA.

## Outline

Chapter 1 gives a short introduction into Classic OPC before starting with the motivation for OPC UA and giving a short overview of OPC UA.

The next three chapters focus on information modeling, that is, how data can be represented using OPC UA. Chapter 2 introduces the modeling concepts. We start with the fundamental concepts to provide data, and later introduce more sophisticated constructs such as type hierarchies. Chapter 3 introduces a real-life example of how to model information in OPC UA and then generalizes modeling by explaining some best practices. Standard information models are introduced in Chap. 4. Starting by explaining what an information model is and how it can be specified as well as how OPC UA deals with information models. Continuing, the base OPC UA information model is introduced followed by more specialized information model extensions of the OPC UA specification. Finally, we will look at the current state of additional information model standards provided by other organizations.

The next two chapters focus on the way how to access the information modeled in OPC UA. In Chap. 5, the abstract Services are described, which are used to access or manipulate data. In Chap. 6, the mapping of those Services to concrete technology is introduced. It is described how data is serialized, how messages are secured, and what transport protocol is used.

In Chap. 7, the security considerations of OPC UA are discussed. This includes the theoretical thoughts behind the security model of OPC UA as well as the practical implications for developers and administrators of OPC UA applications.

Chapter 8 explains the application architecture of OPC UA. Here, the different components needed to implement OPC UA are introduced.

In Chap. 9, the system architecture of OPC UA is described. Included are descriptions of how you can deploy and configure OPC UA applications in your systems, and how to handle redundancy, aggregation of servers, etc.

In the next chapters, we focus on migration of existing applications to OPC UA. In Chap. 10 we explain how concepts of Classic OPC map to the concepts of OPC UA. This chapter is especially useful for readers having a deep knowledge of Classic OPC. Chapter 11 provides strategies of how to migrate your Classic OPC applications to OPC UA and how components, provided by the OPC Foundation, can help you in this effort.

OPC UA specifies a large number of features, but not every application will make use of all of them. OPC UA provides profiles to deal with this fact. Profiles specify a subset of features a product ensures to support. Applications exchange these profiles to know what they can expect from the other application. Details on profiles and how they are organized are described in Chap. 12.

Performance is a critical factor in the scenarios where Classic OPC is typically used today. In Chap. 13, performance considerations of OPC UA are given. This includes a comparison of OPC UA performance to Classic OPC.

We close with Chap. 14 where we summarize OPC UA and discuss the complexity of OPC UA, pointing out that it is simple in most cases and explain why some parts must have some complexity. We also provide an outlook of what we expect to happen in the near future regarding OPC UA.

In addition, some Appendices provide a quick reference when you need to find some details of OPC UA.

# About the Authors

### Dr. Wolfgang Mahnke

Wolfgang Mahnke works at the ABB Corporate Research Center in Germany in the field of Industrial Software Technology. In recent years, he has been the project leader of several projects related to the OPC Unified Architecture. Those projects target the specification of OPC UA, the implementation of the infrastructure provided by the OPC Foundation as well as the application of OPC UA inside ABB, for example, in ABB's major DCS 800xA. He is editor of the Address Space Model and the Information Model parts of the OPC UA specification and has conducted several OPC UA training sessions and given several presentations over the last years.

Wolfgang holds a Diploma in Computer Science from the University of Stuttgart. During his work at the University of Kaiserslautern he gained his Ph.D. in the area of Databases and Information Systems.

### Stefan-Helmut Leitner

Stefan-Helmut Leitner works at the ABB Corporate Research Center in Germany in the area of Industrial Software Technologies. He has been involved in various research and development topics regarding OPC Unified Architecture inside and outside ABB, such as the development of the ANSI-C protocol stack, certificate management for OPC UA, and held several trainings and presentations. In addition, he has the editing responsibility for the Security Model part of the OPC UA specification.

Stefan-Helmut holds a Diploma in Information Technology from the University of Corporate Education Mannheim.

**Matthias Damm**

Matthias Damm is Executive Director and founder of ascolab, where he is responsible for OPC consulting and certification. Since the last 10 years, he has been actively involved in OPC work especially in the areas of compliance testing and OPC Unified Architecture.

Before founding ascolab, Matthias worked as manager of the OPC competence centre in the Siemens division Industrial Services and Solutions.

Matthias is manager of the OPC Foundation Certification Test Lab at ascolab and his team is responsible for the development and maintenance of the OPC Foundation Compliance Test Tools since several years.

He is editor of the Service part of the OPC UA specification and has conducted OPC UA training sessions and given several presentations over the last years. He was involved in the design of the portable ANSI C UA Stack developed by ascolab that was donated to the OPC Foundation. He was was also responsible for the design and development of the C++ UA Server SDK used by many early OPC UA products, which is distributed by Unified Automation GmbH.

Matthias has a Dipl. Ing. (FH) degree in Electrical Engineering from University of applied Science in Schweinfurt/Germany.

# Acknowledgements

Writing a book is a time consuming task that requires many extra after-office hours and weekend hours. First of all, we thank our families and friends for their patience and support. Helmut and Wolfgang thank Martin Naedele from ABB for sponsoring some of our time at the office for this book project. Matthias thank his co-executives at ascolab, Gerhard Gappmeier and Uwe Steinkrauß.

The topic of this book – OPC Unified Architecture – was created by the OPC UA working group of the OPC Foundation. We gained our knowledge and thereby the foundation for writing this book by being part of this working group. We always enjoyed the positive atmosphere of the group focusing on technology issues and not on politics. A lot of people have participated in the working group meetings, some from the beginning to the present and some only for a while. We thank all of them for the excellent cooperation. We specially thank Jim Luth of the OPC Foundation as the leader of the working group, and those who where involved in so many discussions: Randy Armstrong and Tom Burke (OPC Foundation), Jeff Harding and Paul Hunkar (ABB), Karl-Heinz Deiretsbacher (Siemens), Lee Neit-zel (Emerson), Ayana Craven (OSIsoft), Erik Murhpy (Matrikon), Christian Zugfil (ascolab), Jörg Allmendinger (Allmendinger), and Betsy Hawkinson (Honeywell), to name a few.

Several reviewers helped improve the quality of this book. We thank Randy Armstrong (OPC Foundation), Karl-Heinz Deiretsbacher (Siemens), Jens Doppelhamer (ABB), Gerhard Gappmeier (ascolab), Jeff Harding (ABB), Paul Hunkar (ABB), Emanuel Kolb (ABB), Heiko Koziolek (ABB), Claude Lafond (ABB), Jim Luth (OPC Foundation), Uwe Steinkrauß (ascolab), and Roland Weiss (ABB) for their assistance.

Thanks also to our publisher for their support, especially to Dorothea Glaunsinger, Hermann Engesser, and the native speakers who greatly improved our English.

Finally, we thank all those people we have had discussions with about OPC UA at DevCons, workshops, trainings, and other occasions. Those discussions helped us a great deal identifying key problems with understanding OPC UA and gave us the motivation to write this book.

To the readers of this book: We encourage you to contact us if you find errors or unclear statements in this book or if you have suggestions for improvement. We will post corrections and additional information on www.opcuabook.com.

October 2008
Wolfgang Mahnke (wolfgang.mahnke@de.abb.com)
Stefan-Helmut Leitner (stefan.leitner@de.abb.com)
Matthias Damm (matthias.damm@ascolab.com)

# Table of Contents

# 1 Introduction

## 1.1 OPC Foundation

The use of PC- and software-based automation systems in industrial automation rapidly increased since the early nineties. Especially, Windows-based PCs are used for visualization and control purposes. One of the major efforts for the development of standardized automation software in the past years was the access to automation data in devices where an uncountable number of different bus systems, protocols, and interfaces are used.

A similar problem for software applications did exist for the access to printers, where in old DOS days, every application needed to write its own printer drivers for all supported printers. Windows solved the printer driver problem by incorporating printer support into the operating system. This one printer driver interface served all applications that needed printer access. And these printer drivers are provided by the printer manufacturer and not by the application developers.

Since vendors of Human Machine Interface (HMI) and Supervisory Control and Data Acquisition (SCADA) software had similar problems, a task force initiated by the companies Fisher-Rosemount, Rockwell Software, Opto 22, Intellution, and Intuitive Technology was founded in 1995. The goal of the task force was to define a Plug&Play standard for device drivers providing a standardized access to automation data on Windows-based systems.

The result was the OPC Data Access specification released after short time in August 1996. The nonprofit organization that is maintaining this standard is the OPC Foundation. Nearly all vendors providing systems for industrial automation became member of the OPC Foundation. The OPC Foundation was able to define and adopt praxis relevant standards much quicker than other organizations. One of the reasons for this success was the reduction to main features and the restriction to the definition of APIs using the Microsoft Windows technologies Component Object Model (COM) and Distributed COM (DCOM). The focus on important features and the use of base Windows technologies allowed a quick adoption of the standard for the addressed use case.

As a result of the experience from product developments, multi-vendor demonstrations, and interoperability workshops, version two of the OPC Data Access specification was introduced in 1998. Based on this version, a large number of products implemented the standard. OPC Data Access version two is still the most important interface for OPC products.

SCADA and HMI systems, process management and Distributed Control Systems (DCS), PC-based control systems, and Manufacturing Execution Systems (MES) must support OPC interfaces today. OPC is the one – universally accepted – standard delivering the ability to exchange data between different industrial automation system in manufacturing and process industry.

W. Mahnke et al., *OPC Unified Architecture*,
DOI: 10.1007/978-3-540-68899-0_1, © Springer-Verlag Berlin Heidelberg 2009

After 12 years, the OPC Foundation has over 450 members including all relevant automation system suppliers around the world. Figure 1.1 shows the OPC Foundation member demography classified with membership classes and region. The membership class is based on sales number for corporate members and the classes for end user and non-voting members like universities or other organizations. The OPC Foundation is governed by a Board of Directors elected by the membership. The Board, in turn, appoints the Foundation's Officers and the OPC Chief Architect. A Marketing Committee, a Technical Advisory Council, and various working groups have been established.

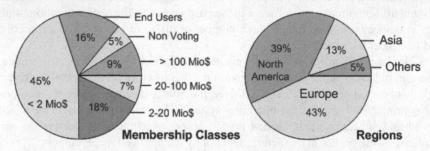

**Fig. 1.1** OPC Foundation member demography

The OPC Foundation has listed over 1,500 OPC-based products in its product catalog containing only products from OPC members. The total OPC market has over 2,500 vendors providing over 15,000 OPC-enabled products.

This great success requires verification mechanisms to make sure that all OPC products interoperate with each other and to ensure a certain level of quality. For this reason the OPC Compliance Program is, beside the development of new standards, the main focus of the OPC Foundation working groups.

The OPC Compliance Program defines two certification levels. The first level combines self certification and interoperability workshops. The OPC Foundation offers Compliance Test Tools for all relevant OPC standards. These tools are used for testing and the encrypted results are sent to the OPC Foundation. These test tools cover the functional tests on the interface level. Interoperability workshops are yearly events in Europe, North America, and Japan, where different vendors can test the interoperability of their OPC products against each other. Products passing self-certification can use the Self-Tested logo to indicate a basic level of OPC Compliance.

The second level is the product certification in independent Certification Test Labs. Accredited third party test labs are verifying OPC products with broader test coverage. In addition to the basic functional tests executed by the Compliance Test Tools, the test labs are running behavior tests, load and stress tests, interoperability tests as well as environment and usability tests. For products passing third party certification, the OPC Certified logo indicates a high level of quality and OPC Compliance.

End users are encouraged to buy only OPC Compliance tested products to reduce interoperability problems and to ensure reliability and performance of their OPC-based solution.

## 1.2 Classic OPC

In recent years, the OPC Foundation has defined a number of software interfaces to standardize the information flow from the process level to the management level. The main use cases are interfaces for industrial automation applications like HMIs and SCADA systems to consume current data from devices and to provide current and historical data and events for management applications.

According to the different requirements within industrial applications, three major OPC specifications have been developed: Data Access (DA), Alarm & Events (A&E), and Historical Data Access (HDA). Access to current process data is described in the DA specification, A&E describes an interface for event-based information, including acknowledgement of process alarms, and HDA describes functions to access archived data. All interfaces offer a way to navigate through the address space and to provide information about the available data.

OPC uses a client–server approach for the information exchange. An OPC server encapsulates the source of process information like a device and makes the information available via its interface. An OPC client connects to the OPC server and can access and consume the offered data. Applications consuming and providing data can be both client and server. Figure 1.2 shows a typical use case of OPC clients and servers.

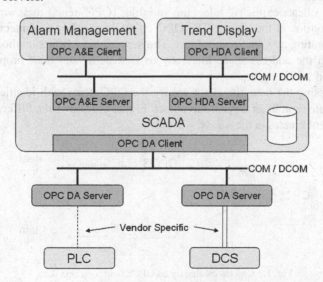

**Fig. 1.2** Typical use case of OPC clients and servers

Classic OPC interfaces are based on the COM and DCOM technology from Microsoft.

The advantage of this approach was the reduction of the specification work to the definition of different APIs for different specialized needs without the requirement to define a network protocol or a mechanism for interprocess communication. COM and DCOM provide a transparent mechanism for a client to call methods on a COM-object in a server running in the same process, in another process, or on another network node. Using this technology available on all PC-based Windows operating systems reduced the development time of the specifications and products and the time-to-market for OPC. This advantage was important for the success of OPC.

The two main disadvantages are the Windows-platform-dependency of OPC and the DCOM issues when using remote communication with OPC. DCOM is difficult to configure, has very long and non-configurable timeouts, and cannot be used for internet communication.

## 1.2.1 OPC Data Access

The OPC Data Access interface enables reading, writing, and monitoring of variables containing current process data. The main use case is to move real-time data from PLCs, DCSs, and other control devices to HMIs and other display clients. OPC DA is the most important OPC interface. It is implemented in 99% of the products using OPC technology today. Other OPC interfaces are mostly implemented in addition to DA.

OPC DA clients explicitly select the variables (OPC items) they want to read, write, or monitor in the server. The OPC client establishes a connection to the server by creating an OPCServer object. The server object offers methods to navigate through the address space hierarchy to find items and their properties like data type and access rights.

For accessing the data, the client groups the OPC items with identical settings such as update time in an OPCGroup object. Figure 1.3 shows the different objects the OPC client creates in the server.

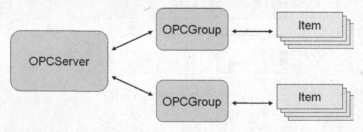

**Fig. 1.3** Objects created by an OPC client to access data

When added to a group, items can be read or written by the client. However, the preferred way for the cyclic reading of data by the client is monitoring the value changes in the server. The client defines an update rate on the group containing the items of interest. The update rate is used in the server to cyclic check the values for changes. After each cycle, the server sends only the changed values to the client.

OPC provides real-time data that may not permanently be accessible, for example, when the communication to a device gets temporarily interrupted. The Classic OPC technology handles this issue by providing timestamp and quality for the delivered data. The quality specifies if the data is accurate (good), not available (bad), or unknown (uncertain).

## 1.2.2 OPC Alarm & Events

The OPC A&E interface enables the reception of event notifications and alarm notifications. Events are single notifications informing the client about the occurrence of an event. Alarms are notifications that inform the client about the change of a condition in the process. Such a condition can be the level of a tank. In this example, a condition change can occur when a maximum level is exceeded or is fallen below a minimum level. Many alarms include the requirement that the alarm has to be acknowledged. This acknowledgement is also possible via the OPC A&E interface.

OPC A&E thus provides a flexible interface for transmitting process alarms and events from different event sources.

To receive notifications, the OPC A&E client connects to the server, subscribes for notifications, and than receives all notifications triggered in the server. To limit the number of notifications, the OPC client can specify certain filter criteria.

The OPC client connects by creating an OPCEventServer object in the A&E server in the first step and by generating an OPCEventSubscription used to receive the event messages in the second step. Filters for these event messages can be configured separately for each subscription. Figure 1.4 shows the different objects the OPC client creates in the server.

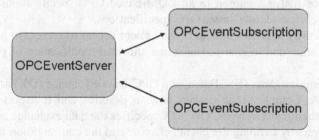

**Fig. 1.4** Objects created by an OPC client to receive events

In contrast to OPC DA, there is no explicit request for specific information like reading values; however, all process events are supplied and the client can limit the quantity of the events by setting certain filter criteria, for example, filter by event types, by priority, or by event source.

### 1.2.3 OPC Historical Data Access

Where OPC Data Access gives access to real-time, continually changing data, OPC Historical Data Access provides access to data already stored. From a simple serial data logging system to a complex SCADA system, historical archives can be retrieved in a uniform manner.

The OPC client connects by creating an OPCHDAServer object in the HDA server. This object offers all interfaces and methods to read and update historical data. A second object OPCHDABrowser is defined for browsing the address space of the HDA server.

The main functionality is the reading of historical data in three different ways. The first mechanism reads raw data from the archive, where the client defines one or more variables and the time domain he wants to read. The server returns all values archived for the specified time range up to the maximum number of values defined by the client. The second mechanism reads values of one or more variables for specified timestamps. The third read mechanism computes aggregate values from data in the history database for the specified time domain for one or more variables. Values include always the associated quality and timestamp.

In addition to the read methods, OPC HAD also defines methods for inserting, replacing, and deleting data in the history database.

### 1.2.4 Other OPC Interface Standards

OPC specified several additional standards as base specifications or for specialized needs. Base specifications are OPC Overview and OPC Common defining interfaces and behavior that is common to all COM-based OPC specifications. Figure 1.5 gives an overview for all Classic OPC specifications.

OPC Security specifies how to control client access to servers to protect sensitive information and to guard against unauthorized modification of process parameters.

- OPC Complex Data, OPC Batch, and OPC Data eXchange (DX) are extensions to OPC DA. Complex Data defines how to describe and transport values with complex structured data types. OPC DX specifies the data exchange between Data Access servers by defining the client behavior and the configuration interfaces for the client inside a server. OPC Batch extends DA for the specialized needs of batch processes. It provides interfaces for the exchange of equipment capabilities

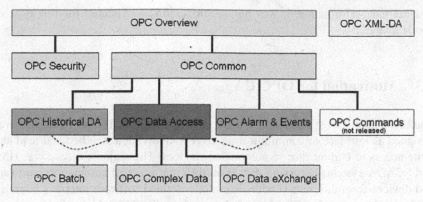

**Fig. 1.5** Classic OPC interface standards

corresponding to the S88.01 Physical Model [ISA88] and current operating conditions.

OPC Commands defines mechanisms to call methods or to execute programs via OPC. This specification was never released since it was finished after OPC UA was started. But its content and functionality is completely incorporated into UA.

## 1.2.5 OPC XML-DA

OPC XML-DA was the first platform-independent OPC specification replacing COM/DCOM with HTTP/SOAP and Web Service technologies. Thus a vendor- and platform-neutral communication infrastructure was introduced and widely accepted functionality of OPC Data Access was retained.

Since typical Web Services are stateless, the functionality was reduced to the minimum set of methods to exchange OPC Data Access information, without the need for methods to create and modify a context for communication. Only eight methods were needed to cover the key features of OPC Data Access.

The eight services are the following:

- GetStatus to verify the server status
- Read to read one or more item values
- Write to write one or more item values
- Browse and GetProperties to get information about the available items
- Subscribe to create a subscription for a list of items
- SubscriptionPolledRefresh for the exchange of changed values of a subscription
- SubscriptionCancel to delete the subscription.

OPC XML-DA was designed for internet access and enterprise integration. But based on its platform-independence, it was mainly implemented in embedded systems and on non-Microsoft platforms. But due to its high resource consumption and limited performance, it was not as successful as expected for this type of applications.

## 1.3    Motivation for OPC UA

The first and still most successful Classic OPC standard – OPC Data Access – was designed as interface to communication drivers, allowing a standardized read and write access to current data in automation devices. The major use case was HMI and SCADA systems accessing data from different types of automation hardware and devices from different vendors using one defined software interface supplied by the hardware vendor. Standards following later like OPC Alarm & Events and OPC Historical Data Access were also designed to access information provided by SCADA systems.

With the successful adoption of OPC in thousands of products, OPC is used today as standardized interface between automation systems in different levels of the automation pyramid. It is even used in a lot of areas where it was not designed for, and there are many more areas where manufacturers want to use a standard like OPC but are not able to use it because of the COM dependency of OPC or because of the limitations for remote access using DCOM.

OPC XML-DA was the first approach of the OPC Foundation to maintain successful features of OPC but to use a vendor and platform neutral communication infrastructure. There are several reasons why just creating Web Service versions of the successful OPC specification did not cover the requirements for a new OPC generation. One reason was the poor performance of XML Web Service compared with original COM version. Furthermore, using different XML Web Service stacks caused interoperability problems.

But besides the issue of platform independence, the OPC member companies brought forward the requirement to expose complex data and complex systems, removing the limitations of Classic OPC.

The OPC Unified Architecture was born out of the desire to create a true replacement for all existing COM-based specifications without losing any features or performance. Additionally it must cover all requirements for platform-independent system interfaces with rich and extensible modeling capabilities being able to describe also complex systems. The wide range of applications where OPC is used requires scalability from embedded systems across SCADA and DCS up to MES and ERP systems. The most important requirements for OPC UA are listed in Table 1.1.

The requirements can be grouped into the ones for the communication between distributed systems being able to exchange information and the requirements for modeling of data describing a system and the available information.

Classic OPC was designed as device driver interface. OPC is used as system interface today; therefore, the reliability for the communication between distributed systems is very important. Since network communication is not reliable by definition, robustness and fault-tolerance are the important requirement, including redundancy for high availability. Platform-independence and scalability is necessary to be able to integrate OPC interfaces directly into the systems running on many different platforms. To replace proprietary communication, an important requirement is always high-performance in intranet environments. But also internet communication through firewalls must be possible out of the box, which makes security and access control another important requirement. And first and foremost the interoperability between systems from different vendors is still the most important requirement.

**Table 1.1** Requirements for OPC UA

| Communication between distributed systems | Modeling Data |
|---|---|
| • Reliability by<br>   • Robustness and fault tolerance<br>   • Redundancy<br>• Platform-independence<br>• Scalability<br>• High performance<br>• Internet and firewalls<br>• Security and access control<br>• Interoperability | • Common model for all OPC data<br>• Object-oriented<br>• Extensible type system<br>• Meta information<br>• Complex data and methods<br>• Scalability from simple to complex models<br>• Abstract base model<br>• Base for other standard data models |

Modeling of data was very limited in Classic OPC and needed to be enhanced by providing a common, object-oriented model for all OPC data. This model must include an extensible type system to be able to offer meta information and to describe also complex systems. The availability of methods provided and described by servers and callable by clients is a powerful feature needed to make OPC flexible and extensible. Complex data is required to support the description and consistent transport of complex data structures. It was an important requirement to enhance the modeling capabilities, but it was equally important to support simple models with simple concepts. For this reason it is required to have a simple and abstract but extensible base model to be able to scale from simple to complex models.

In addition to the functional requirements for a new OPC generation, the initial group of over 40 representatives defining the requirements and use cases for OPC Unified Architecture was not only composed of OPC members. Other standardization organizations like IEC and ISA interested in using OPC as transport mechanism for their information were involved in the early design process. In this group the OPC Foundation defines HOW to describe and transport data, and the collaborating organizations define WHAT data they want to describe and transport depending on their information model.

Another important design goal was to allow an easy migration to OPC Unified Architecture to protect the investment in the very successful Classic OPC standards and to build upon the large installed base of OPC.

## 1.4    OPC UA Overview

To reach the defined goals, the OPC Unified Architecture builds on different layers shown in Fig. 1.6.

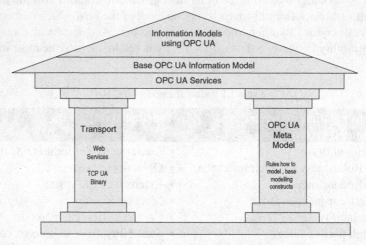

Fig. 1.6 The foundation of OPC UA

The fundamental components of OPC Unified Architecture are transport mechanisms and data modeling.

The transport defines different mechanisms optimized for different use cases. The first version of OPC UA is defining an optimized binary TCP protocol for high performance intranet communication as well as a mapping to accepted internet standards like Web Services, XML, and HTTP for firewall-friendly internet communication. Both transports are using the same message-based security model known from Web Services. The abstract communication model does not depend on a specific protocol mapping and allows adding new protocols in the future. The transport mechanisms are described more detailed in Chap. 6.

The data modeling defines the rules and base building blocks necessary to expose an information model with OPC UA. It defines also the entry points into the address space and base types used to build a type hierarchy. This base can be extended by information models building on top of the abstract modeling concepts. In addition, it defines some enhanced concepts like describing state machines used in different information models. The basics of information modeling are described in Chap. 2 and an example and best practices are introduced in Chap. 3.

The UA Services are the interface between servers as supplier of an information model and clients as consumers of that information model. The Services are defined in an abstract manner. They are using the transport mechanisms to exchange the data between client and server.

This basic concept of OPC UA enables an OPC UA client to access the smallest pieces of data without the need to understand the whole model exposed by complex systems. OPC UA clients also understanding specific models can use more

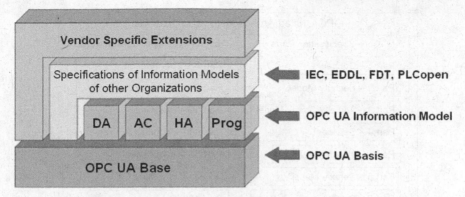

**Fig. 1.7** OPC UA layered architecture

enhanced features defined for special domains and use cases. Figure 1.7 shows the different layers of information models defined by OPC, by other organizations, or by vendors.

To cover all successful features known from Classic OPC, information models for the domain of process information are defined by OPC UA on top of the base specifications. DA defines automation-data-specific extensions such as the modeling of analog or discrete data and how to expose quality of service. All other DA features are already covered by the base. Alarm & Conditions (AC) specifies an advanced model for process alarm management and condition monitoring. Historical Access (HA) defines the mechanisms to access historical data and historical events. Programs (Prog) specifies a mechanism to start, manipulate, and monitor the execution of programs.

Other organizations can built their models on top of the UA base or on top of the OPC information model, exposing their specific information via OPC UA. Examples for standards already working on mappings to OPC UA are Field Device Integration (FDI) combining Electronic Device Description Language (EDDL), and Field Device Tool (FDT) both used to describe, to configure, and to monitor devices and PLCopen, a standard for PLC programming languages.

Additional vendor-specific information models will be defined using directly the UA base, the OPC models, or other OPC-UA-based information models.

## 1.5   OPC UA Specifications

The OPC UA specifications are partitioned in different parts also required for IEC standardization. OPC UA will be known as IEC 62541 standards. Figure 1.8 shows an overview of all specification parts split into the core specifications defining the base for OPC UA and the access type specific parts mainly specifying the OPC UA information models.

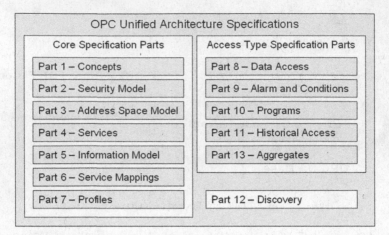

Fig. 1.8 OPC UA specifications

The first two parts are not normative. The concepts part [UA Part 1] gives an overview about OPC UA and [UA Part 2] describes the security requirements and the security model for OPC UA.

Most important to understand how to model and access information are part 3 and 4. These two specifications are the key documents for the design and development of OPC UA applications.

The Address Space Model [UA Part 3] specifies the building blocks to expose instance and type information and thus the OPC UA meta model used to describe and expose information models and to build an OPC UA server address space.

The abstract UA Services defined in [UA Part 4] represent the possible interactions between UA client and UA server applications. The client uses the Services to find and access information provided by the server. The Services are abstract because they are defining the information to be exchanged between UA applications but not the concrete representation on the wire and also not the concrete representation in an API used by the applications. Figure 1.9 shows the layered communication architecture of OPC UA.

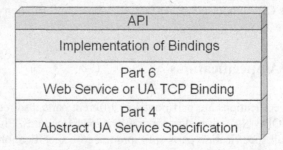

Fig. 1.9 Layered OPC UA communication architecture

The mapping of the UA Services to messages, the security mechanisms applied to the messages, and the concrete wire transport of the messages are defined in [UA Part 6]. Only implementers of UA stacks need to completely understand this specification. Since the OPC Foundation supplies proper UA stacks, typical UA application architects and programmers do not need to read this specification.

The base information model specified in [UA Part 5] provides the framework for all information models using OPC UA. It defines the following:

- The entry points into the address space used by clients to navigate through the instances and types of an OPC UA server
- The base types building the root for the different type hierarchies
- The built-in but extensible types like object types and data types
- The Server Object providing capability and diagnostic information.

The profiles are defining useful subsets of OPC UA features in [UA Part 7]. Such a subset must be implemented completely by an UA application to ensure interoperability for the defined subset. The specification defines the subsets on two levels. The first level are Conformance Units defining a small set of functionality that is always used together and can be tested with Compliance Test Tools and verified as unit. The second level are Profiles composed of a list of conformance units. A profile must be implemented completely and will be verified as complete set during the certification of OPC UA products. The list of supported and used Profiles is exchanged during the connection establishment between client and server and allows the applications to determine if the needed features are supported by the communication partner.

The DA information model defines how to represent and use automation data and specific characteristics like engineering units in [UA Part 8].

The AC information model specifies process alarm and condition monitoring specific state machines and types of events in [UA Part 9].

The Programs information model defines a base state machine for the execution, manipulation, and monitoring of programs in [UA Part 10].

The HA information model in [UA Part 11] specifies the use of the history access Services and how to present information about the configuration of data and event history.

The aggregates used to compute aggregated values from raw data samples are specified in [UA Part 13]. The aggregates are used for historical access as well as the monitoring of current values.

[UA Part 12] defines how to find servers in the network and how a client can get the necessary information to be able to establish a connection to a certain server.

## 1.6   OPC UA Software Layers

OPC UA uses a similar client–server concept like Classic OPC. An application that wants to expose its own information to other applications is called UA server and an application that wants to consume information from other applications is called UA client. But it is expected that much more applications will be both UA server and UA client in one application than in Classic OPC. One reason is that more UA servers will be integrated directly in devices. Implementing also a UA client enables device to device communication. Another reason is the use of OPC UA as configuration interface, where UA clients are also UA servers to be configured via OPC UA.

A typical OPC UA application is composed of three software layers shown in Fig. 1.10. The complete software stack can be implemented with C/C++, .NET, or JAVA. OPC UA is not limited to these programming languages and development platforms, but only these environments are currently used for implementing the OPC Foundation UA Stack deliverables.

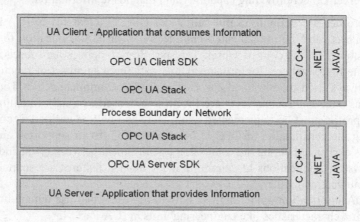

**Fig. 1.10** OPC UA software layers

An OPC UA Application is a system that wants to expose or to consume data via OPC UA. It contains the specific functionality for the application and the mapping of this functionality to OPC UA by using an OPC UA Stack and an OPC UA Software Development Kit (SDK).

An OPC UA client or server SDK implements common OPC UA functionality that is part of the application layer, since the UA Stacks implement only the communication channels. An OPC UA SDK reduces the development effort and facilitates faster interoperability for an OPC UA application.

An OPC UA Stack implements the different OPC UA transport mappings defined in [UA Part 6]. The Stack is used to invoke UA Services across process or network boundaries. OPC UA defines three Stack layers and different profiles for each layer. The message encoding layer defines the serialization of Service parameters in a binary and a XML format. The message security layer specifies how the messages must be secured by using the Web Service security standards or a UA binary version of the Web Service standards. The message transport layer defines the used network protocol, which could be UA TCP or HTTP and SOAP for Web Services. Figure 1.11 illustrates the different UA communication stack layers. The implementation of the layers in a UA Stack and the resulting API for the applications is not part of the OPC UA specification. The UA Stacks provide language-dependent APIs for UA client and UA server applications, but the Services and their parameters are similar and based on the abstract Service definition in [UA Part 4].

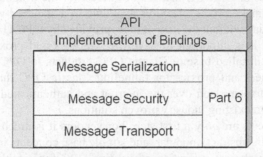

**Fig. 1.11** UA communication stack layers defined in UA Part 6

With implementations in ANSI C/C++, .NET, and JAVA, the main development environments and programming languages are covered by UA Stacks developed and maintained by the OPC Foundation.

## 1.7    Evolution Not Revolution

OPC UA is much more flexible and has much more features than all Classic OPC specifications together, but it incorporates all successful concepts of existing OPC specification, fixes known issues in existing standards, and adds standardization for a lot of additional use cases.

It was an important design goal to allow an easy migration from Classic OPC to OPC UA. For this reason most features known from Classic OPC can be found in OPC UA using sometimes slightly different terminology. It is not possible to expose all UA features with Classic OPC interfaces, but it is no problem to map Classic OPC features to OPC UA.

OPC UA allows a simple mapping and offers migration strategies to integrate OPC products based on previous OPC standards. One part of the migration strategy does not even require a change in existing products. Wrappers and proxies provided by the OPC Foundation are able to translate the different Classic OPC interfaces into OPC UA and vice-versa. This first level in the migration strategy can be used by vendors to support OPC UA for legacy products.

The second level of migration to OPC UA is the integration of OPC UA directly into existing products without adding OPC UA specific features. This step does not require changes in interfaces used between systems and their OPC communication components today. It is much easier to integrate new components if the existing interfaces of a system do not have to be changed. The advantage over the use of wrappers or proxies is a better performance and less configuration and engineering efforts by removing an additional software layer. The direct integration will make it easier to remove potential limitations of wrappers and proxies and allows an iterative development approach by adding OPC UA features step by step.

The third level may require changing internal interfaces of the product to support all features of OPC UA that are of interest for the product. OPC UA will allow systems to make product features available in a standard way, which they can not expose today without the new options provided by OPC UA.

For end users, it is important to have the wrappers and proxies available to migrate the large installed base of Classic OPC products to OPC UA. End users can install wrappers and proxies for tunneling Classic OPC through firewalls, including secure transmission over the internet and authenticated access, so they simply add value to existing industry proven solutions.

These components are only a first step. For vendors it is much more important that OPC UA offers abstract, modular, and simple base concepts in all areas of the standard, allowing an easy migration of existing OPC functionality to OPC UA. The very powerful concepts for extending this base enable vendors to expose more and more of their system features via OPC UA. This leads to an iterative development and improvement process.

## 1.8    Summary

### 1.8.1 Key Messages

The OPC Foundation provides standards for data exchange in industrial automation. This includes the very successful OPC DA specification for current data, as well as OPC A&E for alarms and events and OPC HDA for historical data. All those specifications are based on the retiring COM/DCOM technology. A first step moving forward to state-of-the-art technologies was OPC XML-DA, which used only XML as data transport format and therefore did not meet the performance requirements of typical OPC applications.

With the lessons learned from OPC XML-DA the OPC Foundation created a new standard called Unified Architecture. Here, the transport can be done either using firewall-friendly Web Services by standards like SOAP and HTTP or an optimized binary TCP protocol for high performance communication. OPC UA provides interoperable and platform-independent, high-performing, scalable, secure, and reliable communication between applications. The technology switch from Microsoft's COM/DCOM to state-of-the-art and platform-independent transport protocols allows OPC UA applications to run on intelligent devices and controllers as well as in DCS and SCADA systems and up to the enterprise level with MES and ERP systems. This immensely increases the range of use compared to Classic OPC application

Besides the transport, the second big achievement of OPC UA is information modeling. OPC UA unifies the functionality of the different Classic OPC specifications by exposing current data, event notifications, and the history of both in one address space. It additionally provides a rich and extensible information model using object-oriented concepts, allowing meta data as well as complex data of your applications to be exposed. The extensible mechanisms allow defining standard information models by other organizations that can make use of the OPC UA communication infrastructure and focus on standardizing the information to be exposed. There are already initiatives going on defining standard information models, for example, FDI for device descriptions by mapping EDDL and FDT to OPC UA or for PLC programming languages by PLCopen. Like the transport capabilities the modeling capabilities of OPC UA scale well. You can keep the offered information simple, similar to Classic OPC, but you can also enrich the information with a type system and thus providing more information useful in many application scenarios.

## 1.8.2    Where to Find More Information?

Information about Classic OPC can be found at the OPC Foundation web site (www.opcfoundation.org). There is also a book on Classic OPC [IL06]. Several vendors provide Classic OPC products and toolkits. A list can be found at www.opcconnect.com; here you will find overview information about OPC, including OPC UA. Additional links and information can be found on the book website www.opcuabook.com.

General information about OPC UA can be found at the OPC Foundation web site, including a special section on OPC UA (www.opcfoundation.org/ua). The web site also offers access to the OPC UA specifications where [UA Part 4] and [UA Part 6] focus on the data transport and [UA Part 3] and [UA Part 5] focus on modeling information.

## 1.8.3    What's Next?

In the next three chapters, we will focus on how to provide information using OPC UA before we go into details on how to access those data (starting with Chap. 5).

In Chaps. 2 and 3, we introduce the base modeling concepts and give examples and best practice for these concepts. Standard information models are described in Chap. 4. This includes an introduction on how to create models: the description of the OPC defined models and an overview of standard information models defined by other organizations.

In Chap. 5 we will introduce the abstract Services of OPC UA, and Chap. 6 describes the mapping of those Services to concrete technologies like Web Services.

# 2 Information Modeling: Concepts

## 2.1 Why Information Modeling?

The fundaments of OPC UA are data transport and information modeling. Compared to Classic OPC, the data transport was changed to state-of-the-art, platform-independent, secure, and reliable technologies and the capabilities to model information are highly improved. In Classic OPC, only "pure" data is provided, for example, the temperature measured by a temperature sensor. The only information available to understand the semantic of the provided data is the tag name and some rudimentary information like the engineering unit of the measured value. OPC UA provides more powerful possibilities exposing the semantic of the provided data. In addition to the data provided by Classic OPC, it allows exposing information like that the measured temperature is provided by a specific type of sensor device and allows to expose in a type hierarchy what kind of devices are supported. Thereby, OPC UA clients can get the information that they are dealing with the same kind of device at different places. By exposing much more semantics, OPC UA servers allow clients to process highly sophisticated tasks by interpreting the semantic of the provided data. That includes the automated integration of data provided by an OPC UA server as well as engineering an OPC UA server from a generic OPC UA client.

The base OPC UA specifications provide only the infrastructure to model information. The information can be modeled by vendors - which of course would lead to different ways how to model similar information and thus makes the life hard for OPC UA clients. To avoid that situation, the OPC UA specification provides possibilities to define Information Model specifications based on OPC UA. The OPC Foundation already started activities to generate these specifications. For example, there are efforts to define a base model exposing device information and device types in OPC UA [UA Devices]. A vendor will use this base model and extend it with vendor-specific information about its devices. Clients can access device information provided by different, vendor-specific OPC UA servers in the same manner, since they are exposed in a similar way using the same base model. In addition, a vendor may integrate third-party devices exposing their data via OPC UA into its OPC UA server easily and seamlessly since both use the same base model. This of course does not only apply for device models, but for other scenarios as well, for example, providing data to MES or ERP systems by exposing the ISA 95 model [ISA95] in OPC UA.

The base principles of information modeling in OPC UA are the following:

- *Using object-oriented techniques including type hierarchies and inheritance.* Typed instances allow clients to handle all instances of the same type in the same way. Type hierarchies allow clients to work with base types and to ignore more specialized information.

W. Mahnke et al., *OPC Unified Architecture*,
DOI: 10.1007/978-3-540-68899-0_2, © Springer-Verlag Berlin Heidelberg 2009

- *Type information is exposed and can be accessed the same way as instances.* The type information is provided by the OPC UA server and can be accessed with the same mechanisms used to access instances. This is similar to the information schema of relational database systems, where information about the database tables is managed in database tables and accessible with normal SQL statements [ISO08b].
- *Full meshed network of nodes allowing information to be connected in various ways.* OPC UA allows supporting several hierarchies exposing different semantics and references between nodes of those hierarchies. Thus the same information can be exposed in different ways, providing different paths and ways to organize the information in the same server depending on the use case.
- *Extensibility regarding the type hierarchies as well as the types of references between nodes.* OPC UA is extensible in several ways regarding the modeling of information. Beside the definition of subtypes, it allows, for example, to specify additional types of references defining relations between nodes and methods extending the functionality of OPC UA.
- *No limitations on how to model information in order to allow an appropriate model for the provided data.* OPC UA servers targeting a system that already contains a rich information model can expose that model "natively" in OPC UA instead of mapping the model to a different model.
- *OPC UA information modeling is always done on server-side.* OPC UA information models always exist on OPC UA servers, not on client-side. They can be accessed and modified from OPC UA clients and OPC UA servers can also have a client-part accessing other OPC UA servers. But in general, an OPC UA client is not required having an integrated OPC UA information model and it does not have to provide such information to an OPC UA server.

Let us examine the modeling capabilities of OPC UA by looking at an example. A device vendor provides a temperature sensor as shown in Fig. 2.1. The device has some configuration parameters and some measurement values that may differ depending on the configuration. It provides that information in an OPC UA server using the base device model mentioned earlier.

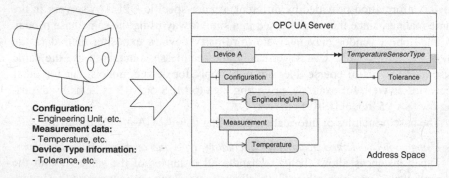

**Fig. 2.1** Temperature sensor and provided data in OPC UA

To understand the example, it is not important to know where the OPC UA server is running and what additional information is provided by it. In the simplest case, the OPC UA server would directly run on the device; for a simple device like a temperature sensor it is more likely that the OPC UA server would run on the controller or a PC on top of the controller. Any OPC UA client can provide an appropriate user interface exposing the measured values of the device as well as configuring the device by using the device model provided by the server. The model can include events and historical data. The client can use a generic user interface (showing lists of parameters) or a specialized one showing a graphical representation of the device and the main parameters. Those specific user interfaces can be created based on the type information. They have to be implemented or configured only once for a type and can be used for each instance of the type or instances of subtypes. Thus such a user interface can be defined for the base types of the device model without exposing any vendor-specific extensions. It can also be defined for a vendor-specific type tailored to the vendor-specific device and its extensions. The most common use-case of integrating device data is aggregating them in a DCS and providing them via the DCS to the client. In that case, a DCS should act as an OPC UA client to receive the data and as an OPC UA server to expose the data. Any OPC UA client could access the device data through the DCS without loosing any functionality. The scenario in which the server contains the information of several devices demonstrates the power of programming with knowledge of the type information. For example, the same graphical element can be used several times in one graphic, showing a process in the factory. Figure 2.2 outlines the afore mentioned use cases for OPC UA clients.

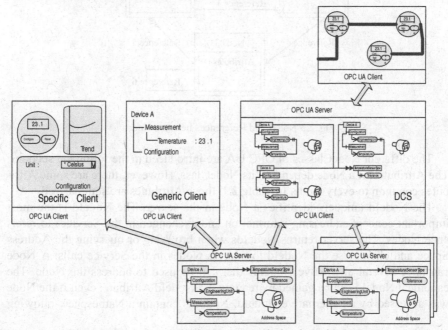

**Fig. 2.2** Different scenarios how to access device data with OPC UA

This chapter gives an overview of how information is modeled in OPC UA. The following sections describe the concepts of OPC UA used for modeling, starting from the base concepts of nodes and references between them, explaining the Object Model of OPC UA containing typed objects with variables, methods and events, and finishes with describing the differences between the OPC UA Address Space Model as the meta model of OPC UA and Information Models tailored to certain domains. In the next chapter, a detailed example on how to model information in OPC UA is given and some best practices are provided.

## 2.2    Nodes and References

The base modeling concepts of OPC UA are *Nodes* and *References* between Nodes. Nodes can be of different *NodeClasses*, depending on the purpose of a Node. There are Nodes representing instances, others representing types, etc. *Attributes* are used to describe Nodes, and depending on the NodeClass a Node can have a different set of Attributes. In Fig. 2.3, an example is given. Node1, Node2, and Node3, all containing Attributes, are connected with several References (Reference 1–6).

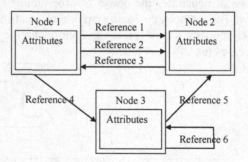

**Fig. 2.3** Nodes and References between Nodes

The different NodeClasses of OPC UA are introduced in the following sections. The Attributes of a Node depend on its NodeClass. However, there are some Attributes common to every Node. In Table 2.1, those Attributes are summarized.

The NodeId uniquely identifies a Node in the server. The NodeId is the most important concept addressing information and exchanged in the Services to reference Nodes. The server returns NodeIds when browsing or querying the Address Space and clients use the NodeId to address Nodes in the Service calls. A Node can have several alternative NodeIds that can be used to address the Node. The canonical NodeId can be gained by reading the NodeId Attribute, even if the Node was accessed by an alternative NodeId. NodeIds contain a Namespace, allowing

Table 2.1 Common Attributes

| Attribute | DataType | Description |
|---|---|---|
| NodeId | NodeId | Uniquely identifies a Node in an OPC UA server and is used to address the Node in the OPC UA Services |
| NodeClass | NodeClass | An enumeration identifying the NodeClass of a Node such as Object or Method |
| BrowseName | QualifiedName | Identifies the Node when browsing the OPC UA server. It is not localized |
| DisplayName | LocalizedText | Contains the Name of the Node that should be used to display the name in a user interface. Therefore, it is localized |
| Description | LocalizedText | This optional Attribute contains a localized textual description of the Node |
| WriteMask | UInt32 | Is optional and specifies which Attributes of the Node are writable, i.e., can be modified by an OPC UA client |
| UserWriteMask | UInt32 | Is optional and specifies which Attributes of the Node can be modified by the user currently connected to the server |

different naming authorities to uniquely define NodeIds. Naming authorities can be organizations, vendors, or systems. Details about the NodeId and its data type are described in Sect. 2.8.5.

The BrowseName is used only for browsing purposes and should not be used for displaying the name of a Node. BrowseNames have a special meaning for Properties (see Sect. 2.6) and for programming with the knowledge of type information (see Sect. 2.5.4). Like the NodeId, the BrowseName is a structure containing a Namespace and a nonlocalized string as described in Sect. 2.8.5.

The DisplayName and Description are localized. Section 2.8.5 describes details about localization and the data type LocalizedText.

In theory, a Reference describes the relation between exactly two Nodes. Therefore, a Reference is uniquely identified by the source Node of the Reference, the target Node, the semantic of the Reference (the ReferenceType, see Sect. 2.3), and the direction of the Reference.

In practice, a server may expose a Reference only in one direction and the Reference may point to a Node in another OPC UA server or a nonexisting Node. Therefore, it makes sense to think about a Reference as a pointer living in a Node and pointing to another Node by storing the NodeId of the other Node. In Fig. 2.4, this view on References is shown.

Such a Reference pointer contains the NodeId of the referenced Node, the OPC UA server where the referenced Node is managed, the type of Reference defining the semantic of the Reference (see Sect. 2.3), and the direction of the Reference. References are distinguished between symmetric and nonsymmetric References.

A nonsymmetric Reference is, for example, "has-parent" in one direction and "is-child-of" in the other direction, whereas a symmetric Reference has the same semantic in both directions like "is-sibling-of." In the first case, the direction of the Reference is important, whereas in the second case it does not matter.

Looking at References as pointers to other Nodes helps understanding the constraints or missing constraints defined for References in OPC UA. Although References connect two Nodes OPC UA servers may expose only one direction of the Reference, for example, only the pointer from Node 1 to Node 2 in Fig. 2.4, not the inverse direction. If only one direction is exposed, the Reference is called unidirectional, otherwise bidirectional. The pointers may refer to Nodes that do not exist (anymore) in the server or to Nodes in other servers that may not be available at a specific point in time or maybe not at all anymore. Clients must expect that they may be able to browse a Reference in one direction but not in the inverse direction or that the referenced Node does not exist.

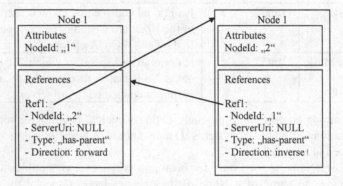

**Fig. 2.4** References as pointers to Nodes

References are not ordered, that is, asking a Node for its References two times may lead to differently ordered sets of References. However, there are types of References that define an order for References of that type, like HasOrderedComponent [UA Part 3]. The server has always to return those References in the same order.

**What's allowed and what's not?**
The set of Attributes of a Node is defined by the OPC UA specifications and cannot be extended. If additional information describing a Node is needed, Properties (see Sect. 2.6) have to be used instead.
The set of writable Attributes indicated by the WriteMask must be the same or a superset of the writable Attributes indicated by the UserWriteMask, since the WriteMask defines which Attributes may be modified by any user.
In general, the requirements on the integrity of References are very low. References may point to none-existing Nodes in the same server or to other servers that are not accessible for the client. References may be exposed in only one direction, and References may lead to loops. Clients must be able

to deal with those inaccurate data. Specific References may restrict this and define much higher constrains on References (see the next section).
References do not contain any Attributes or Properties. In the case that some additional information should be added to the relation of two Nodes, a Proxy-Node must be added and connected by both Nodes instead of using a single Reference (see Sect. 3.3.8 for details on how to use a Proxy-Node).

## 2.3  ReferenceTypes

A Reference is a connection between two Nodes. A Reference cannot directly be accessed, only indirectly by browsing a Node and thus following References. References are not represented as Nodes and cannot contain any Attributes or Properties. However, References are used to expose different semantics on how the Nodes are connected. To expose the semantic of References OPC UA uses *ReferenceTypes*. A ReferenceType defines the semantic of a Reference and every Reference is typed and therefore has a defined semantic. The OPC UA specification defines a set of *ReferenceTypes*. Some of them are used in very fundamental places, for example, to expose a type hierarchy. But the concept of ReferenceTypes is an extensible concept, that is, an OPC UA server can define its own ReferenceTypes exposing a specific semantic for References. To organize ReferenceTypes they are managed in a type hierarchy.

Although References are no Nodes and have no Attributes, the ReferenceTypes are exposed as Nodes in the Address Space. That allows clients to gain the information about the References used by an OPC UA server by accessing Nodes in the Address Space of the OPC UA server. In Table 2.2, the Attributes used to describe a ReferenceType are summarized.

**Table 2.2** Additional Attributes for ReferenceTypes

| Attribute | DataType | Description |
|---|---|---|
| Containing all the common Attributes defined in Table 2.1 | | |
| IsAbstract | Boolean | Specifies if the ReferenceType can be used for References or is only used for organizational purposes in the ReferenceType hierarchy |
| Symmetric | Boolean | Indicates whether the Reference is symmetric, i.e., whether the meaning is the same in forward and inverse direction |
| InverseName | LocalizedText | This optional Attribute specifies the semantic of the Reference in inverse direction. It can only be applied for nonsymmetric References and must be provided if such a ReferenceType is not abstract |

In addition to those Attributes, the common Attributes used for all Nodes described in Table 2.1 are valid for ReferenceTypes as well. Some of those Attributes have some additional constraints when used for ReferenceTypes. The BrowseName of a ReferenceType must be unique in an OPC UA server in order to avoid confusion having several ReferenceTypes with different semantic but the same name. The DisplayName must contain a localized representation of the BrowseName. The BrowseName, and thus the DisplayName as well, defines the semantic of the ReferenceType in forward direction, like the InverseName defines the semantic in inverse direction.

References are managed in a ReferenceType hierarchy. This allows specializing existing ReferenceTypes with more specialized types. In Fig. 2.5, the base ReferenceType hierarchy defined by the OPC UA specification is shown. It uses the OPC UA notation to visualize OPC UA related information as described in Appendix A. In Appendix C the complete hierarchy of ReferenceTypes defined by the base OPC UA specifications is shown.

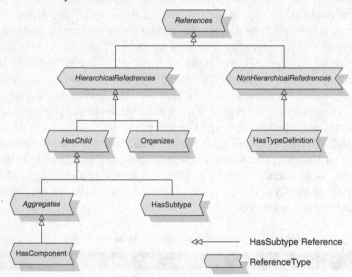

**Fig. 2.5** Base ReferenceType hierarchy

The ReferenceTypes using italic letters are abstract and only used for organizational purposes and for filtering. Chapter 5 describes where you can apply filtering. The "References" ReferenceType is used if all References should be considered in a filter. It has two subtypes distinguishing References in hierarchical References and non-hierarchical References. Hierarchical References should be used when a hierarchy should be modeled, non-hierarchical for other purposes like exposing relationships between different hierarchies. For example, the non-hierarchical HasTypeDefinition references from an instance to its type in the type hierarchy. Clients are expected to use References according to that, for example, displaying hierarchical References in a tree control and filtering out the non-hierarchical References.

To simplify the filtering on ReferenceTypes, the ReferenceType hierarchy supports only single-inheritance, that is, each ReferenceType has exactly one supertype.[1] This guarantees, for example, that each ReferenceType[2] is either a hierarchical ReferenceType or a non-hierarchical ReferenceType and never both of them.

In Fig. 2.5, some subtypes of hierarchical References are shown. The Organizes ReferenceType is used when two Nodes should be connected in a hierarchical way, without defining any additional semantic. An example using this ReferenceType is when a file system is mapped to OPC UA. Folders could be exposed as Nodes and could reference their subfolders using Organizes References. The Organizes

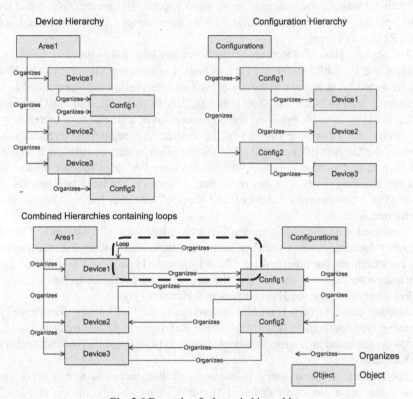

**Fig. 2.6** Example of a loops in hierarchies

---

Reference or any hierarchical Reference does not guarantee that there is no loop when following those References.[3] In Fig. 2.6, such an example is given. In the example, two hierarchies exist. One is organizing devices and one contains configuration information. The devices reference some configuration objects containing their configuration, but several devices can use the same configuration like Device1 and Device2, both using the configuration Config1. In the configuration hierarchy, several configurations are organized having the devices beneath them that are using the configuration. If you look at those hierarchies in a combined view, you can see that there are loops in that hierarchy. Looking at that example also shows that Organizes is not always the best choice for referencing Nodes in a hierarchical way. In the example, some more specific ReferenceTypes could have been applied. We will take another look at the example after introducing some more ReferenceTypes.

The abstract HasChild Reference disallows any loop following only subtypes of it. Thus, the HasChild ReferenceType defines a nonlooping Hierarchy. The Nodes can be organized in another hierarchy as well and thus following hierarchical References may lead to Nodes as shown in Fig. 2.7. In that case, the HasComponent ReferenceType is used, exposing the configuration of a device as a component of the device. As a concrete subtype of the abstract Aggregates ReferenceType, it inherits the "is-part-of" semantic. The nature of an is-part-of relation is that it is not looped, that is, that a part of "A" cannot have "A" as a subpart. Please note that not allowing loops does not mean that a Node cannot have two parents, like Config1 is a component of Device1 and Device2 and thus having two parents in the hierarchy.

Combined with the configuration hierarchy, loops are still possible. The configuration hierarchy cannot use HasComponent References; otherwise, the nonlooping constraint on the inherited HasChild ReferenceType would be broken. Since configurations logically do not have the devices they configure as part of them, it makes no sense to use the HasComponent ReferenceType.

Another example of a HasChild Reference is the HasSubtype ReferenceType exposing type hierarchies (used, e.g., in the ReferenceType hierarchy in Fig. 2.5). Loops do not make any sense in this case since types cannot be (indirect) subtypes of themselves.

The Reason to allow loops in hierarchical References is that a server may expose the same Nodes in different Hierarchies as already shown in Fig. 2.7. Servers may define their own ReferenceTypes under HierarchicalReferences used to expose additional Hierarchies. They can choose to make those hierarchies nonlooping as well, but loops are possible in combination with other hierarchies, for example, the hierarchy using HasChild References. When no additional hierarchy needs to be defined, but only a more specific semantic of the References should be specified, the additional ReferenceTypes should become subtypes of the HasChild ReferenceType.

---

[3] However, it is not allowed that a Node references itself directly with a hierarchical Reference.

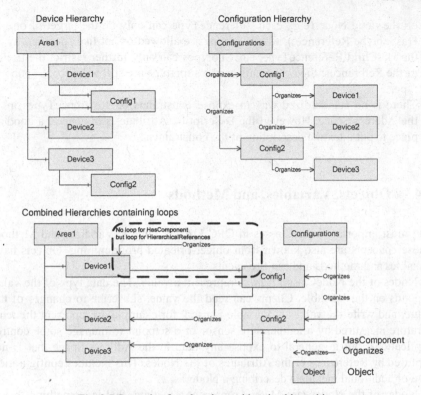

Device Hierarchy

Configuration Hierarchy

Combined Hierarchies containing loops

**Fig. 2.7** Example of nonlooping and looping hierarchies

**What's allowed and what's not?**

References between Nodes are restricted. It is not allowed to provide a Reference of the same type in the same direction between the same Nodes twice. This includes subtypes of the ReferenceType, but not supertypes. For example, it is allowed having References of different types of hierarchical References, but not using HasComponent and a subtype of HasComponent. The restriction regarding the same type is inherent by the model, since References are defined by the source and target Node and the ReferenceType. To avoid that servers provide a Reference of type "A" as well as the more specialized subtype of "A" called "B" it is not allowed to provide both References. Only the most appropriated ReferenceType should be used. Using the subtype always implies that the supertype is valid as well. Clients must consider this when browsing or querying the Address Space using filters on References.

Specific ReferenceTypes further restrict the use of the ReferenceType. That may include the allowed source Node and the target Node (e.g., restricting the NodeClass or a concrete type), the number of times a Reference is used on the same Node (e.g., each ReferenceType can only be the target of one HasSubtype Reference[4]), whether loops are allowed or not like specified by the HasChild ReferenceType, etc. Subtypes can only further restrict the use of the References; the constraints on the supertype are still valid for the subtype.

There is no standardized way to expose constraints on ReferenceTypes in the Address Space. However, the Description Attribute is in general a good place to put a textual description of the constraints.

## 2.4    Objects, Variables, and Methods

The most important NodeClasses in OPC UA are Object, Variable, and Method. These concepts are also known from object-oriented programming. Objects have variables and methods and can fire events.

Nodes of the NodeClass *Variable* represent a value. The data type of the value depends on the Variable. Clients can read the value, subscribe to changes of the value, and write the value. A Variable is used, for example, to represent the temperature measured by a temperature sensor or a setpoint to manage some control applications, but in general to expose any data in the Address Space that is not captured by References or the Attributes of the Nodes. This includes configuration data or additional metadata describing a Node.

Nodes of the NodeClass *Method* represent a method, that is, something that is called by a client and returns a result. Each Method specifies the input arguments a client shall use and the output arguments a client shall expect as a result. The intention of a Method is that it executes relatively fast. The client uses the Call Service to invoke the Method (see Chap. 5) and the response of this Service call already contains the result. When servers need to expose long running processes that are started and controlled by the client, they should use Programs (see Sect. 4.8). Examples are Methods to open a valve or starting a motor, as well as more complex tasks like calculating some simulation results based on provided input values. In general, using a Method makes sense when a set of arguments is used as input or output or both or a special action should be triggered in a defined way in the server. A Method in OPC UA does only provide the signature of a Method. There is no standardized way to get or set the implementation of a Method of an OPC UA server.

Nodes of the NodeClass *Object* are used to structure the Address Space. Objects do not contain data other than describing the Node with Attributes like Display-Name and Description. Values of Objects are exposed using Variables. Objects

---

[4] Please be aware that the HasSubtype Reference is modeled pointing from the supertype to the subtype. It is a hierarchical Reference and therefore it makes sense to expose a type hierarchy in that direction. However, typically in modeling languages like UML the subtype points to its supertype.

contain no Value Attribute like Variables. Objects can be used to group Variables, Methods, or other Objects. Although OPC UA does not define a clear concept of ownership, Methods and Variables always belong to an Object (or ObjectType, see Sect. 2.5). Methods are always called in the context of an Object. In addition to the contained Methods and the Variables, an Object can be an EventNotifier. Clients can subscribe to an EventNotifier to receive Events (see Sect. 2.10).

In Fig. 2.8, the concept of an Object containing Objects, Variables, and Methods and generating Events is summarized. The Object Motor contains a Variable Status identifying if the motor is running or not. Clients can subscribe to this Variable and thus always get Notifications when the status of the motor changes. In addition, the Motor has some configuration Variables, grouped under another Object called Configuration. A client can read or subscribe to those Variables, but also change the configuration by writing the Variables. The Methods Start and Stop can be invoked by the client to start or stop the motor. In addition, clients can subscribe to Events of the Motor. The motor can, for example, generate Events when it goes into a maintenance state and is not working properly anymore. The Motor Object can be connected to other Objects using specific ReferenceTypes, in

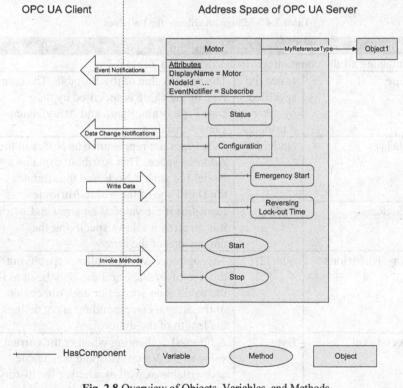

**Fig. 2.8** Overview of Objects, Variables, and Methods

the example it just references another Object Object1 with a Reference of MyReferenceType. In that case, the referenced Object is not considered to be part of the motor.

The only additional Attribute of the Object NodeClass is used to identify if an Object can be used as EventNotifier, that is, whether clients can subscribe to the Object to receive Events or to read or update the history of Events. This is captured in Table 2.3.

**Table 2.3** Additional Attributes for Objects

| Attribute | DataType | Description |
|---|---|---|
| Containing all the common Attributes defined in Table 2.1 | | |
| EventNotifier | Byte | This Attribute represents a bit mask that identifies whether the Object can be used to subscribe to Events and whether the history of Events is accessible and changeable |

Variables provide real data and thus the number of additional Attributes is much higher. These Attributes are summarized in Table 2.4.

**Table 2.4** Additional Attributes for Variables

| Attribute | DataType | Description |
|---|---|---|
| Containing all the common Attributes defined in Table 2.1 | | |
| Value | Is not fix; specified by other Attributes | The actual value of the Variable. The data type of the value is specified by the DataType, ValueRank, and ArrayDimensions Attributes |
| DataType | NodeId | DataTypes are represented as Nodes in the Address Space. This Attribute contains a NodeId of such a Node and thus defines the DataType of the Value Attribute |
| ValueRank | Int32 | Identifies if the value is an array and when it is an array it allows specifying the dimensions of the array |
| ArrayDimensions | UInt32[] | This optional Attribute allows specifying the size of an array and can only be used if the value is an array. For each dimension of the array a corresponding entry defines the length of the dimension |
| AccessLevel | Byte | A bit mask indicating whether the current value of the Value Attribute is readable and writable as well as whether the history of the value is readable and changeable |

*(Continued)*

| UserAccessLevel | Byte | Contains the same information as the AccessLevel but takes user access rights into account |
| MinimumSampling-Interval | Duration | This optional Attribute provides the information how fast the OPC UA server can detect changes of the Value Attribute. For Values not directly managed by the server, e.g., the temperature of a temperature sensor, the server may need to scan the device for changes (polling) and thus is not able to detect changes faster than this minimum interval |
| Historizing | Boolean | Indicates whether the server currently collects history for the Value. The AccessLevel Attribute does not provide that information, it only specifies whether some history is available |

The data type of the Value Attribute is defined by the DataType, ValueRank, and the ArrayDimensions Attribute. The reason having three Attributes is that the support of multidimensional arrays is built into OPC UA. Clients can read or write only parts of an array or subscribe to parts of an array. Thus the DataType specifies only the base type and the other Attributes define whether an array or a matrix of the DataType is used and optionally the size of the array or matrix. More details about DataTypes are described in Sect. 2.8. The reason for not using References to indicate a DataType is that some Variables may often change the DataType and thus clients may want to subscribe to them. Tracking changes on References is much harder in OPC UA, as described in Sect. 2.11.3.

To avoid confusion regarding the Attributes defining the data type of the Value, we provide examples of how to use those Attributes showing allowed Values in Table 2.5.

**Table 2.5** Examples of how to use the Attributes of a Variable defining the type of the Value

| Possible Values | DataType | ValueRank | ArrayDimensions |
| --- | --- | --- | --- |
| "Just a String" | String | −1 (Scalar) | − |
| {1,2,3} {4,7,9,12} | Int16 | 1 (OneDimension) | − |
| {1,2,3} {3,4,8} | UInt16 | 1 (OneDimension) | {3} |
| 1 {1,4,9} {1,2}{1,5} | UInt32 | −2 (Any) | − |
| {3,4}{1,2}{3,4} | Int32 | 2 (two dimensions) | {2, 3} |
| {123,123} {1,2}{1,1}{2,4} | UInt64 | 0 (OneOrMoreDimensions) | − |

The main difference between the WriteMask and the AccessLevel, respectively, UserWriteMask and UserAccessLevel is that the AccessLevel is only related to the Value Attribute. In addition to the write access indicated by the WriteMask, it captures the read access of current data as well as the read and write access to historical data. Thus the optional WriteMask Attribute excludes the Value Attribute of Variables, which means the information is not duplicated and clients must always access the mandatory AccessLevel Attribute to receive that information.

The additional Attributes of a Method are summarized in Table 2.6. For the Method NodeClass, a concept introduced in the Address Space Model is already used to form the Address Space Model. The input- and output-arguments of a Method are not described in Attributes but in OPC UA Variables belonging to the Method. That allows keeping all Attribute data types simple except for the Value Attribute, since the complex argument structure defining Method arguments is provided in the Value Attribute of a Variable. Since those Variables are needed for most Methods, Table 2.6 does not only contain the Attributes of the Method NodeClass but also the standard Variables used to define the arguments of the Method (or more precise standard Properties which are special Variables described in Sect. 2.6).

**Table 2.6** Additional Attributes and standard Properties for Methods

| Attribute | DataType | Description |
|---|---|---|
| Containing all the common Attributes defined in Table 2.1 | | |
| Executable | Boolean | A flag indicating if the Method can be invoked at the moment |
| UserExecutable | Boolean | Same as the Executable Attribute taking user access rights into account |
| Property | | |
| InputArguments | Argument[] | This optional Property defines an array of input arguments for the method. The order of the array defines the order of the arguments. If the Property is not provided the Method has no input argument |
| OutputArguments | Argument[] | Same as InputArguments for the output of a Method |

The structure of the data type Argument is summarized in Table 2.7. The description of each argument of a Method contains a name, a textual description, and the definition of the data type. Here, the same mechanisms are used as in the Variable NodeClass.

Let us take a look on how a method in an object-oriented programming language is mapped to the Method NodeClass. At the moment we do not consider how the Method is bound to an Object, and this will be done in Sect. 2.5 when ObjectTypes are introduced. In Fig. 2.9, a method signature is shown using pseudo code. This method, called Encrypt, takes a key and some data as input and returns the encrypted data and the length of the encrypted data. The mapping to OPC UA is shown in Fig. 2.9 as well. In OPC UA, a Method is created called Encrypt having Variables for input- and output-arguments. The description of the input arguments of the Method is provided by the Value Attribute of the InputArguments Variable. The return value of the method and the out parameter called length are both provided by the Value of the OutputArguments Variable. Since the return value of a method is not named, a name has to be generated for that Argument. In the example, all Arguments have no description. Of course it is reasonable to put in a description if available, for example, from the comments of the method.

The full functionality of Classic OPC can be provided by using only Objects and Variables. By using OPC UA Methods, you can avoid workarounds having

**Table 2.7** Structure of the Argument DataType

| Name | DataType | Description |
|---|---|---|
| Name | String | Name of the Argument |
| DataType | NodeId | NodeId of a DataType Node |
| ValueRank | Int32 | Indicates if the argument is a scalar value, an array, or a matrix |
| ArrayDimensions | UInt32[] | Optionally defines the size of the array or matrix |
| Description | LocalizedText | Description of the argument |

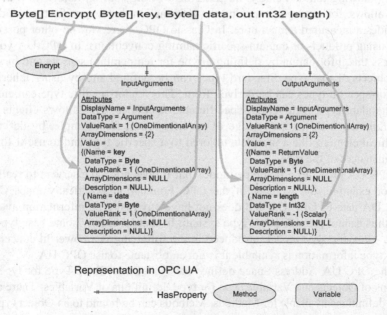

**Fig. 2.9** Mapping of a method in pseudo code to OPC UA

write-only items to specify input arguments and to start a method and using read-only items as output parameters.

**What's allowed and what's not?**

Variables must always belong to another Node. Therefore, they must be referenced by at least one HasComponent or HasProperty Reference from another Node. In Sect. 2.6, details are described for the different kinds of Variables, called Data Variables and Properties.

Methods must belong to an Object (or ObjectType) and therefore referenced from one of those with at least one HasComponent Reference. Methods can only be invoked on Objects (or ObjectTypes) referencing the Method with a HasComponent Reference.

Each Object and each Variable must be typed, that is, pointing with exactly one HasTypeDefinition Reference to an ObjectType, respectively, VariableType (details can be found in Sect. 2.5). However, this requirement can be fulfilled very easily. If no real type information is available or shall not be exposed for some reasons, the base types defined by OPC UA can be used.

## 2.5    Types for Objects and Variables

A main feature of OPC UA is providing type information not only on data type level (knowing that a Value is an Int32 or a String) but on object level as well. This allows, for example, exposing the information that a specific type of device provides a measured temperature. In Classic OPC, there was no other possibility then using product- or domain-specific naming conventions. In OPC UA you can express this information by defining a type for temperature sensors and by creating objects of that type. Standard types can be defined and by using inheritance vendor-specific types can be derived from. The vendor-specific type can enhance the standard type with vendor-specific characteristics. This allows clients to be programmed with the knowledge of specific types, for example, by defining a graphical element like a faceplate tailored to a specific type and to use it for several instances of the type.

OPC UA provides a rich type model, but it does not force servers to really use it. For example, the wrapper of the OPC Foundation generically maps Classic OPC DA data to OPC UA and does not have any real type information available and thus cannot provide a real type system. In that case, only some base types are used. Thus, the type model introduced in the following is a powerful concept, but if no type information is available it is not an obstacle to use OPC UA.

The OPC UA Address Space defines the NodeClass ObjectType for type definitions of Objects and VariableType for type definitions of Variables. There are no type definitions available for Methods. Methods can be bound to an ObjectType and are thus available on Objects, but they are defined by their BrowseName and its arguments and thus no type is needed.

If we are generalizing ObjectTypes and VariableTypes to explain common characteristics, we will call them *TypeDefinition*.

## 2.5.1 Simple ObjectTypes

*ObjectTypes* can be simple or complex. Complex types expose some structure of Nodes beneath them that are present on each instance of the type, whereas simple types define only some semantic for the Object. An example of a simple type is the FolderType defined by OPC UA [UA Part 3]. Here the semantic is defined that the purpose of a folder is to organize other Nodes in the Address Space. No additional structure is defined beneath the FolderType.

The Attributes of an ObjectType are summarized in Table 2.8. The only additional Attribute specifies if the type is abstract. An abstract type cannot be referenced as type definition by an Object and is only used to organize the types in the type hierarchy.

**Table 2.8** Additional Attributes for ObjectTypes

| Attribute | DataType | Description |
| --- | --- | --- |
| Containing all the common Attributes defined in Table 2.1 | | |
| IsAbstract | Boolean | This Attribute indicates whether the ObjectType is concrete or abstract and therefore cannot directly be used as type definition |

Let us examine how the type system for Objects works. In Fig. 2.10, you can see the simple ObjectType FolderType defined by OPC UA and some Objects using the type. An Object references its type using the HasTypeDefinition ReferenceType. Each Object is typed and has exactly one type, thus each Object is the source of exactly one HasTypeDefinition Reference. In Fig. 2.10, the Objects "Root" and "Objects" references the FolderType using a HasTypeDefinition Reference and therefore are of type FolderType. Both Nodes are actually standard entry points into the Address Space and defined in [UA Part 5].

When the NodeManagement Services (see Chap. 5) are used to create a new Object, the type definition has to be provided. Some Attributes for the new Object do not have to be specified but can be filled with default values of the ObjectType. For Objects only[5] the Description and the DisplayName Attributes are by default

---

[5] The WriteMask and UserWriteMask can be used as well; however, here something may need to be changed by some server-internal logic since Objects and ObjectTypes have different Attributes.

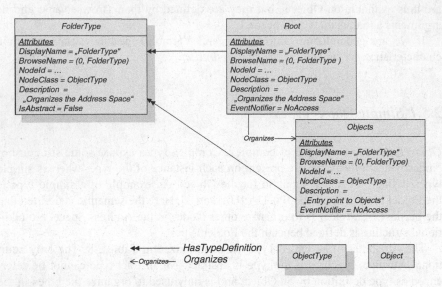

**Fig. 2.10** Example of a simple ObjectType

filled with default values from the ObjectType. This is exemplified on the Root Object where the Description of the FolderType is used.

Other than providing the semantic, the FolderType does not restrict the usage of its instances. In theory, all Attributes of the Node can be changed (which typically does not make sense for some Attributes like the NodeClass). New References can be added to the Node (like Root is now referencing Objects in Fig. 2.10) and later on they can be removed from the Object. However, this may not be true for all kinds of References. Even if the FolderType does not restrict the usage of References, there may be a ReferenceType that restricts its usage to certain ObjectTypes or NodeClasses. In addition, other ObjectTypes may restrict how instances of it are referenced as we will see when we talk about complex ObjectTypes.

ObjectTypes support inheritance and thus there is a type hierarchy of Object-Types. In Fig. 2.11, you can see an excerpt of a type hierarchy where the simple type BranchType is derived from FolderType. This type could be used by a wrapper of OPC DA servers to represent OPC DA branches.[6] They have the same purpose then Objects of FolderType, that is, they are just organizing the Address Space. However, making a subtype makes sense, so clients know that they are accessing wrapped Classic OPC DA data. Clients can ignore the subtype and based on the knowledge that it is a subtype of FolderType handle every Object of type Branch-Type like an Object of type FolderType.

---

[6] Please be aware that the actual OPC DA Wrapper implementation of the OPC Foundation does not use a subtype but directly uses the FolderType for DA branches.

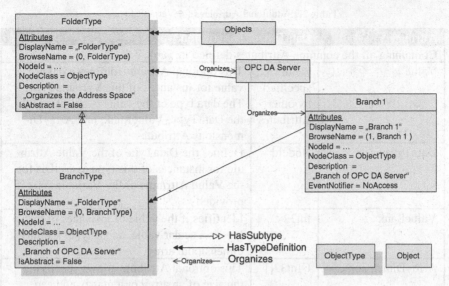

**Fig. 2.11** Inheritance of a simple ObjectType

## 2.5.2 Simple VariableTypes

Like ObjectTypes, VariableTypes can be simple or complex as well. The complex type exposes a structure of Nodes beneath it that is available at the instances, whereas the simple VariableType defines only the semantic of a Variable or restricts the usage of the data type of the Value Attribute on the instances. For example, the OPC UA specification defines a base type for Variables called BaseDataVariableType not restricting the usage of the data type [UA Part 5]. A subtype could define a Counter Variable having a typical counter semantic and restricting the usage of the data type to a scalar integer value.

Before we go into the details of the example, let us examine the Attributes of the VariableType NodeClass in Table 2.9.

The Attributes of the VariableType NodeClass are very similar to the Variable NodeClass. It contains the Value Attribute and the definition of the data type for the Value Attribute. It does not contain those Attributes providing information about the runtime behavior of the Value (is it currently historized, is it readable, what is the minimum sampling rate, etc.), but it contains the IsAbstract Attribute identifying if the VariableType can directly be used by instances or is only used to organize the VariableType hierarchy. Unlike for Variables, the Value Attribute is only optional since it has no real use for VariableTypes since it is expected that the Value will have no real meaning on the VariableType. The only reason for providing the Value is to define a default value for instances of the VariableType. Thus providing the data type information for the value on the VariableType is used mainly to define the data type for instances of the VariableType.

In Sect. 2.8, you will learn that there is also a hierarchy of DataTypes. A VariableType may use only some base types of that hierarchy and instances of the VariableType may offer more concrete types. Let us examine a concrete example.

**Table 2.9** Additional Attributes for VariableTypes

| Attribute | DataType | Description |
|---|---|---|
| Containing all the common Attributes defined in Table 2.1 | | |
| Value | Is not fix; specified by other Attributes | This optional Attribute defines a default value for instances of this VariableType. The data type of the value is specified by the DataType, ValueRank, and ArrayDimensions Attributes |
| DataType | NodeId | Defines the DataType of the Value Attribute for instances of this type as well as for the Value Attribute of the VariableType if provided |
| ValueRank | Int32 | Identifies if the value of instances of this type is a scalar value, an array, or a multi-dimensional array |
| ArrayDimensions | UInt32[] | This optional Attribute allows specifying the size of an array or a matrix and can only be used if the value is an array. For each dimension of the array the corresponding entry into this array defines the size of the dimension |
| IsAbstract | Boolean | This Attribute indicates if the VariableType is abstract and therefore cannot directly be used as type definition or concrete |

In Fig. 2.12, you can see the BaseDataVariableType. It uses the BaseDataType (the root of the DataType hierarchy) and does not restrict the usage of arrays. Thus instances of this VariableType can restrict their data type to their needs (like Variable1 uses a scalar Int32).

But the restriction of the data type does not have to be made on instances. It is also valid that Variables use only abstract base data types. In that case, the client must expect that any subtype of that data type is returned. For example, Variable2 only restricts the data type to be a scalar, thus valid retuned values are a String "Test1," the Int32 "123," etc. The data type can change every time the value changes and clients must be able to handle this behavior. In Sect. 2.8, you will see that there are more abstract DataTypes. This allows, for example, to expose that a number is provided as value without specifying the concrete type of number.

For subtyping simple VariableTypes, the same rules apply as for instantiating a VariableType. The data type can be made more concrete, but of course not be expanded. In Fig. 2.13, you can see an example of subtyping the BaseDataVariableType. The subtype Counter of the BaseDataVariableType restricts the usage of the data type (only scalar integers are allowed) and also defines the semantic for instances of that VariableType. It uses the name (Counter) and the Description Attribute to define the semantic.

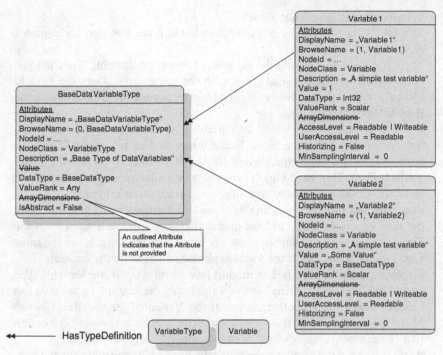

Variable 1

Attributes
DisplayName = „Variable1"
BrowseName = (1, Variable1)
NodeId = ...
NodeClass = Variable
Description = „A simple test variable"
Value = 1
DataType = Int32
ValueRank = Scalar
~~ArrayDimensions~~
AccessLevel = Readable | Writeable
UserAccessLevel = Readable
Historizing = False
MinSamplingInterval = 0

BaseDataVariableType

Attributes
DisplayName = „BaseDataVariableType"
BrowseName = (0, BaseDataVariableType)
NodeId = ...
NodeClass = VariableType
Description = „Base Type of DataVariables"
~~Value~~
DataType = BaseDataType
ValueRank = Any
~~ArrayDimensions~~
IsAbstract = False

An outlined Attribute indicates that the Attribute is not provided

Variable 2

Attributes
DisplayName = „Variable2"
BrowseName = (1, Variable2)
NodeId = ...
NodeClass = Variable
Description = „A simple test variable"
Value = „Some Value"
DataType = BaseDataType
ValueRank = Scalar
~~ArrayDimensions~~
AccessLevel = Readable | Writeable
UserAccessLevel = Readable
Historizing = False
MinSamplingInterval = 0

◄───── HasTypeDefinition    VariableType    Variable

**Fig. 2.12** Example of a simple VariableType

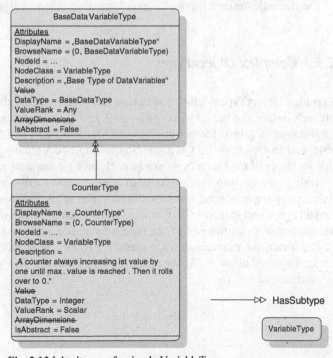

BaseDataVariableType

Attributes
DisplayName = „BaseDataVariableType"
BrowseName = (0, BaseDataVariableType)
NodeId = ...
NodeClass = VariableType
Description = „Base Type of DataVariables"
~~Value~~
DataType = BaseDataType
ValueRank = Any
~~ArrayDimensions~~
IsAbstract = False

CounterType

Attributes
DisplayName = „CounterType"
BrowseName = (0, CounterType)
NodeId = ...
NodeClass = VariableType
Description =
„A counter always increasing ist value by
one until max . value is reached . Then it rolls
over to 0."
~~Value~~
DataType = Integer
ValueRank = Scalar
~~ArrayDimensions~~
IsAbstract = False

───────▷▷ HasSubtype

VariableType

**Fig. 2.13** Inheritance of a simple VariableType

**What's allowed and what's not?**

The following rules apply not only for simple types but also for complex types.

There are no rules keeping the names of Object- or VariableTypes unique. A server can provide several types with the same name. Only the NodeId makes a type unique. However, it is not recommended using the same BrowseName twice.

It is not forbidden that Object- or VariableTypes have multiple supertypes; however, it is not recommended. Each Object- and each VariableType must have at least one supertype, except for the BaseObjectType and the Base-VariableType. Thus each ObjectType must be a subtype of BaseObjectType and each VariableType must be a subtype of BaseVariableType.

Instances and subtypes of VariableTypes can further restrict the data type, but they cannot leverage it. That means that they can use a subtype of the DataType but not use a supertype or any other DataType that is not the same DataType or a subtype. If the ValueRank does not specify the concrete characteristic, it can be specified in the instance or subtype. If the VariableType specifies, for example, "Any" in the ValueRank, the subtype or instance can choose "Scalar" or any other choice. If the VariableType specifies OneOr-MoreDimensions the instance or subtype can specify a concrete dimension (e.g., OneDimension); however, it cannot specify "Any" or "Scalar."

Any semantic defined by a supertype still has to be applicable for the subtypes. VariableType CounterType used in the example may be subtyped but the semantic defined for the CounterType must still be valid for the subtype.

## 2.5.3 Complex ObjectTypes

Complex ObjectTypes define a structure of Nodes beneath them that is available on each instance of the ObjectType as well. In Fig. 2.14, an example of a complex ObjectType is given. MotorType has the Methods Start and Stop, a Status Variable, and an Object called Configuration having two Variables. Figure 2.14 shows that Instances of the MotorType like Motor1 have the same structure beneath them.

Before we go into more details of how complex ObjectTypes work, let us debate why we may need complex ObjectTypes at all. A server exposing complex ObjectTypes and instances of that type gives clients the possibility program their application with knowledge of the type information and use this on all instances. A client can, for example, have a specific part of a user interface tailored to the ObjectType and displays this for each instance of the type. In Fig. 2.15, this scenario is summarized.

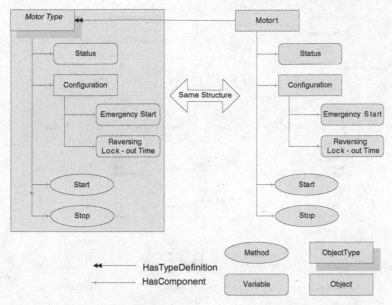

**Fig. 2.14** Example of a complex ObjectType

The graphical element of the client is programmed with knowledge of the MotorType. In the user interface of the client, this graphical element is used two times representing the two instances of the MotorType, called Motor1 and Motor2. The knowledge about the type is used to access and display the information provided by the instances. Using the knowledge about the type is not restricted to complex ObjectTypes. For example, a client can implement a special handling for the FolderType by using a specific icon for it in a tree control. Nevertheless, the real power comes into play when programming with knowledge of complex types considering the structure of Nodes beneath the types.

Another advantage of having complex ObjectTypes is that they are defined once and can be used in several places. When a server creates a new instance of the ObjectType, it is guaranteed that it has the structure defined by the ObjectType. An ObjectType can be defined in a project where it is used several times, in a vendor-specific library, or even in a standard Information Model. Several instances of the ObjectType can be instantiated, using the AddNodes Service (see Chap. 5). Only the ObjectType and the base Attributes of the instance have to be specified. This scenario is shown in Fig. 2.16. The client calls the AddNodes Service to create a new Object Motor1. All newly created Nodes and References based on this call are exposed in a bold line style. In the AddNodes Service, the client has to specify the ReferenceType and Node to which the new Node should be connected. In our example the Area1 Object is chosen and Organizes ReferenceType. In addition, it specifies the Attributes for the new Node like the DisplayName Motor1 and it specifies the ObjectType. Based on the specified ObjectType, the HasType-Definition Reference to the ObjectType is created and the structure defined by the ObjectType is automatically created beneath the new Object.

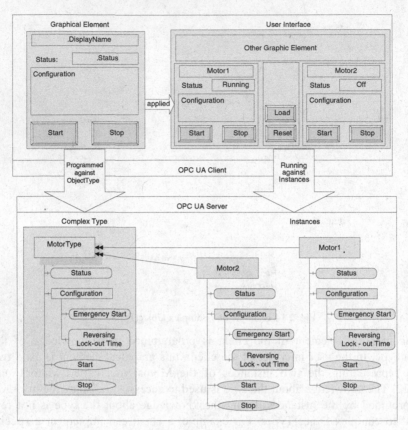

**Fig. 2.15** Programming against complex ObjectType

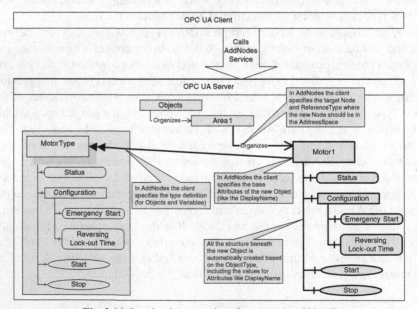

**Fig. 2.16** Creating Instances based on complex ObjectTypes

## 2.5.4 InstanceDeclarations

After explaining why complex ObjectTypes can be a very useful feature, let us examine them a little closer. As you can see in Fig. 2.14, the ObjectType Motor-Type uses the NodeClass ObjectType. All Nodes beneath it are of the Node-Classes Object, Variable, or Method and thus instances and not types. However, they are typically no real instances having real values behind them and thus they are called *InstanceDeclarations*. An InstanceDeclaration is a named entity used to define a complex ObjectType. The InstanceDeclarations are defined as Variables, Objects, and Methods exposed beneath the ObjectType. Since beneath something is not that obvious in a full-meshed network of Nodes exposing several hierarchies, the more precise definition is InstanceDeclarations are referenced from the ObjectType by a hierarchical Reference in forward direction, either directly or indirectly by another InstanceDeclaration. In addition, the InstanceDeclaration must have a ModellingRule (see Sect. 2.5.6).

A key feature of InstanceDeclarations is that they can be uniquely identified relative to the ObjectType. The same relative identifier applies for instances of the ObjectType and the counterpart of the InstanceDeclaration. This allows programming using the knowledge of the ObjectType. NodeIds cannot be used for that purpose since the InstanceDeclaration is typically a different Node than its counterpart on the instance and thus must have a different NodeId. Instead the Browse-Name is used, or for indirectly referenced InstanceDeclarations the *BrowsePath* which is a list of BrowseNames. This requires that an InstanceDeclaration must have a unique BrowsePath starting from the ObjectType. The path must be unique independent of the NodeClass, which means that an ObjectType cannot have an Object and a Variable with the same BrowseName directly referenced as InstanceDeclaration. The BrowsePath is exemplified in Fig. 2.17.

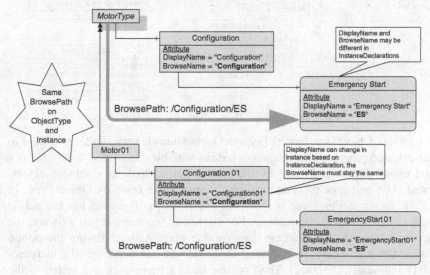

**Fig. 2.17** Unique BrowsePaths for InstanceDeclarations

Clients can detect the BrowsePath of an InstanceDeclaration starting at the ObjectType and following hierarchical References in forward direction. They have to add the BrowseName of each Node before they reach the target InstanceDeclaration. Clients can store that information and when they use their display or other application to access a concrete instance of the ObjectType, they can call a special Service called TranslateBrowsePathsToNodeIds (see Chap. 5 for details). This Service takes the NodeId of the instance and the BrowsePath as input and returns the NodeId of the counterpart of the InstanceDeclaration. By using this NodeId, clients can do the appropriate action with the Node, like subscribing to the data or writing them.

Please be aware that the constraint on unique BrowseNames only applies for InstanceDeclarations, not for instances. In Fig. 2.18 you can see that MotorX references another Configuration Object containing the default Configuration settings having the same BrowseName as the Configuration Object based on the Motor-Type. In that case, the TranslateBrowsePathsToNodeIds Service will return an array of NodeIds, having the NodeId of the Node based on the TypeDefinition as first entry.

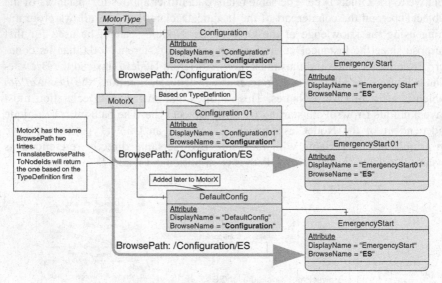

**Fig. 2.18** Nonunique BrowsePaths for Instances

A complex ObjectType having InstanceDeclarations is very similar to a class in object-oriented programming languages having variables. In a class, a variable is a named entity that is addressed by the name. Let us look at a sample object-oriented class and how this can easily be mapped to a complex ObjectType. In Fig. 2.19, the class Employee is shown in pseudo-code. The class has the public variables Name, Salary, and Address. For simplicity the name is just a String, the Salary an Integer, but the address uses another class Address having the public variables Street and City. In addition, the Employee has two methods, Increase-Salary() and SalaryAfterTax(). The first one takes a percentage and increases the salary of the employee; the second returns the salary of the employee after taxes. The mapping to ObjectTypes is straight forward. The Address class is mapped to an ObjectType AddressType having two Variables. The class Employee is mapped to the ObjectType EmployeeType having two Variables for Salary and Name and an instance of AddressType to represent the Address.[7] In addition, there are two Methods IncreaseSalary and SalaryAfterTax, one having only input arguments and ments and the other having only output arguments.

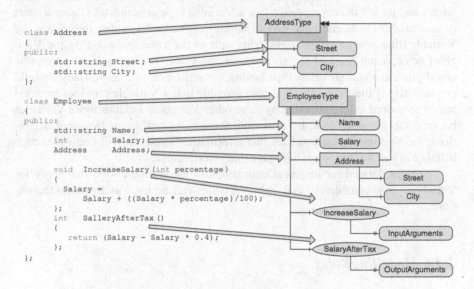

Fig. 2.19 Mapping an object-oriented class to an ObjectType

Of course, there are also differences between classes of typical object-oriented programming languages and ObjectTypes. One difference is that there is no standard way to expose the implementation of a Method. On the other hand, OPC UA is more flexible. It is allowed to add components to an instance independent of the type definition. For example, an instance of Employee could have a Variable called Award storing information about an award received by the employee, without altering the ObjectType or creating a subtype of it. That is also allowed on InstanceDeclarations, thus the EmployeeType could add a Variable ZipCode beneath the Address Object. In an object-oriented programming language, you would typically have to subtype Address to add information in that place.

---

[7] Please note that all Objects and Variables used as InstanceDeclarations are typed, although the type is not exposed in most of the examples shown so far. All constraints valid for Objects and Variables used as instances are valid for Objects and Variables used as InstanceDeclarations as well.

## 2.5.5 Complex VariableTypes

Before we consider ModellingRules and how subtyping works, let us take a look at complex VariableTypes. They are very similar to complex ObjectTypes. The main difference is that they can only use Variables as InstanceDeclarations and not Objects or Methods. Methods are defined for Objects; thus it is obvious that they do not fit to a VariableType. Variables are always parts of Objects or other Nodes and thus it makes no sense that a VariableType contains an Object as part of it. VariableTypes can only expose additional Variables, either describing the Variable (like providing the engineering unit of the value provided by the Variable) or exposing parts of the structure of the value. For example, the Variable could provide a complex data type having several fields and sub-variables would expose each of the fields. But it is also possible that a Variable provides an average of measured values provided by three other Variables and thus those Variables become sub-variables of it. By providing those sub-variables as InstanceDeclarations, the VariableType formalizes this information so clients will know that each instance of the VariableType will have that information.

The rules defined for InstanceDeclarations in the section above also apply for VariableTypes, considering that only Variables can be used as InstanceDeclarations.

## 2.5.6 ModellingRules

Each instance referenced by a TypeDefinition (i.e., ObjectType or VariableType) becomes an InstanceDeclaration if it has a *ModellingRule*. A ModellingRule specifies what happens to the InstanceDeclaration with respect to instances of the ObjectType. There are three fundamental choices, also called the NamingRule of the ModellingRule.

1. The first choice is to make the InstanceDeclaration *Mandatory*, which means that each instance must have a counterpart of the InstanceDeclaration having the same BrowsePath and must be of the same type as the InstanceDeclaration (when it is an Object or Variable) or a subtype of that type.
2. The second choice is to make it *Optional*, that is, each instance may have such a counterpart. But it is not required that each instance has such a counterpart.
3. The third choice is to make it a *Constraint*, which means that the Instance-Declaration defines a constraint for instances of the TypeDefinition. We will see later on more details on what constraints are possible. An example is a cardinality restriction specifying that an instance of the TypeDefinition shall reference a defined range of instances having the same type as the Instance-Declaration.

ModellingRules is an extensible concept in OPC UA, that is, servers or standard Information Models may define their own ModellingRules. However, they always have to specify one of the earlier mentioned NamingRules.

### 2.5.6.1  ModellingRules in the Address Space

ModellingRules are represented as Objects of the type ModellingRule. Each ModellingRule has a Variable (more precisely Property, see Sect. 2.6) called NamingRule. It contains the NamingRule of the ModellingRule. InstanceDeclarations reference a ModellingRule Object with the ReferenceType HasModellingRule to specify their ModellingRule. Each Node can reference only one ModellingRule using the HasModellingRule Reference. How ModellingRules are used in the Address Space is shown in Fig. 2.20 on the left side. To simplify the figures, we use in this book the notation shown on the right side, where the ModellingRule is added to the Node as text in brackets.

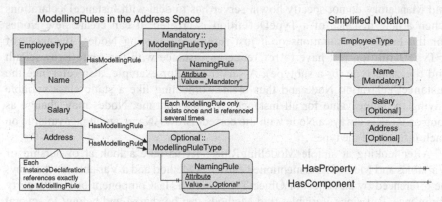

**Fig. 2.20** ModellingRules in the Address Space

### 2.5.6.2  ModellingRules Mandatory and Optional

There are two standard ModellingRules called Optional and Mandatory, named equally to their NamingRule. Let us take a look at an example how these two ModellingRules work. In Fig. 2.21, the AddressType has the InstanceDeclarations Street with the ModellingRule Optional and City with the ModellingRule Mandatory. This means that each instance must have a City and may have a Street. In Fig. 2.21 you can see that Address1 has both. In that case, both instances have ModellingRules as well. As long as they are not referenced by a TypeDefinition, they are no InstanceDeclarations. In that case it is allowed that any ModellingRule is used for the instances. Typically, normal instances have no ModellingRules like in Address2-4. Address2 omits the Street and only provides the City. In Address3

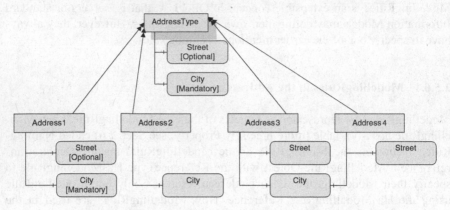

**Fig. 2.21** Applying Optional and Mandatory ModellingRules

and 4 you can see that both share the same City. The ModellingRules Optional and Mandatory do not specify how a server has to deal with InstanceDeclarations when a new instance of a TypeDefinition is created. It can create new Nodes for the InstanceDeclarations or it just references existing Nodes. Instances of a TypeDefinition just have to reference an instance with the same BrowsePath and the same type (or a subtype). A server can, for example, also reference the InstanceDeclaration Node and thus create something like a static class variable having the same value for all instances. During runtime, Nodes may change as long as there is always a Node with the correct BrowseName and type available on each instance of the type.

After looking at simple ModellingRules, let us take a look at ownership of Variables and Methods. As mentioned earlier, a Method and a Variable must always be referenced by an Object or ObjectType using a HasComponent or HasProperty Reference. But since Variables and Methods can be shared and belong to several Objects, they are not *owned* by one Object. Thus, if Address3 in Fig. 2.21 is deleted, the Street beneath it must be removed[8] since it does not have a Node referencing it, but the City cannot be deleted since it is still used by Address4.

Instances of complex TypeDefinitions can be used as InstanceDeclarations, again. In Fig. 2.22, you can see that Address is used as an InstanceDeclaration. Therefore, the instances based on the InstanceDeclarations City and Street become InstanceDeclarations as well. This means that there are rules regarding the ModellingRules. The ModellingRules may change; however, the NamingRule must stay the same. The only exception is Optional, which can be replaced by Mandatory. In general, ModellingRules may only be replaced if their contraints are tightened, not loosened. In Fig. 2.22, the ModellingRule of Street changed from Optional to Mandatory. Thus, a valid instance is Employee1 having both. It would not be

---

[8] There is no clear responsibility defined who has to delete the Node. It could be either done automatically by the server or by a client. However, if a client requests to delete only Address3, the server either has to delete the Street Node as well or reject the request.

allowed having an Employee2 not providing the Street, also the AddressType does not require it.

In Fig. 2.22, another rule regarding ModellingRules is exposed. The Address Object has the ModellingRule Optional and is on the only path to Street and City. This means that when Address is not provided, Street and City do not have to be provided as well as you can see in the valid Employee3 Object.

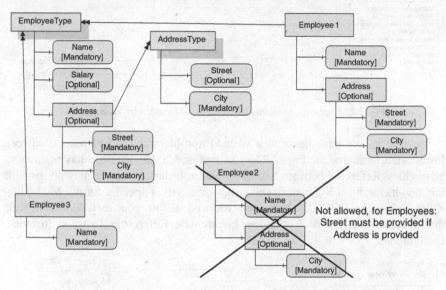

**Fig. 2.22** Instances used as InstanceDeclarations and based on InstanceDeclarations

Before we look at how to use the NamingRule Constraint and how to create our own ModellingRules, let us consider some more complex examples. First let us take a look at what happens if there is more than one BrowsePath from the TypeDefinition to the InstanceDeclaration. In Fig. 2.23, an example is given. A Temperature-SensorType having the EngineeringUnit Variable organized under the Folder Configuration and the Temperature Variable under Measurement. The Temperature Variable uses the EngineeringUnit Variable to expose its engineering unit.

There are two special cases; first two different References are connecting the same source with the same target. In Fig. 2.23, you can see that Measurement references Temperature two times. In that case, on each instance the counterpart to Measurement must reference the same Node with those two References; it is not allowed to point to two different Nodes.

The second case is that there are two different indirect paths. In Fig. 2.23, the EngineeringUnit is referenced by two different paths. In that case, it is allowed that an instance references one Node from Configuration and a different one from Temperature. In the example that probably does not make sense, but there are other use cases where this is a reasonable approach, for example, when shared (static) class variables are used.

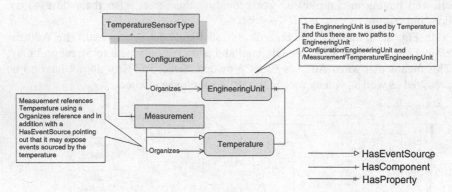

**Fig. 2.23** Example of InstanceDeclarations referenced by several paths

Now let us see what happens if we add non-hierarchical References between InstanceDeclarations. In Fig. 2.24. you can see a DeviceType having a non-hierarchical Reference between two sub-devices. Instances may or may not provide this non-hierarchical Reference. This behavior is server-specific for the Modelling-Rules defined by OPC UA. However, you may define your own ModellingRule that specifies how to deal with non-hierarchical References between Instance-Declarations.

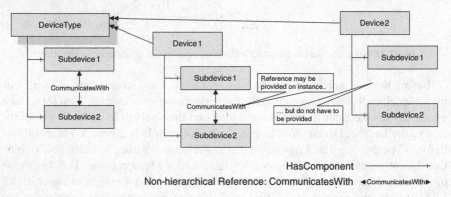

**Fig. 2.24** Non-hierarchical References between InstanceDeclarations

### 2.5.6.3 ModellingRules as Constraints

After looking at Mandatory and Optional InstanceDeclarations, let us take a look at InstanceDeclarations used to define constraints, and thus having the Naming-Rule Constraint in their ModellingRule. We will first take a look at the only ModellingRule defined by the current OPC UA specification defining a constraint. The ModellingRule is called ExposesItsArray and can be used for VariableTypes having an array as data type. The semantic is that each entry of the array is also exposed as a sub-variable. In Fig. 2.25, this is exemplified. The TeamType contains an array of Strings and a Constraint Variable using the ModellingRule ExposesItsArray. Instances of that type must have a sub-variable for each entry of the array as you can see in the UABookTeam Variable in Fig. 2.25. Exposing the sub-variables allows referencing single entries of the array since they are exposed as Nodes in the Address Space. Please be aware that it is not necessary to expose arrays to allow access to single entries of an array (subscribing to them, reading or writing them). This can be done with the OPC UA Services directly by addressing parts of the array (see Chap. 5).

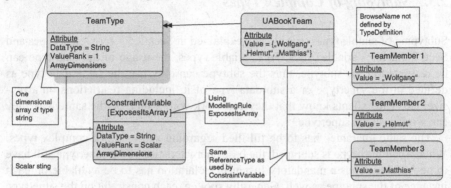

**Fig. 2.25** Using the ExposesItsArray ModellingRule

ExposesItsArray is just an example of Constraint ModellingRules. You can define your own ModellingRules needed to define constraints in your model. A typical constraint in modeling is a cardinality restriction. An instance of one type shall reference between *n* and *m* instances of another type. Such a constraint can be exposed by a Constraint ModellingRule. An InstanceDeclaration having such a ModellingRule can be used as a proxy Object (see Sect. 3.3.8) between two TypeDefinitions containing the min and max values and also reference the addressed ReferenceType. Such a ModellingRule will probably be integrated into version two of OPC UA. Therefore, we will not expose any details of such a ModellingRule, since we might model it slightly different then it will be in the specification.

Finally let us discuss why the ModellingRules defined by OPC UA do not cover every facet like what happens with non-hierarchical References or how instances are created based on the InstanceDeclarations. The OPC UA working group started defining all those things. But it turned out that there are different ways of how to handle this and different use cases where either one or the other possibility was more appropriate. Specifying all those possibilities would lead to a relatively large amount of ModellingRules that would become hard to understand. In addition, it is questionable how useful this additional information would become. In the case of programming against types you just need to know the hierarchical path to the target Node and you have to know if the Node is optional or mandatory. This is all provided by the defined ModellingRules. When creating instances based on types, the server is responsible that counterparts of all InstanceDeclarations exist based on the ModellingRules. Whether new Nodes are created or Nodes are shared is in the responsibility of the server and does not necessarily has to be exposed to the client. Thus the ModellingRules provided by OPC UA are a good foundation that can be extended with additional ModellingRules, especially with those that are constraint-related.

## 2.5.7 Subtyping of Complex Types

Subtyping of simple types was already explained in Sect. 2.5.1 for ObjectTypes and Sect. 2.5.2 for VariableTypes. For VariableTypes, the usage of the data type can be restricted in the subtype, thus the subtype can only use the same data type as defined in the supertype or a sub(data)type of it, including restrictions on array-size, etc. Thus clients know that they can work with a subtype the same way they can work with the supertype.

The same guarantee has to be fulfilled regarding subtyping of complex types. When a complex type is subtyped, the base characteristics of the supertype still have to be fulfilled. Thus a mandatory InstanceDeclaration has to be available on each instance of the subtype as well. Generally spoken, each constraint on the supertype has to be fulfilled on the subtype as well and can only be further restricted. This means that an optional InstanceDeclaration can be made mandatory on the sub-type, but no mandatory InstanceDeclaration can be made optional.

There have been two possibilities how to expose subtypes of complex types in the Address Space. Since each InstanceDeclaration of the supertype is valid on the subtype, one solution is that each subtype copies all InstanceDeclarations of the supertype or references the same Nodes. The other solution is that they are not copied but clients need to request the InstanceDeclarations of the supertypes as well to get a full picture of the subtype. The second approach is typically being used in object-oriented programming languages where variables of the supertype are inherited without the need to copy the code to the subtype. OPC UA has chosen the second approach as well to avoid an explosion of Nodes in a type hierarchy having several levels. Thus InstanceDeclarations do not have to be duplicated on subtypes unless you want to override them. In Fig. 2.26, subtyping of a complex type is shown in comparison to subtyping an object-oriented class. The object-oriented class Address is subtyped by InternationalAddress. Here, only an additional variable Country is added, the other variables are not specified but inherited by Address. The same is applied on the ObjectType InternationalAddressType. Only the InstanceDeclaration Country is added, the other InstanceDeclarations are inherited. To get the full picture of a TypeDefinition, you need to combine the InstanceDeclarations of the supertypes with the TypeDefinition. This combi-nation is called *fully-inherited InstanceDeclarationHierarchy*, and is shown for

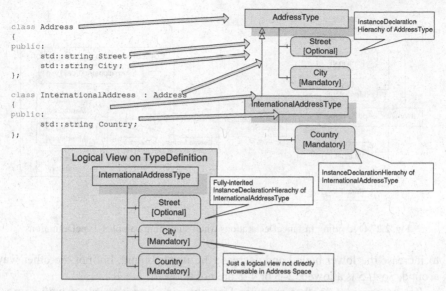

```
class Address
{
public:
    std::string Street;
    std::string City;
};

class InternationalAddress : Address
{
public:
    std::string Country;
};
```

**Fig. 2.26** Subtyping object-oriented classes and complex types

InternationalAddressType in Fig. 2.26. Here all information is captured to program against the type or to get the knowledge what would be instantiated as a minimum.

To use the fully-inherited InstanceDeclarationHierarchy, all InstanceDeclarations must have unique BrowsePaths. Thus subtypes cannot use the same Browse-Path for a different InstanceDeclaration. However, subtypes are able to override an existing InstanceDeclaration of the supertype (Fig. 2.27). For example, in an international address it may be required that a Street is provided. Therefore, the ModellingRule Optional is not appropriated anymore. As we have learned earlier, it is allowed to change Optional to Mandatory in an InstanceDeclaration. This is also true for subtyping. Thus a modified InternationalAddressType would create its own Street Variable defining it to be mandatory. Since the same BrowsePath is used then in the supertype, it is not an additional InstanceDeclaration, but the InstanceDeclaration of InternationalAddressType is overriding the one from AddressType. So the fully-inherited InstanceDeclarationHierarchy has still only one Street Variable, but this time the ModellingRule has changed since the over-ridden InstanceDeclaration is used. In [UA Part 3], the detailed algorithm how to get the fully-inherited InstanceDeclarationHierarchy is defined, considering a chain of supertypes.

Of course, when overriding InstanceDeclarations some rules have to be applied. In general, constraints can only be tightened, not loosened. This means that the same type or a subtype of the overridden InstanceDeclaration must be used, and that ModellingRules may only be further restricted. For example, if there was a constraining ModellingRule saying a Reference must exist 3–6 times, it is allowed

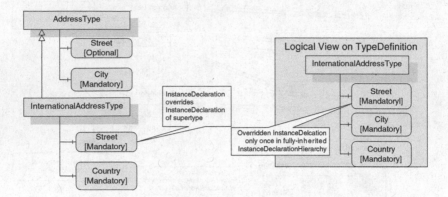

**Fig. 2.27** Overriding InstanceDeclarations when subtyping complex TypeDefinitions

to increase the lower bound and decrease the upper bound, but not the other way around. So 4–5 is allowed, 2–5 or 4–8 are not allowed.

Let us consider another example for subtyping and overriding with a more complex InstanceDeclarationHierarchy. In Fig. 2.28, there is the Temperature-SensorType we have already introduced in Fig. 2.23. The EngineeringUnit Variable is referenced by two BrowsePaths as well as by the Temperature Variable. The subtype MyTemperatureSensorType derives from the TemperatureSensorType. In this subtype, the optional EngineeringUnit of the Temperature has to be made mandatory. Since the EngineeringUnit Variable is not directly referenced by the ObjectType, it cannot directly be overridden. Instead the first InstanceDeclaration on the path to EngineeringUnit must be overridden and beneath that Node the full path to EngineeringUnit must be duplicated to be able to override Engineering-Unit. In Fig. 2.28, you can see that the path starting from Measurement and in addition the Temperature Variable are overridden and beneath it the Engineering-Unit, changing its ModellingRule to Mandatory.

Let us see what that means for the fully-inherited InstanceDeclarationHierarchy. As you can see, only one Reference between the ObjectType and Measurement is provided in the subtype. However, since both References must always refer to the same Node, they reference one Node in the fully-inherited InstanceDeclaration-Hierarchy. The EngineeringUnit is accessible by two paths in the supertype and only overridden in one path. In that case, the fully-inherited InstanceDeclaration-Hierarchy has to duplicate the EngineeringUnit, for the overridden path providing the changed ModellingRule and the original ModellingRule for the not overridden path. Please be aware that although the fully-inherited InstanceDeclarationHierarchy references two different Nodes called EngineeringUnit, instances of MyTemperatureSensorType can reference the same Node in both paths.

In OPC UA, each ObjectType must be a subtype of the BaseObjectType defined in [UA Part 5], thus there is only one type hierarchy. The specification does not restrict the type hierarchy to single inheritance. Thus multiple inheritance,

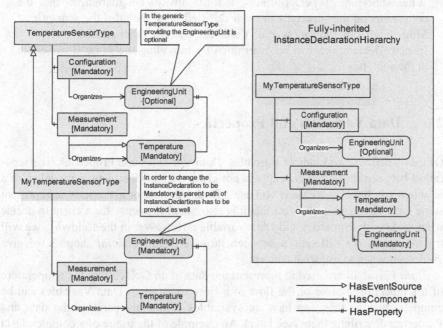

**Fig. 2.28** Overriding InstanceDeclarations having multiple BrowsePaths

that is, having several supertypes, is an option. However, the specification does only specify the rules for single inheritance (only needed for complex types).[9] Therefore, it is recommended to use single inheritance when possible.

---

**What's allowed and what's not?**

Complex TypeDefinitions have InstanceDeclarations with unique Browse-Paths. The ModellingRules define what's allowed on instances of the TypeDefinitions and what is not allowed.

Instances can have the same BrowsePath pointing to different Nodes; the TranslateBrowsePathsToNodeIds Service can be used to gather the Nodes based on the TypeDefinition.

OPC UA defines an open model. As long as it is not defined by some constraints on the TypeDefinition, it is possible to add References to instances of a TypeDefinition and thus adding Variables, Methods, etc. to those instances. However, servers may always restrict those capabilities without making them explicit on the TypeDefinition.

---

[9] Since there are different strategies how to deal with conflicts when using multiple inheritance, providing one specific semantic would exclude the simple mapping for models using a different semantic.

When subtyping TypeDefinitions, it must always be guaranteed that the constraints on the supertype are still fulfilled. That includes the semantic of ModellingRules, the data type of Variables, and any other constraint. InstanceDeclarations can be overridden by providing the same BrowsePath in the subtype.

## 2.6    Data Variables and Properties

OPC UA defines two kinds of Variables: Data Variables and Properties. The separation between those two concepts is not always easy when data is modeled, that is, when you have to decide if you use a Data Variable or a Property to represent some data. This leads to the fact that it is also not always easy for a client to decide what to do with Properties and Data Variables. However, in the following we will try to explain the differences between those concepts and in Chap. 3 we give guidelines when to use what concept.

*Data Variables* are used to represent the data of an Object, like the temperature of a temperature sensor or the flow of a flow transmitter. Data Variables can be complex, that is, they can have sub-variables containing parts of the data and Properties describing them (see later). An example of the usage of a complex Data Variable is when a Data Variable provides a complex type containing all data measured by a device and sub-variables only containing part of the measured data. The device could, for example, measure the temperature and the flow. Both values are captured in one Data Variable and are also exposed separately in sub-variables. Another example is a temperature calculated by the average of measured values from three temperature sensors. The Variables representing the individual measured values can be exposed as sub-variables of the aggregated Variable.

*Properties* are used to represent the characteristics of a Node, for example, containing the engineering unit of a measured temperature, whether it is measured in °C, °K, or Fahrenheit. In general, Properties are used whenever some characteristics of a Node should be described, which are not captured by the Attributes of a Node. InputArguments and OutputArguments of a Method are another example for Properties. Properties are simple. They cannot be complex exposing sub-variables and are always the leaf of each hierarchy, that is, cannot be the source of any hierarchical Reference.

This is the brief definition of Data Variables and Properties. Although this definition makes it very clear for some data to distinguish them between Data Variables and Properties, there is a large grey area in the middle where this is not clear. Is a writeable flag indicating whether a device generates real data or simulates data a Data Variable or a Property? Is the address of a vendor stored in your OPC UA server a Data Variable or a Property?

Another way to look at Data Variables and Properties is where the data is stored and how often it is changed. It is expected that Data Variables typically change their values often and are typically provided by underlying devices, whereas the values of Properties do not change so often and are stored in some configuration database. However, this is not specified by the OPC UA standard, since it cannot be clearly specified what it means that data changes often or not. Is it once per millisecond, per second, or per day? And depending on the mode of the server this behavior may be very different. When engineering a system, the temperature of a temperature device may not change at all since the device is not connected or activated. The engineering unit may change several times due to different engineering tasks. During runtime, it is different. Nevertheless, thinking about online data vs. configuration data may help you in your thinking.

Beside those semantic considerations, there are also syntactic differences between Data Variables and Properties.

Each Node may have Properties. They are connected using the HasProperty Reference. A Property must belong to at least one Node by being the target of at least one HasProperty Reference. Properties are not typed or more precise all Properties point to the same VariableType called PropertyType. The semantic of the Property is defined by its BrowseName. Since the semantic is defined by the BrowseName, each Property of a Node must have a unique BrowseName. Properties cannot be the source of any hierarchical Reference, which implies that Properties cannot have Properties.

Data Variables must belong to an Object or ObjectType. Therefore, they must be referenced by a HasComponent Reference coming from an Object, an ObjectType, a Variable, or a VariableType. References from a Variable or VariableType are allowed because they are used to expose complex Data Variables, and the root of such a complex Data Variable is again part of an Object or ObjectType. Data Variables are typed. Each Data Variable is of the type BaseDataVariableType or a subtype. In turn, the BrowseName of Data Variables does not have to be unique since the semantic is defined by the type.

Data Variables is the more powerful concept, whereas Properties are very simple to use. If you have to make the decision whether to use a Data Variable or a Property and you cannot make the decision based on the semantic differences described in this section, you should consider the syntax. If you need to use some features not provided by Properties directly or potentially in the future (e.g., extensibility through subtyping), your choice has to be Data Variables. Otherwise, you should consider using Properties since they are simpler to handle.

**What's allowed and what's not?**
A Property cannot be a Data Variable and vice versa. This means that a Property cannot be referenced by a HasComponent Reference and must be of the type PropertyType, whereas a Data Variable cannot be referenced by a HasProperty Reference and must be of type BaseDataVariableType or a subtype.
Properties cannot be the source of any hierarchical Reference. However, they can be the source of non-hierarchical References. Whenever you need to add information to a Property, you must use non-hierarchical References. This implies that when you need to add information the same way for Data

Variables and Properties you must use non-hierarchical References. This is used by the OPC UA specification, for example, when the historical configuration of a Variable is referenced.

Properties must have unique BrowseNames, that is, no Node may reference two Properties with the same BrowseName using the HasProperty Reference.

## 2.7    ModelParent for Objects, Variables, and Methods

ReferenceTypes like HasComponent give you a good indication that the referenced component contains or describes some characteristics of its parent. However, when looking at a TypeDefinition and its instances, you can see that some Nodes may be shared by several Nodes, for example, a static class variable containing the same value for all instances. As long as a client reads only the data of that Node, it should not care whether the Node is shared or not. But as soon as the client intends to change the Node, it is desirable that the client knows in what scope the Node is changed. Of course, the client can browse for inverse References to figure out how often the Node is referenced. However, the inverse Reference may not be provided, which is expected when having a static class variable since you typically do not want to reference every single instance of a type. In addition, having the Node referenced by several other Nodes does not provide you with information which Node was used to define the scope of it.

For that purpose OPC UA introduced the concept called *ModelParent*. It is modeled by a HasModelParent Reference pointing from the contained Node to the parent Node defining the scope of the contained Node. In the example of the class variable it would be the TypeDefinition Node. Let us look at a concrete example. The DeviceType in Fig. 2.29 has a Property called Icon representing an Icon,[10] for example used in a tree control exposing the type. Instances like Device1 share this Icon, that is, they are pointing to the same Node. If a client wants to change the Icon for a single instance Device1, it cannot just write a new Icon, since this would affect the TypeDefinition and all other instances like Device2 as well. The client could create a new Icon Node and let Device1 reference that Node. Thus the client can make a change in the scope of Device1 without changing the TypeDefinition of other instances. If a client wants to change the Icon for the TypeDefinition, it can realize that the Icon is in the right scope by following the HasModelParent Reference. In that case the change of the Icon affects the instances as well, but that is the intended use when changing the Icon for the TypeDefinition.

---

[10] By the way: Icon is an optional standard Property for Objects and ObjectTypes defined in [UA Part 3]

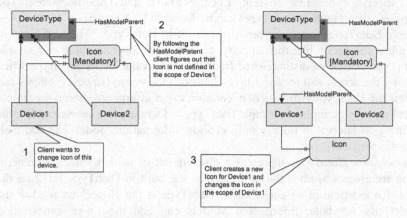

**Fig. 2.29** Example of the usage of ModelParents

**What's allowed and what's not?**
HasModelParent References must be provided for all instances using the standard ModellingRules Optional, Mandatory, and ExposesItsArray. It is allowed to provide the Reference for Objects, Variables, and Methods with other ModellingRules or without ModellingRules, but this is not required. Thus clients should make use of the feature if it is available, but they cannot expect the feature to be provided on Nodes using no ModellingRules or ModellingRules not defined by OPC UA.

## 2.8 DataTypes

All Attributes except for the Value Attribute of Variables and VariableTypes have a fixed data type. The DataType Attribute of Variable and VariableTypes is used together with the ValueRank and ArrayDimensions Attribute to define the data type of the Value Attribute of a specific Variable or VariableType. Variables are used to define Event fields and thus this also applies for Event fields. The same mechanism is used to define the data type of Methods in the Argument DataType. The ValueRank and ArrayDimensions Attributes are used to define whether the data type is a scalar or an array. The DataType Attribute is used to define the type used as scalar or array. The Attribute contains a NodeId of a DataType Node. DataTypes are represented as Nodes in the Address Space. This allows servers to define their own DataTypes and clients to access the information about the DataTypes. OPC UA distinguishes four kinds of DataTypes:

1. *Built-in DataTypes* are a fixed set of DataTypes defined by the OPC UA specification that cannot be extended by standardized or vendor-specific Information Models. They provide base types like Int32, Boolean, Double, and also OPC

UA specific types like NodeId, LocalizedText, and QualifiedName. The complete list of built-in DataTypes can be found in [UA Part 6].

2. *Simple DataTypes[11]* are subtypes of the Built-In DataTypes. They are handled on the wire exactly like their supertypes, that is, a concrete value of a simple DataType cannot be distinguished from the same value of its supertype when sent by the server and received by a client or vice versa. However, clients can access the DataType Attribute of a Variable to get information about the simple DataType. An example of a simple DataType is Duration as a subtype of Double defining an interval of time in milliseconds. Information Models can add their own simple DataTypes.

3. *Enumeration DataTypes* represent a discrete set of named values. Enumerations are always handled the same way as the built-in DataType Int32 on the wire. An example of an enumeration DataType is the NodeClass used in the NodeClass Attribute. Information Models can add their own enumeration DataTypes.

4. *Structured DataTypes* represent structured data. They are the most powerful construct specifying user-defined, complex DataTypes. An example of a structured DataType is the Argument DataType used to define an argument of a Method. It contains the name, data type, and a description of the argument. Information Models can add their own structured DataTypes.

In addition to those DataTypes, there is a set of abstract DataTypes that do not fit into these categories and are only used to organize the DataType hierarchy.

## 2.8.1 DataType NodeClass

All DataTypes are represented as Nodes of the NodeClass DataType in the Address Space. The Attributes of this NodeClass are summarized in Table 2.10.

**Table 2.10** Additional Attributes for DataTypes

| Attribute | DataType | Description |
|-----------|----------|-------------|
| Containing all the common Attributes defined in Table 2.1 | | |
| IsAbstract | Boolean | Indicates whether the DataType is abstract. An abstract DataType can be used in the DataType Attribute. However, concrete values must be of a concrete DataType |

Depending on the characteristics of the DataType, additional information is provided. All DataTypes are managed in a DataType hierarchy. This hierarchy only supports single inheritance, that is, each DataType has exactly one supertype except for the BaseDataType used as root of each hierarchy.

---

[11] In SQL [ISO08a] similar types are called distinct types.

## 2.8.2 Built-in and Simple DataTypes

In Fig. 2.30, the DataType hierarchy for the built-in DataTypes and some simple DataTypes is shown. Since the handling of the built-in DataTypes is defined by the OPC UA specification, there is no need to add additional information about these DataTypes into the Address Space. The handling of the simple DataTypes is defined by their supertypes. In Sect. 2.8.5, we will describe the characteristics of some of the built-in DataTypes having a special handling, like NodeId and LocalizedText.

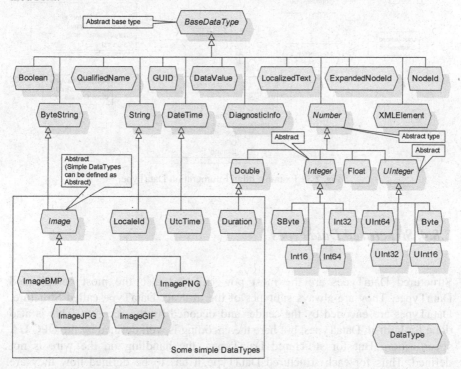

**Fig. 2.30** DataType hierarchy for built-in and simple DataTypes

## 2.8.3 Enumeration DataTypes

Enumeration DataTypes are identified in the DataType hierarchy as subtypes of the abstract DataType Enumeration. Since enumeration DataTypes are always handled as Int32, the only additional information needed in the Address Space is the mapping of the discrete set of named values to the integer values. Therefore, a standard Property called EnumStrings is added to the DataType Node holding an array of LocalizedText. Each integer value can be mapped to an entry in the array.

In Fig. 2.31, this is exemplified by a user-defined enumeration DataType called MotorStatus. The DataType Node has a Property called EnumStrings containing an array of LocalizedText with the discrete set of named values. Variables using this DataType provide a zero-based Int32 value that points into the array, as, for example, the Variable Status of Motor1 in Fig. 2.31.

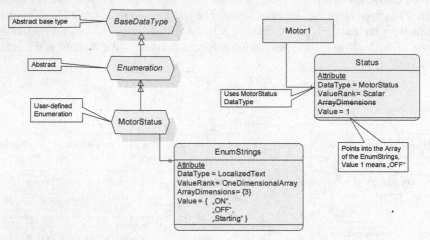

**Fig. 2.31** Example of an Enumeration DataType

## 2.8.4 Structured DataTypes

Structured DataTypes are the most powerful and also the most complicated DataTypes. They are always subtypes of the abstract DataType called Structure. DataTypes are encoded by the sender and decoded by the receiver. This is also done for built-in DataTypes, but here the encoding is well defined by the OPC UA specification. But for structured DataTypes, the handling on the wire is not defined. Thus for each structured DataType it has to be defined how they are encoded. Servers have to provide this information, so that clients can decode the data when they receive this information and can encode the data if they want to write values to the server. Before we go into details, let us take a look on how this works. In Fig. 2.32, you can see OPC UA Client1 connected to an OPC UA server using OPC UA Binary as data encoding (see Sect. 6.2 for details). Client1 requests data (1.1). The server gets this data from its data source in an internal format and converts it to OPC UA Binary (1.2). Then it sends the encoded data to the Client1 (1.3). Client1 has to decode the data into its internal format to make use of it (1.4). The handling is similar for Client2 connected to the OPC UA server using XML data encoding. Client2 requests the data (2.1) and the server uses its internal format and encodes the data (2.2). But in that case the data is encoded into OPC UA

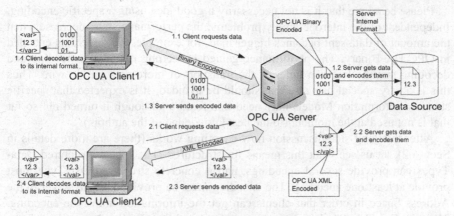

**Fig. 2.32** Encoding and decoding data

XML format and sent that way to the client (2.3). Client2 must decode these data into its internal format (2.4). Thus you can see that there are two encodings used depending on the data encoding of the connection.

The above described scenario is used for all built-in DataTypes and thus also for enumeration and simple DataTypes. The encoding of each built-in DataType is defined for binary and XML in [UA Part 6]. For structured DataTypes, the encoding is not defined and thus has to be provided by the server providing those DataTypes. Looking at the above described scenario, it seems like the server has to provide an XML encoding and a binary encoding for each structured DataType. This is desirable but not required. It is also possible to send a XML encoded value via a binary encoded connection and vice versa. Thus a server only has to provide one encoding that can be used in both data encoding choices of connections. The possibility to use a different encoded value in connections allows another scenario. For specific clients and servers both using the same internal format for their data, it may be desirable to use that format on the wire as well in order to reduce the effort of encoding and decoding data. OPC UA offers this possibility by allowing servers to provide and clients to choose additional encodings. The scenario is outlined in Fig. 2.33. Here, the client requests the data (1.1) and the server can get its internal data without encoding them (1.2). When sending them (1.3) they are embedded in an encoded message and can directly be used by the client without decoding them (1.4).

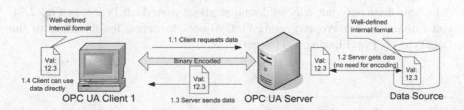

**Fig. 2.33** User-defined encodings

Please be aware that it is not necessarily a good idea using a specific encoding. Independent of the interoperability problems, the performance may decrease when the amount of data sent becomes bigger than, for example, the same data encoded in OPC UA Binary. The performance gained by getting rid of the encoding and decoding may be lost two times in the transport of more data on the wire. Thus this is a very special use case that should be avoided. It is expected that specific standard Information Models may need this feature, although it turned out so far that is not used at the moment (to the best knowledge of the authors).

After this long side-discussion how encoding works (there are more details in Sect. 6.2), let us see what this means for structured DataTypes. Structured Data-Types can provide several encodings, and a concrete structured DataType must provide at least one encoding. The encoding must be provided by the server in the Address Space in order that clients can get the information about the encoding. Thus the DataType Node representing a structured DataType points to *DataType-Encoding* Objects representing the encodings (see Fig. 2.34 for an example). The NodeId of such an Object is sent together with each value on the wire and so the receiver knows what encoding was used by the sender. Clients can choose what encoding they want to receive for a concrete value and can also leave this open to get the default encoding. Therefore, two BrowseNames are defined: "Default Binary" and "Default XML," both with the NamespaceIndex 0 (see Sect. 2.8.5 for details on Namespaces). A concrete structured DataType must reference at least one of those. If both are provided, "Default XML" is used as default for a connection using XML data encoding and "Default Binary" for a connection using OPC UA Binary. If only one is provided, this is used as default in both cases.

Of course, the client needs to get the information how the encoding is working. Therefore, the server provides a DataTypeDictionary Variable containing the information about the encoding of several DataTypes. This can become a large amount of data and typically a client should read a DataTypeDictionary once and cache it persistently. When reconnecting to a server, clients need only to check if the information has changed[12] and only then need to update the cached information. For each DataType stored in the DataTypeDictionary, a DataTypeDescription Variable is exposed having a pointer into the DataTypeDictionary to the DataType. In Fig. 2.34, this is exemplified by MyTypeDictionary, containing the encoding information of MyType1 and MyType2. In addition to the pointer into a DataTypeDictionary, a DataTypeDescription can provide the optional Property DictionaryFragment directly containing the encoding information. This is useful when the DataTypeDictionary becomes large and some clients do not want to read the whole dictionary but only information about some DataTypes. In Fig. 2.34, you can see such a Property using OPC Binary to define the encoding of the DataType MyType1 having two integers.

---

[12] There is a standard Property called DataTypeVersion, indicating if the information has changed. While the Value of that Property has not changed, clients can use their cached version.

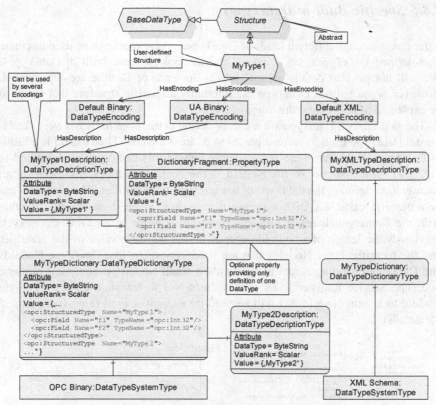

**Fig. 2.34** Example of a structured DataType

Since a DataTypeEncoding represents a concrete encoding, it points to a Data-TypeDescription Variable. This is an indirection; the pointer into the DataType-Dictionary is not directly stored in the DataTypeEncoding. It is done since several DataTypeEncodings may choose the same DataTypeDescription as you can see in Fig. 2.34. You can think of the DataTypeEncoding Object as a proxy Object that is only used to put some information (in that case name and NodeId) into a Reference (see Sect. 3.3.8 for details on proxy Objects).

Finally the server has to specify how the DataTypes are defined inside the DataTypeDictionary. The "how" is specified by the DataTypeSystem. The Data-TypeSystems predefined by the OPC UA specification are *OPC Binary* defined as an Appendix in [UA Part 3] and *W3C XML Schema* defined in [W3C04a] and [W3C04b]. However, servers may use additional DataTypeSystems to define specific encodings for their DataTypes. When the server provides only those encodings – also as the default encodings – they cannot expect that generic clients are able to interpret those data. The format of the pointer into the DataTypeDictionary used by the DataTypeDescription depends on the DataTypeSystem. For OPC Binary it is the name of the data type, for XML Schema it is an XPath expression pointing to a schema element.

## 2.8.5 Specific Built-in DataTypes

After going through different kinds of DataTypes where most can be used to create user-defined DataTypes, let us take a shorter look at some built-in DataTypes. We will not go into details of how Int32, Boolean, or Double are represented. However, some built-in DataType use internally a specific structure that needs to be explained to understand the usage of them.

The first built-in DataType we are considering is the *NodeId*. It is a very fundamental DataType used in various places to address a Node. The NodeId is a built-in DataType. However, there is a structure behind this DataType as described in Fig. 2.35. The first part of the NodeId is the NamespaceIndex, followed by an enumeration defining the data type of the last part, the identifier. The identifier can be a numeric value, a GUID, a string, or an opaque value (byte string). Together with the NamespaceIndex it uniquely identifies a Node in an OPC UA server. Obviously the length of a NodeId depends on the concrete value of the identifier and the IdentifierType. NodeIds that are used very often like DataType NodeIds and DataTypeEncoding NodeIds should use a small NodeId, preferable a numeric one. The Service RegisterNodes allows the server to translate a relatively long NodeId to a short NodeId that will be used by a client several times (see Chap. 5 for details).

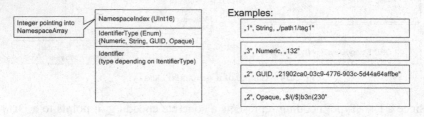

**Fig. 2.35** Structure of NodeId

The *NamespaceIndex* of the NodeId (and also the QualifiedName) is introduced for optimization purposes. The NamespaceIndex is used instead of a Namespace URI like "http://opcfoundation.org/UA/," the Namespace URI of OPC UA. The Namespace URI is used in combination with the identifier to create unique IDs in the Address Space of an OPC UA Server. The Namespace URI identifies the naming authority defining the identifiers. Naming authorities are the OPC Foundation, other organizations defining standard Information models, server vendors, or systems using an OPC UA server to expose their information.

The NamespaceIndex is a pointer to the NamespaceArray provided by each OPC UA server. Thus a client only needs to read the NamespaceArray once and later on only uses small integer values instead of large string values in NodeIds. Using the Namespace URI instead of the NamespaceIndex in the NodeId would lead to a huge overhead. NodeIds are used very often in Service calls since they are used to address Nodes. In Fig. 2.36, an example is shown how the NamespaceIndex is used.

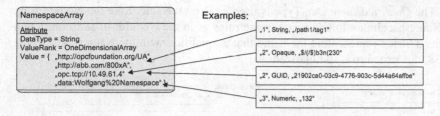

Fig. 2.36 NamespaceArray and NamespaceIndex

Clients have the guarantee that no entry of the NamespaceArray is deleted while they are connected. However, new entries may be added and thus clients should subscribe to changes of the NamespaceArray. When a client disconnects from the server, it does not have any guarantees on the NamespaceArray. The NamespaceArray may have changed completely, including the order of the array. Thus a Namespace URI represented by index "3" could be represented by index "5" when the client reconnects. Therefore, clients shall not persist a NodeId or Qualified-Name without storing the Namespace URI as well. There is one exception to that rule: the NamespaceIndex "0" is always reserved for the Namespace URI of OPC UA.

Let us take a look at the built-in DataType *ExpandedNodeId* that uses a concept similar to the NamespaceIndex. The ExpandedNodeId is mainly used as Service parameter, but in some use cases it is also reasonable to use it as value of a Variable, like for AuditEvents (see Sect. 9.5). An ExpandedNodeId allows referencing Nodes of another OPC UA server. An example is some vendor contact information stored only in one company-wide OPC UA server but referenced from several other OPC UA servers. TypeDefinitions could also be managed in one server and referenced by several other servers using those types (i.e., having instances of those types). Therefore, the ExpandedNodeId has a similar structure as the NodeId with two additional fields (see Fig. 2.37). The NamespaceURI field allows storing the real Namespace URI if it is not in the NamespaceArray of the server providing the ExpandedNodeId. Second, the ServerIndex points to the server actually managing the Node. Like the NamespaceIndex, the ServerIndex points into the ServerArray. The same constraints as for the NamespaceArray apply. The Server-Index 0 is reserved for the local server, that is, if the ServerIndex of an Expanded-NodeId is 0 then a local Node is referenced.

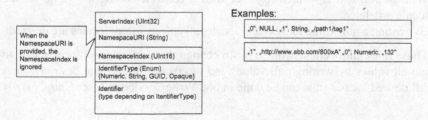

Fig. 2.37 Structure of ExpandedNodeId

The *QualifiedName* DataType is used as BrowseName. Like the NodeId it has a NamespaceIndex following the same rules as in the NodeId. In addition, it contains a String representing the name that is qualified with the Namespace. In Fig. 2.38, this structure is summarized.

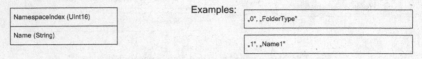

**Fig. 2.38** Structure of QualifiedName

The *LocalizedText* DataType provides a localized text. The structure is exposed in Fig. 2.39. It contains the localized text as string and the identifier of the locale as second String following the RFC 3066 [Al01].

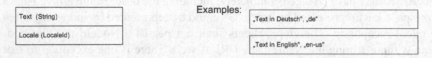

**Fig. 2.39** Structure of LocalizedText

Although the structure of LocalizedText is relatively simple, there are some thoughts to follow when dealing with LocalizedText. When a client connects to a server, it specifies a prioritized list of requested locales. The server returns all values of the type LocalizedText based on that list. It tries to return the value using the first locale in the list, if that is not available, the next, etc. If no locale specified by the client is available, the server will use the default locale that is available for a value. Thus a client should always check the returned locale of a value of the type LocalizedText.

Writing a LocalizedText value is a bit more complicated. By writing a LocalizedText the client only changes the value for the locale specified in the value to be written. This can lead to the situation that a value is changed in one locale but has still the old value in another locale. To avoid this situation, the following rules apply for writing LocalizedText.

1. Writing a value with a concrete locale will either change an existing value, or the value with the locale is added when not available before.
2. When a null text is written together with a concrete locale, the value for the locale is deleted.
3. By writing a null value for text and locale, all entries for all locales are deleted.

These rules allow clients who want to change the values for all locales first to delete all values by writing null values and afterwards adding the desired values for all desired locales (this can be done in one Write Service call, see Chap. 5).

### 2.8.6  Summary on DataTypes

The encoding for built-in, simple, and enumeration DataTypes is fixed and optimized in the OPC UA protocol. Applications should use those types when it is appropriate. However, to support complex user-defined types structured DataTypes must be used. Structured DataTypes allow user-defined encodings. But they have a small overhead on the wire because the DataTypeEncoding NodeId is send with each value. Simple DataTypes are put on the wire like their built-in DataTypes and are thus optimized for transport. On the other hand, they are not type-save, that is, a client receiving that value cannot distinguish them from the built-in DataType. The DataType information can be gained from the DataType Attribute of the Variable, but in case the Variable only defines a supertype and values use subtypes, this information is lost. An example is a Variable providing the simple DataType Money, where individual values would be of the subtypes US-Dollar, Euro, etc. The client would not be able to recognize the subtypes and sending values using the subtypes would not be recognized by the server. For those scenarios it is required to use structured DataTypes where the type information is sent with each value.

> **What's allowed and what's not?**
> Servers should expose the DataType Nodes in their Address Space, but that is not a requirement. Thus clients must be able to deal with the fact that not every server provides them.
> Variables may point to abstract DataTypes. Concrete values must always be of a concrete DataType. It is allowed that concrete values are of subtypes of the DataType specified by a Variable. Thus clients must deal with the fact that they receive not exactly the DataType specified by a Variable but a subtype of it. For built-in DataTypes this makes no difference, but for structured DataTypes the structure of subtypes can be different.
> Clients can choose what encoding they want to receive for structured DataTypes independent of the data encoding chosen when establishing a connection.

## 2.9  Views

We are finally coming to the last NodeClass of OPC UA, the *View*. A View is used to restrict the number of visible Nodes and References in a large Address Space. By using Views servers can organize their Address Space and provide views on it tailored to specific tasks or use cases. For example, the server can provide a View for maintaining the server. For that task, only Nodes containing maintenance information are important and other Nodes can be hidden.

There are two ways to look at Views in OPC UA:

1. A View is represented as a Node in the Address Space. This Node gives an entry point into the content of the View. All Nodes that are part of a View must be accessible starting from the View Node. However, they do not have to be directly referenced by the View Node; they can also be indirectly referenced by other Nodes that are connected to the View Node.
2. The NodeId of the View Node can be used as filter parameter when browsing the Address Space. By using the View as filter, servers may restrict the References to other Nodes. Thus clients browsing the Address Space in the context of a View will only see an excerpt of the Address Space. Be aware that the View context is only used in the Services when browsing and querying the Address Space, not when reading or writing a concrete Node.

By combining those two ways of how to look at Views, you get the full picture. When you want to access the content of a View you typically start at the View Node and then browse in the context of the View by using the View as a filter. Let us take a look at an example. In Fig. 2.40, you can see an Address Space with some devices containing maintenance information. A View called Maintenance references all devices and when browsing in the context of the View only the References exposed in bold are returned. A user responsible for maintenance can start at the View Node and browse in the context of the View to get all relevant information. It is not required that the user starts browsing on the View Node. He could also come to the device using a different starting Node (or has the NodeId of the device available) and thus starts browsing in the context of the View from the device Node.

There are several different ways of how to use Views to organize the Address Space. The first approach was just shown in Fig. 2.40. Here, there is one organization

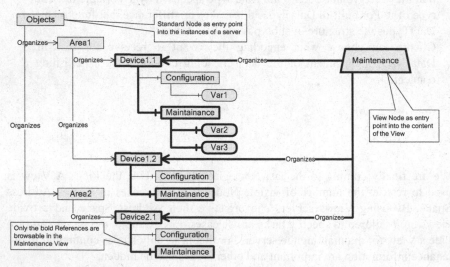

**Fig. 2.40** Example of an View organizing the Address Space

of Nodes and the View gives an additional entry point into those Nodes hiding some information. Another approach is that all Nodes are organized beneath View Nodes and thus clients always access the Address Space starting from a View Node. This is exemplified in Fig. 2.41, where the Views Engineering and Online are the only entry points into the Address Space. Not all clients may be capably of browsing in the context of a View. In that case they should treat View Nodes as Folder Objects to allow accessing those Address Spaces.

Of course, it is possible to combine both approaches, as pointed out in Fig. 2.42. Here, the Engineering and Online Views are the entry points into Address Space and the Maintenance View is used as additional View pointing inside those other Views.

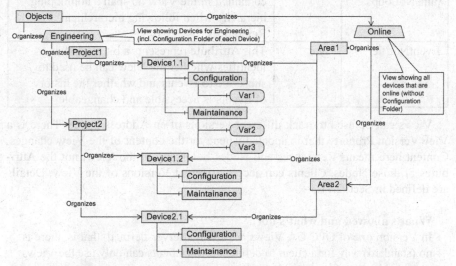

**Fig. 2.41** Example of Views as only entry points into the Address Space

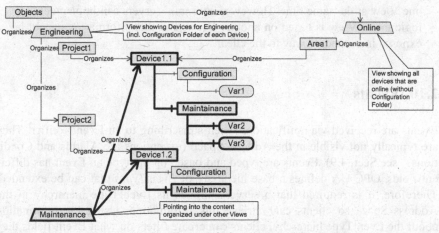

**Fig. 2.42** Combined usage of Views in the Address Space

In Table 2.11, the additional Attributes of the View NodeClass are summarized. When the ContainsNoLoops Attribute is set, clients can use this information to optimize their display since they know that no loop will occur. When the View is an EventNotifier, it is guaranteed that the Events of all EventNotifier Objects that are part of the View are also sent through the View Node.

**Table 2.11** Additional Attributes for DataTypes

| Attribute | DataType | Description |
|---|---|---|
| Containing all the common Attributes defined in Table 2.1 | | |
| ContainsNoLoops | Boolean | This Attributes indicates whether the Nodes contained in the View do span a nonlooping hierarchy when following hierarchical References |
| EventNotifier | Byte | This Attribute represents a bit mask that identifies whether the View can be used to subscribe to Events and whether the history of Events is accessible and changeable |

Views can be used to track different versions of an Address Space. There is a ViewVersion Property that is updated whenever the content of the View changes. Content here means References and Nodes belonging to the View, not the Attributes of those Nodes. Clients can access different Versions of the View. Details are defined in Sect. 2.11.3.

**What's allowed and what's not?**
In Version one of OPC UA Views are always server-defined, that is, there is no (standard) way for a client to define Views. Clients can only use the Views provided by the server.
Views cannot be combined, that is, a client can only browse in the context of one View at the same time. However, internally servers can implement their logic that a View is based on another View. But this information cannot be exposed in a standard way to the client.

## 2.10  Events

Events are received via notifications when subscribing to an EventNotifier. They are typically not visible in the Address Space (exceptions are Alarms and Conditions – see Sect. 4.9). Events are typed and based on the type an Event has different fields. OPC UA defines a base hierarchy of *EventTypes* that can be extended. Therefore, it is required that a server exposes its EventType hierarchy in the Address Space so clients can retrieve this information. Using the information about the EventType hierarchy, clients can create filters on what Event fields they are interested in as well as what kind of Events they want to receive. This is illustrated in Fig. 2.43.

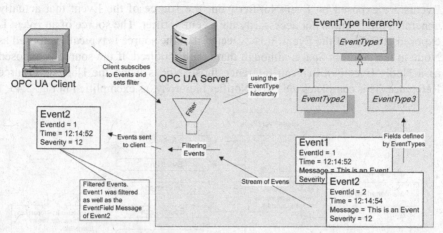

**Fig. 2.43** Subscribing to Events using the EventType hierarchy

Details on how Event filers work can be found in Chap. 5. To represent Event-Types in the Address Space, no new NodeClass is introduced but the NodeClass ObjectType is used. This makes sense for several reasons.

1. There is no additional information needed to expose EventTypes and thus ObjectTypes are a reasonable approach supporting inheritance and Variables used to expose the available fields of Events.
2. No additional NodeClass has to be introduced and clients can use their mechanisms they have to handle ObjectTypes to also handle EventTypes.
3. Some Events will be represented as Objects in the Address Space, and thus ObjectTypes have to be created for them anyhow.

For normal EventTypes, that is, EventTypes of Events that are not visible as Nodes in the Address Space, abstract ObjectTypes are used. OPC UA defines the BaseEventType; all other EventTypes must inherit directly or indirectly from it. In Fig. 2.44, the BaseEventType is shown with its Variables and some example EventTypes as well to point out the possibilities of EventTypes. The BaseEvent-Type uses Properties to expose its field directly beneath it. This is expected for most EventTypes. However, it is allowed to use Data Variables, for example, to expose complex Variables and to use Objects to group Variables as shown in the example EventType MaintenanceType. The type information of an Event defines categories of Events and can be used for filtering Events. EventTypes without additional InstanceDeclarations can be introduced for that purpose. A client may, for example, subscribe to all Events of type CriticalMaintenanceEventType.

Another mechanism to group Events is by providing a hierarchy of EventNoti-fiers. The ReferenceType HasNotifier is used for that purpose. When an EventNo-tifier references another EventNotifier, it is guaranteed that all Events exposed by the referenced EventNotifier are exposed by the referencing EventNotifier as well.

Events are exposed by EventNotifiers, but the source of the Event that actually generated the Event is not necessarily the EventNotifier. The source of an Event is exposed in fields of the Event. It is expected that the source is typically exposed as Node in the Address Space, although that is not required. If the source is exposed as a Node, EventNotifier can reference those Nodes using the HasEventSource Reference. This completes the EventNotifier hierarchy, as exemplified in Fig. 2.45.

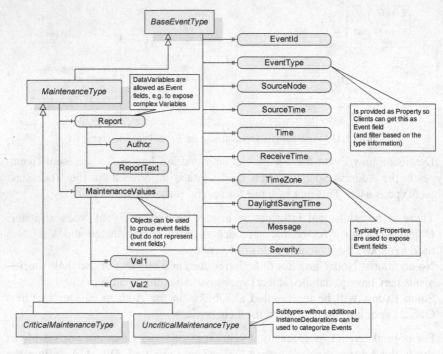

**Fig. 2.44** EventType hierarchy

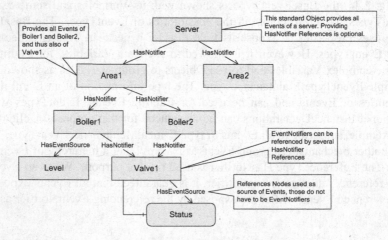

**Fig. 2.45** Hierarchy of EventNotifiers

There is one EventNotifier, which logically references all other EventNotifiers with a HasNotifier Reference, the Server Object. A client can subscribe to that Object to get all Events of the server (except for Events bound to Views like ModelChangeEvents, see Sect. 2.11.3).

Finally, a TypeDefinition Node can already expose what types of Events may be generated by instances of it by referencing from the TypeDefinition Node to the EventType using a GeneratesEvent Reference. It is not guaranteed that instances will generate Events of the referenced EventType, but it is expected in most cases. For example, there may be a device that is intended to generate a Maintenance Event, but the concrete hardware is built in a way that this is not happening as long as the system is running.

**What's allowed and what's not?**
It is required to expose the EventType hierarchy. It is not required to expose an EventNotifier hierarchy or GeneratesEvent References in the TypeDefinitions.
EventTypes are modeled as ObjectTypes and thus must follow the rules of ObjectTypes (like unique BrowsePath for InstanceDeclarations, or inheritance of InstanceDeclarations). InstanceDeclarations of the NodeClass Variable define the fields of the Event. Here, the same rules apply as for components of an instance based on the ObjectType. If the whole BrowsePath has Mandatory InstanceDeclarations, the field must be provided in the Event. If it is Optional, it does not have to be provided.

## 2.11  Historical Access

There are three facets of dealing with history in OPC UA. First of all there is the history of current data. This answers questions like: What was the value of the temperature sensor in the last three days? This is similar to what was captured in OPC HDA. Second, there is the history of Events. It answers questions like: What have been the Events in the last hour? This was not captured in Classic OPC. The third facet is the history of the structure of the Address Space. This answers questions like: How has the structure of the Address Space changed the last two weeks? We will take a short look into those three facets in the following subsections.

### 2.11.1  Historical Data

OPC UA allows accessing and changing the history of the Value Attribute of a Variable. Special Services are introduced for that purpose (and for accessing event-related history as described in the next section). In Chap. 5, it is described how these Services are working. The OPC UA Address Space Model has three different Attributes on Variable Nodes dealing with the history of the Value Attribute.

The AccessLevel and the UserAccessLevel indicate whether the history is accessible and changeable, the first one in general and the second one taking the access rights of the current connected user into account. These Attributes indicate whether some history is available, but not if currently history is collected. Therefore, the Historizing Attribute is used, indicating whether the history is currently collected. All three Attributes work on the granularity of a Variable. The model is summarized in Fig. 2.46. In addition to those Variables, there is the possibility to expose (and allow manipulations) of the configuration of how the data is historized. This is described in Sect. 4.6.

OPC UA only allows historizing the Value Attributes of Variables. If a server collects the history of other Attributes and wants to expose that and makes it accessible in the Address Space, the most appropriate way is to create a Property for each historized Attribute and add those historized Attributes to the Node.

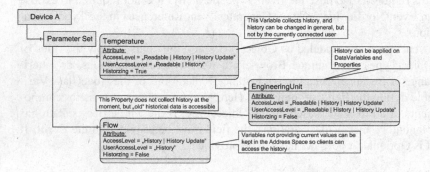

Fig. 2.46 Historical data in the Address Space

## 2.11.2 Historical Events

The history of Events can be gained from EventNotifiers, that is, Objects and Views. The EventNotifier Attribute indicates whether the history of Events can

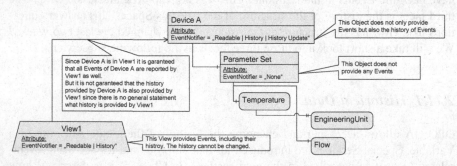

Fig. 2.47 Historical data in the Address Space

be accessed and manipulated. It is not standardized how to expose what Events are historized in an EventNotifier and thus there is also no Historizing Attribute like on Variables. However, there is the possibility to expose the configuration of how Events are historized and this can contain that information (see Sect. 4.6 for the configuration of Event history). In Fig. 2.47, the model of Historizing Events is shown.

## 2.11.3  Historical Address Space

Besides dealing with the history of current data and events, the third facet is about dealing with changes in the Address Space. Nodes and References in the Address Space may be added or deleted over time. OPC UA allows clients to track those changes and to access different versions of the Address Space by referencing different points of time. Please note that this is an optional feature that many servers will not support.

To track changes of the Address Space, OPC UA supports the NodeVersion Property and ModelChangeEvents. A server must always support either both, ModelChangeEvents and NodeVersion, or none of them for a Node. The NodeVersion is a Property on a Node that is updated every time a Reference is added or deleted from the Node. Please be aware that the relation of a Variable or VariableType to its DataType is not modeled as a Reference but as an Attribute, which is considered as a Reference in this case. Thus changes on the DataType Attribute lead to a changed NodeVersion and to a ModelChangeEvent. The NodeVersion is provided per Node, that is, clients can cache the References of a Node and as long as the NodeVersion has not changed they do not need to re-browse the Node.

The ModelChangeEvent is generated in the context of a View (or the Server Object for the whole Address Space) and allows the tracking of several changes in one ModelChangeEvent. Clients interested in changes in the Address Space in general should subscribe for ModelChangeEvents; clients interested in small excerpts may look at individual NodeVersion changes. In Fig. 2.48, the handling of NodeVersions and ModelChangeEvents is exemplified. On the left side, you can see an Address Space before some changes occur. Then, some References are added and deleted, and on the right side, you can see the new Address Space including the updated NodeVersions and the generated ModelChangeEvent. OPC UA provides the BaseModelChangeEvent only indicating that something has changed and the GeneralModelChangeEvent containing the changes as well. In Fig. 2.48, the second type of Event is used indicating the changes as well.

With NodeVersion and ModelChangeEvents it is relatively easy to track changes of the References. When this feature is not provided by a server, the only possibility for a client getting information about changes on the References is by periodically browsing or querying the Address Space.

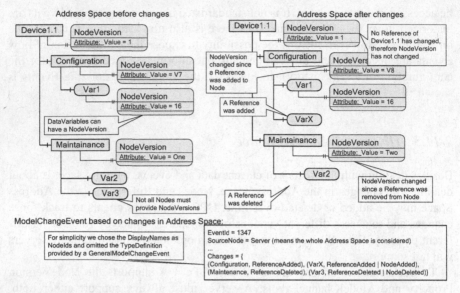

**Fig. 2.48** NodeVersion and ModelChangeEvent to track changes of the Address Space

To access different versions of the Address Space, the browse and query Services allow to specify a certain version or a certain point of time of the Address Space they want to access. This only affects querying and browsing, meaning that not the concrete Attribute values of a Node are managed in different versions of the Address Space, but the References and thereby indirectly whether specific Nodes where accessible in a concrete version of the Address Space. This implies that clients cannot make a direct connection between the different versions of the Address Space and the tracking of changes of the Address Space. When clients access an older version of the AddressSpace, they still only read the current value of the NodeVersion of a Node, not the value that was valid in the old version of the Address Space. In Fig. 2.49, different versions of an Address Space are exemplified. On the left side you can see the References you get when browsing the View in ViewVersion 1 and on the right side when browsing the ViewVersion 2. As soon as the content of a View changes, the ViewVersion has to be increased. But like the ModelChangeEvents, several changes can be captured by increasing the ViewVersion only once. The ViewVersion Property is different than the NodeVersion Property. Here, also changes in the content of the View are tracked that do not affect References directly connected to the View Node. For example, when the Reference from the Maintenance Object to Var3 is deleted from the View, the ViewVersion must be increased although the NodeVersion Property of the View Node would not change.

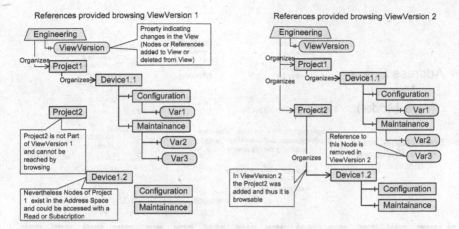

References provided browsing ViewVersion 1

Engineering
  └─ ViewVersion — Proerty indicating changes in the View (Nodes or References added to View or deleted from View)
Organizes
  └─ Project1
       └─ Organizes → Device1.1
              ├─ Configuration
              │      └─ Var1
              └─ Maintainance
                     ├─ Var2
                     └─ Var3
Project2 — Project2 is not Part of ViewVersion 1 and cannot be reached by browsing
       └─ Device1.2 — Nevertheless Nodes of Project 1 exist in the Address Space and could be accessed with a Read or Subscription
              ├─ Configuration
              └─ Maintainance

References provided browsing ViewVersion 2

Engineering
  └─ ViewVersion
Organizes
  └─ Project1
       Organizes → Device1.1
              ├─ Configuration
              │      └─ Var1
              └─ Maintainance
                     ├─ Var2 — Reference to this Node is removed in ViewVersion 2
                     └─ Var3
  └─ Organizes → Project2
Organizes
       └─ Device1.2 — In ViewVersion 2 the Project2 was added and thus it is browsable
              ├─ Configuration
              └─ Maintainance

**Fig. 2.49** Different Versions of an Address Space

**What's allowed and what's not?**
Details on how to access and manipulate the history of current data and events can be found in Chap. 5. How the configuration can be accessed is described in Sect. 4.6. The rules how to deal with the Attributes described in this section have already been captured before. The UserAccessLevel must be a subset of AccessLevel, and Historizing can only be set if the Access-Level defines access to history. Nodes can provide only the history without providing current data or current events.
There are no standard ways defined what Events are provided in the Event history. It can be any subset of the Events accessible by an Event subscription, and since the history of Events can be manipulated it can also provide additional Events. The rules defined for HasNotifier do not apply for the history of Events.
If a NodeVersion is provided, the ModelChangeEvent must be generated and vice versa. Address Spaces may only provide NodeVersions for some Nodes in the Address Space and not for other Nodes.

## 2.12 Address Space Model and Information Models

The concepts introduced in this chapter build the foundation to model data in OPC UA. The different NodeClasses with their fixed set of Attributes define the meta model of OPC UA. In addition to the NodeClasses, some standard Nodes are used inside the meta model and thus can be seen as part of the meta model as well. In particular, these are base ReferenceTypes like HasSubtype and base TypeDefinitions like PropertyType, but also standard Properties like the Input- and Output-Arguments of Methods. In terms of OPC UA, the meta model is called Address Space Model.

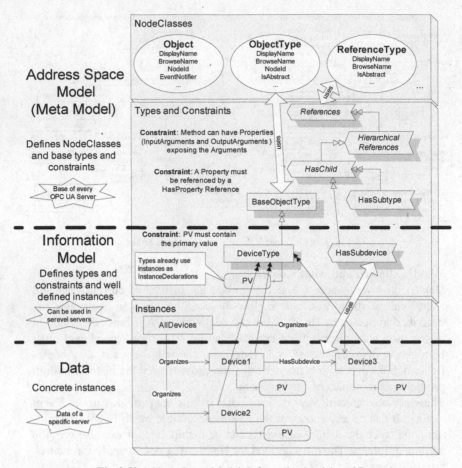

**Fig. 2.50** Address Space Model, Information Model, and Data

An OPC UA Information Model uses the concepts of the Address Space Model to define its own, domain-specific types and constrains as well as well-defined instances. Finally, the concrete data of a server is created based on the Information Model as shown in Fig. 2.50.

Typically, a server will support several Information Models where some may be based on other Information Models. The OPC UA specification already defines the base Information Model containing base types. Some of those are already part of the OPC UA meta model, whereas other parts are additional information, for example, used as entry points into the Address Space of the server or for exposing diagnostic information of the server. Based on the base Information Model, other Information Models can be derived for domain specific purposes. Finally the server may extend those to define some server-specific types and thus a server-specific Information Model used by the specific data provided by the server. This is exemplified in Fig. 2.51. The base Information Model is extended by a Topology and a Device Information Model. The Device Information Model is extended by

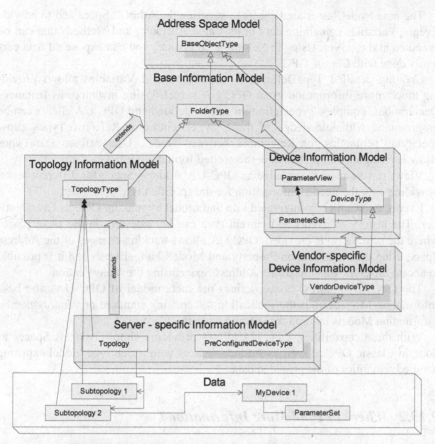

**Fig. 2.51** Address Space Model and several Information Models

the vendor-specific Device Information Model containing vendor-specific types of devices. Finally, the server-specific Information Model extends Topology and vendor-specific Information Model and is used by the instances of the server. In the server-specific Information Model, some preconfigured Device Types and entry points into the Address Space are provided. In Chap. 4, details on standard Information Models and how to deal with them are given.

## 2.13 Summary

### 2.13.1 Key Messages

The OPC UA Address Space is composed of Nodes and References between them. Nodes are of different NodeClasses for different purposes. Each NodeClass has a fixed set of Attributes, whereas References do not have Attributes.

The base NodeClasses are Objects to structure the Address Space and to provide Events, Variables containing data in its Value Attribute, and Methods that can be executed in the server. Using these simple constructs, you can expose all data currently done with Classic OPC.

Creating detailed TypeDefinitions for Objects and Variables allows providing much more information in an OPC UA server. Using instances as Instance-Declarations, complex TypeDefinition can be defined and OPC UA clients can be programmed with knowledge of those TypeDefinitions. ReferenceTypes allow specifying semantics for References between Nodes. User-defined DataTypes allow exchanging complex data in the needed format.

Views can be used to organize an OPC UA Address Space for different tasks, providing only the needed information for the specific task.

Events are seamlessly integrated into that model by making Objects EventNotifier. The history of events and current data can be accessed on the same places where the actual data is provided. OPC UA allows tracking changes of the Address Space using the NodeVersion Property and ModelChangeEvents and it is possible to access different versions of the Address Space using the ViewVersion.

The OPC UA Address Space defines the meta model of OPC UA. The base Information Model builds the foundation for creating standard or vendor-specific Information Models tailored for specific domains.

With these capabilities, OPC UA allows providing simple Address Spaces as done in Classic OPC as well as Address Spaces with a rich type model exposing detailed semantics of the provided data.

### 2.13.2  Where to Find More Information?

The Address Space Model is defined in [UA Part 3]; the base types used in the Address Space are defined in [UA Part 5]. In Appendix A of this book, you can find a description of the notation used in this chapter. In Appendix B, a summary of the NodeClasses and their Attributes is given. The base Information Model including ReferenceTypes that are part of the Address Space Model is provided in Appendix C.

### 2.13.3  What's Next?

In the next chapter, we will look at an example how to use the modeling concepts you just learned in this chapter. Afterwards, we describe some best practice on how to use those modeling concepts. In Chap. 4, we will take a look at standard Information Models including the base Information Model and specific Information Models for Data Access, Programs, Alarms and Conditions, etc. provided by the OPC UA Specification. After that chapter, you should know everything about modeling information in OPC UA and we will take a look at the Services of OPC UA to see how you can actually access and manipulate your OPC UA data.

# 3 Information Modeling: Example and Best Practice

## 3.1 Overview

In Chap. 2 you learned the concepts of modeling information in OPC UA. In this chapter we will tighten your knowledge by looking at a concrete example showing how to apply the concepts. We will start with a simple scenario only exposing data similar to Classic OPC. Then we will go forward by adding type information, multiple references, etc. to demonstrate the full power of information modeling in OPC UA. This already shows a way of how to migrate existing Classic OPC applications to OPC UA with respect to the modeling. However, in Chap. 10, we talk about more details on how to migrate from Classic OPC to OPC UA.

In the example, we target an application scenario typical for Classic OPC applications. However, in the second part of this chapter we will generalize the example by looking at some general best practices on how to model information in OPC UA. In the example, we will not consider standard Information Models other than using types of the base Information Model. In Chap. 4, we will introduce standard Information Models. When modeling your information, you should consider using those Information Models and extend them rather than creating your own Information Model from scratch when this is appropriate in your domain.

The notation used in the example to expose details on the Information Model is described in Appendix A of this book. The Appendix does not only describe the notation but also discusses its relation to UML.

## 3.2 Example

The application scenario of the example is described in the following section. Afterwards, the modeling of this example in OPC UA is discussed. It is separated in two sections, one describing a simple application comparable to Classic OPC and the other extending that simple application to provide the full power of OPC UA.

### 3.2.1 Application Scenario

The application we want to model is an air conditioner similar to the one you might find in your office or at home. We do not want to go into details on how an air conditioner is working internally, but focus on the external communication and how to model that information. In Fig. 3.1, a typical air conditioner application is

W. Mahnke et al., *OPC Unified Architecture*,
DOI: 10.1007/978-3-540-68899-0_3, © Springer-Verlag Berlin Heidelberg 2009

shown. There is a control module in which the controller application is running. The controller provides two set points to define the requested temperature and humidity. In addition, you can turn the air conditioner on or off. It offers the actual temperature and humidity as well as the power consumption, the fan speed, and the cooler state as measured values. It provides events generated internally as well as externally from the devices it is using. An internal event is, for example, generated if the communication to a device fails; an external event is, for example, forwarded from the fan, indicating a maintenance request. The controller provides a short-term history of measured temperature and humidity also used internally to optimize the process. We do not show details on the internal logic of the controller, but you can see that it uses some sensors on the left hand and some actors on the right hand. Using Classic OPC, you would have a PC-based client on top of the control module using a proprietary protocol talking to the control module and providing the data as a Classic OPC server. Clients to this server can run on the same machine as on other machines using DCOM to communicate.

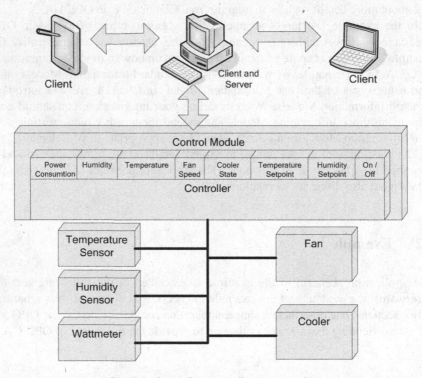

**Fig. 3.1** Air conditioner application scenario

There are different ways how to migrate this scenario to OPC UA. You could provide an OPC UA server on the client machine targeting the Classic OPC server(s), you could natively access the control module, or you could implement your OPC UA server on the control module. In the following, we do not go into those deployment issues but focus on the information modeling of this scenario.

### 3.2.2 Simple Scenario: Similar to Classic OPC

In Classic OPC, you would provide an OPC DA server allowing to access the measured values and to set the set points. An OPC A&E server would provide the events and an OPC HDA server the history of the temperature and humidity. The history of events could not be provided in a standard way. We will focus on current data to expose how to model the above described data.

In OPC DA, you would provide a structure as shown on the left hand of Fig. 3.2. As long as you only want to provide the similar information in OPC UA, your Address Space would look very similar as shown on the right hand in Fig. 3.2. Here, only the BaseObjectType, the BaseDataVariableType, and the PropertyType are used and the standard HasComponent and HasProperty References.

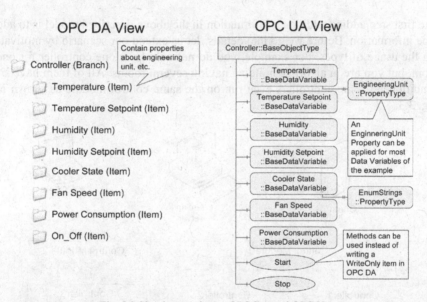

**Fig. 3.2** Simple mapping to OPC DA and OPC UA

To extend this scenario to events and history, you would make the Controller Object an EventNotifier and change the AccessLevel Attribute of the Temperature and Humility Variables supporting history as well. The history of events can also be made available on the Controller Object. In addition, you need to provide the configuration of the historical data by adding this information to the Nodes. How this can be done is described in Sect. 4.6.

If you look at this scenario, you can see that you provide the same information as in Classic OPC. Using Methods make things a little bit clearer although this is not required in the described scenario. You can provide the history of events, and in general events and history are integrated to the current data and not separated in different servers as done in Classic OPC. You have your secure and reliable communication, and your OPC UA applications can run on different platforms, including the control module. However, the information is still the same. On the one hand, this means that you do not need to put in any additional effort in providing more information, but on the other hand, you are not using the full power of OPC UA regarding information modeling. The above described modeling of information in OPC UA is a compliant application of OPC UA and may be sufficient for your needs. Nevertheless, in the following section we will see what the next steps regarding the modeling of information can be and how this can help your applications.

### 3.2.3 Advanced Scenario: Providing Full Power of OPC UA

The first step adding additional information in the above described model is to add type information. Before we go into details, let us extend our scenario by motivating the usage of types. For example, you do not only have one controller for one room, but you are in an office building having several rooms. All of them have air conditioners, some controllers even run on the same control module as shown in Fig. 3.3.

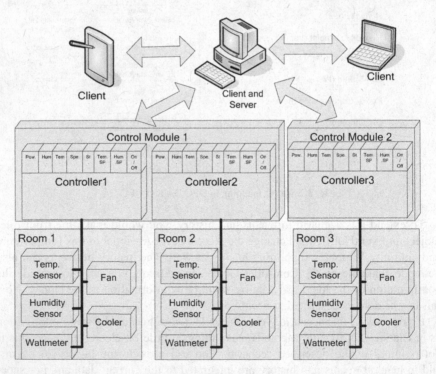

**Fig. 3.3** Multiple air conditioner

However, they all work the same way and your client applications always look the same for each room. Thus the client application should be developed only once and be applied to all air conditioner controllers. In OPC UA, this can easily be done by creating a TypeDefinition for the controller and program your client application with knowledge of the TypeDefinition. Creating a type for the controller is very simple by using the structure we have seen earlier and put them under an ObjectType Node instead of an Object. All Nodes in the structure reference a ModellingRule, and since they are referenced by a TypeDefinition Node they become InstanceDeclarations. In the example, it makes sense to use the Mandatory ModellingRule for all InstanceDeclarations. This is shown in Fig. 3.4. Now your client application can be programmed by using the TypeDefinition. You use the TranslateBrowsePathsToNodeIds Service to access the instance Nodes based on the knowledge about the InstanceDeclarations.

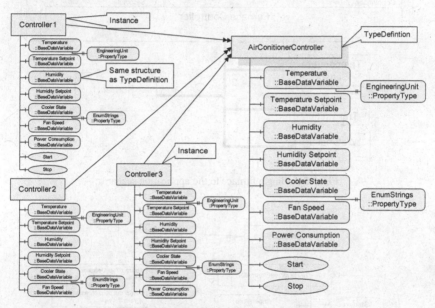

**Fig. 3.4** TypeDefinition for the controller

To expose the power of using type hierarchies, we extend the example described earlier. Let us assume your office building does not only have an air conditioner, but also a furnace. A furnace is shown in Fig. 3.5. Again, we do not want to go into technical details but focus on the provided data. The controller of the furnace provides the temperature, the power consumption as well as the gas consumption by measuring the gas flow. It provides the state of the burner and allows setting the temperature and turning it on and off. It uses a temperature sensor to measure the temperature, a wattmeter to measure the power consumption, and a flow transmitter to measure the gas consumption. Thus in a way it is very similar to the controller of the air conditioner. It provides the measured temperature and the temperature can be controlled by a set point; it can be started or stopped. The power consumption is measured in both cases. So when you think about it, there may be client applications that can handle both controllers in the same manner using only the common information provided by both controllers.

In OPC UA, you can use a type hierarchy to expose that information and make it possible for client applications to be more general by using some base TypeDefinition and be programmed based on those supertypes. The type hierarchy that could be created in our advanced scenario is exposed in Fig. 3.6. On top we have an abstract base type for controllers that could, for example, be referenced by control modules. Then we have an abstract temperature controller providing

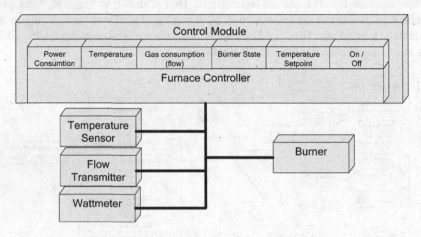

**Fig. 3.5** Adding a furnace to the application scenario

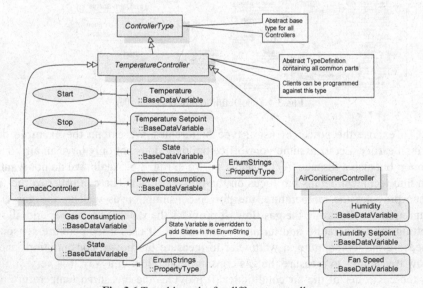

**Fig. 3.6** Type hierarchy for different controller

all the common features of a temperature controller, like the measured temperature and a set point as well as the start and stop methods. It already contains a state. FurnaceController is a subtype of the TemperatureController inheriting the base features. It is overriding the state to add additional states to the Enum-Strings.

The AirConditionerController inherits the same features without overriding the state. The FurnaceController adds the gas consumption and the AirConditioner-Controller the humidity and the humidity set point. Applications focusing only on the temperature can be programmed based on the abstract TemperatureController and use concrete instances of the FurnaceController or AirConditionerController at runtime.

After looking at the use of types and inheritance, let us look what additional information could be useful for client applications and thus should be provided by your OPC UA server. In the description of this scenario, we have seen that beneath the controller devices are providing data (sensors) or are controlled by the controller (actors). From the maintenance point of view as well as from the engineering point of view (e.g., when you engineer your controller), this is important information. In our example, we will focus on the maintenance use case, although activities have started from PLCopen for an OPC UA Information Model for IEC 61131-3, the only global standard for industrial control programming (see Chap. 4).

The devices shown earlier do not necessarily belong to one single controller – they can, for example, also be used by several controllers. In the end, the devices can span a hierarchy independent of the controllers as shown in Fig. 3.7. On the

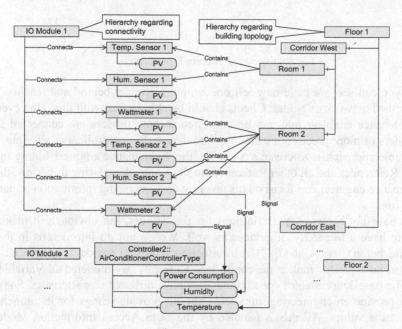

**Fig. 3.7** Devices in the Address Space

left hand, a hierarchy representing the communication to the devices is shown. The hierarchy on the right hand side provides the topology of your building. Of course, the devices are connected to the controllers as well since they are used by them.

You can see that we use several new ReferenceTypes exposing all those information. The connectivity hierarchy uses Connects References from the IO modules to the devices and the building topology uses Contains References to point from rooms to the devices. The Variables of the controllers point to the Variables of the devices using a non-hierarchical Reference called Signal. References of this type imply that the measured value of the device is used by the controller and thus both Variables have the same value. All those ReferenceTypes are newly created and not contained in the OPC UA specification. You do not always need to provide new ReferenceTypes, for example, you could use Organizes References from rooms to devices. However, creating new ReferenceTypes makes the semantic more explicit. In Fig. 3.8, the newly created ReferenceTypes are shown in the ReferenceType hierarchy.

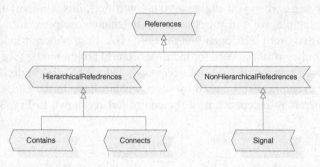

**Fig. 3.8** Extended ReferenceType hierarchy

As you can see, we have now left one simple hierarchy behind and reached a full-meshed network of Nodes. Clients should be able to deal with this. However, a maintenance engineer may not be interested in how devices are connected to controllers or more precisely he may not be interested in controllers at all. Thus a reasonable approach is to create a View for the maintenance engineer hiding the Signal References and all other References to the Controllers. Using this View, the maintenance engineer can focus on his tasks by only accessing information important to him.

We have not shown TypeDefinitions for the devices, but obviously it makes sense to have a hierarchy of devices as well. We do not go into details in this example, but in Chap. 4, an OPC UA Information Model for devices is introduced.

Let us take another look at the controllers. Currently, we modeled all Variables using the BaseDataVariableType although they have different characteristics. Some should provide an engineering unit; some should provide strings for its numeric enumeration values. All this is handled by the Data Access Information Model provided by the OPC UA specification [UA Part 8]. It standardizes where to find

Properties on the Variable for the engineering units, etc. However, since we did not look at that model so far, we will not go into details on VariableTypes in this example.

In the example, we have not considered the data types of the Variables at all. It is expected that in the described use case, built-in DataTypes can be used and thus no special considerations have to be made. In the next section we will consider complex DataTypes as well.

We do not need to consider history in this example. History is just provided by the Variables and you have to provide a history configuration as described in the Historical Access Information Model in Set. 4.6. Events can be gained from Objects setting their EventNotifier Attribute to eventing. In the example, the Controller Objects are good places for EventNotifier. Clients can subscribe to them to receive Events. However, you have to provide an EventType hierarchy, which enables clients to define a filter specifying the fields they want to receive as well as limiting the Events they want to receive.

The base EventTypes are defined in [UA Part 5]. You can either just use those or extend the hierarchy by subtyping in order to add fields for the Events or to categorize the Events. In our example, we want to support two types of Events. One is for exposing communication errors to a device and one is for maintenance information coming from the devices. There is already a standard EventType called DeviceFailureEventType, which applies to the communication failure to the device. So after finding the right standard EventType, you have to consider two aspects: First, are the Event fields of the standard EventType suitable for the Events you need to generate or do you need more? Second, do you need to categorize Events? In our case, the Event fields are suitable but we want to categorize the Events so you can filter only for communication Events. Therefore, you have to create a subtype of DeviceFailureEventType without additional InstanceDeclarations. In our scenario, we call it DeviceCommunicationFailureEventType. For the second type of Events, the maintenance-related Events, we do not have a more concrete EventType than the BaseEventType. But the fields of the BaseEventType are not sufficient, so we need to create a subtype called MaintenanceEventType to define additional fields. In addition, the subtype is also needed for categorization purposes, allowing clients to filter for all maintenance Events. In Fig. 3.9, the extended EventType hierarchy is shown.

In the example you have seen how to apply the OPC UA information modeling concepts. You can start by only providing simple Objects and Variables as well as Events and the history of current data and Events. This is very similar to Classic OPC. You can add TypeDefinitions allowing clients to be programmed using the knowledge of TypeDefinitions. You can use different ReferenceTypes to expose different kinds of relations between Nodes and thus expose multiple hierarchies for multiple purposes. By using Views you can hide parts of the Address Space, so clients see only the information they need to fulfill certain tasks. Thus you can model your information appropriately for your scenario. In the next section, we will generalize from the example and provide some best practices of how to use the different modeling concepts of OPC UA.

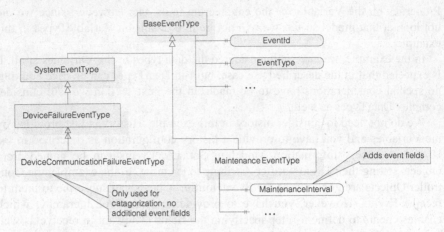

**Fig. 3.9** Extended EventType hierarchy

## 3.3    Best Practices

In the following, we give you some hints how to use the modeling concepts of OPC UA. There is some flexibility in modeling information in OPC UA, so there is not always a strong rule that must be applied. We will provide the pros and cons of different solutions so you can judge which solution fits best for your concrete application.

We start with some general advice before we go into the details. Model your OPC UA server according to your requirements and appropriate to the data sources you are accessing. If you are not expecting clients to browse your Address Space but they are only accessing some Variable values getting the NodeIds from some other sources, it is not necessary to provide a rich information model. If your underlying data source is a generic OPC DA server and you have no additional information available, you cannot provide a rich information model.

Try to use standardized types if possible instead of creating your own types. This applies for Nodes defined by the base Information Model of OPC UA or standard Information Models specified by other organizations. When there is a standard Information Model in your domain try to use it. Clients that have knowledge of those models can make use of this instead of just generically accessing the data. But it also makes sense for generic clients to use standard Information Models as the user of the client may be aware of the model and thus knows better how to deal with the provided information. In Chap. 4, we introduce standard Information Models.

## 3.3.1  Structuring with Objects, ReferenceTypes, and Views

Objects are used to structure the Address Space. They are the entry points to Variables having values and Methods that can be called. How you want to structure your Address Space depends on your application. If you expect that clients will browse the Address Space to find information, it is probably not a good idea having one Object with 10,000 Variables beneath. It would be better to structure them with several Objects. Nodes can be structured according to different criteria, for example, by devices or similar constructs like controllers. Beneath them, the Variables can be grouped by Objects considering the different purposes of the Variables (configuration data, measured data, etc.). Devices can be ordered by the geographical location in the factory, by the functionality of a process, etc. Since OPC UA does not only provide one hierarchy, you can provide several different structures in one Address Space. This all depends on your use cases.

As soon as you are not providing a simple hierarchy with a well-defined semantic, you should consider using different types of References. In our example, you have seen that we used different ReferenceTypes for the building and the communication hierarchy. This makes sense as both hierarchies imply a specific semantic between the connected Nodes. And they are referencing the same Nodes. When browsing a device, you can filter for inverse References regarding the communication, so you know which IO module is connected to it without getting the room in which the device is located. You can also provide non-hierarchical References between Nodes. This does not expose a hierarchy, but some other relation between them. The example uses this also for the signal References between Variables of the device and the controller. Here, and also as for hierarchical References, you should first check if an existing ReferenceType is suitable for that purpose. Existing ReferenceTypes include the ReferenceTypes defined by the OPC UA specification and potentially other ReferenceTypes defined by standard Information Models. When you need to create your own ReferenceType, you have to use the most appropriate supertype in the existing ReferenceType hierarchy. Always consider that clients might apply filters based on standard ReferenceTypes when they browse and query the Address Space.

As long as your server only provides a small amount of Nodes, it is not necessary to use any Views. However, if your server provides hundred of thousands of Nodes, it may be suitable using Views to show excerpts of the Address Space tailored to specific tasks. There are two ways of how Views can be applied.

A View can hide subcomponents of a Node but the Nodes are not organized in a View-specific hierarchy. In our example, an engineer may have the task to configure devices. Here, it would be interesting to browse the building hierarchy or the communication hierarchy. However, on the device he is only interested in the configuration parameters and neither in other parameters nor the signals to the controllers. You have to provide the View Node which could, for example, just reference the Objects[1] Node as the standard entry point into the Address Space. But when browsing the Objects in the context of that View, it would hide certain References to Nodes that do not belong to the View. Please be aware that you have to be able to access each Node that is part of the View starting from the View Node. On the left side of Fig. 3.10, this is exemplified by using an abstract example.

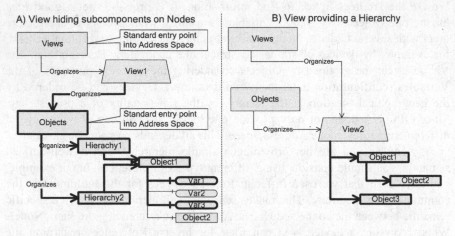

**Fig. 3.10** Two ways of providing Views

The other scenario for Views is that they span a View-specific hierarchy in the Address Space. In that case it makes sense that the View Node is the only entry point into that hierarchy and it is therefore referenced by the Objects Node. So you would not provide an Object called BuildingHierarchy but a View. Clients not capable of handling View Nodes in a special way should handle them as normal Objects to access hierarchies only accessible via the View Node. On the right side of Fig. 3.10, this is exemplified using an abstract example.

You have to decide what kind of View you want to use in order to know where to place it in the Address Space. View Nodes always have to be accessible from the standard Views Object, but in addition you might want to add the View Node under the standard Objects Node used as browse entry point for instances.

### 3.3.2 TypeDefinitions (ObjectTypes and VariableTypes)

All Objects and Variables have to be typed in OPC UA. But there is a simple solution for servers without type information. They can use the BaseObject-Type for their untyped Objects and the BaseDataVariableType for their untyped

---

[1] In Chap. 4, we will learn more about the entry points into the Address Space.

DataVariables. Properties are always of the PropertyType, anyhow. However, there are mainly two reasons providing type information for Objects and Data-Variables. First, it provides a specific semantic for a Node defined by the Type-Definition. Having an Object of type TemeratureSensorType gives clients a hint that the Object represents a temperature sensor. If the Object is of type Production-ScheduleType, it is not representing a device but a production schedule. Second, by using complex TypeDefinitions you are also defining the structure beneath each instance. In other words, you are defining a specific syntax for Nodes of this type. Clients can use this knowledge based on the TypeDefinition on each instance of the type, without the need to reconfigure or reprogram the client. Through this information, clients are able to assign instances of client-side objects like graphics very efficient to corresponding Objects in the server.

Therefore, it is often useful to provide specific TypeDefinitions for your Objects and DataVariables. The benefit becomes even bigger if you use TypeDefinitions specified by standard Information Models, as client applications may already be aware of those types. Those client applications include aggregating OPC UA servers, providing the information of many OPC UA servers in its Address Space (see Chap. 9 for details on aggregating servers).

However, it only makes sense to provide a TypeDefinition when it is expected that it will be used more than once. This is not restricted to one server. It may make sense to provide a TypeDefinition that is only used once in a server but many servers use the same TypeDefinition. This provides interoperability on the modeling level.

Before creating a specific TypeDefinition, you should ask yourself the following questions:

1. *Is there already a TypeDefinition I can use instead of?*
   It is always preferable to use TypeDefinitions of standard Information Models (including the base Information Model of OPC UA) instead of defining a similar type for yourself. However, the drawback of a standard Information Model is that it may not fit to the information you want to provide. If you can provide the information required by the standard Information Model you should consider using it, if you cannot provide that information then obviously you cannot use it. In the case that you can provide the expected information but you want to provide more information you have the following choices: add the additional information on each instance without providing it on the TypeDefinition or specialize the standard TypeDefinition with a subtype. Here you have to consider what additional information you want to provide and whether this is needed on the TypeDefinition.

2. *Is there already a specialized ObjectType I can use as supertype?*
   Each ObjectType has to inherit from the BaseObjectType so you always have to inherit your ObjectTypes from another ObjectType. Same is true for Type-Definitions of DataVariables and the BaseDataVariableType. However, there may be more specialized TypeDefinitions available you can inherit from. You have to verify whether the semantic of the supertype fits to the TypeDefinition

you want to create. You are only allowed to specialize the semantic, not generalize it. If your supertype is specifying a temperature sensor, your subtype must be a sensor providing temperature as well. It can add semantic, for example, a specific type of temperature sensor. You also have to consider if the information that is mandatory on the supertype can be provided in your scenario as well. If the TemperatureSensorType requires providing an engineering unit and you do not have that information available, you cannot use it as a supertype. For VariableTypes, you also have to consider the data type. Only the same data type or subtypes can be used.

There is no rule how deep type hierarchies should be and rules from object-oriented programming languages can not be applied, since an ObjectType or VariableType does not contain any code (at least from the OPC UA point of view). As long as it makes sense from the information point of view, you can create subtypes.

There is a specialty to consider when creating subtypes. It is the question on single or multiple inheritance. OPC UA does not forbid multiple inheritance in the Object- and VariableType hierarchies. However, it only specifies inheritance rules for single inheritance. One reason for this is that there are different ways of how to work with multiple-inheritance. Defining one single way means that the server cannot use a different one. Another reason is that multiple-inheritance can become quite complex and hard to handle. Therefore, you should try to avoid multiple-inheritance in type hierarchies. There are some drawbacks on that. For example, if you want to expose that all of your Objects support the NodeVersion Property, you could create a server-specific ObjectType having the NodeVersion as mandatory Property and let all ObjectTypes inherit from that server-specific ObjectType in addition to their normal supertype. To overcome this use case, the base Information Model of OPC UA allows servers to add InstanceDeclarations to well-defined TypeDefinitions. This means that you are allowed to add a mandatory Property to the BaseObjectType. This, in turn, requires that all Objects of the server must support the Property. This can become a hassle for aggregating servers and therefore should be well considered whether it makes sense to add this information.

### 3.3.2.1 ObjectTypes

After this general view, let us take a short look at some considerations specific to ObjectTypes before we look into more detail on VariableTypes.

*Should I create simple or complex ObjectTypes?*

Complex ObjectTypes define a base structure of each Object of the ObjectType, whereas simple ObjectTypes only define the semantic. For example, you can create an ObjectType called AirConditionerController either as a simple ObjectType without InstanceDeclarations or as a complex ObjectType as shown in the example. This decision depends on answering the following question: do I expect my instances always to have the same structure beneath and do I expect to have several instances (not necessarily in the same server)? In that case it makes sense to have a complex ObjectType. If each instance of the ObjectType has a different structure beneath, it does not make sense to have a complex type. If the type is only used once it is questionable why to create an ObjectType for it at all. In our example, we expect each AirConditionerController to have the same structure beneath so we created a complex ObjectType. An example where a complex ObjectType does not make sense is an ObjectType representing an area in a factory. Here, each area has typically a different structure beneath. So a complex ObjectType does not make sense. However, providing the semantic that an Object represents an area makes sense.

Of course, the question is not always to create a simple or complex Object-Type. The question is for each potential InstanceDeclaration whether it should be placed on the ObjectType or not. In the example with the area, there may be some Properties common to each area, for example, the coordinates. This can be captured in a Property defined on the ObjectType. However, most parts of an area should not be defined on the ObjectType.

### 3.3.2.2 ObjectTypes or VariableTypes

For complex ObjectTypes only providing one Variable, you can consider using a VariableType instead. For example, a simple temperature sensor could be represented as a Variable instead of an Object containing a Variable. However, you should consider the extensibility and the handling of other, similar constructs. When you want to define a more complex temperature sensor that supports measuring the flow in addition, you cannot just subtype the VariableType since you need two DataVariables instead of one. It can also be considered as bad design if you model your simple devices as Variables and having your complex devices modeled as Objects containing Variables. Clients (and their users) would have to handle those devices in different ways.

### 3.3.2.3 VariableTypes (for DataVariables)

VariableTypes should only be specified to add semantic to Variable instances. It is not needed to define VariableTypes just reflecting the data type of the Variables. This applies for the pre-defined DataTypes as well as for user-defined DataTypes. The Attributes of the Variable provide this information, so it is not needed to duplicate it in the VariableType. An example where it may make sense defining the semantic is to specify a setpoint.

However, in the Data Access part there are some standard VariableTypes defined that can be applied in many scenarios, including specifying a setpoint. If you want to use the VariableTypes introduced in the Data Access Information Model and add a VariableType for setpoints, you would have to create subtypes on each of those types. You can either define a base SetpointVariableType and let all newly created VariableTypes inherit from it or you can leave the base Set-PointVariableType out to avoid multiple inheritance. In the second case, you loose the information that all newly created types have some commonality.

The better approach is using composition instead of subtyping. In Fig. 3.11, this is exemplified. For the composition you can use an ObjectType instead of a VariableType, since you do not need an additional place to put the value to. It is expected that instead of extending the VariableType hierarchy of the Data Access Information Model composition using ObjectTypes is used instead. However, there is a good reason to provide additional VariableTypes, which is explained in the next section.

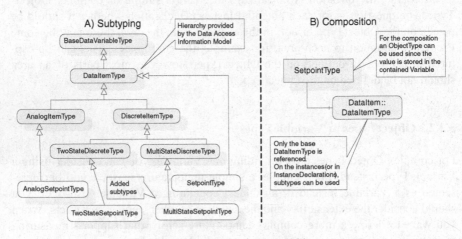

**Fig. 3.11** Subtyping vs. composition

## 3.3.3 Providing Complex Data Structures

Let us consider how to provide complex data structures. In Sect. 2.5.4, we already introduced an example for providing an address with the street and the city. In that section we used an Object with Variables beneath to model that information. Actually you have three different possibilities of how to model that information:

1. *Provide several Variables with pre-defined DataTypes*
   You are grouping the information by using an Object and provide variables beneath containing the information using pre-defined DataTypes. This is similar to the solution we used in Sect. 2.5.4.
2. *Provide one Variable with a structured DataType*
   You can create a complex DataType and use this DataType in one Variable to provide the information.

3. *Provide one Variable with a structured DataType and sub-variables with built-in DataTypes*

   A combination of both approaches is providing a structured DataType and use the DataType in a Variable, but in addition expose the information in sub-variables using pre-defined DataTypes.

The above described solutions imply that the complexity is only one level deep, that is the street and the city can be represented in a pre-defined DataType. Otherwise, you can recursively use the above described approaches again.

All choices are valid ways to model your information. However, there are different pros and cons for each solution. When you want to access individual elements of the complex structure, you can do this easily with solution one and three. For the second solution, you always access all data at once. It is possible to get the individual data, but there is always an overhead. Referencing individual elements is not possible with solution two, but it works well with one and three. You can access all data at once with all solutions; however, you have a small overhead in solution one, since you have to access several Variables in one request. If you need to access or manipulate all elements at once in a transaction context, you cannot use solution one. OPC UA does not specify any explicit transaction context. This means that each Variable access will be executed individually (unless your server implements some proprietary transaction handling). In solution two and three, all data are in one Variable and therefore an implicit transaction context is given. On the other hand, complex DataTypes may not be supported by every OPC UA client. Those clients cannot access the data provided in solution two. In Table 3.1, the pros and cons are summarized.

**Table 3.1** Pros and cons for structuring data

|  | Several variables | Structured DataType using one Variable | Structured DataType and several Variables |
|---|---|---|---|
| Reading and writing individual values | + | o | + |
| Subscribing to individual values | + | o | + |
| Referencing individual values in the Address Space | + | – | + |
| Reading and writing all values at once | + | + | + |
| Subscribing to all values at once | + | + | + |
| Reading or writing all values in a transaction context | – | + | + |
| Access possible with built-in DataTypes | + | – | + |

When you model your data and you do not need a transaction context, you should consider using solution one. This allows access from all clients and you can add References to individual entries. If you need transaction context or you know that many clients will always access the whole structure, you should consider solution three. If you expect all clients always accessing the whole structure, you can go for solution two. However, you have to be aware that an individual access is not possible in that solution.[2]

When you use the third solution, it typically makes sense to define complex VariableTypes with mandatory sub-variables so clients know what to expect.

### 3.3.4 Providing User-Defined DataTypes

As we just discussed the usage of structured DataTypes, let us look into some more details. As discussed, structured DataTypes provide an implicit transaction context. But they are harder to use by a generic client as the client needs to get and interpret the type description, which may not be supported by all clients. In addition, there is a slight overhead on the wire because the encoding information has to be put on it.[3] Therefore, you should use numeric NodeIds for all Encoding Objects in order to keep the overhead low.

When talking about encoding, you can use OPC Binary or XML Schema to define your structured DataTypes or your own mechanism for your own encoding. You should avoid using proprietary encoding mechanisms and use the standard mechanisms instead, since your own encoding will not be interpretable by most clients. When proprietary encoding would highly improve your performance, you might consider using it. But in that case you should also provide the standard encodings so that generic clients are able to access the data as well.

### 3.3.5 Properties

We already had a discussion about DataVariables and Properties in Sect. 2.6, which should provide enough information for a decision whether to use a Property or a DataVariable.

---

[2] We are considering this issue only from the modeling perspective. Of course, providing sub-variables may be some coding effort for you, so you may want to go for solution two based on those considerations.

[3] The overhead is compared to one built-in DataType. Since a structured DataType often contains the data of several built-in DataTypes, providing the same data in a structured DataType is typically more efficient. You only get one set of status code and timestamps (see Chap. 5 for details).

If your choice is a Property and you are applying Properties on Variables and Objects, you can decide whether you want to make it available on TypeDefinitions or not. Defining mandatory Properties makes sense as it gives the client additional information. An optional Property is not that useful. The semantic is defined by the BrowseName and Properties may show up on the instances or not. However, providing optional Properties give clients a hint that those Properties may exist. Properties are not defined by specific TypeDefinition Nodes, so you do not know that certain Properties may exist on your server unless you have seen an instance of it. Therefore, it is reasonable to use optional Properties in your type information to point out the existence of such Properties.

## 3.3.6 Methods

Methods should be used whenever something is executed on the server triggered by the client. For long-running processes you should use Programs. But that implies using Methods as well since Programs are controlled using Methods.

In Classic OPC, there is no concept of a method so you have to write some values to start a Method. This should be avoided in OPC UA and Methods should be used instead. Especially, if you have input or output parameters, a Method should be preferred. In a Method call, the input arguments have to be specified and the output arguments are returned. This means that those values are directly connected to the Method call and it is unambiguous when the Method was called several times and what value belongs to what call.

You can define a Method on an Object or an ObjectType. If you define a Method on an ObjectType, you have to decide whether all Objects share the same Method Node or you provide additional copies of that Node. In the first case, you can reduce the number of Nodes in the Address Space. However, the Method contains Attributes specifying if it can be executed. If you want to provide this information on the granularity of the Objects, you should create copies. If this information is always the same for each Object you should share the Method Node.

If you have Methods that are not related to a specific Object, you should put them on the Server Object. Clients are expected to look at the Server Object for those global Methods.

## 3.3.7 ModellingRules

You should use the standard ModellingRules whenever they are applicable. However, there is only a small set of ModellingRules defined. When you need to have a new constraint or some semantic that cannot be expressed in enough detail with the existing ModellingRules, you can define your own ModellingRules.

Examples for new constraints are cardinality restrictions. OPC UA is an open model meaning that you can add References of any type to instances of your TypeDefinition as long as the constraints of the ReferenceType allow this. If you want to express, that your car can only have three or four wheels, you have to create a new ModellingRule.

If you want to expose that a Method on an ObjectType is always shared on the instances, you have to create your own ModellingRule as the standard Modelling-Rules do not define this behavior.

However, you always have to consider whether it makes sense to provide this additional information, since you expect client applications to make use of it. A client who executes Methods is looking at the Attributes of the Method Node, but it does not care if the Node is shared or not. If your client is creating new Type-Definitions and wants to specify whether the server should share the Methods, you need such a ModellingRule.

Creating additional ModellingRules may make more sense for other standard Information Models than for vendor- or server-specific ones, since more clients may be able to interpret those standard ModellingRules.

### 3.3.8  Proxy Objects (Properties on References)

References are simple constructs in OPC UA only connecting two Nodes. The only information they provide is their ReferenceType and the direction. If you need to add any additional information to a Reference, you cannot do this directly in OPC UA. But there is a simple workaround. Instead of providing one Reference with additional information, you can create an Object which references the target and the source Node. This is exemplified in Fig. 3.12.

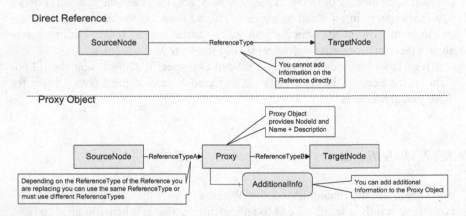

**Fig. 3.12** Usage of a Proxy Object instead of a reference

On the proxy Object, you can add your additional information. It already provides some base information like a NodeId and a name. Thus the relation represented by the proxy can be referenced by other Nodes and you can add Data-Variables or Properties on the proxy. Of course, browsing the relationship becomes more cumbersome. So you should only use a proxy when you really need it.

## 3.4 Summary

### 3.4.1 Key Messages

In our example you have learned that you can use the OPC UA modeling concepts to model your information similar to Classic OPC. Only using the base types you do not have to define your own type system and you can focus simply on providing data.

However, you have also seen how you can provide much more information using the advanced features and how this can help clients and users with their tasks. You can reuse client code or configuration data specified with the knowledge of your OPC UA TypeDefinitions by applying them on several instances of the same type. By using different ReferenceTypes you can expose different semantics and span multiple hierarchies. Views help you organizing large Address Spaces with potentially hundred thousands of Nodes.

In the best practices section you have learned that Objects, ReferenceTypes, and Views are the key features for organizing your Address Space. You should use standard TypeDefinitions instead of your own TypeDefinitions when possible. There are different ways of how to provide complex data structures in OPC UA. If possible you should expose them as a set of Variables using pre-defined Data-Types. If transaction context is needed, you can additionally provide complex DataTypes. Optional Properties on TypeDefinitions make clients aware of the existence of those properties. Methods should be shared if the execution is not restricted per Object. In general, standard ModellingRules should be preferred. However, there are not enough standard ModellingRules defined to capture common use cases like cardinality restrictions. If you provide additional information to a relationship between Nodes, you need to use a proxy instead of a simple Reference.

### 3.4.2 Where to Find More Information?

There are power-point presentations and videos of the OPC UA DevCon 2007 available at the OPC Foundation web site (www.opcfoundation.org/ua). The presentation about "Information Model and Services" contains another example modeled in OPC UA. The scenario includes a boiler having controls, flow transmitters, and valves.

There is an Appendix in [UA Part 3] providing some best practices and an Appendix in [UA Part 5] explaining the design decisions regarding the modeling of the diagnostics information.

### 3.4.3  What's Next?

In the next chapter, we will explain how to create Information Models and how servers support multiple Information Models. We will introduce the base Information Model and the more specific Information Models like Data Access and Programs, provided by the OPC UA specification. Afterwards, we will look at current activities regarding the development of standard Information Models defined by other organizations. Starting with Chap. 5, we will finally explain how to access and manipulate the data modeled in OPC UA.

# 4 Standard Information Models

## 4.1 Overview

In this chapter, the base Information Model of OPC UA is introduced. This model provides the foundation for OPC UA information modeling and is always used as foundation to define additional Information Models. We will also look at the extensions of this model defined by the OPC UA specification. Those extensions are used to define a standard way to represent capabilities and diagnostic information of an OPC UA server in its Address Space and how specific information for current data, historical data, state machines, programs, alarms, and conditions are modeled. Depending on your application you should use those extensions (for example, in the case of Data Access) or you must use them (for example, in the case of Historical Data where it is required to provide certain information). Finally, we take a look at what standard Information Models are currently in development by other organizations based on OPC UA. Maybe there are already activities in your domain that you can use or should join.

Before looking at those standard Information Models, we start this chapter by considering how to handle standard Information Models. What is defined by an OPC-UA-based Information Model, how you can actually define such a model, and what mechanisms are built into OPC UA allowing servers and clients to work simultaneously with different Information Models?

## 4.2 Handling Information Models

### 4.2.1 What is Specified by an Information Model?

From the OPC UA Address Space point of view, an Information Model mainly defines Nodes. This includes well-defined NodeIds for the Nodes. Different kinds of Nodes can be defined. Typically an Information Model defines TypeDefinitions (incl. EventTypes), ReferenceTypes, and DataTypes. It can also define Modelling-Rules when the standard ModellingRules are not sufficient. An Information Model can define standard Properties and Methods by defining a specific BrowseName and the semantic of it. An Information Model can also define standard Objects and Views as standard entry points into the Address Space and standard Variables containing well-defined data.

Beside this, an Information Model can define constraints that are not visible in the Address Space. For example, it defines rules that restrict the usage of ReferenceTypes.

W. Mahnke et al., *OPC Unified Architecture*,
DOI: 10.1007/978-3-540-68899-0_4, © Springer-Verlag Berlin Heidelberg 2009

In theory it can define any kind of constraint. It can specify that every device targeted by a system must be represented in the OPC UA server by a specific ObjectType. In the Capabilities and Diagnostics Information Model of OPC UA, for example, you have to represent each session of a server as an Object of a specific type in the Address Space. Table 4.1 summarizes the different concepts that can be defined by an Information Model.

**Table 4.1** What can be specified by an Information Model

| Concept | Description | Example |
| --- | --- | --- |
| ObjectType | Simple or complex ObjectTypes including constraints on the instances of the type, e.g., when the type should be applied (semantic) and where instances of the type should be referenced in the Address Space (syntax).<br>Some constraints can only be defined textual, either in the description or some additional Variables; some constraints can be defined by InstanceDeclarations and ModellingRules | ObjectType representing devices |
| Modelling-Rule | For complex TypeDefinitions, additional ModellingRules can by defined specifying specific constraints | Cardinality restriction between instances of two types |
| EventType | EventTypes can be specified either to categorize Events or to add additional Event fields. In addition, constraints can be defined when Events of the type must be generated. Some constraints can be exposed by references in the Address Space (see the State Machine Information Model), others only by a textual description | EventType for level alarms |
| Variable-Type | VariableTypes can be specified as subtype of the BaseDataVariableType. They can restrict the usage of data types, they can define a specific semantic, and they can be complex (containing sub-variables). Constraints can define where the VariableType can or must be applied and where it can be found in the Address Space | VariableType with specific Properties like engineering unit |

*(Continued)*

| Property semantic | By defining a concrete BrowseName for a Property, a specific semantic for the Property is defined. Information Models can define constraints on allowed data types, and where the Property can or must be defined. Typically these constraints are defined only textually; however, adding the Property on a base TypeDefinition allows defining some constraints like the BrowseName and the data type more explicitly. When a Property is not used as InstanceDeclaration, the actual support of this Property in a server cannot be detected in the Address Space[1] | A Property for the engineering unit of a DataVariable |
|---|---|---|
| Method semantic | By defining a concrete BrowseName for a Method, a specific semantic for the Method is defined. Additional constraints like specifying where such Methods are applied or on the arguments of the Method can be defined. Like Properties there is no standard way exposing supported Methods | A Method applicable on each Type Definition creating an instance of the type with specific input-arguments defining specific default values, whether optional InstanceDeclarations should be applied, etc. |
| Reference-Type | Hierarchical or non-hierarchical Refer-enceType defining specific semantic between two Nodes. Each Refer-enceType has constraints where it can be applied, for example, the NodeClass and potentially the TypeDefinition of the source and target node, or how often it can be used for the same source. Those constraints are typically only visible as textual descriptions; at least there is no standard way to expose them | A ReferenceType identifying that two Nodes representing devices communi-cate with each other |

*(Continued)*

---

[1] At least in a standard way. Information Models may define a place where they expose all sup-ported Properties in the Address Space.

| DataType | Simple DataTypes can be defined providing a specific semantic, and enumeration DataTypes specifying a specific enumeration. Structured DataTypes can be defined for complex data. In addition, abstract DataTypes can be defined organizing the DataType hierarchy and providing places to extend the hierarchy | A DataType representing a Status of a device |
|---|---|---|
| DataType encodings | For specific applications, a specific way how to encode a structured DataType can be defined. This is a sophisticated feature that should be avoided or used together with a standard encoding because of interoperability issues | An encoding providing the data in exactly the same format as provided by a device |
| Object | Standard Objects can be defined as entry points into the Address Space. Clients can use those Objects and start browsing from the Object. Objects can also be defined as EventNotifiers and thus as standard sources to subscribe to Events | Server Object as entry point into the diagnostics, but also as entry point to all Events of the server |
| View | Similar to Objects, Views can be defined as entry points into the Address Space. In addition, it can be defined what should be contained in the View | A View providing all devices represented in a server |
| Variable | Variables contain a value and thus standard Variables define specific information. Clients can directly read, write, or subscribe to the value of the Variable without the need to find it first | Variable containing the status of the server |
| Method | A standard Method can directly be called by a client without the need to find it first | A Method to shut down the server |
| Constraint | A variety of constraints can be defined by an Information Model. These constraints can define how the Address Space is organized, but also what must be provided by the Address Space or how a server must behave. This behavior must not conflict with what is defined by OPC UA, but it may define a more restrictive behavior, like a server must be redundant | All events generated by the devices represented by the server must be provided as Events in OPC UA |

## 4.2.2 How is an Information Model Specified?

At the moment there is no standard way how to specify an Information Model. If you look at the Information Models defined by the OPC Foundation, for example, for Data Access and Programs, a text document is used. Standard Nodes are defined in tables and constraints by text in the document.

For constraints we expect that there will always be the use case where plain text is needed. However, for standard Nodes it is desirable to have a more machine-friendly way to provide this information. This could be used by a server to populate its Address Space and by test tools checking if the Nodes exist. The SDKs provided by the OPC Foundation already use XML documents based on a specific XML Schema to generate code out of those documents. We expect that a similar XML Schema will be standardized by the OPC Foundation in the long-term and can be used as base to define Information Models. However, constraints that cannot be easily exposed in the Address Space need to be defined as well. And – of course – there must be some introduction where the Information Model should be applied. Thus you will always need to create a text document, but in the long-term you may use an XML document to specific standard Nodes.

## 4.2.3 How are Multiple Information Models Supported?

Servers can support several Information Models at the same time. OPC UA provides some very simple mechanisms to accomplish this. In the end, an Information Model defines unique Nodes in the Address Space, standard Properties and Methods. The uniqueness of Nodes is provided by the NodeId, the uniqueness of standard Properties and Methods by the BrowseName. To avoid the risk that two Information Models use the same NodeId or the same BrowseName, both contain a NamespaceURI (optimized by the NamespaceIndex, see Sect. 2.8.5). Each organization uses its own NamespaceURI (which, by definition, is unique). Thus, NodeIds and BrowseNames become unique to the organization defining them. This allows servers to expose several Information Models without "name conflicts."

However, different Information Models may define global constraints that exclude each other. For example, one Information Model may define that all devices accessed by a server must be exposed; another one that devices only used for communication shall not be exposed. Those scenarios can be avoided when Information Models are more specific, for example, specifying that all communication devices are not exposed using their specific types.

## 4.3    Base OPC UA Information Model

The base Information Model is defined in [UA Part 3] and [UA Part 5]. In [UA Part 3], the Nodes used in the meta model of OPC UA are introduced like Nodes representing specific ReferenceTypes. The Nodes are formally defined together with additional Nodes in [UA Part 5]. In this book, we distinguish between the base Information Model of OPC UA and the Nodes defining the capabilities and diagnostics of the server. Both are defined in [UA Part 5]. All NodeIds defined by the OPC Foundation use the Namespace URI of OPC UA and NamespaceIndex zero.

In Fig. 4.1, the base TypeDefinitions of the base Information Model is shown. All ObjectTypes must inherit from the BaseObjectType and all VariableTypes from the BaseVariableType. However, you can define only additional DataVariableTypes inheriting from the BaseDataVariableType. All EventTypes must inherit from the BaseEventType. The FolderType can be used for Objects only organizing the Address Space without providing additional semantic, and the PropertyType must be used for all Properties. The ModellingRuleType is used to define ModellingRules. There are several TypeDefinitions used to define the encoding of structured DataTypes as described in Sect. 2.8.4. The full list of audit-related EventTypes is given in Appendix C.

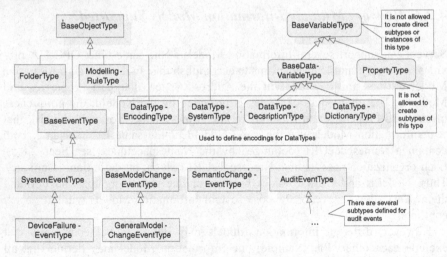

**Fig. 4.1** Base TypeDefinitions

In Fig. 4.2, an overview of ReferenceTypes and DataTypes of the base Information Model is given. The base Information Model defines all built-in DataTypes. The complete list of base ReferenceTypes and DataTypes is given in Appendix C.

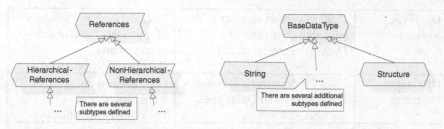

**Fig. 4.2** Base DataTypes and ReferenceTypes

There is one standard Method called "Create". It is used on ObjectTypes to create instances with different default values or specifying what optional Instance-Declarations should be applied. Standard Method means that the BrowseName is defined. Each ObjectType using this Method must define its own Method Node and offer input- and output arguments suitable for the type. There are several standard Properties. In Table 4.2, they are summarized.

**Table 4.2** Standard properties

| Property | Description | Constraint |
| --- | --- | --- |
| NodeVersion | Used to track changes of the Address Space, see Sect. 2.11.3 | Can be applied on all Nodes (except for Properties) |
| ViewVersion | Used to track changes in a View, see Sect. 2.9 | Only defined on View Nodes |
| Icon | An icon that can be used by clients when displaying the Object or ObjectType | Only defined on Objects and ObjectTypes |
| NamingRule | NamingRule of the ModellingRule, see Sect. 2.5.6 | Only for Objects of type ModellingRuleType |
| LocalTime | The time difference (in minutes) between the Source-Timestamp (UTC) associated with the value and the standard time at the location in which the value was obtained | Only defined on DataVariables |
| AllowNulls | Specifies whether a NULL value is allowed for the value of the DataVariable | Only defined on DataVariables |

(*Continued*)

| DataType-Version | Used as version number of the encoding of structured DataTypes, see Sect. 2.8.4 | Only defined on Variables of type DataTypeDescriptionType and DataTypeDictionaryType |
|---|---|---|
| Dictionary-Fragment | Used for describing the encoding of structured DataTypes, see Sect. 2.8.4 | Only defined on Variables of type DataTypeDescriptionType |
| EnumStrings | Used to define the string representation of an enumeration, see Sect. 2.8.3 | Only defined for enumeration DataTypes (in the Data Access Information Model it is also defined for DataVariables) |
| Input-Arguments | Input arguments of a Method | Only defined on Methods |
| Output-Arguments | Output arguments of a Method | Only defined on Methods |

In addition to the standard types, Methods, and Properties, the base Information Model defines some standard Nodes as entry point into the Address Space. It also defines the Server Object as the EventNotifier providing all Events of the Server. The Server Object contains the Namespace- and ServerArray and is the entry point into the diagnostic information and the Variables describing the capabilities of the server. In Fig. 4.3 you can see the Objects and Variables defined by the base Information Model. There are no Views or standard Methods defined by the base Information Model.

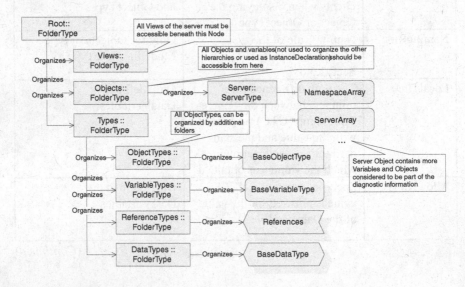

**Fig. 4.3** Objects and Variables of the base Information Model

## 4.4    Capabilities and Diagnostics

The Capabilities and Diagnostics Information Model contain information about the status of the server, the capabilities of the server, what clients are connected to the server, and what Service was called how many times. It offers entry points to which vendor-specific information can be added as well. Details of the provided information can be found in [UA Part 5]. The diagnostic information is split into information per server, per session, and per subscription. The general handling of this is shown in Fig. 4.4.

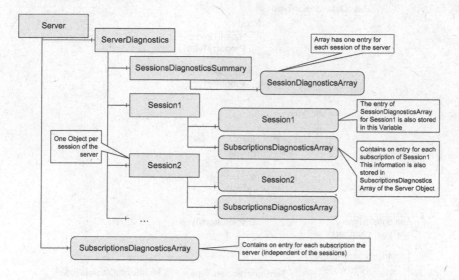

**Fig. 4.4** Diagnostic information

## 4.5    Data Access

The Data Access Information Model [UA Part 8] mainly defines standard Vari-ableTypes and adds mandatory and optional Properties to them. The VariableType hierarchy is shown in Fig. 4.5. The DataItemType is used to represent arbitrary automation data. Two optional Properties are defined: definition contains a human-readable string that specifies how the value of the DataItem is calculated and Value-Precision specifies the maximum precision of the value. The AnalogItemType is used to represent continuously-variable physical quantities. It only applies for Number DataTypes and defines Properties for the InstrumentRange, the EURange, and EngineeringUnits. The abstract DiscreteItemType is specialized to TwoState-DiscreteType for Booleans and MultiStateDiscreteType for unsigned integers. Both contain Properties for the localized text representation of the numeric value. In that way they are enumerations, not by the DataType Attribute but the VariableType.

You should use an enumeration DataType when you expect the enumeration to be used several times and a DiscreteItemType when the enumeration is only used once or a few times or the enumeration text may change often. Of course, this decision may also depend on the source the server is accessing.

The Data Access Information Model also defines some DataTypes used in the Properties of the DataItemTypes, for example, defining the range structure used in the EURange Property or the engineering unit structure used in the Engineering-Units Property.

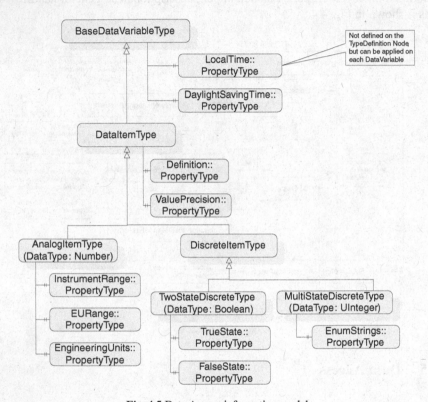

**Fig. 4.5** Data Access information model

## 4.6    Historical Access and Aggregates

Historical Access defines the representation and access of historical time series data and historical event data in OPC UA.

The Historical Access Part of the OPC UA specification was released in a first version in 2007 [UA Part 11]. Later, the document has been split into two documents, one for Historical Access [UA Part 11Draft] and one for Aggregates [UA Part 13]. We will give only a brief overview since both may change in details until release.

More details on Historical Access are described in the Service chapter (see Sect. 5.9) where also a list of Aggregates is provided in Table 5.48.

The Historical Access Information Model mainly describes where to find configuration information of historical data. It extends the Capabilities and Diagnostics Information Model, with details on how history is supported. In addition, it defines how EventNotifiers and Variables expose their configuration and how historical data are collected. Many EventNotifiers can use the same configuration; the same is true for Variables. In turn, each EventNotifier and Variable can have several configurations when a server collects the history in different ways (e.g., a more detailed history for 2 weeks and a less detailed history for 2 years). This is shown in Fig. 4.6.

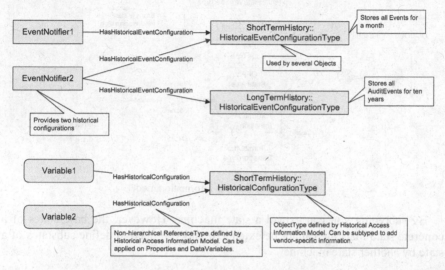

**Fig. 4.6** Historical access information model

With respect to information modeling, the Aggregates specification mainly extends the capabilities model of the server exposing the supported Aggregates. Those can be used for historical data or current data. Primarily, the Aggregates specification defines the behavior of the aggregate functions.

## 4.7  State Machine

The State Machine Information Model defines how to expose state machines in the OPC UA Address Space. This model is used by Programs as well as Alarms and Conditions. It is defined in an Appendix of [UA Part 5]. The model is summarized in Fig. 4.7. It defines two base types. The StateMachineType exposes only the current state of the state machine, whereas the FiniteStateMachineType also provides information about the states and transitions of the state machine. It allows specifying causes triggering transitions and effects that are executed when a transition is triggered. It is defined how to use a Method call as cause and the generation of an Event as effect, but this can be extended to other causes and effects. An instance of a State Machine provides only the information about the current state, whereas the description of the possible states and transitions can be found at the type.

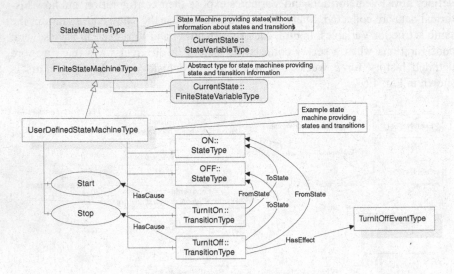

**Fig. 4.7** State machine information model

By subtyping you can extend a state machine. However, the base states of a concrete state machine cannot be extended, and you need to define substates of a state by another state machine.

## 4.8    Programs

A Method is invoked by a client, executed by the server, and the result is directly (in the Method call response) returned to the client. In contrast, a Program is used for more complex, long running, and stateful functionality. A Method may be called to calculate a value, whereas a Program may be used to run and control a batch process or a machine tool program. Programs can be controlled by a client (e.g., starting and stopping) and intermediate results can be returned to the client using Events. To control a Program, it is desirable to know its state (whether it is already running, interrupted, etc.). Therefore, the Programs Information Model uses the State Machine Information Model as base to model Programs. It defines a concrete subtype of the FiniteStateMachineType called ProgramType having four states as shown in Fig. 4.8. It also defines several transitions between them and optional Methods to control the Program. In addition, specific Variables containing capabilities and diagnostics of the Program are defined. The ProgramType can be subtyped and substates can be added to the four states of the ProgamType.

The first version of the Programs specification was released in 2007 [UA Part 10]. Although no updated release or release candidate is available while writing this section, it is not expected that there are major changes to the document.

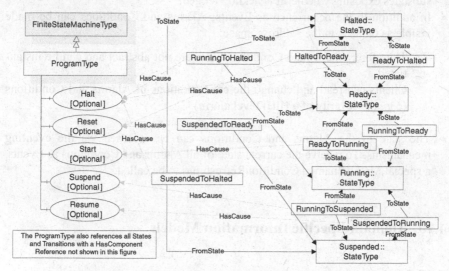

**Fig. 4.8** Programs information model

## 4.9    Alarms and Conditions

The Alarms and Conditions specification defines an Information Model for Conditions, acknowledgeable Conditions, confirmations, and Alarms. This Information Model can also be extended to support the needs of other domains.

While writing this section the Alarms and Conditions specification [UA Part 9] was not jet released. To avoid providing you instable information, we just outline the ideas of the Alarms and Conditions Information Model.

- Conditions are specific Events that are not transient but always maintain a state (e.g., enabled or disabled).
- There are acknowledgeable conditions where entering a specific state requires a client to acknowledge this state. The acknowledgement is done by a Method call. For example, if a level reaches a certain value, this may have to be acknowledged by an operator.
- Alarms are acknowledgeable conditions that can be suppressed and shelved to avoid an explosion of Alarms in a system when a critical error occurs. The most important state of an Alarm is the active state. For example, if a level reaches a critical value like 95% the Alarm changes to active.

- Dialogs represent another subtype of Conditions. They allow a server to pop up different types of dialogs at the client.
- Alarms and Conditions use state machines describing their states. Most types of Alarms and Conditions defined in the Alarms and Conditions specification uses several states and substates. An acknowledgeable Condition has, for example, substates exposing whether it is acknowledged.
- In addition to the occurrence as Events, Alarms and Conditions can be made visible as Objects in the Address Space:

  – Therefore, Alarm- and ConditionTypes are not abstract and can be instantiated.
  – Clients can read and change the configurations of Alarms and Conditions (e.g., the severity of a HiHi level alarm).

- The state of the Alarms and Conditions can be accessed via the eventing mechanisms. To receive the current state of all Alarms and Conditions as Events, a special Method named ConditionRefresh has to be called.

## 4.10    Domain-Specific Information Models

### 4.10.1    Overview

The OPC UA Information Model provides a means to describe the semantics related to a specific domain. ISA-S88, ISA-S95, and IEC TC 57 – CIM are examples of existing information models for specific domains. The OPC Foundation is collaborating with these and other standard organizations to become the how for moving the other standard organizations what. In the following, we introduce activities done by other organizations in cooperation with the OPC Foundation defining domain-specific Information Models based on OPC UA.

A common Information Model for devices is currently available in a draft version [UA Devices]. Details of the model are described in Sect. 4.10.2. The EDD Cooperation Team (ECT) defined a mapping from an EDD to a device representation in OPC UA based on this model [ECT06]. The FDT group also defined a mapping of DTMs to OPC UA using the same model [FDT08].

While the devices Information Model specifies only a generic model how to represent devices, the ADI (analyzer device integration) initiative of the OPC Foundation brings the vendors and customers of analyzer devices together to define concrete types for different kinds of analyzers. The resulting Information Model is based on the devices Information Model. Currently there is a draft version available of this model as well [UA Analyzer].

The Field Device Integration (FDI) initiative brings together ECT and FDT group defining the future of device integration. The devices Information Model will be used in that approach, but also other facets like user interfaces are considered.

Discussions have started with several other organizations regarding Information Models based on OPC UA:

- PRODML (www.prodml.org) for the vertical integration of oil values (drilling)
- MIMOSA (Machinery Information Management Open Systems Alliance – www.mimosa.org) for plant operations and maintenance
- ISA-88 (www.isa-88.com) for batch control
- ISA-95 (www.isa-95.com) for the integration of control systems with enterprise systems (vertical integration)
- OMAC (Open Modular Architecture Control – www.omac.org) for the integration of different packaging line functions
- PLCopen (www.plcopen.org) for standard PLC programming languages

We are currently not aware of additional standard Information Models initiatives, although we know that other organizations are evaluating OPC UA as well figuring out whether it can be applied for their purposes.

## 4.10.2  Devices Information Model

The device Information Model [UA Devices] defines the Information Model associated with devices providing a unified view irrespective of the underlying device protocols. It defines a device as entity that provides sensing, actuating, communication, and/or control functionality.

At the time of writing this book the device Information Model has been in draft state. Therefore, we will provide only the idea behind the model. A device is represented by an Object. All the parameters of the device are gathered with another Object called ParameterSet. Objects of type ParameterView can be used to group related parameters (e.g., all configuration parameters). The parameters use the VariableTypes defined by the Data Access Information Model. Sub-devices and function blocks are provided beneath the device as additional Objects. The devices Information Model defines ObjectTypes, for example, for the devices, blocks, and parameter sets. It is illustrated in Fig. 4.9. You can see that the devices Information Model is derived from the base Information Model. Specific types of devices are modeled as sub-types of the DeviceType, like the motor starter type in the figure. As specified by the devices Information Model, the motor starter uses VariableTypes specified by the Data Access Information Model.

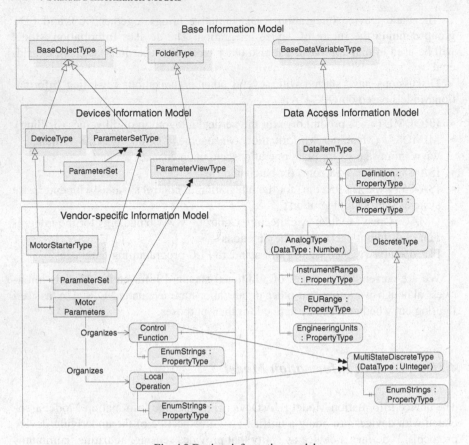

**Fig. 4.9** Devices information model

The devices Information Model also provides entry points for bus-specific extensions (like HART, FF, and PROFIBUS).

## 4.11    Summary

### 4.11.1    Key Messages

Information Models define standard Nodes, including types, Properties, and Methods. In addition, they define constraints on the Address Space. These constraints may reference the environment of the server, like all sessions of the server must be provided as Objects in the Address Space. Information Models are currently defined by text documents; in the future there will be an XML Schema that can be used to define standard Nodes. The NamespaceURI contained in

BrowseNames and NodeIds allows providing several Information Models in one server.

The base Information Model defines the foundation of all types and standard entry points into the Address Space. The Capabilities and Diagnostics Information Model defines standard places to find the capabilities of a server and diagnostic information. The Data Access Information Model provides VariableTypes having standard Properties storing Data Access related information like the engineering unit. The Historical Access Information Model defines where to find the configuration of historical data and events. The State Machine Information Model provides a generic model for state machines used by the Programs and the Alarms and Events Information Models.

There are several initiatives going on defining standard Information Models for specific domains. Make use of those models when they are appropriate in your domain or try to define additional standard Information Model when there is the need for it in your domain.

### 4.11.2 Where to Find More Information?

The documents defining the Information Models are already referenced in the corresponding sections. URLs to the organizations cooperating with the OPC Foundation defining Information Models have been provided as well.

### 4.11.3 What's Next?

In the next chapters we will leave the information modeling and look at how the information modeled in OPC UA can be accessed. This is done by the OPC UA Services described in Chap. 5. Chapter 6 discusses the mapping of those Services to concrete technologies.

# 5 Services

## 5.1 Overview

The OPC UA Services are defining the data communication on application level. Services are methods used by an OPC UA client to access the data of the Information Model provided by an OPC UA server. Similar to Classic OPC, where the OPC specifications just defined Application Programming Interface (APIs) between applications, the Services define the communication interface between UA applications. The definition of the Services is independent of the transport protocol and the programming environment that is used to develop an OPC UA application. This is the fundamental difference to Classic OPC where the definition of the APIs was bound to a specific transport mechanism – Microsoft Component Object Model (COM).

The independence of the transport protocol and the programming environment requires an abstract definition of the Services. This abstract definition [UA Part 4] can be applied to different transport mechanisms (see Chap.6) defining the representation of the Services on the wire [UA Part 6] and to different implementations of the transport mechanisms in OPC UA Stacks (see Sect. 6.5) in different programming languages. The language specific APIs for the application development are defined by the OPC UA Stacks based on the abstract UA Service definition. The different communication layers are shown in Fig. 5.1.

Like Classic OPC, the OPC UA Services are designed for exchanging bulk data between UA applications running in different processes or on different network nodes to reduce the roundtrips between the applications. For example, a Read method does not read one Variable but allows defining a list of Variables to read. OPC UA Services are reduced to a generic set of methods. There are two main reasons for this reduction. On the one side a lot of information provided in Classic OPC is now modeled in the server Address Space and accessed with a generic method like read instead of having specific methods to access the information. A simple example is the server status information. In Classic OPC, this information was obtained by a special GetStatus Method. In OPC UA, this information is modeled as server status Variable and can be accessed with the Read Service or monitored for changes. Another reason was the design goal to provide only one generic Service for a specific functionality and not a long list of specialized methods for different variations of information.

This chapter describes the general Service behavior and the functionality provided by the different Services. They are partitioned into Service Sets in the corresponding OPC UA specification [UA Part 4]. The grouping in this chapter is based on use cases summarized in Table 5.1 and does not exactly match the Service Set partitioning. Each Service is described in this chapter with its key parameters. A complete list of parameters and their detailed description can be found in [UA Part 4] or in API documentations.

W. Mahnke et al., *OPC Unified Architecture*,
DOI: 10.1007/978-3-540-68899-0_5, © Springer-Verlag Berlin Heidelberg 2009

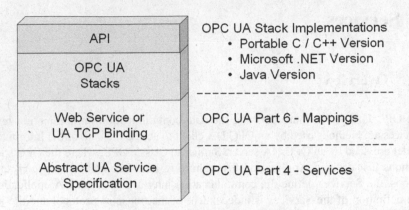

**Fig. 5.1** OPC UA communication layering

**Table 5.1** Services grouped by use cases

| Use case | Service sets or services |
|---|---|
| Find servers | Discovery Services Set |
| Connection management between clients and servers | Secure Channel Service Set Session Service Set |
| Find information in the Address Space | View Service Set |
| Read and write data and metadata | Read and Write Service |
| Subscribe for data changes and Events | Subscription Service Set Monitored Item Service Set |
| Calling Methods defined by the server | Call Service |
| Access history of data and Events | HistoryRead and HistoryUpdate Service |
| Find information in a complex Address Space | Query Service Set |
| Modify the structure of the server Address Space | Node Management Service Set |

## 5.2   General Service Concepts

The Service definition uses the request and response pattern known form Web Services where each Service is composed of a request and a response message. To invoke a Service in the server, the client sends a request message to the server. After processing the request, the server sends a response message back to the client. Since this message exchange is asynchronous, all Service invocations are asynchronous by definition. After sending the request message, the client application can process other functionality until the response message arrives. Most UA Stack APIs provide synchronous versions of the APIs for convenience. This is a general enhancement compared to Classic OPC where all functions are synchronous and only a few functions where provided as asynchronous versions in addition.

## 5.2.1 Timeout Handling

The OPC UA data communication is designed for data exchange between different systems, typically running on different network nodes or in different processes. Especially network communication can be interrupted at any time and it is important to detect and handle these failures correctly.

An important concept in such an environment is configurable timeouts for Service invocations to get a timely detection of communication failure. For this reason each single Service call has individual timeouts defined by the client. This is an important enhancement over Classic OPC.

The communication stack on the client side returns the call to the API or sends the callback with a timeout status if the timeout expires. But the timeout set on the client-side UA stack is also send to the server to detect Service invocations that are not longer expected to return to the client side.

## 5.2.2 Request and Response Headers

Each Service contains the same headers for request messages and for response messages. For this reason they are not listed for each Service in this chapter. They are containing common Service parameters like the token for the Session context or the result of the Service call. The request header parameters are described in Table 5.2 and response header parameters are described in Table 5.3.

**Table 5.2** Request header parameters

| Parameter | Description |
|---|---|
| AuthenticationToken | The secret Session identifier used to assign the Service call to the Session context created between client and server application |
| RequestHandle | A client defined handle assigned to the Service call |
| Timestamp | The time the client sent the request |
| TimeoutHint | The timeout set in the client side UA Stack for the call. This hint can be used by the server to cancel long running calls if the timeout expires |
| ReturnDiagnostic | Indicates if the client requests the server to return additional detailed diagnostic information in the case of an error instead of returning only a status code |
| AuditEntryId | A string that identifies the client or user that initiated the action. The string is empty if this parameter is not used. It is used for auditing (see Sect. 9.5) |

**Table 5.3** Response header parameters

| Parameter | Description |
|---|---|
| ServiceResult | UA defined result code for the Service call |
| RequestHandle | The client defined handle assigned to the Service call |
| Timestamp | The time the server sent the response |
| ServiceDiagnostics | Client requested detailed diagnostic information |

## 5.2.3 Error Handling

Error handling is an important part of the Service parameters and Service handling since communication between distributed systems from different vendors can cause errors on different levels and in different scenarios. Errors can happen in normal operation, for example, when a client is using wrong parameters like NodeIds of Nodes that are no longer available or they can happen in communication error scenarios when the connection between client and server or between server and the underlying system[1] is interrupted.

There are two types of error information used in the Services. The one type is an error code called *StatusCode*. The StatusCode is a 32-bit unsigned integer. The most significant 16 bits represent the numeric value of the code that shall be used for detecting specific errors or conditions. The least significant 16 bits are bit flags that contain additional information but do not affect the meaning of the Status-Code. The two most significant bits are indicating the overall severity which could be *Good* for success, *Uncertain* for warning, and *Bad* for failure. Status codes are only defined by OPC UA and cannot be extended by vendors or other organizations.

The second type of error information is the *DiagnosticInformation*. This structure contains additional information for a StatusCode including vendor-specific error codes, a localized description of the error, and a text field for additional information. The diagnostic information can be nested to be able to provide an error stack. There is a DiagnosticInformation field available for each StatusCode field in a Service, but the additional information is only returned by the Server if requested by the client. The DiagnosticInformation fields are not contained in the Service descriptions in this chapter.

The error information[2] is provided on two levels. The first level is the result of the Service call. The second level is the list of operations inside the Service call. Since OPC UA supports bulk operations for all Services used to exchange data, some operations in a Service call can fail while others succeed. An example is the Read Service where the client can read a list of Variable values in one Read Service call. Each Variable in the Read is an operation.

---

[1]For example devices connected to the server by an interrupted network.

[2]Combination of StatusCode and DiagnosticInformation.

Clients must check the results always on both levels since both can fail. In the first step, the client must check if the Service call succeeded. If not, none of the result fields is valid. If the Service succeeded, each operation StatusCode must be verified by the client before using the result data of the operation.

Compared to Classic OPC, the error handling was simplified in OPC UA. Classic OPC provided a result code and a quality code for read and data change methods. Clients needed to check first the result code and then the quality code but only one field was able to contain error information. OPC UA provides only one StatusCode field which contains general error codes and also quality codes for values in the same field.

### 5.2.4 Extensible Parameters

Extensible parameters are used to add flexibility and variations to Services without having the need to extend the number of Services. Extensible parameters are used everywhere where a Service parameter can contain different structures for different use cases. Samples for the use of extensible parameters are the Subscriptions where different types of information like data and Events are handled with the same Services using extensible parameters for the filters and the transport of the notifications from server to client. Another sample is the history access Services where only two Services are defined for the read and update access to different type of data and Events.

### 5.2.5 Communication Context

OPC UA Services are not stateless and cannot be called without establishing a communication context on different levels. For this reason a lot of Services are not used for data transfer but to create, maintain, and modify these different levels of communication context illustrated in Fig. 5.2.

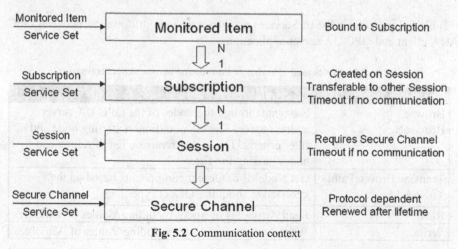

**Fig. 5.2** Communication context

The Secure Channel is the low - level and protocol - dependent channel to secure the communication and the exchanged messages. This level is handled completely by the UA communication stacks hiding the different possible protocols. The Secure Channel must be renewed after the lifetime negotiated during the first establishment of the Secure Channel to reduce the risk of compromising the channel security.

The Session is the connection context between the two applications created on the top of and in the context of a Secure Channel. The lifetime of the Session is independent of the Secure Channel and another Secure Channel can be assigned to the Session. A Session has a timeout that allows the server to free the resources for a Session after a defined time period. The timeout gets reset with each Service invocation in the Session context received by the server.

Multiple Subscriptions can be created in the context of a Session. A Subscription is the context to exchange data changes and Event notifications between server and client. A Subscription requires a Session to transport the data to the client but it can be transferred to another Session for example to be used in a Session created by a redundant backup client if the client that created the Subscription is no longer available. Therefore the Subscription lifetime is independent of the Session lifetime and a Subscription has a timeout that gets reset every time data or keep-alive messages get sent to the client.

Multiple Monitored Items can be created in a Subscription but they are bound to this Subscription. A Monitored Item is used to define the Attribute of a Node that should be monitored for data changes or to define the Event source that should be monitored for Event notifications.

OPC UA defines 37 Services whereof 21 Services are used to manage the communication infrastructure and context and only 16 Services are used to exchange different types of information.

### 5.2.5.1    Services Used to Exchange Information

Table 5.4 provides a list of Services used to exchange information between OPC UA client and OPC UA server applications.

**Table 5.4** Services used to exchange information between client and server

| Service | Description |
|---|---|
| Browse BrowseNext | Navigate through the nodes of the OPC UA server address space. The client defines a starting node and filter criteria. The server returns a list of referenced nodes passing the filter |
| TranslateBrowsePaths-ToNodeIds | Get NodeIds of Object components based on the knowledge about the ObjectType |
| Read | Read Attributes of nodes including Values of Variables |
| Write | Write Attributes of nodes including Values of Variables |

*(Continued)*

| Publish Republish | Send changed data or Events for a Subscription from the OPC UA server to the OPC UA client |
|---|---|
| Call | Call a Method in the server |
| HistoryRead | Read the history of Variable Values or the history of Events |
| HistoryUpdate | Update the history of Variable Values or the history of Events |
| AddNodes | Adding nodes to the server address space. This includes the instantiation of Object instances |
| AddReferences | Adding references between nodes in the server address space |
| DeleteNodes | Deleting nodes in the server address space |
| DeleteReferences | Deleting references between nodes in the server address space |
| QueryFirst QueryNext | Returns a list of nodes and Attribute values based on complex filter criteria operating on the whole address space of a server |

### 5.2.6 Conventions for Describing Services in this Chapter

The following sections are using tables to describe the Service paramters. Not all parameters are contained since some parameters like the diagnostic information are described as general concepts and other parameters are not important for understanding the Services. The data types of parameters are also not contained as general information in the tables. They are mentioned when it is important for understanding the Service. A complete list of parameters, data types, and their detailed description can be found in [UA Part 4] or in API documentations.

## 5.3   Finding Servers

The Discovery Service Set is used by clients to find available OPC UA servers and to get information about the available Endpoints of a server. It is used by the server to register with a Discovery server. The Discovery server maintains the list of available servers. The available Endpoints are provided by each server.

An Endpoint defines the used network protocol and the necessary security settings to be able to connect to the Endpoint of a server. Fig. 5.3 shows the interaction between UA client, Discovery server, and UA server.

Like all other Services, the Discovery Services can be invoked over the network and thus allow a network-wide discovery. Nevertheless OPC UA defines only the behavior of a local Discovery Server expecting that each node with more than one OPC UA server is running a Discovery Service. The definition of network-wide discovery will be added in a future release of OPC UA.

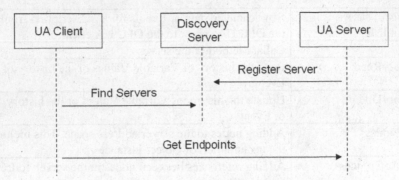

**Fig. 5.3** Use of Discovery server and the Discovery Service Set

## 5.3.1 Service FindServers

The FindServers Service is implemented by the Discovery server returning a list of registered servers and by each UA server returning only itself. This feature is necessary to ensure the same behavior if only one server is running on a network node without an additional Discovery server. The parameters are described in Table 5.5.

This Service can be called on a Secure Channel without security enabled and without having a Session context created since this is not possible without the information returned during the discovery process.

**Table 5.5** FindServers Service parameters

| Request parameters | Description |
|---|---|
| LocaleIds [ ] | A list of locales for the server name returned in the application description. The server should use the first locale in the list that it supports |
| ServerUris [ ] | A list of server URIs to allow the client to request information about specific servers. All available servers are returned if an empty list is passed in |
| **Response parameters** | **Description** |
| Servers [ ] | A list of application description structures for each returned server |
| ApplicationUri | Globally unique identifier for the server instance |
| ApplicationName | Human readable name for the server |
| ProductUri | Globally unique identifier for the server product |
| ApplicationType | The type of application which could be server, client, client and server and discovery server |
| DiscoveryUrls [ ] | The available URLs of the server that allow calling GetEndpoints without requiring a secure connection |

## 5.3.2 Service GetEndpoints

This Service returns the Endpoints supported by the server implementing this Service. An Endpoint description contains all information that is necessary to establish a Secure Channel and a Session between the client and the server. The main parts are the network address of the server and the security settings like the server instance certificate, the security policy defining the used algorithms, and the type of user authentication used to create a Session.

Like FindServers this Service does not require a secure connection or a Session to be called. The parameters are described in Table 5.6.

**Table 5.6** GetEndpoints Service parameters

| Request parameters | | Description |
|---|---|---|
| LocaleIds [ ] | | A list of locales for human readable strings returned in the endpoint descriptions. The server should use the first locale in the list that it supports |
| ProfileUris [ ] | | A list of profile URIs to allow the client to request Endpoints supporting specific transport profiles. All available Endpoints are returned if an empty list is passed in |
| Response parameters | | Description |
| Endpoints [ ] | | A list of endpoint description structures for each returned Endpoint |
| | EndpointUrl | Network address of the Endpoint used by the client to establish a Secure Channel |
| | ServerCertificate | The server instance certificate used for the Endpoint. This is the public key of the server used by the client for securing the message exchange with the server |
| | SecurityPolicy | The security policy URI defining the algorithm sets and key length used for the Secure Channel. The security policy URIs are defined in [UA Part 7] |
| | SecurityMode | The message security mode used to secure the messages exchanged between client and server. Messages can be signed to detect changes of the message content and to ensure the right sender and messages can be encrypted to ensure privacy. The possible modes are SignAndEncrypt, Sign, and None |
| | UserIdentity Tokens [] | A list of user identity tokens supported by the server to authenticate a user during the creation of a Session. Possible tokens are for example the combination of username and password, a certificate, or anonymous |
| | TransportProfileUri | URI of the network protocol used by the Endpoint. The transports profiles are defined in [UA Part 7] |

### 5.3.3 Service RegisterServer

This Service registers a server with a discovery server. This Service will be called by a server or a separate configuration utility. Applications that are only client will not use this Service.

This Service requires a secured connection to make sure that only trusted servers can be registered. The registration call is done periodically by the server to indicate the availability. It is also called during shutdown to indicate that the server is shutting down and gets offline.

The Server passes all information to the Service that is necessary to return the application description in FindServers. In addition, the online status is sent to the Discovery Server.

## 5.4    Connection Management Between Clients and Servers

OPC UA requires establishing different levels of communication channels to ensure that all requirements for a secure, flexible, and reliable data communication are fulfilled (see Fig. 5.4).

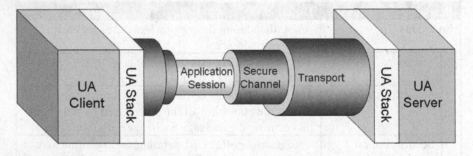

**Fig. 5.4** Different levels of communication channels

The low - level network transport channel for exchanging the messages and the logical Secure Channel to secure the messages are handled by the UA Stacks. The Session on the application level used to authenticate users is handled by the client and server applications.

Most of the security handling is implemented by the UA Stacks provided by the OPC Foundation. On the application level, security handling is only necessary during handshaking for the Session establishment.

A client SDK will typically hide all of the security handling and combine the connection handling in connect and disconnect methods.

A server SDK implements all Session and connection handling without the need for a server implementer to do anything for the Secure Channel and Session Service Sets other than providing the configuration information.

## 5.4.1 Secure Channel Establishment

The SecureChannel Service Set is used to establish the low - level transport channel and the Secure Channel. Since most of the functionality is implemented in the UA Stacks, these Services are described from a Stack API point of view instead of the definition in the Service specification. These are the only two Services where the Stack APIs parameters are different than the parameters defined for the Services.

More details for the security related parts of the Secure Channel can be found in Chap. 7.

The Stack API parameters for OpenSecureChannel are described in Table 5.7. The Stack API parameters for CloseSecureChannel are described in Table 5.8. These Stack API parameters are different than the ones defined in [UA Part 4].

**Table 5.7** Stack API parameters to open a Secure Channel

| Stack API in parameters | Description |
| --- | --- |
| EndpointUrl | Network address of the server Endpoint used by the client to establish a Secure Channel |
| SecurityPolicy | The security policy URI defining the algorithm sets and key length used for the Secure Channel. The security policy URIs are defined in [UA Part 7] |
| SecurityMode | The message security mode used to secure the messages exchanged between client and server. Messages can be signed to detect changes of the message content and to ensure the right sender and messages can be encrypted to ensure privacy. The possible modes are SignAndEncrypt, Sign, and None |
| ServerCertificate | The server instance certificate used for the Endpoint. This is the public key of the server used by the client for securing the message exchange with the server |
| ClientCertificate | The client instance certificate. This is the public key of the client used by the server for securing the message exchange with the client |
| ClientPrivateKey | The private key for the client instance certificate. This private key is used by the client side UA stack to secure the message exchange with the server |
| RequestedLifetime | Requested lifetime for the security token. The security token must be renewed by the UA Stack before the lifetime expires. A renew starts after 75% of the lifetime has expired |
| Stack API Out parameters | Description |
| SecureChannelId | Identifier for the created Secure Channel |
| RevisedLifetime | Revised lifetime of the channel |

**Table 5.8** Stack API parameters to close a Secure Channel

| Stack API In parameters | Description |
|---|---|
| SecureChannelId | Identifier for the Secure Channel to close |
| Stack API Out parameters | Description |
| No relevant out parameters | |

## 5.4.2 Creating an Application Session

Like the Secure Channel Service Set, the Session Service Set is only used to establish a secure and reliable communication channel and not to transfer information from one system to another.

There are two Services for the handshaking to create a Session between two applications, one Service to close the Session and one Service to cancel Service calls in this Service Set.

The handshaking with the Services CreateSession and ActivateSession is necessary to ensure that the client can validate with CreateSession that the application he connects to is the server he wants to connect to and trusts in the further communication before sending sensitive data in ActivateSession like user name and password for the user authentication. The Service ActivateSession is also used to impersonate a user on the active Session and to assign another Secure Channel to the Session if the used Secure Channel is no longer valid.

### 5.4.2.1   CreateSession Service

This Service is used by an OPC UA client to create a Session and the server returns the identifier that is used in all the following Service invocations to assign them to the Session context.

A Session is not valid until the Service ActivateSession was called successfully. Sessions are terminated by the server if he did not receive Service calls during the negotiated timeout period. This ensures that the server can free resources in a defined way if the client is no longer available, for example based on a network interruption. This is a big advantage over Classic OPC specifications where the error handling is relying on fixed COM timeouts. Sessions should be closed gracefully by the client using the Service CloseSession if the communication channel is no longer needed.

A flag in the CloseSession Service indicates if all associated Subscriptions should be deleted. Each Subscription has its own lifetime and can be transferred to another Session if the Session is terminated or closed without deleting the associated Subscriptions.

There are several parameters in this Service only used for additional security validations and security handling. Examples are the EndpointDescription and the application certificates. They are already exchanged during Discovery or Secure Channel establishment but must be also validated in the context of a secure application Session. Since these parameters are typically handled by the UA SDKs and not visible to the application programmers, they are not listed here. See ref. [UA Part 4] for all parameters of this Service and Sect. 7.5.2 for more details on the security aspects of the secure communication channel (Table 5.9).

**Table 5.9** CreateSession Service parameters

| Request parameters | Description |
| --- | --- |
| SessionName | Name for the Session assigned by the client. The name is shown in the diagnostics information of the server |
| ClientDescription | Application description for the client application containing information like application and product URI or the application name |
| Requested SessionTimeout | Timeout of the Session requested by the client. If the client fails to issue a Service request within the interval negotiated with the server, the Session will automatically be terminate by the server |
| **Response parameters** | **Description** |
| SessionId | A unique public identifier assigned by the server to the Session. It is used to identify the Session in server diagnostic objects or in audit logs |
| AuthenticationToken | A unique private identifier assigned by the server to the Session. This identifier is only used for assigning Service calls to the Session and must be kept private between the client and the server application |
| Revised SessionTimeout | Timeout of the Session assigned by the server. This time typically matches the requested timeout of the client if it falls into the valid range defined by the server |
| ServerSoftware Certificates [ ] | The list of software certificates of the server application identifying the product, the supported profiles, and the compliance test level for each profile |

### 5.4.2.2   ActivateSession Service

The ActivateSession Service is used as the second part of the handshaking to establish an application Session. It is also used to change the user of the Session, to change the used language settings for a Session, and to assign a new Secure Channel to the Session (Table 5.10).

Table 5.10 ActivateSession Service parameters

| Request parameters | Description |
|---|---|
| ClientSoftware Certificates [ ] | The list of software certificates of the client application identifying the product, the supported profiles, and the compliance test level for each profile |
| LocaleIds [] | List of locales that should be used by the server to provide localized strings. The server uses the first locale he supports in the list |
| UserIdentityToken | User identity token to validate and logon a specific user to the Session. There are different token types like user name and password or certificates supported. Section 7.5.3.4 describes the different token types |
| Response parameters | Description |
| Results [ ] | Validation results for the client software certificates |

## 5.4.3 Closing an Application Session

If a client does no longer need the connection to the server, he must use the Service CloseSession to start disconnecting from the Server and to free the Session resources in the server. The second step to disconnect is closing the Secure Channel. Both steps are typically combined in one disconnect method of a client SDK (Table 5.11).

Table 5.11 CloseSession Service parameters

| Request parameters | Description |
|---|---|
| DeleteSubscriptions | A flag that indicates if the Server must delete all Subscriptions associated with the Session. Subscriptions can exist independent of a Session and can be transferred to another Session |
| Response parameters | Description |

## 5.4.4 Cancel Outstanding Service Requests

A client is able to cancel outstanding Service requests by using the Service Cancel. To cancel requests can be helpful for potentially longer running Services like Query (Table 5.12).

**Table 5.12** Cancel Service parameters

| Request parameters | Description |
|---|---|
| RequestHandle | Request handle assigned by the client to one or more requests in the request header |
| Response parameters | Description |
| CancelCount | Number of canceled requests |

## 5.5   Find Information in the Address Space

OPC UA provides capabilities to describe information and to transport this information. This section describes how to find different types of data in the Address Space of the server. The two main Services for this purpose are Browse to navigate through the Nodes in the Address Space and Read to access the metadata of the Nodes. Browse and the more specialized Services such as TranslateBrowsePathsToNodeIds, RegisterNodes, and UnregisterNodes are explained in this section. For a better understanding of how to use these generic Services, this section describes also the use of the Services and the Service parameters based on different typical use cases and types of information clients are interested in.

Since the Services are used to access the Information Model provided by the server, it is necessary to understand the concepts described in Chap. 2. For the simple use cases it is enough to know how Objects and Variables are connected together to provide data access capabilities. For the more enhanced use cases it is necessary to read Chaps. 2 – 4 completely.

### 5.5.1 Services Used for Discovering the Address Space

One of the main design goals of OPC UA was the combination of all types of Classic OPC information in one Address Space and the generic access to this model. Each of the Classic OPC specifications defined different ways to navigate through the Address Space and to access the available, but in most cases limited, type and metadata information. OPC DA, A&E, and HDA defined different but similar methods for browsing. DA and HDA defined completely different concepts of accessing properties of OPC variables and A&E defined eight methods to get information about the available event types. OPC UA covers all these different use cases with the flexible information modeling capabilities and the two Services Browse and Read.

### 5.5.1.1    Browse Service

The Browse Service is used by a client to navigate through the Address Space by passing a starting Node and browse filters and the server returns the list of Nodes connected to the starting Node by references.

The Browse Service takes a list of starting Nodes and returns a list of connected Nodes for each starting Node. Nevertheless, most clients will only pass one starting Node for the main purpose of building a tree hierarchy. Since the OPC UA Address Space can be a full-meshed network and is not limited to a pure hierarchy, the capability to pass in a list of starting Nodes is mainly used to browse metadata like the Properties of a list of Variables. A client SDK will provide different browse methods, one for a single starting Node and one for a list of starting Nodes.

Table 5.13 describes the parameters of the Browse Service.

**Table 5.13** Browse Service parameters

| Request parameters | | Description |
|---|---|---|
| View | | Passing a View allows limiting the browse to a specific View. For browsing the entire Address Space this parameter is not set |
| RequesteMax-ReferencesPerNode | | Allows the client to limit the returned Nodes to protect against an unlimited number of results. BrowseNext can be used to get more results |
| NodesToBrowse [ ] | | Defines a list of starting Nodes and browse filters |
| | NodeId | NodeId of the starting Node |
| | BrowseDirection | Indicates if the server should follow references in the forward, the inverse, or both directions |
| | ReferenceTypeId | NodeId of the ReferenceType the server should follow. This parameter is typically combined with the IncludeSubtypes set to filter for a whole set of ReferenceTypes. This is for example Hierarchical-References to fill a tree control |
| | IncludeSubtypes | Indicates if also subtypes of the specified ReferenceTypeId should be returned by the server. Clients should set this value to true. Only in very seldom use cases it makes sense setting it to false |
| | NodeClassMask | Filter on the NodeClass of the returned Nodes, for example only requesting Objects and Variables |
| | ResultMask | Filter on the results returned per Node. The only information that is always returned is the NodeId of the target Node. All other result values can be excluded with this mask. This allows the client to reduce the server effort to find and return information the client is not interested in and reduces also the amount of data on the wire |

*(Continued)*

| Response parameters | | | Description |
|---|---|---|---|
| Results [ ] | | | List of results for the passed starting Nodes and filters |
| | StatusCode | | Result code for the passed starting Node and filter. This status code indicates only invalid filters or an unknown starting Node. An empty result list does not cause a failed status code |
| | ContinuationPoint | | A continuation point is returned when the server was not able to deliver all results in the Browse response. The limitation can be set by the client in the request or by the server during Browse processing. The continuation point can be passed to BrowseNext to get the remaining results |
| | References [ ] | | List of references and target Node information for the Nodes passing the filter criteria set in the request |
| | | Reference-TypeId | NodeId of the ReferenceType followed from the starting Node to the target Node |
| | | IsForward | Indicates if the server followed a forward Reference or the inverse Reference from the starting Node to the target Node |
| | | NodeId | NodeId of the target Node passing the filter criteria set in the request. This could be also a Node in another server indicated by the server information in the ExpandedNodeId |
| | | BrowseName | The qualified name of the target Node. This name provides in some use cases a relation to the type system |
| | | DisplayName | The localized name of the target Node used for display purposes. The locale depends on the Session setting defined in ActivateSession |
| | | NodeClass | Indicates the NodeClass of the target Node |
| | | TypeDefinition | NodeId of the Object or Variable type of the target Node. This parameter is only set if the target Node is a Variable or an Object |

### 5.5.1.2  BrowseNext Service

This Service is only used to continue a Browse started with the Browse Service if not all results could be returned by the Browse or a following BrowseNext Service call. The number of Nodes to return can be limited by the client in the Browse request or by the Server during processing the Browse Service call. The parameters of the BrowseNext Service are described in Table 5.14.

**Table 5.14** BrowseNext Service parameters

| Request parameters | Description |
|---|---|
| ReleaseContinuation-Points | A flag that indicates if the Service is called only for releasing the memory associated with the continuation point in the server or if the next set of results should be returned Clients should always call this Service even if they do not want to continue browsing. In this case this flag is set to true |
| ContinuationPoints [ ] | List of continuation points returned from a previous Browse or BrowseNext Service call |
| Response parameters | Description |
| This Service returns the same parameters like the Browse Service described in Table 5.13 | |

### 5.5.1.3   Read Service

The Browse Service returns already the Attribute values normally needed for filling up a browse tree like the display name, the NodeClass, or the TypeDefinition needed to display different icons for the different types of Nodes.

Additional Attributes needed for completing necessary information about Nodes like the data type or access level of Variables can be accessed using the Read Service. All available Attributes can be read by passing a list of NodeIds and AttributeIds as request parameters of the Read Service and the Server returns a list of Values for the requested NodeId and AttributeId combinations. The Read Service is described more detailed in Sect. 5.6.1.

### 5.5.1.4   TranslateBrowsePathsToNodeIds Service

This Service is used to access components of an Object based on the knowledge about the ObjectType. Since the NodeId of a Node is needed to access information provided by the Node like subscribing for Variable Value changes or to call a Method, it is necessary to know the NodeIds of components of Objects. Since OPC UA allows programming software components with built-in knowledge of ObjectTypes, UA needs to provide a mechanism to return the NodeIds for components of an Object instance based on the knowledge about the ObjectType. This mechanism is built on the requirement that the BrowseNames of components in the instance must be the same like BrowseNames of components in the type.

Figure 5.5 shows an example with the components of air conditioner controllers where the BrowseNames like Temperature or EngineeringUnit are defined by the ObjectType and the same BrowseNames are used on the two instances Controller1 and Controller2.

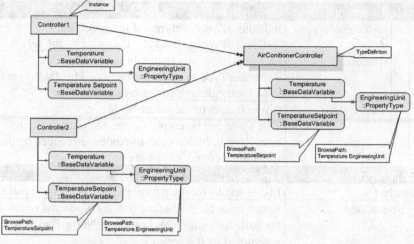

**Fig. 5.5** Browse path in type definition and instance

Based on the requirement to have the same BrowseName, the browse path from the object type to a component is the same like the browse path from an instance to the same component.

For example a client wants to display the status of Controller1 in an air conditioner graphic. The graphic monitors the Value of the Variable Temperature and reads the Property EngineeringUnit to display the Value together with the unit. To get the NodeIds of the Variable and the Property, the graphic uses the Service TranslateBrowsePathsToNodeIds to pass in the starting Node Controller1 and the browse path "Temperature" for the Variable and the browse path "Temperature. EngineeringUnit" for the Property. The server returns then the NodeIds of the target Nodes. If more than one Node matches the browse path, the first Node in the list is the Node that is based on the type. The parameters of the Service are described more detailed in Table 5.15.

**Table 5.15** TranslateBrowsePathsToNodeIds Service parameters

| Request parameters | | | Description |
|---|---|---|---|
| BrowsePaths [ ] | | | The list of browse paths for which NodeIds are requested |
| | StartingNode | | NodeId of the Node where the server should start following the browse path |
| | RelativePath [ ] | | The browse path the server should follow. It is composed of a list of browse elements |
| | | ReferenceTypeId | NodeId of the ReferenceType the server should follow. This parameter is typically combined with the IncludeSubtypes set to filter for a whole set of ReferenceTypes<br>This is for example HasComponent to find the components of an Object |

*(Continued)*

| Response parameters | | | Description |
|---|---|---|---|
| | IncludeSubtypes | | Indicates if also subtypes of the specified ReferenceTypeId should be followed by the server |
| | IsInverse | | Indicates if the server should follow the ReferenceType in inverse direction. This flag is set to false for the default forward direction |
| | TargetName | | BrowseName of the target Node. This name can be empty for the last element in the browse path. In this case all Nodes referenced by the specified ReferenceType are returned |
| **Response parameters** | | | **Description** |
| Results [ ] | | | List of results for the passed starting Nodes and paths |
| | StatusCode | | Result code for the passed starting Node and paths. If the path does not result in a target Node, BadNoMatch is returned by the server |
| | Targets [ ] | | List of target Nodes for each starting Node browse path combination. This list contains typically only one Node if the browse path is build with information from the type system |
| | | TargetId | NodeId of the target Node |
| | | RemainingPath-Index | Servers can have references to Nodes in other servers. In that case the full browse path cannot be processed by one server. Therefore the TargetId contains the starting Node in the other server and the client must pass the remaining path to this other server. This parameter defines the index of the starting element for the remaining path |

### 5.5.1.5  RegisterNodes Service

This Service allows clients to optimize the cyclic access to Nodes for example for Writing Variable Values or for calling methods. There are two levels of optimization.

The first level is to reduce the amount of data on the wire for the addressing information. Since NodeIds are used for addressing in Nodes and NodeIds can be very long, a more optimized addressing method is desirable for cyclic use of Nodes. Classic OPC provided the concept to create handles for items by adding them to a group. RegisterNodes provides a similar concept to create handles for Nodes by returning a numeric NodeId that can be used in all functions accessing information from the server. The transport of numeric NodeIds is very efficient in the OPC UA binary protocol.

The second level of optimization is possible inside the server. Since the client is telling the server that he wants to use the Node more frequently by registering the Node, the server is able to prepare everything that is possible to optimize the access to the Node.

The handles returned by the server are only valid during the lifetime of the Session that was used to register the Nodes. Clients must call UnregisterNodes if the Node is no longer used to free the resources used in the server for the optimization. This method should not be used to optimize the cyclic read of data since OPC UA provides a much more optimized mechanism to subscribe for data changes. The parameters of the Service are listed in Table 5.16.

Clients do not have to use the Service and servers can simply implement the Service only returning the same list of NodeIds that was passed in if there is no need to optimize the access.

**Table 5.16** RegisterNodes Service parameters

| Request parameters | Description |
|---|---|
| NodesToRegister [ ] | The list of Nodes to register. For each Node the NodeId of the Node is passed in |
| Response parameters | Description |
| RegisteredNodeIds [ ] | List of NodeIds identifying the registered Node. This NodeId is typically an optimized numeric Node used as handle to the registered Node. This NodeId is only valid in the Session context it was created in. If the server does not know the NodeId or he is not able to optimize the access to the Node, he simply returns the NodeId provided in the request |

**UnregisterNodes Service**

Handles created with the Service RegisterNodes must be freed by the client using the Service UnregisterNodes to free the resources in the server. The parameters of the Service are listed in Table 5.17.

**Table 5.17** UnregisterNodes Service parameters

| Request parameters | Description |
|---|---|
| NodesToUnregister [ ] | The list of Nodes to unregister. For each Node the registered NodeId is passed in |
| Response parameters | Description |

## 5.5.2 Use Cases for Finding Information in the Address Space

OPC UA provides different information in different levels of complexity in one generic and extensible model accessed by a small set of generic Services. For a better understanding about the use of the Services to find information necessary for different use cases, this section describes the use of the Services for specific use cases. Some of the use cases are known from Classic OPC, other use cases are only possible with the new features provided by OPC UA.

### 5.5.2.1   Search Data Variables for Reading and Monitoring Data

The most common use case for OPC is to access Variable Values to read and write the current Value or to monitor the Value for data changes. In most cases, a user must select the list of Variables the client software uses for read, write, and monitoring data changes. This selection includes navigating through the Address Space to find the available Variables and to select the right Variables by checking the Attributes like data type and access level.

The Browse Service is used to navigate through the Address Space to find Variables. Table 5.18 describes the Browse parameters used to fill a browse tree.

Table 5.18 Browse parameters used to find Variables

| Parameter | Value |
|---|---|
| View | Not set for browsing the whole Address Space, otherwise set to a view restricting the Address Space |
| RequestedMax ReferencesPerNode | 500 is a good compromise between an efficient transport and a protection of the client. This should be adapted to the needs or restrictions of the tree display. If the server has more than 500 Nodes in one level, BrowseNext can be called with the returned continuation point |
| NodeId | Objects folder or one of the server Views as starting point for the browse. Following Browse requests use objects returned by previous Browse requests |
| BrowseDirection | Forward |
| ReferenceTypeId | HierarchicalReferences |
| IncludeSubtypes | True |
| NodeClassMask | Object and View – Building the hierarchy Variable – Variables providing Values |
| ResultMask | DisplayName – Used to display the name in the tree NodeClass – Used to distinguish between Objects and Variables TypeDefinition – Can be used to display different icons for different ObjectTypes or VariableTypes. For example to distinguish between Folder objects and other Objects or between Properties and DataVariables. ReferenceTypeId – Used to filter results for HasNotifier and HasEventSource since they are used to build an Event hierarchy and they are not relevant for data access |

Only one starting Node is needed which allows using a simplified client SDK browse method that is reduced to one starting Node.

The information returned by the Browse can be used to identify a Node as Variable with the information NodeClass and TypeDefinition and provides the addressing information NodeId also returned by the Browse.

In addition a client needs other information like the data type of the Variable and the access level or the user access level to know if the Variable is readable or writable. The Read Service can be used to read this information for a list of Variables with one Read call. Table 5.19 provides a list of Attributes containing important metadata about a Variable. If a client wants to read these 5 Attributes for 10 Variables, he needs to call Read with a list of 50 elements containing a NodeId and AttributeId pair for each possible combination.

**Table 5.19** Variable Attributes containing metadata

| Attribute | Use |
| --- | --- |
| DataType | NodeId of the DataType. This could be one of the UA defined built-in types or a complex data type |
| ValueRank | Points out if the value is scalar, an array or a multidimensional array indicating the dimension |
| ArrayDimensions | An array of integers indicating the length of each dimension |
| AccessLevel | A bit mask indicating if the Value is readable or writable in the system. There are additional bits defined indicating the historical access capabilities |
| UserAccessLevel | The same bit mask used for AccessLevel but this Attribute can differ from the AccessLevel based on the user that is logged into the Session. For example is the AccessLevel for a set point typically readable and writable but the UserAccessLevel is only readable for a normal user that is not allowed to change a set point |

In addition to reading the metadata of the Variables, a client may also be interested in Properties containing additional metadata for the Variables. To find such Properties, a Browse is called with a list of starting Nodes for each Variable that should be checked for availability of Properties. The same mechanism can be used to get the Properties of Objects or other Nodes (Table 5.20).

For the returned Property Nodes the Property Value can be determined by reading the Value Attribute of the Nodes with the Read Service.

Table 5.20 Browse parameters used to find Properties

| Parameter | Value |
|---|---|
| NodesToBrowse [ ] | List of Variables and filters |
| NodeId | NodeId of the Variable |
| BrowseDirection | Forward |
| ReferenceTypeId | HasProperty |
| IncludeSubtypes | True |
| NodeClassMask | Variable – Properties have the NodeClass Variable |
| ResultMask | DisplayName – Localized name of the Property BrowseName – Type name of the Property |

### 5.5.2.2    Find Variables with Historic Data

The Variables providing historical data can be found in the same way like described in Sect. 5.5.2.1 for the current data. The only difference is that different flags must be checked for the AccessLevel and UserAccessLevel Attribute of the Variables. The additional flags are indicating if the history of data is available for reading and if the history can be updated.

There is another history - specific Attribute with the name Historizing. This flag indicates if the server is currently collecting history for the Value. Additional information can be found in the HistoricalConfiguration Object available for each Variable containing history by following the HasHistoricalConfiguration Reference from the Variable to the configuration Object.

### 5.5.2.3    Get Information to Call a Method

Methods are typically the target of a HasComponent Reference starting from an Object. Methods can be requested together with Variables and Objects when browsing an Object like described in Table 5.18. The NodeClass Method must be added to the NodeClassMask parameter settings described in this table. The parameters used to Browse only for Methods are described in Table 5.21.

Table 5.21 Browse parameters used to find Methods

| Parameter | Value |
|---|---|
| NodeId | NodeId of the Object that provides Methods |
| BrowseDirection | Forward |
| ReferenceTypeId | HasComponent |
| IncludeSubtypes | True |
| NodeClassMask | Method – Filter for Methods |
| ResultMask | DisplayName – Used to display the name in the user interface BrowseName – Used to distinguish between known Methods from the ObjectType |

The necessary information to call a Method is the NodeId of the Method and of the Object in which context the Method should be called. Both NodeIds are known after browsing for the available Methods. If the Method is not a well-known Method, the clients need to get also the description of the input and the output arguments for example to populate a user interface with this information.

There are two steps necessary to get this information, the first step is to find out the NodeIds of the Properties containing the argument descriptions and the second step is to read the values of the Properties to get the argument description. For the first step the most efficient way to get the NodeIds is to use the Service Translate-BrowsePathsToNodeIds since we know the BrowsePath from a Method to the Properties InputArgument and OutputArgument and the Service returns exactly the information we need. If we would use the Browse Service instead we may get additional Nodes we are not interested in. The necessary parameters for the Trans-lateBrowsePathsToNodeIds Service call are described in Table 5.22.

The client must check the result StatusCode for both BrowsePaths since the server will return the BadNoMatch StatusCode for a path if the Method does not have input or output arguments.

**Table 5.22** TranslateBrowsePathsToNodeIds Service parameters

| Request parameters | | | Description |
|---|---|---|---|
| BrowsePaths [0] | | | BrowsePath for Property InputArguments |
| | StartingNode | | NodeId of the Method |
| | RelativePath [0] | | Browse path with one element |
| | | Reference-TypeId | HasProperty to find the Property of the Method |
| | | IncludeSubtypes | True since the server may use a subtype of HasProperty |
| | | IsInverse | False |
| | | TargetName | BrowseName with the text InputArguments and the namespace index zero |
| BrowsePaths [1] | | | BrowsePath for Property OutputArguments |
| | StartingNode | | NodeId of the Method |
| | RelativePath [0] | | Browse path with one element |
| | | Reference-TypeId | HasProperty to find the Property of the Method |
| | | IncludeSubtypes | True since the server may use a subtype of HasProperty |
| | | IsInverse | False |
| | | TargetName | BrowseName with the text OutputArguments and the namespace index zero |

For the returned NodeIds the client can call the Read Service to read the Value Attribute of the Properties. The Read returns an array of Argument structures for both Properties. The Argument structure describes a Method argument and contains the information argument name, description, and data type. The DataType of an argument can be complex. This allows using nested structures in Method arguments.

### 5.5.2.4   Find the Type Description for a Structured DataType

There are different use cases where a client needs to get the type description of a complex DataType but we assume that the NodeId of the type is already known from one of the following places:

- DataType Attribute of a Variable
- DataType parameter of an Argument structure describing the parameters of a Method
- DataType Attribute of an Event Field Variable.

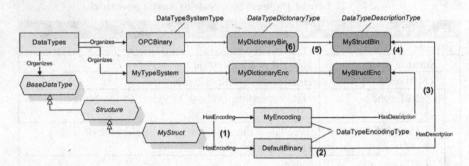

**Fig. 5.6** Nodes involved to describe complex data types

Since OPC UA allows the support of different encodings for a complex DataType, the type description is not directly available through the DataType Node. Section 2.8.4 provides more details on structured DataTypes. The example used to explain the Service calls necessary to get the type description is shown in Fig. 5.6. The server in the sample has two DataTypeSystems, one is the OPCBinary and one is a vendor specific type system. The structured DataType MyStruct has the two corresponding encodings.

The DataType NodeId for MyStruct is used as starting point to find the type description with the following steps and Service calls:

1.   To get the available data encodings for the DataType, the Browse Service is called to follow the ReferenceType HasEncoding from the DataType Node to the available DataTypeEncoding Objects.

2.  The client must select an encoding from the list of returned DataTypeEncoding Objects. The selection can be done based on the preferred encoding or based on a user selection. In our example, the client is a generic client and therefore selects the DefaultBinary encoding.
3.  From the DefaultBinary encoding the DataTypeDescription Variable can be browsed by following the HasDescription ReferenceType.
4.  The client must read the Value Attribute of the DataTypeDescription Variable MyStructBin to get the identifier of the description used to find the entry in the DataTypeDictionary.
5.  To find the DataTypeDictionary containing the description, the Browse Service needs to be called following the inverse HasComponent ReferenceType from the DataTypeDescription Node to the DataTypeDictionary:
6.  The client must first check if the returned DataTypeDictionary MyDictionaryBin is already in the client cache to avoid multiple reads of potentially large dictionaries. If the dictionary is not available, the client can read the dictionary by calling Read for the Value Attribute of the Variable MyDictionaryBin. The description can be found in the dictionary with the identifier read from the MyStructBin Variable.

### 5.5.2.5    Find Object Components Based on ObjectType Knowledge

If a client software component was built with the knowledge about an ObjectType, the component knows the path from the type to InstanceDeclarations. This knowledge is necessary to find the used components of an Object instance based on this knowledge.

If the Object has for example three Variables the software component needs to monitor, the NodeIds of these three Variables are needed. To get the NodeIds the client calls the TranslateBrowsePathsToNodeIds Service with three browse paths containing the Object instance NodeId as starting Node and the relative path from the ObjectType to the InstanceDeclaration of the Variable.

### 5.5.2.6    Search Event Hierarchy and Fill up an Event Filter Display

The rules to create a filter are defined by OPC UA and are described in the Sect. 5.7.5 for Event monitoring. The server - specific parts of the Event filters are Event Types and the Event fields defined by the EventTypes and sources for Events which can be found in the Object and Variable instances Nodes.

Most of the information necessary to populate an Event filter dialog can be found in the EventType hierarchy. There is a well-known NodeId for the BaseEventType which is the root Node for the EventType hierarchy. Table 5.23 describes the Browse parameters used to fill a tree control with the EventType hierarchy.

The Event fields from the tree are used to select the fields delivered with an Event notification and are used together with the EventTypes to filter Events.

**Table 5.23** Browse parameters used to find EventTypes and the Event Fields

| Parameter | Value |
|---|---|
| NodeId | BaseEventType ObjectType as starting point for the browse<br>Following Browse requests use derived EventType Nodes returned by previous Browse requests |
| BrowseDirection | Forward |
| ReferenceTypeId | HierarchicalReferences |
| IncludeSubtypes | True |
| NodeClassMask | ObjectType – Building the Type hierarchy<br>Object – Potentially used to structure Event Types and Event Fields in the Address Space. Only InstanceDeclarations, i.e. Objects referencing a ModellingRule with the HasModellingRule, should be considered<br>Variable – Variables representing the fields of an Event Type. These Variables are typically Properties. Only InstanceDeclarations should be considered |
| ResultMask | DisplayName – Used to display the name<br>NodeClass – Used to distinguish between ObjectTypes,[3] Objects and Variables<br>TypeDefinition – Can be used to display different icons for different Object or Variable types. For example to distinguish between Folder objects and other Objects or between Properties and DataVariables |

A second tree control can be populated with EventNotifiers[4] and Event sources provided by the server. The References used to build such a hierarchy are Organizes, HasNotifier, and HasEventSource. Starting points for such hierarchies are the Server Object, the Objects Folder, or Views. Table 5.24 describes the Browse parameters used to fill a tree control with the EventNotifier and Event source hierarchy.

The EventNotifiers are used to create Monitored Items which is a preselection of Events provided by this EventNotifier. The Event sources can be used as filter criteria.

---

[3]ObjectTypes represent Event Types in this case.

[4]An EventNotifier is an Object where the SubscribeForEvents flag is set in the EventNotifier Attribute.

**Table 5.24** Browse parameters used to find EventNotifiers

| Parameter | Value |
|---|---|
| NodeId | Server Object, the Objects Folder or Views as starting point for the browse<br>Following Browse requests use Objects returned by previous Browse requests |
| BrowseDirection | Forward |
| ReferenceTypeId | HierarchicalReferences |
| IncludeSubtypes | True |
| NodeClassMask | Object – Building the hierarchy<br>Variable – Variables can be Event sources |
| ResultMask | DisplayName – Used to display the name<br>NodeClass – Used to distinguish between Objects and Variables<br>TypeDefinition – Can be used to display different icons for different Object or Variable types.<br>For example to distinguish between Folder objects and other Objects or between Properties and Data-Variables<br>ReferenceTypeId – Used to filter results for Organizes, HasNotifier and HasEventSource. All other references are not relevant to the Event hierarchy |

### 5.5.2.7   Find Information for a State Machine Display

State Machines are one of the base concepts of OPC UA. The base concept can be used by servers to describe application specific State Machines but it is also used by OPC Information Models like Programs [UA Part 10] and Alarm & Conditions [UA Part 9]. The base concepts and OPC Information Models using these concepts are described in Chap. 4.

This section describes the discovery of a State Machine description based on an abstract example but the same concepts can also be used to discover also Program or Alarm State Machines. Since it is expected that clients understanding the OPC UA Program or Alarms and Conditions Information Model do not need to browse the well-known State Machines, this is only necessary for vendor – specific extensions to these Information Models.

The abstract example used to explain the concepts of browsing a State Machine is shown in Fig. 5.7. The ReadingUaBook State Machine and the corresponding State Machine Type has two states, Idle and Reading and the transitions between the two states.

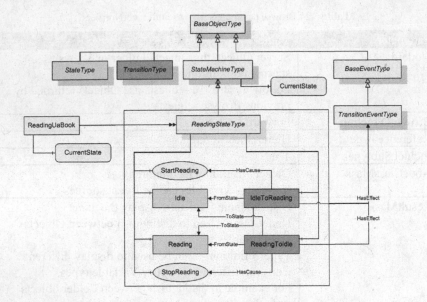

**Fig. 5.7** ReadingUaBook State Machine and its Type Definition

If a client finds a StateMachine instance like the ReadUaBook Object in a server, the information provided by the instance itself is limited to information related to the current state. All information describing the State Machine like possible states and transitions is only available on the StateMachineType.

Two NodeIds are needed as starting points. The NodeId of the State Machine instance ReadingUaBook is necessary to get information about the current state and to subscribe for transition Events. The NodeId of the StateMachineType ReadingStateType is necessary to get the description of the State Machine. The NodeId of the TypeDefinition ReadingStateType is normally known from browsing the instance or can be browsed by following the HasTypeDefinition Reference from the instance ReadingUaBook.

Using the ReadingStateType NodeId as starting point the State Machine description can be discovered with the following steps and Service calls:

1. To get the available states, transitions, Methods, and Variables containing additional information, the Browse Service is called with the following settings:

   - ReadingStateType NodeId as starting Node
   - BrowseDirection set to Forward
   - ReferenceTypeId set to HasComponent
   - IncludeSubtypes set to True
   - NodeClassMask set to Object, Method, and Variable
   - and Result Mask set to DisplayName, BrowseName, and TypeDefinition

2.  To find the relations between the returned components, the client takes the list of NodeIds of the transition Nodes as list of starting Nodes to four Browse calls with the following settings:

    *   IdleToReading and ReadingToIdle Object NodeIds as starting Node
    *   BrowseDirection set to Forward
    *   ReferenceTypeId set to HasCause, HasEffect, FromState, and ToState in the four different Browse calls
    *   IncludeSubtypes set to True
    *   NodeClassMask set to all
    *   and Result Mask set to DisplayName and BrowseName

Based on the information returned from the Browse calls the client can for example display the State Machine with the states and transitions, he can provide a way to trigger state changes with the available Methods and by reading the current state from the instance and subscribing for the transition Events, the client can monitor the state of the State Machine.

## 5.6   Read and Write Data and Metadata

One of the most important features of OPC is to read and write data from another system using a standardized data exchange mechanism.

The Read and Write Services not only allow reading and writing the Values of Variables, but are also used in a generic way to read and write Attributes of Nodes to access metadata in the Address Space. A different way to read data is the subscription for data changes. This is the preferred method for clients needing cyclic updates of variable value changes.

### 5.6.1 Reading Data

The Read Service is used to read one or more Attributes of one or more Nodes. It allows also reading subsets or single elements of array values and to define a valid age of values to be returned to reduce the need for device reads. Like most other Services, the Read Service is optimized for bulk read operations and not for reading single Attribute values. Typically all Node Attributes are readable. For the Value Attribute the Read rights are indicated by the AccessLevel and User-AccessLevel Attribute of the Variable. The parameters of the Read Service are described in Table 5.25.

Table 5.25 Read Service parameters

| Request parameters | Description |
|---|---|
| MaxAge | The maximum age of the value to be read in milliseconds. This parameter allows clients to reduce the communication between server and data source by allowing the server to return a cached value that is not older than the defined time period. Setting a value of 0 forces the server to obtain the current value. This is similar to a device read in Classic OPC |
| TimestampsToReturn | OPC UA defines two timestamps, the source and the server timestamp. This parameter allows the client to define which timestamps the server should return with the value. See the response parameters for a description of the different timestamps |
| NodesToRead [ ] | List of Nodes and Attributes to read |
|      NodeId | Identifier for the Node to read |
|      AttributeId | Identifier for the Attribute of the Node to read. This could be the Value Attribute or any other valid Attribute providing metadata for Nodes. A list of Attributes can be found in Appendix B |
|      IndexRange | This parameter is used to identify a single element of an array or a single range of indexes for arrays |
|      DataEncoding | This parameter is only relevant for reading values with a structured DataType. Structured types can be transported using different data encodings. Default encodings for UA are XML or UA binary format. This parameter allows the client to define the encoding used to transport the complex value |
| Response parameters | Description |
| Results [ ] | List of read results contained in DataValue structures |
|      Value | Contains the read value if the StatusCode parameter indicates a successful read |
|      StatusCode | Success code for the read operation or quality of the read value. The value is only usable if the status is good |
|      SourceTimestamp | Source timestamp assigned to the value if requested by the client. The source timestamp is only available for Value Attributes. The source timestamp is used to reflect the timestamp that was applied to a Variable value by the data source. It should indicate the last change of the value or status code. The source timestamp must be always generated by the same physical clock. This timestamp type was added for OPC UA to cover |

*(Continued)*

| | | the use case to get the timestamp of the last value change which is different than the ServerTimestamp definition |
|---|---|---|
| | ServerTimestamp | Server timestamp assigned to the value if requested by the client<br>The server timestamp is used to reflect the time that the server received a Variable value or knew it to be accurate if the changes are reported by exeption and the connection to the data source is operating.<br>This is the behavior expected by Classic OPC |

## 5.6.2 Writing Data

The Write Service is used to write one or more Attributes of one or more Nodes. It allows also writing of subsets or single elements of array values. Like most other UA Services, the Write Service is optimized for bulk write operations and not for writing single Attribute values. The parameters of the Write Service are described in Table 5.26.

**Table 5.26** Write Service Parameters

| Request parameters | Description |
|---|---|
| NodesToWrite [ ] | List of Nodes, Attributes, and values to write |
|   NodeId | Identifier for the Node to write |
|   AttributeId | Identifier for the Attribute of the Node to write. This could be the value Attribute or any other valid Attribute. A list of Attributes can be found in Appendix B |
|   IndexRange | This parameter is used to identify a single element of an array or a single range of indexes for arrays |
|   Value | Contains the value to write |
|   StatusCode | Status code assigned to the value. A zero value indicates that the status is not set |
|   SourceTimestamp | Source timestamp assigned to the value. A null value indicates that the timestamp is not set |
|   ServerTimestamp | Server timestamp assigned to the value. A null value indicates that the timestamp is not set |
| Response parameters | Description |
| Results [ ] | List of write result status codes for each write operation |

Typically only the Value Attributes of Variables are writable. Other Attributes are only writable if the server allows the configuration of Nodes through OPC UA. For the Value Attribute the Write rights are indicated by the AccessLevel or UserAccessLevel Attribute of the Variable. The Write rights for all other Attributes are indicated by the WriteMask or UserWriteMask Attributes.

This Service allows also writing the status and the timestamps of the value if it is supported by the server. There is a defined error status code returned if the client tries to write these parameters but the server does not support this feature.

## 5.7    Subscribe for Data Changes and Events

A client can subscribe for three different types of information from an OPC UA server. A Subscription is used to group sources of information together. A Monitored Item is used to manage a source of information. A piece of information is called a notification. A Subscription can contain all three different types of Monitored Items and the server will deliver notifications for these Monitored Items until the Subscription or the Monitored Items are deleted.

The first and most common type of Monitored Item is used to subscribe for data changes of Variable Values (Sect. 5.7.4). The second type of Monitored Item is used to subscribe for Events by defining an EventNotifier[5] to monitor and by defining a filter for the Events (Sect. 5.7.5). The third type of Monitored Item is used to subscribe for aggregated Values calculated based on current Variable Values in client-defined time intervals (Sect. 5.7.6).

Most of the Services are used to create the necessary context for the Subscription (Sect. 5.7.2) and Monitored Items (Sect. 5.7.3). Figure. 5.8 shows the relation between the communication context created on top of a Session for subscribing to data changes or Events.

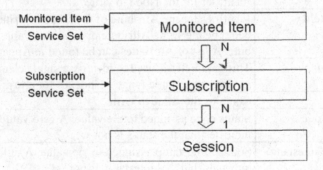

Fig. 5.8 Context necessary to subscribe for data changes and Events

All Monitored Items have common settings like monitoring mode, sampling interval, filter settings, and queue size. The different types of Monitored Items are defined by the type of source assigned to the item and the filter defined for the Monitored Item. Figure. 5.9 shows the different Subscription and Monitored Item settings.

---

[5]An EventNotifier is an Object where the SubscribeForEvents flag is set in the EventNotifier Attribute.

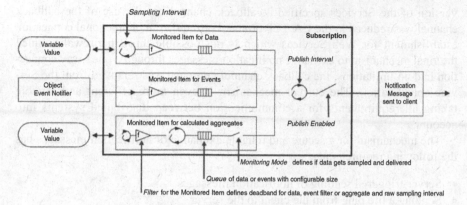

**Fig. 5.9** Settings for Subscription and Monitored Items

The sampling interval defines the rate the server checks Variable Values for changes or defines the time the aggregate gets calculated. The monitoring mode defines if the Monitored Item is active or inactive. The queue size defines how many notifications can be queued for delivery. The default value for data changes is one and the value for Events is infinite where the size of infinite depends on the resources available in the server. The filter settings are different for data changes, Events, and aggregate calculation.

There are two Subscription settings. The Publish interval defines the interval when the server clears the queues and delivers the notifications to the client. The Publish enabled setting defines whether the data gets delivered to the client.

The only two Services used to actually deliver the notifications in a notification message to the client are the Publish Service for transferring the notification messages and the Republish Service to get lost notification messages from the server. The mechanism to deliver the information is described in Sect. 5.7.1. The Services used to create the necessary Subscription and MonitoredItem context are explained afterward.

### 5.7.1 Delivery of Changed Data and Events

The nature of the notifications provided by the Subscription requires a report by exception from the server to the client. It is required to combine notifications to larger notification messages to optimize interprocess or network communication which is the typical use case of OPC. Nevertheless the server needs to be able to send a notification message to the client whenever it is required.

In Classic OPC this was achieved by defining callback interfaces allowing the server to call methods on the client to send data change or event notifications. Based on the requirement to be firewall-friendly and to ensure the same behavior for all transports, OPC UA does not define such a callback interface. An early version of the Services specified a callback channel but the use of the callback channel was reduced to the UA TCP protocol or required a bidirectional connection establishment for Web Services which is not possible through firewalls. Since the final mechanism to exchange notification messages through a one - way connection had no limitations, the callback channel approach was removed from the Service specification. The current mechanism is even more efficient and reliable taking all requirements for a communication between distributed systems into account.

The mechanism for a secure and reliable exchange of notification messages has the following requirements:

- Server-triggered sending of notification messages
- Sending a life ping from the client to the server
- Sending a life ping from the server to the client when no notification messages are available
- Sending sequence numbers together with the notification message from the server to the client to allow the client detecting lost messages
- Acknowledgement of received sequence numbers from the client to the server
- Resending of lost notification messages.

The Services used to implement this mechanism are the Publish and the Republish Services. The Services fulfill all these requirements based on the Service parameters and the special behavior defined for these Services. The parameters of the Services are described in the following sections after describing the base mechanism realized with Publish and Republish.

### 5.7.1.1    Server-Triggered Sending of Notification Messages

The server-triggered sending of notification messages is accomplished by a special rule for the Publish Service. It is the only Service that can be blocked by the Server without doing any processing. It is expected that a client sends a list of Publish requests to the server without expecting an immediate response. The server can queue the Publish requests until a notification message is ready for sending to the client. Since the exchange of request and response messages is asynchronous by definition, the communication is not blocked by these outstanding Publish requests. If the client uses the right algorithm for sending Publish requests, the server is able to trigger the sending of notification messages.

The algorithm for sending Publish requests from the client to the server depends on the following parameters:

- Number of Subscriptions
- Network latency
- Maximum queue size for Publish requests in the server.

The Publish request is not bound to a specific Subscription and can be used by the server for all Subscriptions running in the same Session context. To make sure that all Subscriptions can send a notification message at the same time, the client should make sure that there are more outstanding Publish requests than active Subscriptions.

Additional Publish requests may be required if the latency of the network connection is very high. This can be calculated based on the timestamps contained in the request and response messages. In the case of a large number of Subscriptions and low network latency, the number of outstanding Publish requests can be reduced.

If the Server indicates an overflow of his Publish queue with a Service result of BadTooManyPublishRequests, the client must reduce the calculated number of outstanding Publish requests.

Figure 5.10 summarizes the mechanisms used for the delivery of notification messages.

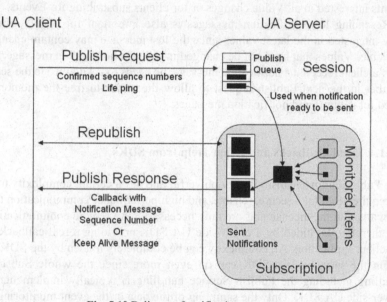

**Fig. 5.10** Delivery of notification messages

### 5.7.1.2  Keep Alive Messages

An important requirement for a quick recovery from error scenarios is a timely detection of communication problems. One important feature is the configurable timeout for Service invocations in OPC UA. But this feature cannot be used to detect connection problems for the Publish since Publish requests are queued in the server and need therefore a much longer timeout than required for a timely detection of communication problems.

For this reason the Publish procedure provides life ping mechanisms in both directions. Every Publish request is a life ping from the client to the server. Every notification message is a life ping from the server to the client. If no notification message is available, an empty Publish response is sent to the client as life ping after the keep-alive interval. This interval is configurable by the client and is a multiple of the publishing interval used to send notification messages.

### 5.7.1.3   Detection and Resending of Lost Notification Messages

Another important requirement for a reliable communication is the detection of lost data. This can be achieved with the exchange of sequence numbers with each notification message. If a client detects missing sequences, he can use the Republish Service to get the lost notification message from the server. This is important for clients interested in all Value changes or for clients subscribing for Events.

Resending lost notification messages is also important for clients which are only interested in the latest values since the lost message may contain changes for Variables Values that have not be changed in the next notification message.

If a client received a notification message, he needs to acknowledge the sequence number in the next Publish request to allow the server to free the memory allocated for the buffered notification messages.

### 5.7.1.4   Real Callbacks and Other Help from SDKs

The Publishing mechanism is very powerful and has a certain complexity to fulfill all requirements for a secure, reliable, and high performance communication through firewalls. But the mechanisms are only necessary for a remote communication and can therefore be hided by a client-side UA SDK providing a real callback inside the client application. All complexity can be completely hidden by the SDK.

On the server-side a SDK can do even more since the whole Subscription handling including the Publish Service handling is typically implemented by a server-side UA SDK. Only the sampling of the data or the event monitoring needs to be done by the server application.

### 5.7.1.5   Publish Service

The parameters of the Publish Service are described in Table 5.27. The relevant Subscription settings for the trigger of the Publish response like the publishing interval or the keep-alive interval are negotiated during the creation of the Subscription.

**Table 5.27** Publish Service parameters

| Request parameters | Description |
|---|---|
| Subscription Acknowledgements [ ] | List of sequence numbers the client received and where the server can free resources for |
|    SubscriptionId | The id of the Subscription that sent the notification message |
|    SequenceNumber | Sequence number of the received notification message to acknowledge |
| Response parameters | Description |
| SubscriptionId | The id of the Subscription sending the notification message |
| Available SequenceNumbers [ ] | A list of sequence numbers available in the Subscription for retransmission and not acknowledged by the client |
| MoreNotifications | A flag that indicates if the server was not able to send all available notifications in this Publish response |
| NotificationMessage | Structure containing the notification message |
|    SequenceNumber | Sequence number of the notification message |
|    PublishTime | The time that this message was sent to the client |
|    NotificationData [ ] | A list of extensible parameters containing the notification data. This could be a DataChange notification or an Event notification. Since only two notification data types are defined yet, this list can have a size of one or two elements |

### 5.7.1.6   Republish Service

The parameters of the Republish Service are described in Table 5.28.

**Table 5.28** Republish Service Parameters

| Request parameters | Description |
|---|---|
| SubscriptionId | The id of the Subscription that sent the notification message |
| Retransmit SequenceNumber | Sequence number of the notification message to resend |
| Response parameters | Description |
| NotificationMessage | Structure containing the notification message |
|    SequenceNumber | Sequence number of the notification message |
|    PublishTime | The time that this message was sent to the client |
|    NotificationData [ ] | A list of extensible parameters containing the notification data. This could be a DataChange notification or an Event notification. Since only two notification data types are defined yet, this list can have a size of one or two elements |

## 5.7.2 Create and Manage Subscriptions

In normal operation the relevant settings for the Subscription are the Publish enabled and the Publish interval. Additional settings are keep-alive count, lifetime count, maximum number of notifications per Publish, and the priority of the Subscription.

The keep-alive count defines how many times the Publish interval needs to expire without having notifications available before the server sends an empty message to the client indicating that the server is still alive but no notifications are available.

The lifetime count defines how many times the Publish interval expires without having a connection to the client to deliver data. If the server is not able to deliver notification messages after this time, it deletes the Subscription to clear the resources. The lifetime count must be at minimum three times the keep-alive count. Both values are negotiated between the client and the server.

The maximum number of notifications per Publish is used to limit the size of the notification message sent from the server to the client. The number of notifications is set by the client but the server can send fewer notifications in one message if his limit is smaller than the client-side limit. If not all available notifications can be sent with one notification message, another notification message is sent.

The priority setting defines the priority of the Subscription relative to the other Subscriptions created by the Client. This allows the server to handle Subscriptions with higher priorities first in high-load scenarios.

### 5.7.2.1    CreateSubscription Service

This Service is used to create a Subscription and to define the initial settings for the Subscription. The Subscription can be deleted using the DeleteSubscriptions Service or by setting the DeleteSubscriptions flag when closing the Session. The parameters of the CreateSubscription Service are described in Table 5.29.

**Table 5.29** CreateSubscription Service parameters

| Request parameters | Description |
| --- | --- |
| Requested PublishingInterval | Client-requested publishing interval for the Subscription |
| PublishingEnabled | Publish enabled setting for the Subscription |
| Requested MaxKeepAliveCount | Client-requested keep-alive count for the Subscription |
| Requested LifetimeCount | Client-requested lifetime count for the Subscription |
| MaxNotifications PerPublish | Client-defined maximum number of notifications per notification message delivered to the client by Publish |

*(Continued)*

| Priority | Priority of the Subscription in the client relative to other Subscriptions created by the client |
|---|---|
| Response parameters | Description |
| SubscriptionId | Id of the subscription set by the server. The client must use this id in all following Service calls related to this Subscription |
| Revised PublishingInterval | Server-revised publishing interval for the Subscription |
| Revised MaxKeepAliveCount | Server-revised keep-alive count for the Subscription |
| RevisedLifetimeCount | Server-revised lifetime count for the Subscription |

### 5.7.2.2   DeleteSubscriptions Service

This Service is used to delete a list of Subscriptions created with the CreateSubscription Service. The parameters of the DeleteSubscription Service are described in Table 5.30.

**Table 5.30** DeleteSubscriptions Service parameters

| Request parameters | Description |
|---|---|
| SubscriptionIds [ ] | List of Subscriptions to delete. The Subscriptions are identified by their ids created in the CreateSubscription Service |
| Response parameters | Description |
| Results [ ] | List of status codes for the passed Subscription ids indicating if the delete was successful |

### 5.7.2.3   ModifySubscription Service

This Service is used to modify the settings of a Subscription. The parameters of the ModifySubscription Service are described in Table 5.31.

**Table 5.31** ModifySubscription Service parameters

| Request parameters | Description |
|---|---|
| SubscriptionId | Id of the Subscription to modify. This id was returned from the CreateSubscription Service |
| Requested PublishingInterval | Client-requested publishing interval for the Subscription |
| Requested MaxKeepAliveCount | Client-requested keep-alive count for the Subscription |

*(Continued)*

| | |
|---|---|
| Requested LifetimeCount | Client-requested lifetime count for the Subscription |
| MaxNotifications PerPublish | Client-defined maximum number of notifications per notification message delivered to the client by Publish |
| Priority | Priority of the Subscription in the client relative to other Subscriptions created by the client |
| Response parameters | Description |
| Revised PublishingInterval | Server-revised publishing interval for the Subscription |
| Revised MaxKeepAliveCount | Server-revised keep-alive count for the Subscription |
| RevisedLifetimeCount | Server-revised lifetime count for the Subscription |

### 5.7.2.4  SetPublishingMode Service

This Service is used to modify the Publish-enabled setting for a list of Subscriptions. The parameters of the SetPublishingMode Service are described in Table 5.32.

**Table 5.32** SetPublishingMode Service parameters

| Request parameters | Description |
|---|---|
| PublishingEnabled | A flag that indicates if the Publish should be enabled or disabled for the list of Subscriptions passed to this Service |
| SubscriptionIds [ ] | List of Subscriptions to modify. The Subscriptions are identified by their ids returned by the CreateSubscription Service |
| Response parameters | Description |
| Results [ ] | List of status codes for the passed Subscription ids indicating if the setting of the Publish -enabled flag was successful |

The Service allows clients to deactivate the delivery of notification messages without deactivating the collection of data and events.

### 5.7.2.5  TransferSubscriptions Service

This Service is used to transfer a list of Subscriptions to the Session that is used to call this Service. This feature is used by redundant clients to transfer a Subscription from the main client to the backup client if the main client is no longer available. It is also used to assign a Subscription to a new Session if the old one is not longer valid but the Subscription is still valid. The parameters of the TransferSubscriptions Service are described in Table 5.33.

**Table 5.33** TransferSubscriptions Service parameters

| Request parameters | Description |
|---|---|
| SubscriptionIds [ ] | List of Subscriptions to transfer. The Subscriptions are identified by their ids returned by the CreateSubscription Service |
| Response parameters | Description |
| Results [ ] | List of transfer results |
|   StatusCode | Result of the transfer operation for one Subscription |
|   AvailableSequence Numbers [ ] | A list of sequence numbers available in the Subscription for retransmission and not acknowledged by the client |

### 5.7.3 Create and Manage Monitored Items

Clients are creating Monitored Items in a Subscription to subscribe for data changes and Events. This section describes the common settings for Monitored Items and the Services to manage Monitored Items. The three different types of Monitored Items are described in more detail in the following sections.

The sampling interval of the Monitored Item defines the rate in milliseconds; the underlying data source is sampled for data changes. The sampling interval can be inherited from the publish interval of the Subscription but can be also set individually for each item. If the server must sample the data source, there is typically a minimum possible rate. If this minimum is known, it is exposed as MinimumSamplingInterval Attribute of the Variable. If the data source delivers the data exception based at changes, the server can also accept sampling intervals of 0. The server can adjust the requested rate to the next possible rate it supports but the server must attempt to sample at the defined rate, however, the server is not allowed to sample faster than the negotiated rate. The sampling interval is 0 for Event Monitored Items.

The monitoring mode defines the states disabled, sampling, and reporting. The difference between sampling and reporting is that for sampling the data source is sampled but the notifications are not sent to the client and for reporting they are also sent to the client. The setting sampling is necessary for the definition of triggered monitored items where the notifications are only reported when a triggering Monitored Item has a new notification. More details on triggering are described for the SetTriggering Service in this section.

Filter settings are specific to the different types of Monitored Items and are described in the following sections. The filter defines if a notification gets queued for transfer to the client.

The queue parameters define the size of the queue for notification message and the discard policy if the queue is full but a new notification message is available and passed the filter criteria. In this case it could be defined that the newest or the oldest notification in the queue will be overwritten. The queue size for Event Monitored Items is unlimited. For data Monitored Items it depends on the use case. A HMI client only displaying the latest value will set the size to one. A size greater than one can be used by clients that do not want to lose data changes even if the sampling is faster than the delivery of the notification message with Publish. This applies for example for a trend display.

### 5.7.3.1  CreateMonitoredItems Service

This Service is used to create Monitored Items in a Subscription and to define the initial settings for the Monitored Items. They can be deleted using the Delete-MonitoredItems Service or by deleting the Subscription. The parameters of the CreateMonitoredItems Service are described in Table 5.34.

**Table 5.34** CreateMonitoredItems Service parameters

| Request parameters | Description |
|---|---|
| SubscriptionId | Id of the Subscription to add the items to. This id was returned from the CreateSubscription Service |
| TimestampsToReturn | OPC UA defines two timestamps, the source and the server timestamp. This parameter allows the client to define which timestamps the server should return with the value. The two different timestamps are described in Sect. 5.6.1 |
| ItemsToCreate [ ] | List of items to create with the requested settings |
|     NodeId | NodeId of the Node to monitor. This is typically a Variable for data and must be an Object for Events. This can be also all other Node classes for data monitoring but this would be an unusual use case |
|     AttributeId | Id of the Attribute to monitor. This could be the Value Attribute of a Variable for data or the Event-Notifier Attribute for Events<br>It is possible to subscribe for data changes of all defined Attributes for all possible Node classes. But there are more efficient methods (see Sect. 5.7.4) to get informed about changes of Attributes other than Value since it is expected that these Attributes change never or only after configuration changes |
|     MonitoringMode | Monitoring mode of the item which could be dis-abled, sampling, or reporting |
|     ClientHandle | Client defined handle for the Monitored Item. This handle gets delivered together with the notification to allow the client to assign the notification to a Monitored Item |

(Continued)

| | |
|---|---|
| Monitoring Parameters | Client requested monitoring parameters sampling interval, filter, queue size, and discard policy |
| Response parameters | Description |
| Results [ ] | List of results for the list of items to create |
| StatusCode | Status code that indicates if the creation of the requested Monitored Item succeeded |
| MonitoredItemId | Id for the Monitored Item assigned by the server This id must be passed in Services used to modify and delete Monitored Items |
| Revised SamplingInterval | Sampling interval accepted by the server. If the requested rate is not available, the server adjusted the interval to the next available longer rate |
| RevisedQueueSize | Queue size used by the server |

### 5.7.3.2   DeleteMonitoredItems Service

This Service is used to delete MonitoredItems created with CreateMonitoredItems. The parameters of the DeleteMonitoredItems Service are described in Table 5.35.

**Table 5.35** DeleteMonitoredItems Service parameters

| Request parameters | Description |
|---|---|
| SubscriptionId | Id of the Subscription to remove the items from. This id was returned from the CreateSubscription Service |
| MonitoredItemIds [ ] | List of Monitored Items to delete. The ids were returned from the CreateMonitoredItems Service |
| Response parameters | Description |
| Results [ ] | List of status codes for each item to delete indicating if the delete succeeded |

### 5.7.3.3   ModifyMonitoredItems Service

This Service is used to modify MonitoredItems in the Subscription. The parameters of the ModifyMonitoredItems Service are described in Table 5.36.

**Table 5.36** ModifyMonitoredItems Service parameters

| Request parameters | Description |
|---|---|
| SubscriptionId | Id of the Subscription to add the items to. This id was returned from the CreateSubscription Service |
| TimestampsToReturn | OPC UA defines two timestamps, the source and the server timestamp. This parameter allows the client to define which timestamps the server should return with the value |

(*Continued*)

| ItemsToModify [ ] | List of items to modify with the requested settings |
|---|---|
| MonitoredItemId | Server defined handle for the Monitored Item used to identify the item in the Subscription. This id was returned from the CreateMonitoredItems Service |
| ClientHandle | Client defined handle for the Monitored Item |
| Monitoring Parameters | Client requested monitoring parameters sampling interval, filter, queue size, and discard policy |
| Response parameters | Description |
| Results [ ] | List of results for the list of items to modify |
| StatusCode | Status code that indicates if the modification of the Monitored Item succeeded |
| Revised SamplingInterval | Sampling interval used by the server. If the requested rate is not available, the server adjusted the interval to the next available longer rate |
| RevisedQueueSize | Queue size used by the server |

#### 5.7.3.4  SetMonitoringMode Service

This Service is used to set the monitoring mode for MonitoredItems in the Subscription. The parameters of the SetMonitoringMode Service are described in Table 5.37.

**Table 5.37** SetMonitoringMode Service parameters

| Request parameters | Description |
|---|---|
| SubscriptionId | Id of the Subscription containing the items to modify |
| MonitoringMode | Monitoring mode of the items which could be disabled, sampling, or reporting |
| MonitoredItemIds [ ] | List of Monitored Items to modify. The ids were returned from the CreateMonitoredItems Service |
| Response parameters | Description |
| Results [ ] | List of status codes for each item to modify indicating if setting the monitoring mode succeeded |

#### 5.7.3.5  SetTriggering Service

The Monitored Items Service Set allows adding items that are reported only when another item, the triggering item, triggers. This is done by creating links between the triggered items and the triggering item. The monitoring mode of the triggered items is set to sampling-only so that it will sample and queue notifications without reporting them. The parameters of the SetTriggering Service are described in Table 5.38.

**Table 5.38** SetTriggering Service parameters

| Request parameters | Description |
|---|---|
| SubscriptionId | Id of the Subscription containing the trigger items |
| TriggeringItemId | The server defined id for the Monitored Item that should be used as trigger item |
| LinksToAdd [ ] | A list of server defined ids of Monitored Items that should be assigned to the triggering item |
| LinksToRemove [ ] | A list of server defined ids of Monitored Items that should be removed from the triggering item |
| Response parameters | Description |
| AddResults [ ] | List of status codes for each trigger link to add indicating if the add succeeded |
| RemoveResults [ ] | List of status codes for each trigger link to remove indicating if the remove succeeded |

## 5.7.4 Monitor Data Changes

Subscribing for data changes of Variable Values is the main use case in Classic OPC. OPC UA allows subscribing for more information than just Variable Value changes but it is expected that it is also one of the most important features of OPC UA. Table 5.39 describes the Value change specific MonitoredItem settings.

The other specific part is the structure of a notification message sent for a data change. The structure contains value, status of the value, the source timestamp, and the server timestamp assigned to the value. The same parameters are returned by the Read Service. They are described more detailed in Sect. 5.6.1.

It is expected that other Attributes than the Value Attribute or Properties of a Variable are changed very infrequently. Therefore the monitoring with a data Monitored Item should be avoided if possible. For this reason OPC UA provides two features used to monitor changes of metadata.

One feature is directly related to Values monitored with a data change Monitored Item. Any changes in the structure or the DataType of the sent data or any semantic changes of the Variable like a change of the engineering units are indicated in the normal data flow with the StructureChanged flag and the SemanticsChanged flag in the StatusCode assigned to each Value sent from the server to the client. If the StructureChanged flag is set, the client should read the data type information or the type description of a structured DataType. If the SemanticsChanged flag is set, the client should check the Properties of the Variable for changes.

Another feature is the SemanticsChange Event indicating changes in the Address Space semantic of the server. The changes covered by this Event are changes of Property Values. The AccessLevel Attribute of a Property indicates with the SemanticsChange bit if the Property is able to trigger such an Event if the Value is changed. Servers will support this typically only for Properties where they get informed by the underlying system about such changes. Otherwise the server needs to monitor all Properties in the system if a client subscribes for such an Event which is even worse than monitoring Properties with a data change Monitored Item for changes.

**Table 5.39** Data Monitored Item settings

| Parameters | Description |
|---|---|
| NodeId | NodeId of the Variable to monitor |
| AttributeId | Value Attribute |
| SamplingInterval | The rate in milliseconds the server checks the underlying data source for changes. The type of change that triggers a notification is defined by the filter. If −1 is used for this interval, the publishing interval of the Subscription is used as for this setting. A client can over sample the Value by setting the SamplingInterval to a smaller value than the publishing interval and the queue size to 1 |
| QueueSize | Maximum number of values stored for the Monitored Item during a publishing interval. After each publishing interval the server will send the values in the queue to the client |
| Filter | Data change filter settings |
|     Trigger | Type of change that triggers a notification message. The possible triggers are change in: <br>• The status of the value <br>• The value or status of the value (default) <br>• The source timestamp, value, or status of the value |
|     DeadbandType | This parameter indicates if a deadband is applied and if applied, which type of deadband. OPC UA defines two type, absolute deadband and percent deadband |
|     DeadbandValue | *Absolute deadband* <br>For this type the DeadbandValue contains the absolute change in a number data value that will cause a notification to be generated. Triggers a value change if abs(last value − new value) > DeadbandValue <br>*Percent deadband* <br>For this type of deadband the DeadbandValue is defined as the percentage of the EURange. This deadband setting is only applied to Variables having a EURange Property. This setting triggers a value change if the value changed more than the percentage of the configured Value range |

## 5.7.5 Monitor Events

The only way to receive current Events from a Server is the creation of an Event Monitored Item in a Subscription. Event and data Monitored Items can be combined in one Subscription. The main difference between an Event and a data Monitored Item is the way to select the subset of information to receive. For data items the client selects exactly one Variable Value and monitors the Value for changes. For an Event Item it is normally not possible to directly select the Event Source since Objects acting as EventNotifiers may combine a large number of Event Sources. For this reason the filter settings are very important to be able to reduce the amount of Events and Event Fields to the needed subset. The Event Monitored Item settings including the filter are described in Table 5.40.

**Table 5.40** Event Monitored Item settings

| Parameters | | | Description |
|---|---|---|---|
| NodeId | | | NodeId of the Object to monitor |
| AttributeId | | | EventNotifier Attribute |
| SamplingInterval | | | 0 |
| QueueSize | | | 0 – this means that the maximum size supported by the server is used |
| Filter | | | Event filter settings |
| | SelectClauses [ ] | | List of select clauses used to select the Event fields to return for each Event notification |
| | | TypeId | NodeId of the Event Type defining the Event field |
| | | BrowsePath [ ] | List of BrowseNames from the Event Type to the Instance Declaration representing the Event field. This list has one element for simple Event Types. If the list has more elements the server must follow forward hierarchical references to find the Event field |
| | WhereClause | | Limits the notifications to those Events that match the criteria defined by this ContentFilter |
| | | Elements [ ] | List of operators and their operands that compose the filter criteria. The filter is evaluated by starting with the first entry in this array |
| | | FilterOperator | Filter operator to be evaluated. Possible operators are described in Table 5.41 |
| | | Filter Operands [ ] | Array of extensible parameters containing the operands used by the selected operator. The number and use depend on the operands described in Table 5.41. This array needs at least one entry |

The *Select* clause is used to reduce the number of data contained in an Event notification. The client must explicitly select Event fields he is interested in. There are no default fields returned like in Classic OPC.

The *Where* clause is used to filter on the Event fields to reduce the number of Events to the ones the client is interested in. Examples for typical filters are:

- EventType = TransitionEventType
- ((SourceNode = DeviceX) OR (SourceNode = DeviceY)) AND (Severity > 200)
- (EventType = MyEventType) AND (Severity > 500)

Figure 5.11 shows the fields of the BaseEventType, a derived Event Type MyEventType, and an Event filter with a select of some fields of both Types and a Where clause using other fields to filter the Events.

The operators and operands are defined by OPC UA. The operators are described in Table 5.41. Additional information can be found in [UA Part 4].
The Operands could be:

- A index of another element in the list used to build a logic tree of elements
- A literal value, e.g., the NodeId of the EventType to filter for
- An operand[6] identifying the field of the new Event used to filter on, e.g., the EventType field defined by the BaseEventType.

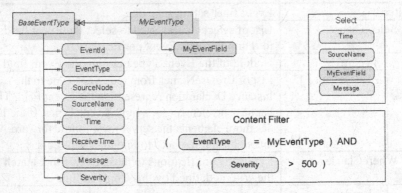

**Fig. 5.11** Example for Event filter

**Table 5.41** Filter operators

| Operator | Description |
|---|---|
| Equals | True if operand one is equal to operand two |
| IsNull | True if operand one is null |
| GreaterThan | True if operand one is greater than operand two |
| LessThan | True if operand one is less than operand two |
| GreaterThanOrEqual | True if operand one is greater or equal to operand two |

*(Continued)*

---

[6]SimpleAttributeOperand containing similar information like a SelectClause element.

| LessThanOrEqual | True if operand one is less or equal to operand two |
|---|---|
| Like | True if operand one matches a pattern defined by operand two.<br>The pattern syntax is defined in [UA Part 4] |
| Not | True if operand one is false |
| Between | True if operand one is greater or equal to operand two and less than or equal to operand three |
| InList | True if operand one is equal to one or more of the remaining operand |
| And | True if operand one AND operand two are true |
| Or | True if operand one OR operand two are true |
| Cast | Converts operand one to a data type identified with a DataType NodeId in operand two |

## 5.7.6 Monitor Aggregated Data

A special version of subscribing for data changes of Variable Values is the monitoring of aggregated data where the server samples on a higher rate, calculates the selected aggregate after the SamplingInterval and sends only the aggregated values to the client. Table 5.42 describes the aggregate specific MonitoredItem settings. More details about aggregate calculation are described in Chapter 5.9.1 in the section for HistoryRead processed and in [UA Part 13].

**Table 5.42** Aggregate MonitoredItem settings

| Parameters | | Description |
|---|---|---|
| NodeId | | NodeId of the Variable to monitor |
| AttributeId | | Value Attribute |
| SamplingInterval | | The interval in milliseconds for which the server calculates the aggregate |
| QueueSize | | Maximum number of values stored for the Monitored Item during a publishing interval. After each publishing interval the server will send the values in the queue to the client |
| Filter | | Aggregate filter settings |
| | StartTime | Start time of the first interval to calculate. The length of the intervals is defined by the SamplingInterval |
| | AggregateType | NodeId of the aggregate type. The list of aggregates is described in Table 5.48 |
| | RawData SamplingInterval | The rate at which values are sampled from the underlining system to be used to compute the aggregate |

The structure of a notification message sent for an aggregate result is the same like for data MonitoredItems.

## 5.8   Calling Methods Defined by the Server

OPC UA allows servers to expose Methods in the Address Space that can be called by clients. Methods are components of Objects and can be called in the context of an Object. All necessary information to call a Method is available in the Method description including the detailed description of the input and the output parameters of the Method. Section 5.5.2.3 describes how to find this information in the use case to get information to call a method.

The Call Service is used to actually call a method with built-in knowledge of the client or based on knowledge the client got through the information available in the Address Space. The Service allows calling a list of Methods to reduce the roundtrips between the client and the server. OPC UA client SDKs will provide simplified functions to call one Method and full featured functions to call a list of Methods in one Service invocation. The parameters of the Call Service are described in Table 5.43.

**Table 5.43** Call Service parameters

| Request parameters | Description |
|---|---|
| MethodsToCall [ ] | List of Methods to call |
|    ObjectId | NodeId of the Object or ObjectType Node that provides the Method |
|    MethodId | NodeId of the Method to call in the context of the Object or ObjectType |
|    InputArguments [ ] | List of input argument values of the Method. The required arguments and the necessary data types for each argument are defined by the InputArgument Property of the Method in the Address Space |
| Response parameters | Description |
| Results [ ] | List of results for each Method to call |
|    StatusCode | Success code for the Method call |
|    InputArgument Results [ ] | List of input argument result codes for the Method call |
|    OutputArguments[ ] | List of output argument values of the Method. The returned arguments and the data types for each argument are defined by the OutputArgument Property of the Method in the Address Space |

## 5.9   Access History of Data and Events

The main difference between the access to current data and Events using Read, Write, and Subscriptions and the access to the history is the definition of a time domain in the history request and the return of an array of information archived for the time period domain of the current data or Events. The availability of history is indicated by the AccessLevel Attribute of a Variable or the EventNotifier Attribute of an Object.

The history access Services HistoryRead and HistoryUpdate are making extensive use of extensible parameters to cover the different use cases for history access with two Services. [UA Part 4] defines only the fixed Service parameters. All extensible parameters are defined in [UA Part 11].

The HistoryRead Service request uses an extensible parameter to define the type of read for raw data, modified data, processed data, data on specific timestamps, and history of Events. The HistoryRead response is using an extensible parameter for the transport of the two types of requested information, data and Events. The HistoryUpdate Service request uses an extensible parameter to insert, to replace, to update, and to delete data or Events.

To describe these different variations of the Services, the following sections are describing first the Service with the common parameters and then the different types of extensible parameters. OPC UA client SDKs will typically expose nine history methods. Their signatures are defined by the different types of extensible parameters.

### 5.9.1 HistoryRead Service

This Service is used to read historical Values or Events of one or more Nodes in an ordered sequence for the defined time domain. Continuation points are used to continue the read of the ordered sequence if not all data can be returned in one HistoryRead response. The returned number can be limited by the client or the server. Table 5.44 describes the general HistoryRead Service parameters. The extensible parameters for the different types of history Read are described in the following Sections.

**Table 5.44** General HistoryRead Service parameters

| Request parameters | Description |
|---|---|
| HistoryReadDetails | Extensible parameter containing the parameters for the different types of history read operations. This could be a read of raw, modified, and processed values, read of Values at certain timestamps or the read of Event history |
| TimestampsToReturn | Indicates if the source timestamp, the server timestamp, or both should be returned<br>The selected timestamp is also used for the selection of the values in the time domain to read. If both are selected, the source timestamp is used |
| Release ContinuationPoint | The flag indicates if the Service call is used to release ContinuationPoints returned from previous calls without returning additional data. This allows clients to free resources in the server if the client does not continue the read |
| NodesToRead [ ] | List of Nodes where the client wants to read history |
|   NodeId | NodeId of the Node that provides historical information<br>For reading data history this must be the NodeId of a Variable Node where the HistoryRead flag is set for the Access Level Attribute<br>For reading Event history this must be the NodeId of an Object Node where the HistoryRead flag is set for the EventNotifier Attribute |
|   ContinuationPoint | Returned by the server in a previous HistoryRead call. It is used by the client to continue the read or to release the continuation point |
| Response parameters | Description |
| Results [ ] | List of results for each Node to read |
|   StatusCode | Success code for the Node and the filter settings |
|   HistoryData | Extensible parameter containing the result data for the different types of history read operations. This could be a list of data values or a list of Event notifications |
|   ContinuationPoint | Set by the server if not all data can be returned in this call. This allows the client to continue the read without exceeding the limits set by the client or the server |

#### 5.9.1.1  Reading Raw or Modified Data

The HistoryRead Service is called with the extensible parameter of type Read-RawModified to read raw or modified data for a specified time domain. It reads the Values, status, and timestamps of one or more Variables. The extensible parameter is described in Table 5.45 and is used in the HistoryReadDetails parameter of the HistoryRead Service.

For raw data the values stored in the history database are returned directly. A modified value is a value that has been replaced by another value at the same timestamp in the history database. If there are multiple replaced values the server must return all of them.

Table 5.45 ReadRawModified extensible parameter

| Parameters | Description |
|---|---|
| IsReadModified | Specifies the type of read. If the flag is set to false, a read raw is performed, if set to true a read modified is performed |
| StartTime | Begin of the time period to read |
| EndTime | End of the time period to read |
| NumValuesPerNode | The maximum number of values returned for each Node. If this maximum is exceeded by the number of available values in the defined time domain, the server returns a continuation point. The value 0 indicates that there is no limit set by the client. The server can also reduce the number of values to return |
| ReturnBounds | A flag that indicates if bounding values should be returned. If set to true, a value before the start time and a value after the end time is returned if no values are available at the specified start and end timestamps |

The extensible parameter type HistoryData is used to return the data for read raw, modified, processed and read at time. The content of the HistoryData structure is described in Table 5.46. The data value structure is also used in the Read Service and data change notifications. The parameters are described more detailed at the Read Service in Table 5.25.

Table 5.46 HistoryData extensible parameter

| Parameters | Description |
|---|---|
| DataValues [ ] | Array of data values containing the result data |
|   Value | Raw or processed value from the history database |
|   StatusCode | Status of the value. There are special historical access status codes and info bits defined providing history specific information |
|   SourceTimestamp | Source timestamp for the value |
|   ServerTimestamp | Server timestamp for the value |

### 5.9.1.2   Reading Processed Data

The HistoryRead Service is called with the extensible parameter of type Read-Processed to Read processed data calculated with the specified aggregate based on the raw data in the history database. It reads the processed Values, status and time-stamps for one or more Variables in the specified time domain. The extensible parameter is described in Table 5.47 and is used in the HistoryReadDetails parameter of the HistoryRead Service. The server must use start time, end time, and the resample interval to generate a sequence of time intervals and then calculate an aggregate for each interval. The aggregates are defined in [UA Part 13] and described in Table 5.48.

Table 5.47 ReadProcessed extensible parameter

| Parameters | Description |
|---|---|
| StartTime | Begin of the time period to read |
| EndTime | End of the time period to read |
| ResampleInterval | Time interval in milliseconds that is used to calculate one aggregated value from the raw values in the history database. The time domain is divided into sub-intervals with the length of the ResampleInterval beginning with the start time<br>If the ResampleInterval is 0, one aggregated value is calculated for the time domain |
| AggregateType | The NodeId of the aggregate used for the calculation of the values. The OPC UA defined aggregates are described in Table 5.48 |

All aggregates in the following table without an additional comment return a timestamp of the start of the interval. If the aggregate returns another timestamp, the specific behavior is described for the aggregate.

Table 5.48 Aggregates used for HistoryRead and monitoring of aggregated values

| Aggregate | Description |
|---|---|
| Interpolative | Returns an interpolated value for the starting time of the interval |
| Data averaging and summation aggregates | |
| Average | Returns the average data over the resample interval. It adds up all values in the interval and divides the sum by the number of values |
| TimeAverage | Returns the time weighted average data over the resample interval. A straight line is drawn between each raw value in the interval. The area under the line is divided by the length of the interval to yield the average. Interpolated values are used at the start and at the end of the interval |

*(Continued)*

| Total | Returns the sum of the data over the resample interval. It adds up all values in the interval |
|---|---|
| Totalize Average | Returns the totalized Value (time integral) of the data over the resample interval |
| Data variation aggregates | |
| Minimum | Returns the minimum value in the resample interval |
| Maximum | Returns the maximum value in the resample interval |
| Minimum ActualTime | Returns the minimum value in the resample interval and the timestamp of the minimum value |
| Maximum ActualTime | Returns the maximum value in the resample interval and the timestamp of the maximum value |
| Range | Returns the difference between the minimum and maximum Value over the sample interval |
| Counting aggregates | |
| Annotation Count | Returns the number of annotations in the resample interval. Annotations are user entered comments in the history database |
| Count | Returns the number of raw values with good status in the resample interval |
| Duration InState0 | The duration of the interval the value was in FALSE state. The value of the aggregate is the time in milliseconds |
| Duration InState1 | The duration of the interval the value was in TRUE state. The value of the aggregate is the time in milliseconds |
| Number OfTransitions | Returns the number of value changes with good quality in the resample interval |
| Time aggregates | |
| Start | Returns the first value in the interval and the timestamp of the first value |
| End | Returns the last value in the interval and the timestamp of the last value |
| Delta | The difference between the first and the last good value in the interval. If the last value is less than the first value, the result will be negative |
| Data quality aggregates | |
| DurationGood | The duration of the interval the value had good quality. The value of the aggregate is the time in milliseconds |
| DurationBad | The duration of the interval the value had bad quality. The value of the aggregate is the time in milliseconds |
| PercentGood | Percentage of the interval the value had good quality (0–100). PercentGood = DurationGood / ResampleInterval * 100 |
| PercentBad | Percentage of the interval the value had bad quality (0–100). PercentGood = DurationGood / ResampleInterval * 100 |
| WorstQuality | Returns the worst quality of the values in the interval. The value of the aggregate is the status code for the worst quality |

### 5.9.1.3   Reading Data at a Series of Timestamps

The HistoryRead Service is called with the extensible parameter of type Read-AtTime to read data for the specified timestamps. When no value exists for a specified timestamp, a value is interpolated from the surrounding values to represent the value at the specified timestamp. It reads the Values, status, and timestamps for one or more Variables. The extensible parameter is described in Table 5.49 and is used in the HistoryReadDetails parameter of the HistoryRead Service.

**Table 5.49** ReadAtTime extensible parameter

| Parameters | Description |
|---|---|
| RequestedTimes [ ] | List of requested timestamps |

### 5.9.1.4   Reading Event History

The HistoryRead Service is called with the extensible parameter of type Read-Event to read Events for the specified time domain. The filter parameter is used to determine which historical Events are returned and selects the Event field returned for an Event. The extensible parameter is described in Table 5.50 and is used in the HistoryReadDetails parameter of the HistoryRead Service.

**Table 5.50** ReadEvent extensible parameter

| Parameters | Description |
|---|---|
| NumValuesPerNode | The maximum number of Events returned for each Node. If this maximum is exceeded by the number of available events in the defined time domain, the server returns a continuation point. The value zero indicates that there is no limit set by the client. The server can also reduce the number of events to return |
| StartTime | Begin of the time period to read |
| EndTime | End of the time period to read |
| Filter | The filter allows reducing the amount of Events returned from the Read by using the same Event filter used for monitoring current Events. The filter is described there in Table 5.40 |

The extensible parameter type HistoryEvent is used to return the Events for Read Events. The content of the HistoryEvent structure is described in Table 5.51.

**Table 5.51** HistoryData extensible parameter

| Parameters | Description |
|---|---|
| Events [ ] | Array of Events being delivered |
|    EventFields [ ] | List of selected Event fields |

## 5.9.2 HistoryUpdate Service

This Service is used to insert, replace, update, or delete historical Values or Events. Table 5.52 describes the general HistoryUpdate Service parameters. The extensible parameters for the different types of history update are described in the following sections.

**Table 5.52** General HistoryUpdate service parameters

| Request parameters | Description |
|---|---|
| HistoryUpdate Details [ ] | A list of extensible parameters containing the information for the different types of history updates. This could be insert, replace, update, or delete of historical Values or Events |
| **Response parameters** | **Description** |
| Results [ ] | List of results for each update detail list entry |
|    StatusCode | Status code for the list entry |
|    OperationResults [ ] | Status code for each operation in the list entry |

### 5.9.2.1  Insert, Replace, or Update Data

The HistoryUpdate Service is called with the extensible parameter of type Update-Data to insert, replace, or update data in the history database. The extensible parameter is described in Table 5.53 and is used in the HistoryUpdateDetails parameter of the HistoryUpdate Service.

**Table 5.53** UpdateData extensible parameter

| Parameters | Description |
|---|---|
| PerformInsert | A flag that indicates if an insert should be performed if no value is available for the passed timestamp in the history database |
| PerformReplace | A flag that indicates if a replace should be performed if a value is available for the passed timestamp in the history database |
| NodeId | NodeId of the Variable to be updated |
| DataValues [ ] | A list of values including status codes and timestamps to update in the history database |

One of the two flags to force insert or replace must be set. Table 5.54 describes the update Event flags usage.

**Table 5.54** Update data flags

| Insert | Replace | Description |
|--------|---------|-------------|
| True | False | The passed value will only be written to the history if no value exists at the specified timestamp |
| False | True | The passed value will only be written to the history if a value exists at the specified timestamp. The existing value will be replaced |
| True | True | The passed value will be inserted if no value exists for the timestamp but will also replace an existing value at the given timestamp |

### 5.9.2.2   Insert, Replace, or Update Event

The HistoryUpdate Service is called with the extensible parameter of type Update-Event to insert, replace, or update, Events in the history database. The extensible parameter is described in Table 5.55 and is used in the HistoryUpdateDetails parameter of the HistoryUpdate Service.

**Table 5.55** UpdateEvent extensible parameter

| Parameters | Description |
|------------|-------------|
| PerformInsert | A flag that indicates if an insert should be performed if no event is available for the passed timestamp in the history database |
| PerformReplace | A flag that indicates if a replace should be performed if an event is available for the passed timestamp in the history database |
| NodeId | NodeId of the Object to be updated |
| Filter | The filter is used to find the event to update or to replace or to insert the Event if PerformInsert is set and the Event was not found. The same Event filter is used like for monitoring current Events. The filter is described there in Table 5.40 |
| EventFields [ ] | List of Event fields for the Event to update |

One of the two flags to force insert or replace must be set. Table 5.56 describes the update Event flags usage.

**Table 5.56** Update Event Flags

| Insert | Replace | Description |
|--------|---------|-------------|
| True | False | The passed Event will only be written to the history if no Event exists at the specified timestamp |
| False | True | The passed Event will only be written to the history if an Event exists at the specified timestamp. The existing Event will be replaced |
| True | True | The passed Event will be inserted if no Event exists for the timestamp but will also replace an existing Event at the given timestamp |

### 5.9.2.3  Delete Raw or Modified Data

The HistoryUpdate Service is called with the extensible parameter of type Delete-RawModified to delete raw or modified data for a specified time domain. The extensible parameter is described in Table 5.57 and is used in the HistoryUpdate-Details parameter of the HistoryUpdate Service.

For raw the values stored in the history database are deleted. A modified value is a value that has been replaced by another value at the same timestamp in the history database. If there are multiple replaced values the server must delete all of them.

**Table 5.57** DeleteRawModified extensible parameter

| Parameters | Description |
|------------|-------------|
| IsDeleteModified | Specifies the type of delete. If the flag is set to false, a delete raw is performed, if set to true a delete modified is performed |
| NodeId | NodeId of the Variable for which the values are to be deleted |
| StartTime | Begin of the time period to delete |
| EndTime | End of the time period to delete |

### 5.9.2.4  Delete Data at a Series of Timestamps

The HistoryUpdate Service is called with the extensible parameter of type Delete-AtTime to delete data for the specified timestamps. The extensible parameter is described in Table 5.58 and is used in the HistoryUpdateDetails parameter of the HistoryUpdate Service.

**Table 5.58** DeleteAtTime extensible parameter

| Parameters | Description |
|---|---|
| NodeId | NodeId of the Variable for which the values are to be deleted |
| RequestedTimes [ ] | List of requested timestamps |

#### 5.9.2.5  Delete Events

The HistoryUpdate Service is called with the extensible parameter of type DeleteEvent to delete specific events. The extensible parameter is described in Table 5.59 and is used in the HistoryUpdateDetails parameter of the History-Update Service.

**Table 5.59** DeleteEvent extensible parameter

| Parameters | Description |
|---|---|
| NodeId | NodeId of the Object for which the events are to be deleted |
| EventId [ ] | An array of Event ids to identify which Events are to be deleted |

## 5.10  Find Information in Complex Address Space

The Browse Service is used to navigate through the Address Space. This mechanism is useful to navigate through known areas and to find information in a small Address Space but it will be difficult or impossible to find the necessary information in a very large or a very dynamic Address Space. Address Spaces of servers providing access to systems with rich Information Models can have millions of Nodes. Address Spaces of MES or ERP systems can have very dynamic Address Spaces representing for example current work orders.

The OPC UA feature used to find information in such Address Spaces is Query. It implements a different approach than Browse. It allows defining filter criteria to retrieve a subset of Nodes and Information based on these filters, whereas Browse defines a starting Node and filters to reduce the list of returned referenced Nodes. The query mechanism of OPC UA is based on type information. The starting point of each query is to specify the type of Objects or Variables the client is interested in. In the SECLECT-Part (DataToReturn) of a query, the client specifies what data should be returned relative to instances of the type and in the WHERE-Part (Filter) the client specifies the filter criteria.

The QueryFirst Service is used to start a Query and QueryNext is used to get the remaining results if too many results are available. The Service parameters of QueryFirst are described in Table 5.60.

**Table 5.60** QueryFirst Service parameters

| Request parameters | | | Description |
|---|---|---|---|
| View | | | Passing a View allows limiting the Query to a specific View |
| NodeTypes [ ] | | | Array of structures containing the type filter for the Query |
| | TypeDefinitionNode | | NodeId of the TypeDefinition VariableType or ObjectType where instances should be returned |
| | IncludeSubtypes | | Indicates whether instances of subtypes should be included |
| | DataToReturn [ ] | | Specifies the Nodes and the Attributes of the instances to return |
| | | RelativePath | Brows Path from the instance of the specified type to the component of the instance |
| | | AttributeId | Id of the Attribute to return for the selected Node |
| Filter | | | Content filter used to reduce the returned instance Nodes and their Attribute values. The content filter is the same filter that is used in the where clause of the Event Monitored Items. The filter settings are described there in Tables 5.40, 5.41 |
| MaxDataSetToReturn | | | This parameter allows the client to limit the number of returned results |
| Response parameters | | | Description |
| QueryDataSets [ ] | | | List of result data |
| | NodeId | | NodeId of the instance Node matching the query defined in the request |
| | TypeDefinitionNode | | TypeDefinition NodeId for the returned instance Node |
| | Values [ ] | | List of Values for the selected Attribute |
| ContinuationPoint | | | A continuation point is returned when the server was not able to deliver all results in the QueryFirst response. The limitation can be set by the client in the request or by the server during Query processing<br>The continuation point can be passed to QueryNext to get the remaining results<br>QueryNext takes the ContinuationPoint as input parameter and returns the same results like QueryFirst |

## 5.11  Modify the Address Space

The NodeManagement Services enables an OPC UA client to create and delete Nodes and References in the Address Space of an OPC UA server. It is expected that this feature is mainly used between OPC UA servers and their configuration clients. Information Models may define the use of these Services more detailed to make them useful for generic clients knowing the Information Model.

## 5.11.1 Adding Nodes

The AddNodes Service is used to add one or more Nodes to the Address Space. The parameters of the Service are described in Table 5.61.

**Table 5.61** AddNodes Service parameters

| Request parameters | Description |
|---|---|
| NodesToAdd [ ] | List of Nodes to add to the server Address Space |
|    ParentNodeId | NodeId of the Node where the new Node should be referenced from |
|    ReferenceTypeId | NodeId of the Reference type used for the Reference to create between the parent Node and the new Node |
|    BrowseName | Browse name of the new Node |
|    NodeClass | Node class of the new Node |
|    NodeAttributes | Extensible parameter containing the additional Attribute values depending on the NodeClass to create |
|    TypeDefinition | TypeDefinition NodeId used to define which type of Object or Variable with its type defined components should be created. This parameter is not set if the NodeClass is not Object or Variable |
| **Response parameters** | **Description** |
| Results [ ] | List of results for each add operation |
|    StatusCode | Result code for the add operation |
|    AddedNodeId | NodeId of the newly created Node |

## 5.11.2 Creating References Between Nodes

The AddReferences Service is used to create one or more References between Nodes in the Address Space. The parameters of the Service are described in Table 5.62.

**Table 5.62** AddReferences Service parameters

| Request parameters | Description |
|---|---|
| ReferencesToAdd [ ] | List of References to create |
|    SourceNodeId | NodeId of the source Node of the new Reference |
|    ReferenceTypeId | NodeId of the Reference type used for the Reference to create between the source and the target Node |
|    TargetNodeId | NodeId of the target Node of the new Reference |
| **Response parameters** | **Description** |
| Results [ ] | List of result codes for each add operation |

### 5.11.3 Removing Nodes

The DeleteNodes Service is used to remove one or more Nodes from the Address Space. The parameters of the Service are described in Table 5.63.

**Table 5.63** DeleteNodes Service parameters

| Request parameters | Description |
|---|---|
| NodesToDelete [ ] | List of Nodes to remove from the server Address Space |
|   NodeId | NodeId of the Node to delete |
|   DeleteTarget Reference | A flag that indicates if the server should also delete the Reference to the target Node |
| Response parameters | Description |
| Results [ ] | List of result codes for each delete operation |

### 5.11.4 Delete References Between Nodes

The DeleteReferences Service is used to remove one or more References in the Address Space. The parameters of the Service are described in Table 5.64.

**Table 5.64** DeleteReferences Service parameters

| Request parameters | Description |
|---|---|
| ReferencesToDelete [ ] | List of References to delete from the server Address Space |
|   SourceNodeId | NodeId of the source Node of the Reference to delete |
|   ReferenceTypeId | NodeId of the Reference type used for the Reference to delete between the source and the target Node |
|   TargetNodeId | NodeId of the target Node of the Reference to delete |
| Response parameters | Description |
| Results [ ] | List of result codes for each delete operation |

## 5.12  Summary

### 5.12.1  Key Messages

There are two types of OPC UA Services. One type is used to create a communication context like the Secure Channel, Session, Subscription, and MonitoredItem Service Sets. The other type is used to exchange information like Browse to get information about the structure of the Address Space, Read, Write, and Publish to access data and Call to execute Methods.

Compared to Classic OPC the number of Services[7] is reduced to a small set based on the design goal to provide only one generic Service for a task and on the design goal to provide information by modeling the information and not by providing a special access method for the type of information.

The Services are defined in an abstract way enabling the implementation of the Service transport with different technologies and different development environments to achieve the requirements for platform-independence, scalability, and high performance but also for Internet access and the capability to cross firewalls.

All Services can be called synchronous and asynchronous since the base mechanism to exchange the messages is asynchronous and the calls to the client API can be made synchronous in the UA Stack. Individual timeouts per Service call can be configured. A communication context like a Session or a Subscription can still be used by the client after short network interruptions but the negotiated timeouts are allowing the server to clear resources after the timeout expires. Together with the Publish mechanisms to ensure no data gets lost and the built-in redundancy features (see Sect. 9.3) a reliable communication between distributed systems is ensured.

### 5.12.2  Where to Find More Information?

The abstract OPC UA Services are defined in [UA Part 4]; the technology mapping is defined in [UA Part 6].

Additional implementation specific information is provided by the documentation of the different UA Stack implementations and OPC UA SDKs.

### 5.12.3  What's Next?

After explaining the abstract Services to access the OPC UA information provided by a server, Chap. 6 describes the different technology mappings of the Services to the different types of message serialization, message security, and message transport and the different available implementations of these mappings.

Other related aspects are the Security concepts described in Chap. 7, the Application Architecture explained in Chap. 8 and the System Architecture described in Chap. 9.

---

[7]Comparable to interface methods in COM.

# 6 Technology Mapping

## 6.1 Overview

When considering developing applications it soon comes to the question which technology to use for the implementation. There are often many different technology options from which one has to be selected. In some cases it is preferable to apply a matured technology and in other cases innovation is more important. However, when developing a standard, the technology question is not easy to answer if you intend to satisfy everyone in the community. For some people performance and reliability are more important than security, for others this is vice-versa. Another issue that has to be considered for answering the technology question is what happens when a technology retires? Technologies are provided and maintained for certain platforms like operating systems. When new versions of such platforms are provided then sometimes older technologies are replaced by newer ones. The backward compatibility is thereby not always given!

In order to be open for future technologies and to provide certain interoperability between OPC UA products the working group decided to define services (see Chap. 5) and concepts in an abstract manner and to specify a technological mapping for implementation. The specified mappings address three tasks necessary for exchanging data between OPC UA applications: data encoding, securing the communication, and transporting the data. This is illustrated in Fig. 6.1. OPC UA applications in general can be separated into several functional layers. There are layers for the application logic, for accessing other components (i.e., interfaces) and there are several layers responsible for encoding, security, and transport which can be composed to a so-called stack. Stacks are mostly generic components separated from the real application since they can be reused by many other applications. Reference [UA Part 6] defines for each of the stack's layer two technologies that can be used for implementation. However, technology evolves and additional technology mappings might be added in the future. In order to develop an OPC UA compliant product (see Chap. 12) at least one of the specified technologies for each layer has to be implemented.[1]

In the following subsections each specified technology is briefly introduced.

---

[1]Note that the OPC Foundation provides deliverables already implementing all the technologies specified in [UA Part 6]; see Sect. 6.5 for some more information.

W. Mahnke et al., *OPC Unified Architecture*,
DOI: 10.1007/978-3-540-68899-0_6, © Springer-Verlag Berlin Heidelberg 2009

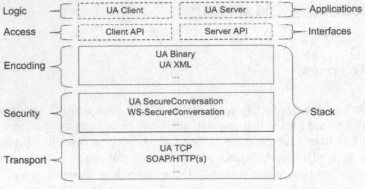

**Fig. 6.1** Mappings

## 6.2   Data Encodings

Data encoding is the serialization of the Service messages including its input and output parameter to a network format OPC UA currently specifies two encodings: OPC UA Binary and XML. Both encodings are introduced in the following. However, there are some aspects common for both encoding types.

For both, OPC UA Binary and for XML, the network representations of a set of primitive types (e.g., Boolean, Byte, and Float) are specified in order to compose structures and more complex types. This specific set of primitive types is called Built-In DataTypes and their encoding is defined in [UA Part 6].

A further aspect that is common for all encoding types is the ExtensionObject. This is a special type container for any complex data independent of the encoding. Beside the encoded data, the ExtensionObject contains also an identifier which indicates what data it contains and how it is encoded. There are two use cases for this special container. One use case is to provide type information for the decoding since the encoded data may not contain meta information about the structure of the data like in the binary encoding. It provides the necessary meta information in all places in the encoded data where different types can be used. The second use case is the transport of proprietary encoded data where the encoding is only known by the application layer.

A Variant, which is also used in both encodings, is a data type that can be used to hold a set of different other types. In OPC UA, a Variant can represent each of the defined Built-In DataTypes mentioned above including an ExtensionObject.

### 6.2.1 OPC UA Binary

Performance and overhead on the wire is often a critical parameter for industrial systems such as for applications embedded in a controller. Therefore the OPC UA working group defined a data format – OPC UA Binary – providing fast encoding and decoding of data by only having a small size and efficient format of encoded data on the wire.

The basic concept of OPC UA Binary Encoding is that a specified set of primitive data types (Built-In DataTypes) are translated into a binary representation by using well-defined rules by sequentially writing it to a binary stream. The serialization and deserialization of the Service parameters to a binary stream is the most efficient way for data exchange between different systems. An example for a binary representation of Built-In DataType is given in Fig. 6.2. In this figure, the String "OPCUA" is encoded according to OPC UA Binary. Thereby a sequence of UTF-8 characters is used beginning with the length of the String (in the present example 5 characters). Note that there is no null terminator contained. Null Strings are indicated by encoding the value "–1" as length.

| 5 | | | | O | P | C | U | A |
|---|---|---|---|---|---|---|---|---|
| 05 | 00 | 00 | 00 | 4F | 50 | 43 | 55 | 41 |

**Fig. 6.2** String example of OPC UA Binary Encoding

More complex data types are composed by combining a set of primitives. The translation to its binary format is performed by sequentially translating the contained primitives.

The abstract Service messages defined in [UA Part 4] are encoded by using ExtensionObjects.

## 6.2.2 XML

Sometimes it is desirable to exchange data in a format that can be easily consumed by different applications, platforms as well as by humans. In such scenarios, XML documents often play an important role since the structure is standardized. This allows every application or platform having an XML parser to interpret such documents. Based on this fact many applications at operations level (such as MES) use XML to exchange data with systems at corporate level (e.g., ERP systems). Since it is expected that OPC UA applications will run at both levels, an XML support has to be provided.

Most of the Built-In DataTypes are encoded according to the common XML specifications [W3C04a] and [W3C04b]. In some cases, restrictions or special usages have to be applied. However, these are not described in this book but they are specified in [UA Part 6]. Figure 6.3 illustrates how a String is represented when applying XML encoding. The upper line represents the XML schema that defines the XML instance at the bottom.

More complex types are composed by nested XML elements composed with primitives. A LocalizedText is a simple example of structure containing primitive types and is depicted in Fig. 6.4.

Messages are represented the same way a structure is encoded and are therefore also defined by a "xs:complexType".

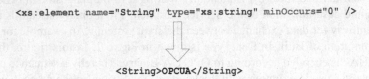

```
<xs:element name="String" type="xs:string" minOccurs="0" />
```

```
<String>OPCUA</String>
```

**Fig. 6.3** Primitive example of XML Encoding

```
<xs:complexType name="LocalizedText">
  <xs:sequence>
    <xs:element name="Locale" type="xs:string" minOccurs="0" />
    <xs:element name="Text" type="xs:string" minOccurs="0" />
  </xs:sequence>
</xs:complexType>
```

```
<LocalizedText>
    <Locale>DE</Locale>
    <Text>OPCUA</Text>
</LocalizedText>
```

**Fig. 6.4** Structure example of XML Encoding

## 6.3    Security Protocols

There are two security protocols defined for OPC UA in order to map the abstract services defined in [UA Part 4]: WS-SecureConversation and UA-SecureConversation. Both are based on a certificate-based connection establishment as described in Sect. 7.5.2.

### 6.3.1 WS-SecureConversation

WS-SecureConversation defined at [OASIS07] is an extension specification to WS-Security specified at [OASIS04] which defines concepts and technologies for securing data exchanged via Web Services. These and other related standards are developed and published by OASIS[2] a nonprofit organization driving open standards in the field of information technology. WS-SecureConversation is used in

---

[2]Organization for the Advancement of Structured Information Standards.

conjunction with WS-SecurityPolicy [OASIS07a] defining the security algorithms and WS-Trust [OASIS07b] negotiating shared secrets for the Secure Channel that has to be established between OPC UA applications (see Sect. 7.5.2). WS-SecurityPolicy is also used as a basis for SecurityPolicies and SecurityProfiles used by OPC UA which are introduced in Sect. 7.5.4. When it comes to encrypting and signing data then XML Encryption [W3C02] and XML Signature [W3C08] are applied. These standards have been chosen since they are approved and already implemented in several products and platforms such as Microsoft's Windows Communication Foundation.[3]

WS-SecureConversation is optimized for securing XML data since it applies XML Encryption and Signature which makes it a good approach for developing OPC UA applications running at operations or corporate level of the automation pyramid.

The connection establishment in OPC UA requires creating a Secure Channel and a Session (see Sect. 7.5.2.1). The abstract OpenSecureChannel request and response are mapped to the concrete RequestSecurityToken (RST) and Request-SecurityTokenResponse (RSTR) messages of WS-SecureConversation. These messages are used to agree upon a shared key which is used for securing all further messages (including the Session establishment) in a symmetric manner (which is better performing than securing messages with Public and Private Keys). In WS-SecureConversation this secret key is called DerivedKeyToken.

Tables 6.1 and 6.2 show in more detail how to map OpenSecureChannel request and response to the WS-SecureConversation equivalents.

Table 6.1 Mapping of OpenSecureChannel request to RequestSecurityToken

| OpenSecureChannel request | RequestSecurityToken |
| --- | --- |
| clientCertificate | BinarySecurityToken |
| requestType (open/renew) | RequestType |
| secureChannelId | SecurityTokenReference |
| securityMode<br>securityPolicyUri | SignatureAlgorithm<br>EncryptionAlgorithm<br>KeySize |
| clientNonce | Entropy |
| requestedLifetime | Lifetime |

Table 6.2 Mapping of OpenSecureChannel response to RequestSecurityTokenResponse

| OpenSecureChannel response | RequestSecurityTokenResponse |
| --- | --- |
| securityToken | RequestedSecurityToken |
| revisedLifetime | Lifetime |
| serverNonce | Entropy |

---

[3]http://msdn.microsoft.com/en-us/netframework/aa663324.aspx.

## 6.3.2 UA-SecureConversation

Why does the OPC UA working group define its own new security protocol? This is a question which we have been asked a lot of times. First of all, UA-SecureConversation is not a new security protocol. It is rather a combination of approved techniques and mechanisms of the standards TLS[4] and WS-SecureConversation. There are several reasons for heading this approach which are discussed in the following.

WS-SecureConversation is a protocol tailored for communication scenarios in which XML documents are exchanged for example via SOAP/HTTP. However, other scenarios have also to be considered in which performance and overhead are quite important such as applications running on controllers. In such cases, something fast and efficient is needed and since XML comes up with a large overhead on the wire WS-SecureConversation is therefore rarely an option.

One idea that came up in the working group was to use TLS for mapping the abstract connection establishment Services since this is widely accepted and used in a diverse range of applications. But after several investigations it turned out that TLS off-the-shelf cannot be used for OPC UA applications because either the specification or the TLS implementations do not meet certain requirement of OPC UA.

TLS implementations do not support the latest security protocols which is quite obvious since these algorithms may have been developed when the products were already on the market. One problem is that updates are not always provided for the specific platform but only for the next release. Another problem is that updates are not always possible since it is not that easy to extend the implemented applications. This could lead to interoperability problems considering an environment with OPC UA applications running on different platforms.

Another problem comes up with the Session handling. Many TLS implementations (such as Microsoft's SSPI[5]) hide the context information of established SSL sessions since they are transparently created to the upper layers. Since OPC UA requires binding Sessions to Secure Channels, this is a problem. This means in addition to that the application above does not have the full control over the SSL session representing the OPC UA Secure Channel and therefore does not know when new sessions are created. Network interruptions causing the creation of a new SSL session would be an interesting event of that an application would like to know about.

A further issue regarding SSL sessions is the lifetime. In many TLS implementations the maximum lifetime of a SSL session can be configured. After that lifetime the session ends and new one has to be created. However, the TLS specification suggests maximum of 24 h causing that most implementations use an even much shorter period. However, in industrial environments this can be far too short.

---

[4]Transport Layer Security; defined at [DR06].
[5]MS Security Support Provider Interface.

Whenever the Secure Channel (in this case the SSL session) is renewed, it has to be bound to an OPC UA Session and during this phase no application-specific data (for example production requests) can be exchanged between clients and servers. This could lead to some problems when production process last longer than 24 h.

One use case of OPC UA is to run several servers on a machine all sharing the same IP address and port. A special addressing mechanism at transport level allows such a scenario. But TLS 1.1 only supports one certificate per IP address and port which does not allow end-to-end security. This means the above described scenario cannot be secured with TLS 1.1.

Finally, it has to be said that although current TLS implementations and standard does not meet the requirements of OPC UA this does not mean that future versions of TLS addressing all those problems cannot be used. Since OPC UA is open for future technologies additional mappings can be defined.

UA-SecureConversation does not directly map the abstract Services but uses the encoded Service messages as the payload and adds additional security-related information in front of and behind this payload. The message chunk structure is shown in Fig. 6.5.

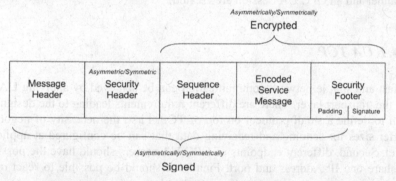

**Fig. 6.5** Message chunk according to UA-SecureConversation

The Message Header contains information identifying the type of the message, for example whether it is an OpenSecureChannel request or a CreateSession request.

This header is followed either by the Asymmetric Security Header or by the Symmetric Security Header. The first variant is only used for OpenSecureChannel requests and responses since OpenSecureChannel is the only Service messages secured with Public and Private Keys (see Sect. 7.5.2.1).This header contains the applied Security Policy identifying the algorithms used for securing the message, the certificate of the sender in order to verify the signature of the message, and a thumbprint identifying the certificate used for encrypting the message. The second variant is applied for all other messages beside the OpenSecureChannel message. In this case the header only contains a TokenId identifying the set of symmetric keys used to sign and encrypt messages.

The Sequence Header contains a number identifying a chunk. This is used when the payload (i.e., the Encoded Service Message) does not fit in a single chunk and therefore the message has to split up into multiple chunks.

Directly after the Encoded Service Message the Security Footer is placed. It contains among others the Signature of the message used to verify whether the signed data has been changed after it is sent and whether the message really comes from the entity (i.e., installed application instance) represented by the certificate in the Security Header. This signature is verified with the Public Key of the sender certificate when an OpenSecureChannel message is exchanged and for all other messages the negotiated symmetric keys identified by the TokenId are used.

## 6.4    Transport Protocols

UA TCP and SOAP/HTTP are the two transport protocols defined by the OPC UA standard. These protocols are used for establishing a connection between an OPC UA client and server at network level. On top of the transport protocol a Secure Channel and an OPC UA Session are created.

### 6.4.1 UA TCP

A fast and simple network communication can be achieved by applying UA TCP for the transport layer. There are different requirements leading to the design decision to define a small protocol on top of TCP: First, the necessity of negotiating buffer sizes for sending and receiving data that can be configured at application level. Second, different endpoints of OPC UA servers should have the possibility to share one IP-Address and port. Finally, it should be possible to react on and recover from errors occurring at transport level.

The general structure of an UA TCP message chunk consists of a Message Header and a Message Body which are depicted in Fig. 6.6.

The Message Header contains information about the type and the length of the message. Note, that when combining UA-SecureConversation with UA TCP the Message Headers are intentionally the same which slightly reduces the overhead

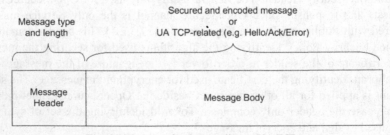

**Fig. 6.6** Message chunk according to UA TCP

on the wire when applying message security and allows the implementation of the Transport Layer to easily distinguish between Transport Layer messages and messages that have to be forwarded to the Security Layer (e.g., OpenSecureChannel messages).

The Message Body either contains the encoded and secured Service messages that are forwarded to the upper layer or contains UA TCP-specific connection messages used for establishing a socket connection or exchanging connection error information.

There are three UA TCP messages types defined which are briefly introduced in the following.

A Hello message is sent by the OPC UA client to the server in order to establish a socket connection to a specific endpoint provided by the server. It thereby also requests certain buffer sizes for sending and receiving data from the server as well as maximum chunk and total message lengths.

As response to the Hello message, the server sends an Acknowledge message confirming or revising the requested buffer sizes as well as chunk and message lengths. An agreement on these numbers is important from reliability and from the security perspective. Clients and servers thereby know what to expect from each other and can resist certain attacks like buffer overflows or Denial-of-Service.

Finally, the third message type is the Error message providing error information to the other application. Such messages are sent around if connection problems occur, for example, if a message cannot be processed since the size is too long or the server is overloaded.

As indicated above, UA TCP defines also a specific error recovery mechanism enabling OPC UA Sessions to survive network interruptions. When a client loses the socket connection then a new socket is created and assigned to the existing Secure Channel which has to be first reauthenticated by the server. Pending requests of the client and responses of the server are buffered until a new socket is available. However, if the error recovery fails (after trying to reconnect a certain number of times) an error message is sent around which enables the Application Layer to react on that.

## 6.4.2 SOAP/HTTP

SOAP/HTTP stands for SOAP over HTTP and is a widely accepted communication scheme in Web Service environments because it is simple and firewall-friendly. Since the standard ports for the Web protocol HTTP is used for transportation, no additional port has to be opened in the firewall. This means that OPC UA applications can securely communicate with each other via Internet in the same manner as Web browsers talk to Web servers.

SOAP in general is a network protocol for exchanging data between systems and calling remote procedures. It thereby relies on several other standards for example XML for data representation and HTTP or TCP for data transportation.

Note that for OPC UA only HTTP is specified in the technological mapping. In principle a SOAP message is structured in a header and in a body which is reflected in Fig. 6.7. The headers contain addressing and routing information whereas the body encloses the payload that has to be transported. OPC UA does not define specific headers but uses headers specified in WS-Addressing defined at [W3C04c]. The encoded and secured Service message is then enclosed by the Body element of a SOAP message. Although the SOAP message is an XML-based data structure it is still capable of transporting both an XML encoded Service message as a child of the Body element and an UA Binary encoded message using Base64 encoding rules. Common structures and exchange patterns for SOAP messages used for OPC UA purposes are defined in [W3C07a] and [W3C07b].

```
<?xml version="1.0"?>
<s:Envelope xmlns:s="http://www.w3.org/2001/12/soap-envelope">
    <s:Header>
    </s:Header>
    <s:Body>
    <!-- Either XML encoded
         or UA Binary encoded service message -->
    </s:Body>
</s:Envelope>
```

**Fig. 6.7** Structure of a SOAP message

As mentioned above HTTP is used for transporting the SOAP messages. This is done by transmitting the OPC UA Service requests embedded in SOAP requests in the body of HTTP POST requests and the OPC UA Service responses the same way in HTTP POST responses. HTTPS which uses TLS for securing the exchanged HTTP data can also be used. However, when already applying one of the above introduced Secure Channels this is an unnecessary overhead. Furthermore, TLS is not meeting all the requirements of OPC UA. But in some scenarios in where not all OPC UA requirements are needed it can make sense to disable UA security and use HTTP over TLS instead.


## 6.5   Available Mapping Implementations

Implementing a protocol stack for OPC UA is admittedly not an easy task and requires a lot of time. But it is not expected that everyone develops its own stack. An OPC UA stack is a generic component that can be used for a diverse range of applications and therefore many vendors can use the same stack and build their applications on top of it. To ensure interoperability on the stack layer and in order to verify the defined mappings the OPC Foundation decided to develop stacks implementing the specified mappings.

Currently there are two stacks available: one implemented in C# and another one in ANSI C which are both part of the UA SDK provided by the OPC Foundation. The C# stack implements all mappings described above. However, the ANSI C stack currently provides UA Binary, UA-SecureConversation, and UA TCP as mapping implementations. A JAVA stack implementation was under development during the time this book was written.

In addition, it is possible generating your own stack for SOAP/HTTP using the WSDL provided by the OPC Foundation.

## 6.6   Summary

### 6.6.1 Key Messages

OPC UA is open to future technologies since it defines abstract concepts and services which are then mapped to different concrete technologies. This allows adding additional mappings to technologies coming up in the future.

A set of various mappings are already provided for the Transport Layer, the Security Layer, and for the Encoding Layer representing the protocol stack of an OPC UA application. A technological mapping of interfaces or applications using the stack is not in the scope of the OPC UA standard.

For the Encoding Layer there are two mappings defined: UA Binary and XML. UA Binary is a fast and efficient encoding tailored for applications running at the Control Level or below (e.g., on the controller) of the automation pyramid whereas the XML provides a flexible and interoperable encoding for applications running at Operations Level or above (e.g., MES, ERP connectivity).

OPC UA defines also two Security Layer mappings: WS-SecureConversation and UA-SecureConversation. WS-SecureConversation is a security protocol speci-fied by OASIS in order to secure XML-based messages exchanged via Web Services. For example MS Windows Communication Foundation is implementing this standard. UA-SecureConversation is not a new protocol but combination of approved techniques and mechanisms of WS-SecureConversation and TLS. This adaptation has to be done, since the actual TLS standard as well as current imple-mentations do not completely meet the requirements of OPC UA. However, this does not mean that future versions of TLS will not be a possible Security Layer mapping of OPC UA.

At the lowest layer – the Transport Layer – OPC UA specifies two transport mechanisms which are namely UA TCP and SOAP/HTTP. UA TCP is a simple protocol on top of TCP providing special mechanisms required by OPC UA such as a special error recovery allowing the OPC UA Sessions to survive from network interruptions. The widely accepted standards SOAP/HTTP are used to provide a firewall-friendly mechanism for OPC UA applications in order to communicate over the Internet with Web Services.

Since implementing all these layers is a lot of work and in order to help appli-cation developers developing OPC UA applications the OPC Foundation provides a set of OPC UA standard deliverables already implementing all the defined mappings. The standard deliverables are offered in the OPC UA SDK of the OPC Foundation which is freely available for members of the OPC Foundation.

## 6.6.2 Where to Find More Information?

All defined mappings are specified in [UA Part 6], whereas the abstract OPC UA Services are defined in [UA Part 4]. More information about XML schemas as a possible Data Encoding for OPC UA can be found at [W3C04a] and [W3C04b]. The specification of WS-SecureConversation is provided at [OASIS07]. The specifications to be supported in order to implement SOAP/HTTP can be found at [W3C07a] and [W3C07b].

## 6.6.3 What's Next?

Chapter 7 is about how OPC UA applications can be secured. Thereby the security concepts of OPC UA are presented and also concepts that are not specified by the OPC UA standard but necessary for running OPC UA applications such as Public Key Infrastructures.

# 7 Security

## 7.1 Why is Security so Important?

The topic "security" gained a lot in importance in the automation domain in the past years although it is still very controversially discussed.

In the IT world, this topic has already been very important for a long time caused by many publications and articles about security incidents of hackers that tried to intrude into systems of banks or credit card organizations. IT-administrators feared that the same could happen to their system and CEOs feared that the customers would not trust the company anymore. Therefore companies decided to invest more money in security measures to resist those attackers. Soon people realized that not only banks and credit card organizations were affected but also any organization that is somehow dependent on distributed IT systems was affected. Excellent examples for that can be found in the field of industrial automation. Today's production processes of manufacturing companies are mostly based on IT systems. Production requests are initiated by Enterprise Resource Planning (ERP) systems, the execution of the process is managed by Manufacturing Execution Systems (MES), special HMIs used to for supervisory of the process, and the documentation of results, quality, and resource consumption are highly dependent on IT systems. And most of these systems do not act in an isolated environment anymore but have interconnections with systems from other areas within a plant, other sites of an organization or even from other organizations (e.g., supply chain). There are companies that have sites all around the world that are interconnected over the Internet. A security incident in such organizations could cause more than only a financial damage. Attacks on a chemical plant for example could also harm the environment and humans as well, which makes it to an attractive target for sabotage and terroristic activities.

But how much security is necessary? This is the controversially discussed aspect of security. Some may state that security is not needed at all because their automation solution acts in an isolated environment, some others would like to secure any part of the system. A realistic answer to this question is that the appropriate level of security depends on many different factors like the concrete target environment, the asset to be protected, and also restrictions by regulation bodies. This means that it has somehow to be investigated how much security a system really needs. There are approved methods and tools available which can be used to simplify this investigation. One of the most important methods is a systematic security assessment which is described in the Sect. 7.4. Once the necessary level of security is identified a security model can be developed in order to integrate security into the system in a proper way. Section 7.5 describes the abstract security model for OPC UA applications integrating measures identified in a security assessment for OPC UA environments described in Sect. 7.4.2. Besides the abstract model, also concrete

W. Mahnke et al., *OPC Unified Architecture*,
DOI: 10.1007/978-3-540-68899-0_7, © Springer-Verlag Berlin Heidelberg 2009

technologies used for the implementation are important to the security of a system. The OPC UA Security implementations are based on certificates managed by Public Key Infrastructures (PKIs). Therefore, Sects. 7.6 and 7.7 point out how these technologies are used for securing OPC UA applications. Finally, Sect. 7.8 gives a summary of security in the context of OPC UA.

## 7.2    Organizational Perspective of Security

Most people think about technical measures like firewalls when they first hear the term security and do not realize that it has also an organizational nature which is quite important to think about and to address in operational environments. However, OPC UA does not specify anything in that area since there are lots of other standards and guidelines mainly dealing with security from the management perspective. Therefore, this chapter only mentions some important aspects and refers to some sources that discuss that topic in more detail.

Organizational security is about how humans deal with security instead of how computers and applications deal with security (which is discussed in Sect. 7.3). Obviously humans do not behave and work like computers since the way they work and act is influenced by feelings, motivation, background, and other social factors. An application can be forced to behave in a special way but this would not work in all cases with humans. For example, if data is encrypted with a certain tool then you can be pretty sure that this tool will not show the plain text to anybody that does not know the correct password (assuming that the tool behaves correctly). But can you be sure that if you tell an employee a password that he will keep it for himself? Or that he will not write it on a piece of paper and place it directly next to the computer as a reminder?

There are a lot of different organizational measures that can be introduced in order to address this and similar problems. At this point only two aspects will be briefly discussed: awareness and responsibilities.

Many people are often not aware of the potential threats at their workplace and the impacts on the organization they work for. Often they do not realize when something is going wrong. Opening an email attachment from an unknown sender is quite risky. There are attachments containing malicious code that can interrupt running production processes when it is executed. Some may argue that in the automation network no emails are allowed and that it is isolated from the office network. But in reality this isolation often does not exist anymore. Enterprise application such as ERP systems from the office network are tightly integrated in the production process. Such incidents can be avoided if an employee knows about the risks and the threats at his workplace and knows about proper measures learned in special trainings. Another problem comes up with the occurrence of anomalies in a system. Let us assume an operator of a production system realizes that the CPU load of his workstation is unusually high but after half an hour it returns to its usual load again. The most often reaction is that he is doing nothing although this could mean that a malicious application is spying on the process and sending the recorded data to a person outside the company. The operator ignores the incident because he does not know what it is and also does not know what to do. A good measure to address this is to define clear responsibilities and duties for such incidents. The operator should know that he has to contact the responsible security team (which can be represented by the system administrator in smaller environments) of the company. The security team should inform the production manager, investigate and identify the problem, and solve the problem.

These are just two typical scenarios the organizational security is dealing with. A broader and more detailed view on organizational security problems and measures can be found in [ISA99].

## 7.3   Technical Perspective of Security

Besides the organizational perspective of security there is the more common technical perspective which more people are aware of. Technical security is about how systems and their infrastructures (e.g., software, computers, devices, and network) can be protected with technical measures. Security measures can thereby be introduced in different phases of a system's lifecycle. There are also approaches defining security measures for each phase of the development lifecycle like the Security Development Lifecycle (SDL) [LH05] defined by Microsoft. This is a good approach for assuring products are already secure before they are deployed at the customer's site. But such an overall lifecycle model is neither in the scope of the book nor in the scope of the OPC UA standard. This book focuses on the requirements analysis and design of secure OPC UA applications.

The first security-related task has to be done when collecting requirements for the system to be developed. Thereby security goals have to be defined (as a part of the requirements specification) addressing rules and regulations dictated by companies or regulatory bodies like the Food and Drug Administration (FDA).[1]
In the design phase, there are two tasks that have to be processed regarding security: protecting the application to be developed and protecting its environment. The challenge for both tasks is to find the appropriate level of security since it has impacts on the characteristics of system such as performance and flexibility. Therefore, a tradeoff has to be made between those factors which are commonly investigated in an assessment. The common steps to be performed in such an assessment are described in Sect. 7.4.1. The results of such assessments are lists of security measures that have to be considered in the system design and implemented in the product.

---

[1]The US Food and Drug Administration (FDA) define requirements for companies developing applications for the consumer industry in the United States.

The measures for the first task – protecting the environment of an OPC UA system – very much depend on the concrete environment. If security measures for the network infrastructure are introduced, then these measures have to be integrated into an existing network infrastructure and have thereby also to be conformant with rules and policies of the site. Therefore, it is hard to suggest concrete security measures on that level but generic concepts can be provided. Such a generic concept is the Defense-in-Depth strategy in which multiple layers of defense in networks are defined. For example, different network segments can be protected by firewalls of different vendors which makes it harder for hackers to intrude into the core of the system. A more detailed view on environment protection is provided in [ISA99].

For the second task – protecting the application – the OPC UA working group identified measures as results of a security assessment that are either suggested as good practices in [UA Part 2] or considered in the normative parts of the OPC UA standard. These measures are described in the Sect. 7.5 and 7.6.

## 7.4    Determining the Appropriate Level of Security

### 7.4.1  Security Assessments

As indicated in the previous sections, the appropriate level of security for a system can be identified with the help of a security assessment.

An assessment, in general, is a process with defined goals and steps that have to be accomplished by a defined group of persons. Each step instructs activities and results that have to be achieved in order to proceed to the next step. A security assessment has the goal to identify a useful set of security measures to protect assets[2] of an environment or a system. Standardized security assessments are already processed for a long time in the "Office-IT-World". However, in the automation domain some bigger companies just start to apply standardized assessments such as defined in [ISA99] for automation systems. There are lots of different standards for security assessments that vary in the amount of steps, the kind of activities, or the granularity of security measures but they all have the same basic procedure as described in the following sections.

#### 7.4.1.1    Defining Security Goals

First of all security goals have to be defined. Security goals describe what of an asset has to be protected. In principle, there are three common security goals:

---

[2]An asset can be nearly anything that has to be protected (e.g., information, communication, hardware, and software).

confidentiality, availability, and integrity. Although these terms are quite well-known varying valid definitions can be found in literature [AL02]. However, it is important that everybody that participates in the assessment has the same understanding of these three basic goals. This can be assured if an understandable and accepted definition is written down and distributed among the participants. But obviously three goals are not sufficient to describe what of an asset should be protected. Therefore, further security goals have to be derived from these basic ones, for example auditability or nonrepudiation. In addition, a context in which the derived goals are used has to be defined, for example the auditability of the user authentication and authorization. Higher level security goals are often dictated by common security policies of companies or rules by regulatory bodies.

At the end of this step a list of security goals for a specific asset has to be created to proceed to the next step.

**Common Security Policies vs. OPC UA Security Policies**

The term Security Policy is used in different contexts within this book. A security policy in general is a document written or at least approved by CIO of a company defining how a company deals with different security-related topics.
In OPC UA a Security Policy is a collection of cryptographic algorithms used for securing the connection between OPC UA clients and servers. Section 7.5.4 provides a more detailed description on that.

### 7.4.1.2    Identifying Relevant Threats

In the second step, the assessment team looks for threats that harm the previously defined security goals. Threats can be of technical nature which means that they are based on a technical system like virus or a hacker that uses a computer for his attacks. But threats can also be of nontechnical nature. In such a case, they are more focusing on manipulating or tricking humans. For example, a hacker could personate himself as a service engineer pretending to repair something in a plant but intends to spy on the system. In many cases it is even a mixture of both. The mentioned service engineer does not only want to get access to the system but also tries to infect the plant network with a trojan that eavesdrop the network traffic.

Three good information sources for identifying potential threats are: vulnerability databases, experience of security experts, and former security issues of previous or similar products.

Vulnerability databases are provided via Web sites by special organizations that collect reports of exposures of security flaws and publish them in order to inform the community about these problems. There is the possibility to search threats by keywords which simplifies the process of getting vulnerabilities that are relevant for a specific target environment. The two famous examples for such vulnerability databases are CVE[3] and CERT.[4]

The involvement of security experts in principle is quite efficient since they have a good knowledge and a long experience with a broad range of security attacks and holes. Therefore, they can quickly identify the most important threats by analyzing the specific target environment and suggest countermeasures as well. But there are also some concerns with common "Office-IT" security experts since they often do not have enough domain knowledge and they may judge threats based on "Office-IT" requirements instead of considering the special requirements for automation systems. Particularly because of this circumstance some consulting companies specialized themselves on securing critical environments used in nuclear power plants and factories.

It is also worth looking at problems and security issues of previous versions of the same product or similar products since they could also be relevant for the current one. These issues should be captured in a kind of bug tracking database[5] or documented in a bug report document or at least in the heads of some end-users or system-integrators that can be interviewed.

As a result of this step, a list of threats has to be created whereby each of them harms at least one of the defined security goals defined in the first step.

### 7.4.1.3    Determining Effective Countermeasures

In the final step of the assessment, countermeasures have to be determined against the threats that were identified in the second step. As described previously, threats can be either of technical or of nontechnical nature – and this is also true for countermeasures. A threat can be mitigated by a technical solution such as an identity management system allowing or denying access to a server room by automatically validating ID-Cards or by a nontechnical solution by security personnel checking employee's ID-Cards. It is also important when processing this assessment phase to realize that there are countermeasures addressing more than one threat and sometimes only several countermeasures together are able to mitigate a threat.

The process of searching countermeasures against specific threats can be very time consuming and therefore it is very helpful to have proper sources. Section 7.4.1.2 mentions some sources for finding threats (vulnerability databases, security consultancy, and experience) and these sources are also interesting for finding counter measures. The vulnerabilities databases for example often give hints and information about advisories, solutions and bug fixes for identified threats.

---

[3]CVE Web site, http://cve.mitre.org/cve/

[4]CERT Web site, http://www.cert.org/advisories/

[5]Bugzilla (http://www.bugzilla.org/) for example is useful open source tool that can be used.

At the end a list of countermeasures has to be generated in a way that for each relevant threat at least one countermeasure is identified. If there is more than one countermeasure for one threat, then a decision has to be made based on defined requirements. Thereby kind and priority of requirements can vary from company to company but most common ones are:

- Effectiveness
- Implementation efforts
- Maintenance
- Usability
- Compliance.

The resulting list of countermeasures after the decision finally represents the definition of the appropriate level of security for the investigated target environment and has to be implemented in the product.

## 7.4.2 The OPC UA Security Assessment

Section 7.4.1 describes what security assessments are and how they are processed for automation solutions in general. Such a security assessment has been processed for OPC UA applications by the OPC UA working group and the results are captured in [UA Part 2] which is an informative part of the OPC UA specification. This part gives also a common understanding of important security terms that are used within this part of the specification and also in other parts. Particularly for the security goals there are various interpretations even among security experts and therefore it is important to commit to one definition that is used throughout the different parts of the OPC UA specification.

A further security assessment on OPC UA [Pet08] has been done by Digital Bond, a company specializing on securing critical infrastructures.

## 7.5    The OPC UA Security Model

### 7.5.1 Security Architecture

#### 7.5.1.1    Environment

OPC UA applications will run in varying environments with different security requirements, threats, and security policies. Figure 7.1 shows an example of how OPC UA applications can be deployed. In this example, OPC.UA is applied at different levels of the automation pyramid which is reflected by the different network segments indicated in the example below.

At the plant floor level an OPC UA server can run in the controllers providing data from field devices to OPC UA clients. Another OPC UA server can be used for gathering data from controllers which is handled by a field engineer working with an OPC UA engineering client. Furthermore an OPC UA server could even run in the controller providing data changes to clients (e.g., HMIs).

On top of the plant floor at operations level an OPC UA application is acting as a client and a server at the same time. It could be the client collecting data from the server running at the lower level and performs special calculations, generates alarms, historizes data, or performs operations whereby the results are presented to other OPC UA clients. A good example for that are applications monitoring the state of the production process.

At the very top level which is represented by the corporate network an OPC UA client integrated in an ERP system could obtain information about the working hours of used devices in the plant floor and if necessary automatically create a maintenance request.

In addition to that the corporate network layer could allow remote access via Internet to OPC UA servers in order to perform service or maintenance tasks.

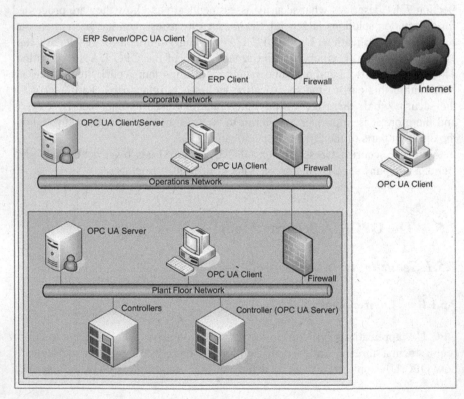

**Fig. 7.1** OPC UA environment

The example scenario above shows that OPC UA can be used at various places and for different purposes within the same environment. The security requirements for these applications may also differ in various ways. The tradeoff between security and performance is a good example. At the very top level security might be more important than performance since this network is connected to the Internet. At the very bottom level the requirements could be completely different: performance could be more important than security when data has to be acquired in very fast and efficient way in order to control a production process.

Therefore, OPC UA has to provide a flexible security model that allows OPC UA applications to be run at different levels in the automation pyramid and at same time meeting the security requirements for each environment. This model is described in the following sections.

### 7.5.1.2    Architecture

The OPC UA security architecture is described in [UA Part 2] and defines a layered approach in which each layer has specific responsibilities regarding security. The security architecture is depicted in Fig. 7.2.

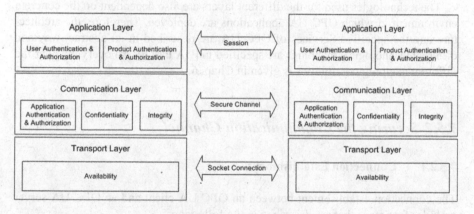

**Fig. 7.2** OPC UA security architecture

The application layer at the very top of the figure is used for transmitting plant information, settings, instructions, and real-time related data from devices between a client and a server in a Session. A Session is used for authenticating and authorizing users working with the client (Sect. 7.5.3.4) as well as for authenticating and authorizing certain products (Sect. 7.5.3.3). The mechanisms for both authorization and authentication mechanisms are addressed by the OPC UA Session Services specified in [UA Part 4] and described in Chap. 5.

An OPC UA Session runs on top of a Secure Channel which is in the responsibility of the communication layer. The Secure Channel secures data exchanged in a session in several ways: first of all it maintains the integrity by applying digital signatures and confidentiality by encrypting sensitive information of the transmitted messages. Furthermore OPC UA introduces the concept of application authentication and authorization which allows applications to identify other applications. This concept is based on the usage of special X.509 certificates in conjunction with the OPC UA Secure Channel Services and is described in sects. 7.5.2 and 7.6.2. The Secure Channel Services are also specified in [UA Part 4].

Both application and communication layer rely on a special infrastructure for managing certificates that are used for securing the application. On the one hand a technical infrastructure is needed for example in order to create such certificates and on the other hand an organizational infrastructure is needed for verifying to whom such certificates are provided. The OPC UA standard does not specify how such an infrastructure looks like since there are many different concepts that all depend on the concrete environments and requirements. Therefore Sect. 7.7 describes some general concepts and use cases as well as some hints for applying them in the industrial automation domain.

At the very bottom the transport layer is responsible for transmitting and receiving the secured data through a socket connection. Here mechanisms for error recovery have to be applied in order to maintain the availability of the system which can be threatened by special attacks such as Denial-of-Service.[6]

The technologies used for the different layers are also dependent on the concrete environment in which OPC UA applications are deployed. Therefore, the architecture and the specified Services of OPC UA are described in an abstract way and different technological mappings are specified in [UA Part 6]. An overview over the different mapping possibilities is given in Chap. 6.

## 7.5.2 Securing the Communication Channel

### 7.5.2.1    Connection Establishment

The connection establishment between an OPC UA client and an OPC UA server includes four steps that are described in the following.

In the first step, an OPC UA client informs itself about the different configuration options of how a connection to the server can be established. If the application is preconfigured and already knows how to connect to the server then this step can be skipped. If the OPC UA client is not preconfigured, it sends an unsecured GetEndpoints request to the Discovery Endpoint of the server in order to obtain the descriptions of the existing Session Endpoints including the security configuration

---

[6]A Denial-of-Service attack prevents authorized access of a resource or a function of a system. A typical example for such an attack is overloading a server by sending a huge amount of messages in a very short period of time which is called as message flooding.

which contains for example the supported Security Policies (Sect. 7.5.4), the Security Modes, User Token Policies and the server's Application Instance Certificate (Sect. 7.6.2.1). This Discovery Endpoint is either well-known or the location information is retrieved by further discovery mechanisms like those described in Chap. 5 and 9 and is specified in [UA Part 12]. As soon as the client receives the response with the desired information, it selects a Session Endpoint with a special security configuration that it can handle and validates the Application Instance Certificate of the server. This is done by requesting the validity status from its associated Validation Authority (VA) which can be for example a local crypto component (e.g., OpenSSL or Microsoft crypto library) or a central service that is consumed for that purpose.

If the certificate is considered as trustworthy, then as the second step an Open-SecureChannel request secured in accordance to the Security Policy and the Security Mode is sent to the selected Session Endpoint of the server. The Security Mode has thereby three possible states: "None", "Sign", and "SignAndEncrypt". If "None" is selected, then the OpenSecureChannel message will not be secured. When "Sign" is chosen then the message is signed with the associated Private Key of the Application Instance Certificate of the OPC UA client. Signing messages allows detecting whether a received message has been manipulated by an untrusted third party. If "SignAndEncrypt" is used, then the message is additionally encrypted with the Public Key of the server's Application Instance Certificate. Encrypting messages prevents or at least makes it very difficult for untrusted third parties to read the content of messages exchanged between two applications. The Security Policy defines thereby which algorithm to choose for signing and encrypting the message. Once the secured message is received by the server it first validates the client's Application Instance Certificate by requesting its VA. The certificate is provided in an unencrypted part of the message and can thereby be read by the server. If the certificate is trustworthy by the server, then the message has to be interpreted according to the Security Policy and the Security Mode. This means the message is decrypted with the associated Private Key of the server's Application Instance Certificate and the signature of the message is verified with the Public Key of the client's Application Instance Certificate. The server sends back the response to this request which is similarly secured. Therefore, the same checks on the message and the server certificate are performed on the client side. The establishment of the Secure Channel is mainly used for exchanging special secret information between clients and servers. This secret is used for deriving Symmetric Keys used for encrypting and signing all further messages instead of using the Public Key Cryptography operations with Asymmetric Keys which are more CPU-intensive. Figure 7.3 illustrates how these secrets are exchanged and used for deriving a Symmetric Key.

If these keys are derived on both client- and server-side then the Secure Channel is established. However, such a Secure Channel has also a finite lifetime. After this lifetime has expired a renewal of this channel has to be initiated. Thereby the same steps have to be processed again in order to derive new Symmetric Keys.

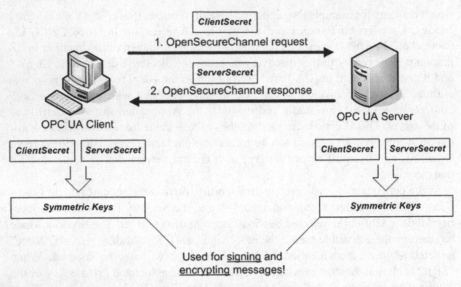

**Fig. 7.3** Creating Symmetric Keys

This is an additional security measure in order to resist long-term attacks on the Secure Channel. But this renewal process is transparent to the Session that is created on top of a Secure Channel. This means that the Session is not affected and remains the same (Fig. 7.4).

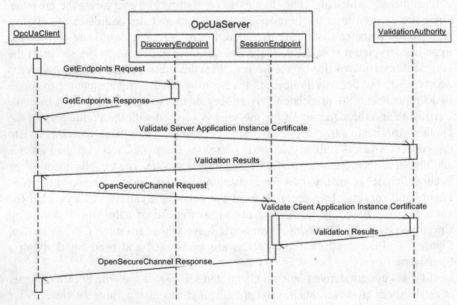

**Fig. 7.4** Creating an OPC UA Secure Channel

The third step is to create a Session on top of the previously established Secure Channel. Therefore, a CreateSession request is sent to the server. This message is secured according to the Security Mode and Security Policy agreed upon for the connection. However, as indicated previously the derived Symmetric Keys are used instead of the Public and Private Keys of the client and the server. In the response to this request the server provides its Software Certificates (Sect. 7.6.2.2) to the client in order to prove its functional capabilities and to prove with challenge–response-test the possession of the certificate used for creating the underlying Secure Channel. Therefore, a nonce is sent with the request which has to be signed with the server's private key. As soon as the client receives and interprets the response it validates the server's Software Certificates. Furthermore it verifies whether the server passed the challenge–response-test by verifying the signed nonce. If the certificates are trusted by the client, the server provides the needed capabilities and proved that it possesses the correct certificate then it proceeds to the fourth and last step.

Before the created Session can be used by the client and the server it has to be activated. This is done by sending an ActivateSession request to the server including the credentials of the current user together with the Software Certificates of the client. One reason for separating the Session establishment in CreateSession and ActivateSession is that it has to be ensured that user credentials are sent to the same server that was used to establish the Secure Channel. This is verified in the CreateSession Service with several checks described above. The ActivateSession Service is mainly for providing the user credentials. Once the request is received

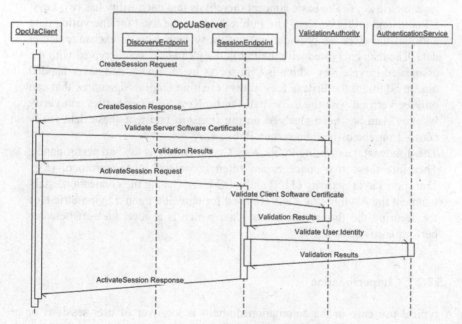

**Fig. 7.5** Establishing an OPC UA Session

by the server it validates the Software Certificates of the client and in addition it validates the user credentials. However, the user credentials can be of different types which imply also different validation mechanisms. The user credentials could be represented by an X.509 certificate which means that it is validated by a Validation Authority like it is done with the Application Instance and Software Certificates. In many other cases, the user credentials are provided in the form of a username and password. The validation of this type of credentials very much depends on the concrete application. In the simplest case it is a simple lookup in a user database. After all validation have succeeded a connection between the client and the server is fully established and process data in the server can be accessed by the client (Fig. 7.5).

**Symmetric Keys vs. Asymmetric Keys**

When using Symmetric Keys for encrypting and signing data then the same keys are used for decrypting and verifying the signature of the data. This means that in the client–server scenario both parties have identical keys for certain cryptographic operations. This kind of securing data is very fast and efficient. However, there is a fundamental key distribution problem: How can a secret key be provided to the communication partner in a secure way? There is always the risk that it gets lost, stolen, or is illegitimately handed to other parties.

That problem can be solved by using the Public Key Cryptography with asymmetric keys. The basic concept thereby is that each entity has two keys: a Public and a Private Key. The Public Key can be used for encrypting data and can therefore be provided to any party intending to exchange secret data. The data encrypted with the Public Key can only be decrypted with the associated Private Key which is kept secret by the owner and never handed out. In addition, the Private Key allows creating Digital Signatures that can only be verified with the associated Public Key. So other parties can verify whether data has been changed during transmit and that these data really comes from the owner of a certain Public Key.

The disadvantage of using Public Key Cryptography is the bad performance. Therefore these two concepts are often combined in one protocol (e.g., Transport Layer Security (TLS) and OPC UA). During the connection establishment the Asymmetric Keys are used for agreeing upon a Symmetric Key for securing the further exchanged data which is a good tradeoff between performance and security.

### 7.5.2.2    Impersonation

A typical use case in the automation domain is log-over of user sessions or in other words user impersonation (see Fig. 7.6). In such a scenario a user "A" with specific permissions is connected with his client to a server. Another user "B" would like to overtake the session of user "A" in order to perform special tasks. A practical example is when an operator supervising a production process hands over a shift in plant to another operator. Thereby a log-over procedure has to be performed in which both operators type in their password in the monitoring application (we assume that this application is an OPC UA client) in order to correctly hand over the shift of user "A" to user "B".

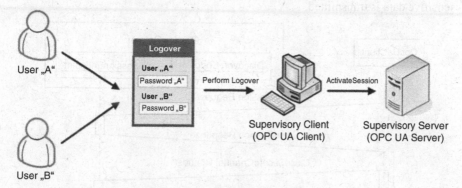

Fig. 7.6 Operator log-over

OPC UA addresses this use case with the ActivateSession Service. Once a Session is already running (Secure Channel and Session is created and activated) a further ActivateSession Request message with the credentials of the new user (in the example above the credentials of the user "B") is sent to the OPC UA server which is shown in Fig. 7.7. The user credentials are validated by an authentication service which could be for example a directory service using LDAP. If the user is authenticated and authorized to overtake the session then the server changes in its local session management the owner of the session and returns a response to the client.

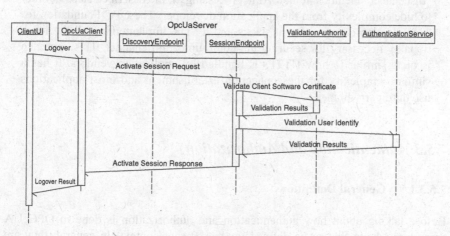

Fig. 7.7 Impersonating a user

### 7.5.2.3    Connection Termination

The whole connection is terminated by exchanging the appropriate closure service messages CloseSession and CloseSecureChannel whose usage is shown in Fig. 7.8. Both closure message types are secured with symmetric keys. However, OPC UA specifies that the CloseSecureChannel messages only have to be signed since no sensitive data is transmitted.

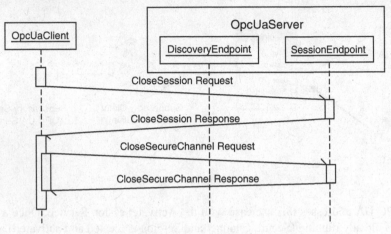

**Fig. 7.8** Terminating an OPC UA connection

**Do I have to implement that all on my own?**

No, note that the connection establishment and termination steps will in most cases be encapsulated by a third-party SDKs offering a "connect" and "disconnect" methods in their APIs processing all the described steps in order to hide complexity from the application developer. The OPC Foundation for example also offers different stacks and a SDK implementing all the functionality necessary for securing the communication channel. This approach is quite similar to how HTTPs is handled by application vendors. It has a similar complexity for the connection establishment and most applications use third party libraries.

## 7.5.3 Authentication and Authorization

### 7.5.3.1    General Definitions

Before talking about how authentication and authorization is done in OPC UA these terms have first to be defined for the present context. In general, they are often considered as the same. However, there are fundamental differences.

Authentication is the process of verifying a claim made by an entity (e.g., person, computer, and certificate). For example a person claims to be operator "A" of a system. The system is verifying that by checking the user name and password provided during the log-in process. If the user is found in the user database and the provided password is correct then the person is identified and therefore authenticated. In another example a certificate (Sect. 7.6) sent to an entity "A" (e.g., a person or an application) contains the claim that the embedded public key belongs to another entity "B". Authentication in this case could be done by verifying whether entity "A" has the private key associated to the embedded public key. A typical mechanism for verifying that is a so-called challenge–response-test. Entity "B" sends entity "A" data to be signed as the challenge. Once entity "B" has signed the data with its private key and sent it back in a response entity "A" can verify the signature of the data with the public key of the provided certificate and confirm the claim.

Authorization is the process of verifying whether an authenticated entity has the permission to perform a special task. For example, user "A" is authenticated since he provided the correct user name and password. But it has still to be verified whether he is allowed to access certain data. Typically he is not allowed to increase his salary in a financial system of an organization.

### 7.5.3.2   Application Authentication and Authorization

Application authentication and authorization means that in the present context an OPC UA server can verify that an Application Instance Certificate belongs to a

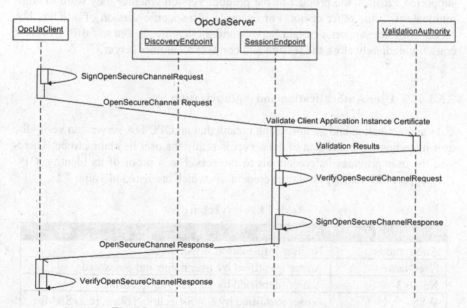

**Fig. 7.9** Application authentication and authorization

certain OPC UA client and can therefore allow the client to establish a Secure Channel and vice-versa. A mutual challenge–response-test is inherently performed in the OPC UA communication protocol when establishing a Secure Channel with the SecurityMode "Sign" or "SignAndEncrpyt" (see Sect. 7.5.2.1) between the client and the server. Figure 7.9 shows how the application authentication process is performed. On the one hand the client proves the possession of the private key associated with its Application Instance Certificate by signing the OpenSecure-Channel request and the server can verify the signed request with the public key of the client's certificate. On the other hand the server signs the response to the OpenSecureChannel request with its private key so that the client can verify whether the certificate received from the server is evidently the server's certificate.

### 7.5.3.3    Product Authentication and Authorization

Products or specific versions of products can also be authenticated and authorized by applications since they have also special certificates associated. When a certain version of a product gets certified by a Certification Authority (CA) of a test lab it obtains Software Certificates (see Sect. 7.6.2.2) containing the test results in terms of tested Profiles (see Sect. 7.5.4).

Software Certificates are exchanged during the session establishment: in the CreateSession response the server provides its certificates to the client and in the ActivateSession request the clients provides its certificates to the server. Both the client and the server validate the Software Certificates and decide based on the supported Profiles, the product or the product version whether they want to communicate with the other or not. For example if a specific version of an OPC UA server does not support a certain Service and a client needs that to fulfill its task it could immediately close the session and connect to another server.

### 7.5.3.4    User Authentication and Authorization

User authentication and authorization means that an OPC UA server can verify the user intending to access data of the server is really the user he claims to be. Therefore the user provides its credentials to the server as a proof of its identity. OPC UA support different types of user credentials which are listed in Table 7.1.

Table 7.1 IdentityToken types

| Symbolic ID | Description |
| --- | --- |
| Anonymous | No user information is available |
| UserName | A user identified by user name and password |
| X509v3 | A user identified by an X509v3 Certificate |
| WSS | A user identified by a WS-SecurityToken. (e.g. SAML, Kerberos-Ticket) |

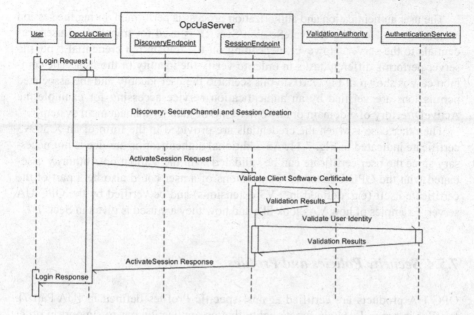

**Fig. 7.10** User authentication and authorization – general

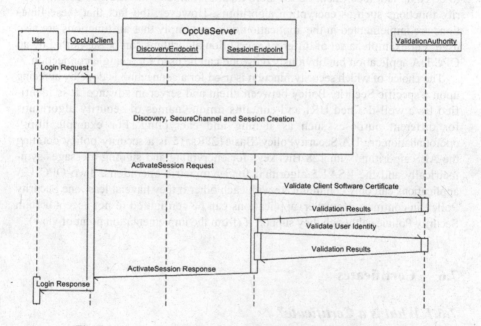

**Fig. 7.11** User authentication and authorization with X.509 certificates

The user authentication and authorization process is performed during the session establishment. Here the ActivateSession Service is used for transferring user credentials to the server. However, depending on the transferred credential type, the server performs different tasks in order to verify the identity of the user. The common case is shown in Fig. 7.10. In this scenario the user identity and the associated permissions are verified by an authentication service accessing for example the ActiveDirectory of a domain or any other kind of identity management system.

The other case is when the credentials are provided in the form of an X.509v3 certificate indicated in Fig. 7.11. An additional authentication service is not necessary since the user certificate can be validated with the Validation Authority associated with the OPC UA server. Permissions of a user could also be a part of the certificate itself (e.g. defined in a V3 extensions) and be verified by the OPC UA server. Examples of how VAs look like and how they are used is given in Sect. 7.7.

### 7.5.4 Security Policies and Profiles

OPC UA products are certified against specific Profiles defined in [UA Part 7]. Profiles in general contain functionality that an application has to support in order to be compliant (see Chap. 12 for more details). Some of the Profiles define security functions such as encryption algorithms. However, the fact that these functions are implemented in the application does not imply that all functions are also used. For example, a set of different encryption algorithms can be supported by an OPC UA application but obviously only one can be used for a single connection.

The choice of which security function is used for a connection is done by agreeing upon a specific Security Policy between client and server in advance. It is identified by a well-defined URI and contains unique names of security algorithms for different purposes such as signing and encrypting. For example http://opcfoundation.org/UA/SecurityPolicy#Basic128Rsa15 is a security policy defining the AES algorithm with 128 Bits keys for encrypting and signing messages symmetrically and the RSA1.5 algorithm for asymmetric operations. Two OPC UA applications can only communicate with each other if they have at least one Security Policy in common. However, applications can be configured to not accept certain Security Policies although they support it (from the implementation point of view).

## 7.6    Certificates

### 7.6.1 What is a Certificate?

Before talking about how to manage certificates it has to be made clear what in the certificates are in the context of OPC UA are.

A certificate in general is an official document affirming some fact. In OPC UA we are talking about so-called digital certificates. These are electronic documents containing different information affirmed by a trusted third party. In principle, certificates are used for distributing public keys of a public/private key pair used for Public Key Cryptography among entities that are using them for different purposes, for example for encrypting data. Public Key Cryptography is quite complicated and a big topic which is not described very detailed in this book. A detailed description is provided in [SF03] and [AL02]. Two main goals are followed with digital certificates: the first is to bind special information and a public key to a specific owner that the receiver of certificate can identify the owner. And the second goal is to ensure the integrity of the public key and the associated data in order to detect manipulations of the certificate by third-parties. When discussing the concepts of a digital certificate it is important to recognize that there are different types and formats like X.509v3 certificates, Simple Public Key Infrastructure (SPKI) certificates, Pretty Good Privacy (PGP) certificates and Attribute certificates. OPC UA focuses on the usage of X.509v3 certificates which is the most common type.

**Table 7.2** Content of a X.509 certificate

| Field | Description |
|---|---|
| Version | Describes the version of the certificate which can be 1, 2, or 3 For OPC UA purposes this should always be 3 |
| Serial Number | Must be positive integer identifying a certificate issued by a particular CA and must therefore be unique in his scope |
| Signature Algorithm | Contains the identifier of the signature algorithm used by the CA for signing this certificate |
| Issuer | Identifies the CA who issued and signed the certificate. The identifier of the CA is represented by a distinguished name (DN) |
| Valid From | The date when the validation period of the certificate begins |
| Valid To | The date when the validation period of the certificate ends |
| Subject | The identifier of the entity that owns the certificate represented with a distinguished name (DN). A V3 extension may also provide an alternative name (subjectAlternativeName) for this entity which may provide addition information or is simply more readable for humans |
| Public Key | Contains the identifier for the type of the public key of the subject as well as the key itself |
| <Extensions> | Extensions are only available when using V3 of X.509 certificates. Standardized extensions are for example Key Usage, Certificate Policies, Subject Alternative Name, and CRL Distribution Point |
| Signature | Contains the digital signature created by the issuer in order to sign the certificate |

X.509v3 is a standard format specified in [HPF+02]. Table 7.2 lists and describes the common content of such a certificate. The main advantage of X.509v3 is that it is extendable which means that additional fields can be added in a well-defined way. Common product-specific extensions like "Subject Alternative Name" or "Enhanced Key Usage" provide additional or more precise information about the embedded public key. Even OPC UA makes use of this concept and defines an addition extension for its Software Certificates which are explained in Sect. 7.6.2.2.

Certificates can be further classified in self-signed and signed by trusted Certification Authority. When the private key associated to the public key of the new certificate is used to sign the certificate (i.e., to generate the signature) then this is called a self-signed certificate. This means the entity generating the certificate is its own Certification Authority (see left side in Fig. 7.12). However, when another entity uses its private key to sign the certificate then it is trusted by a Certification Authority (see right side in Fig. 7.12).

The lifecycle of certificates is managed by a Public Key Infrastructure which is described in Sect. 7.7.

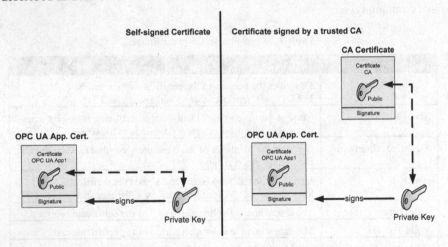

**Fig. 7.12** Self-signed vs. signed by a trusted CA

## 7.6.2 OPC UA Certificates

OPC UA applications use three kinds of X.509 certificates for the connection establishment (see Sect. 7.5.2.1). The different certificate types are described in the following sections.

### 7.6.2.1    OPC UA Application Instance Certificates

Each installation of an OPC UA product requires an X.509v3 certificate named as Application Instance Certificate. Table 7.3 shows the content of an Application

Instance Certificate specified in [UA Part 6] whereby the structure is compliant to [HPF+02]. This certificate identifies a running instance of an OPC UA application on a host and is obtained from either a trusted private or public CA responsible for the concrete environment.

Table 7.3 Fields of an Application Instance Certificate

| Field | Description |
|---|---|
| Version | Shall be "V3" |
| Serial Number | The serial number assigned by the issuer |
| Signature Algorithm | The algorithm used to sign the Certificate |
| Issuer | The distinguished name of the Certificate used to create the signature |
| | The issuer field is completely described in [HPF+02] |
| Valid From | The date when the validation period of the certificate begins |
| Valid To | The date when the validation period of the certificate ends |
| Subject | The distinguished name of the application instance |
| | The Common Name attribute shall be specified and should be the productName or a suitable equivalent. The Organization Name attribute shall be the name of the Organization that executes the application instance. This organization is usually not the vendor of the application |
| | Other attributes may be specified |
| | The subject field is completely described in [HPF+02] |
| Public Key | The public key associated with the Certificate |
| SubjectAltName (Ext) | The alternate names for the application instance |
| | Shall include a uniformResourceIdentifier which is equal to the applicationUri |
| | Servers shall specify a dNSName or IPAddress which identifies the machine where the application instance runs. Additional dNSNames may be specified if the machine has multiple names. The IPAddress should not be specified if the Server has dNSName |
| | The subjectAltName field is completely described in [HPF+02] |
| Key Usage (Ext) | Specifies how the certificate key may be used |
| | Shall include digitalSignature, nonRepudiation, keyEncipherment, and dataEncipherment |
| | Other key uses are allowed |
| Extended Key Usage (Ext) | Specifies additional key uses for the Certificate |
| | Shall specify serverAuth and/or clientAuth |
| | Other key uses are allowed |
| Signature | The signature created by the Issuer |

### 7.6.2.2    OPC UA Software Certificates

Another type of X.509v3 certificate used for OPC UA is the Software Certificate which is also compliant to [HPF+02] and specified in [UA Part 6]. Instead of a running instance this certificate identifies a specific version of an OPC UA product. It has an additional v3 extension field containing the tested and passed OPC UA Profiles defined in [UA Part 7] for this product. By exchanging this information during the connection establishment both applications know whether they can communicate with each other in a proper way and which Services they support. This certificate can be obtained by accomplishing the OPC UA certification process[7] of accredited test laboratory.[8] Table 7.4 lists the fields of OPC UA Software Certificates.

**Table 7.4** Software Certificates

| Field | Description |
|---|---|
| Version | Shall be "V3" |
| Serial Number | The serial number assigned by the issuer |
| Signature Algorithm | The algorithm used to sign the Certificate |
| Issuer | The distinguished name of the Certificate used to create the signature |
| | The issuer field is completely described in [HPF+02] |
| Valid From | The date when the validation period of the certificate begins |
| Valid To | The date when the validation period of the certificate ends |
| Subject | The distinguished name of the product |
| | The Common Name attribute shall be the same as the productName in the SoftwareCertificate and the Organization Name attribute shall the vendorName in the SoftwareCertificate |
| | Other attributes may be specified |
| | The subject field is completely described in [HPF+02] |
| Public Key | The public key associated with the Certificate |
| SubjectAltName (Ext) | The alternate names for the product |
| | shall include a "uniformResourceIdentifier" which is equal to the productUri specified in the SoftwareCertificate |
| | The subjectAltName field is completely described in [HPF+02] |
| Key Usage (Ext) | Specifies how the certificate key may be used |
| | Shall include digitalSignature, nonRepudiation, keyEncipherment, and dataEncipherment |
| | Other key uses are allowed |
| Extended Key Usage | Specifies additional key uses for the Certificate |

*(Continued)*

---

[7]OPC Certification Process Web site, http://www.opcfoundation.org/Certification.aspx.

[8]The first accredited OPC Certification Test Lab is operated by ascolab.

| (Ext) | May specify "codeSigning" |
|---|---|
| | Other key usages are not allowed |
| softwareCertificate | The XML encoded form of the SoftwareCertificate stored as UTF8 text |
| | Reference [UA Part 6] describes how to encode a Software-Certificate in XML |
| | The ASN.1 Object Identifier (OID) for this extension is: 1.2.840.113556.1.8000.2264.1.6.1 |
| Signature | The signature created by the Issuer |

### 7.6.2.3 OPC User Certificates

The third type of certificate is the user certificate identifying the current user intending to access the data of the server during the connection establishment (see Sect. 7.5.2.1). However, user certificates are only one possible credential type supported by OPC UA (see Sect. 7.5.3.4 for other types) and therefore not a requirement for applying OPC UA. The content of the fields should be compliant to [HPF+02] in order to be fully interoperable with other OPC UA products.

## 7.7 Public Key Infrastructure for OPC UA

### 7.7.1 What is a PKI?

A Public Key Infrastructure is used for managing Digital Certificates as described in Sect. 7.6. It provides thereby the technical and organizational basis for accomplishing different tasks with certificates. From an abstract point of view a PKI involves several entities with specific roles and duties such as the Registration Authority (RA), the Certification Authority (CA), Validation Authority (VA), and End-Entities (EE). Figure 7.13 shows how these entities are related to each other and in which PKI use cases they are involved in.

An End-Entity (EE) is the user of a certificate and is represented for example by a person, a computer, or an application. For a better understanding EEs in the context of this book are considered to be OPC UA products, installed instances of OPC UA products, or users of OPC UA applications.

A Registration Authority (RA) which can also be an application or a person or both is the direct contact for the EEs regarding questions on certificates. Certification, certificate renewal, and revocation requests are first processed by a RA of a PKI. Thereby he has to identify the requesting EE and verify the provided information. After that the RA forwards the requests to the Certification Authority for further processing.

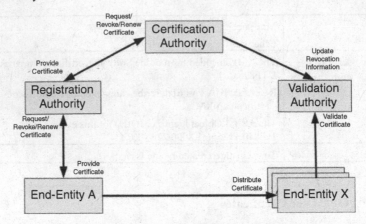

**Fig. 7.13** Entities of a Public Key Infrastructure

The Certification Authority (CA) is the entity (which is mostly a person using special software, but fully automated and rule-based CAs are also possible) that issues, renews, and revokes certificates. In addition to that, it informs other entities like the Validation Authority when certificates are revoked. The RA and CA are often combined together since they have a very strong relation to each other.

The VA is responsible for validating certificates that are provided by EEs in order to verify whether they can trust the certificates or not.

The different approaches for implementing the use cases are described in Sect. 7.7.3.

## 7.7.2 Trust Models

This section describes trust models in general and the different model types. However, it is important to define in advance what trust in the present context means. Adams and Lloyd [AL02] provides the following definition: "trust between two entities in general means that one entity behaves exactly the way another entity expects". This means for the present context that an OPC UA client trusts a CA when the client can assume that the CA will establish and maintain an accurate binding of meta-information and the Public Key. Furthermore an OPC UA client trusts an OPC UA server if the client is convinced that a Public Key contained in the server's certificate really belongs to the OPC UA server. So trust between entities can be established by trusting in the associated certificates. This can be done if the administrator decides that the certificate of the OPC UA server should be trusted and stores it in a database of the OPC UA client containing all the trusted certificates. The OPC UA client now knows that a communication with that certain server can be established since it is trustworthy. Figure 7.14 illustrates the described scenario which is commonly known as a Direct Trust Model.

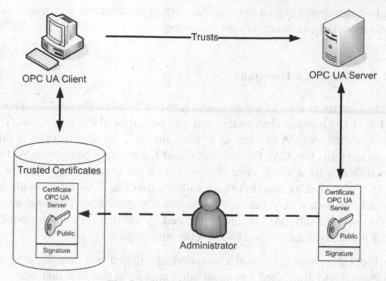

**Fig. 7.14** Establishing Direct Trust

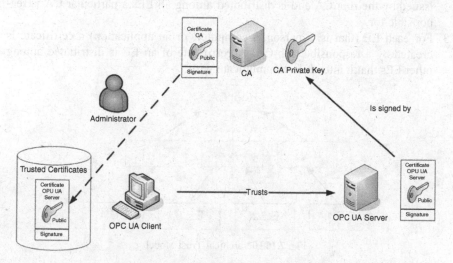

**Fig. 7.15** Establishing Hierarchical Trust

There is also another basic model of how trust can be established. In that model the server certificate is signed by a trusted CA. Instead of the server's certificate the CA's certificate is stored in the client's database. The client trusts the server's certificate since it trusts the CA's certificate which can be seen in Fig. 7.15. This scenario represents a Hierarchical Trust Model.

Trust models show the different trust relationships between entities and provide better understanding and reasoning about the security of the applying system. Therefore, they are used for planning and designing PKIs. The structure of such models varies depending on the requirements of the concrete scenario. Two basic models are briefly introduced in the following.

### 7.7.2.2    Strict CA Hierarchy

The most common form of a trust model is the strict hierarchy of CAs. This model (see Fig. 7.16) is depicted as an inverted tree with special CA as the root. This CA is the so-called root CA and acts as a "trust anchor". All other entities in this trust domain trust this root CA. The root CA could for example be responsible for issuing certificates for a whole organization. For larger organizations that are organized in different units it makes sense to have multiple CAs for example one for each unit. In such a case, the root CA is directly trusted by a defined number of sub-CAs and the sub-CAs are directly trusted by the EEs they are responsible for. Such a hierarchy is established by the following steps:

1. A root CA is established and a so-called self-signed root certificate for the CA is created and distributed among all other entities in this trust domain.
2. A defined number of sub-CAs are established and for each a certificate is issued by the root CA and is distributed among all EEs a particular CA is responsible for.
3. For each EE (that is, a person, a computer, or an application) a certificate is created by a responsible sub-CA. A certificate of an EE is distributed among other EEs that it intends to communicate with.

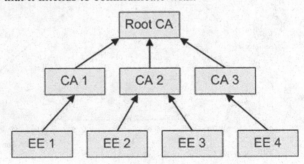

**Fig. 7.16** Hierarchical Trust Model

### 7.7.2.3    User-Centric Trust Model

In a user-centric trust model each user (that is person, computer, or application) is totally responsible for deciding who to trust. Such a decision is made based on different factors such as personal contact, rules or experience. The model of the trust domain results in a full-meshed network of entities with trust relationships (see Fig. 7.17). In principle, there are two approaches leading to such a trust model: by applying Direct Trust and exchanging self-signed certificates or by a Web-of-Trust.

A typical application applying that approach is Pretty Good Privacy (PGP)[9] which builds up a Web-of-trust in which each entity certifies the public key of another entity.

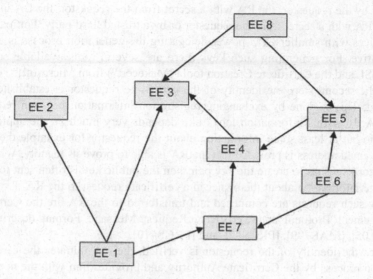

Fig. 7.17 User-Centric Trust Model

## 7.7.3 Certificate Lifecycle Management

In the sections before, we described how a PKI is established and which roles it involves. We also pointed out that PKIs are used for managing certificates which includes use cases like requesting, creating, installing, distributing, revoking, renewing, and validating certificates. This means that certificates are not static objects that are created once and used until a system retires. In other words, certificates have a specific lifecycle that is managed by a PKI. Furthermore, there are different approaches of handling the lifecycle phases. Therefore, in the following sections we will describe and discuss the most important approaches for each phase.

### 7.7.3.1    Request and Create Certificate

The creation of certificates signed by trusted CAs involves in principle four steps:

The first step is to create a Public/Private Key pair. Three important parameters are critical for the security of the keys: the key strength, the algorithm, and the entropy source. Longer keys are more secure but require more time when using them for

---

[9]PGP is a signing and encrypting application used for securing e-mail communication.

example for encrypting data. The most often used Asymmetric Key algorithm is RSA which is part of the Public Key Cryptography Standards (PKCS). Another issue is the location where the keys are generated. The keys can be generated locally by the requestor, the RA with a secret from the requestor, the CA initiated by the RA with a secret from the requestor or by a trusted third-party. For machines or devices with smaller CPU power delegating the generation process is a good alternative. For generating such keys there are several tools available such as OpenSSL and the Certificate Creation tool ("Makecert") from Microsoft.[10]

In the second step, the identity of the certificate requestor is established and verified. This is done by exchanging registration information between requestor and RA. How this information looks like depends very much on the application scenario but at least some information about the requestor for example the name and an email address is provided that the RA is able to prove its identity. When the requestor itself has to create the key pair then the public key is often sent together with the information about the owner in a certificate request to the RA. Examples of how such requests are composed and transferred to the RA are the Certificate Management Protocol and Certificate Request Message Format described in [AFK+05], [MAS+99], [PKCS#7], and [PKCS#10].

Once the identity of the requestor is verified, the RA initiates the certificate creation process by the Certificate Authority and provides him with the necessary data. Thereby the public key, the information about the requestor, and sometimes also some additional proprietary information is signed with the private key of the CA. The signature together with the other information represents the signed certificate that is now trusted by the CA and handed to the certificate requestor.

However, there is also the possibility of generating self-signed certificates. These certificates are not signed by other trusted CAs but with the private key associated with it. Thereby no central CA or RA is needed since the roles are maintained by the entity created the self-signed certificate. It is expected that there will be OPC UA-based products generating such certificates during the setup routine in order to provide a secure out-of-the-box installation. If necessary, this certificate can be replaced by another one signed by a trusted CA.

### 7.7.3.2    Install Certificate

Once the requestor receives the signed certificate from the CA the certificate has to be installed and the associated application has to be configured for using it. Certificates reside in a certificate repository (e.g., certificate store) in which own certificates as well as certificates from third-parties or root certificate are stored. Since it only contains the public key of the key pair putting all these certificates together in one store is not critical to the security of the whole system. In addition to that, the associated application has to know which certificate it should use for

---

[10]This tool is provided with the .NET Framework 2.0 and higher.

cryptographic operations. Therefore, the location in the store of the desired certificate has to be configured. Repositories for certificates can be located on the same machine of the target application or also on a central server which is accessed by the target application.

Besides the certificate containing the public key also the private key has to be installed to a special location. However, this location must only be accessible by the owner of the private key and the access must therefore be secured. However, these locations are mostly on the same machine as the target application or stored on external devices like Smartcards. These locations must be known by the target application as well.

### 7.7.3.3   Distribute Certificate

After the certificate and the private key are installed and the owning target application is configured there must also be the possibility for other applications to retrieve the certificate for performing different cryptographic operations. Basically there are three ways for disseminating a certificate: out-of-band distributions, public repositories, and in-band distributions.

The out-of-band mechanism is for example the manual transportation and installation of certificates by individual users. Thereby a certificate is conveyed via disk or some other storage mediums to each target device, imported into the local repository and the application is configured accordingly. Another example is sending the certificates via email and installing it manually like it is done with Pretty Good Privacy (PGP).[11] One problem with such out-of-band mechanisms is that they do not scale very well. The manual transportation and installation of certificates on hundreds or thousands devices might take a long time until the whole system is ready to operate. Another problem is that such an approach is quite unreliable. It is not assured that certificates that are manually distributed or via email are not revoked or compromised. On the other hand it is also not ensured that every device receives or imports the certificate into the local repository. So this approach might be a quick and easy approach for small environment but comes up with several problems when applying it to bigger environments.

The second dissemination mechanism is publishing certificates in a central repository. The idea behind that concept is to post certificates in a trusted, widely known, publicly available, and easily accessible location. Whenever a special certificate is needed by an application or a device then this repository is consumed. Typical examples for such repositories are LDAP servers, Web servers, or corporate databases. The advantage of this concept is that the effort for distributing and installing of certificates can be reduced since they are automatically downloaded from the repository by the application when they are needed. In addition, this is also a reliable source for certificates since such repository are mostly controlled

---

[11]PGP Web site, http://www.pgp.com/.

and updated by the CA of the trust domain. One disadvantage of this approach is that it introduces another security risk regarding availability. A Denial-of-Service attack run against the repository can block the whole system. Another issue is that the communication overhead in the network is increased since the devices have to communicate with the repository in addition to its normal application-specific communication. In such cases a repository could also be bottleneck when lots of devices try to access the repository all at once.

And finally, the third approach is the in-band distribution which uses the application-specific communication protocol for exchanging certificates. This is the case with Secure/Multipurpose Internet Mail Extensions (S/MIME), TLS, or OPC UA. The advantage when using such an approach is that no additional channel or protocol has to be provided in order to get the necessary certificates. Channels and protocols that are used anyway can be used for the transportation and installation. This does not necessarily mean that this replaces other approaches like the repository. The use of in-band mechanisms can also supplement a repository when for example different certificates (like the OPC UA Software, User or Application Instance Certificates) are used by the system. One type can be retrieved from the repository; the other one can be provided by the application-specific protocol.

### 7.7.3.4    Validate Certificate

Whenever an application intends to use certificate from another party it has first to validate the certificate. Validation in this context means the process of determining whether a given certificate can be trusted and therefore be used in a given context. A definition of trust and a description of the common trust models are given in Sect. 7.7.2.

The validation process is commonly done with Certificate Path Processing which includes two steps: the path construction and the path validation.

The EE tries to construct the certification path (also called the certification chain) of the certificate in order to aggregate all the certificates for validation step afterwards. Therefore, the CA certificates indicated in the received certificates are searched in the accessible repositories. If not all certificates can be retrieved, then the trustworthiness of the received certificate cannot be fully validated and thus the certificate should not be trusted. However, there are some scenarios in which the user is asked in such a case whether the certificate should be trusted or not. A typical example of such scenarios is a Web browser trying to validate SSL certificates obtained from Web servers.

Once the certificate path is constructed the EE needs verify whether it is valid. If for each certificate in the certification path the following checks succeed, then the certificate can be considered as trustworthy:

- The signature of the certificate can be properly verified
- The certificate is within the specified validation period which is defined in the certificate itself

- The certificate has not been revoked (see Sect. 7.7.3.5 for details)
- The operation that is performed with the certificate is in accordance with the defined purpose, usage, policy, or other rules.

In some special scenarios, there might be some additional checks that have to be passed but the above mentioned are the common ones that are applied in most applications. The order in which these checks are performed is also dependent on the concrete scenario. Some applications are running the less time-consuming operations before the more intensive ones to have a faster response time when a certificate check fails.

### 7.7.3.5   Revoke Certificate and Update Revocation Information

A certificate can be marked as revoked if a further usage has to be prohibited. Reasons for prohibiting the usage depend on many factors. Typical examples are:

- A certificate was renewed or updated before the expiration date is reached
- It is suspected that the certificate or the associated private key is compromised
- The certificate is not needed since for example the using application is not running anymore
- The owner of the certificate has left the company.

Thereby the owner of the certificate or the RA acting on behalf of the owner or an authorized administrator contacts the CA requesting him to revoke a special certificate. This can be done via out-of-band mechanisms like physical presence or telephone or via special communication protocols such as CMP. Once the CA receives the revocation request he marks the certificate as revoked in his repository and informs the VA. The VA provides offline- or online-validation services for end-entities in order to verify whether a specific certificate is revoked.

In the following, one approach for both offline and online certificate validation is introduced. There are a lot of other variations of these concepts that can be applied and are described in detail [AL02].

### Offline Approach

An offline validation is based on publish-subscribe-mechanisms with Certificate Revocation Lists (CRLs). A CRL is a data structure that contains a list of revoked certificates and is signed by the publishing CA. The exact structure and fields of a CRL is defined in [HPF+02]. End-entities like applications or users download these lists typically by using standard protocol like LDAP, FTP, or HTTP from well-known locations. The exact content, the size, and the way how a CRL is processed can vary dependent on the requirements of the concrete target environment.

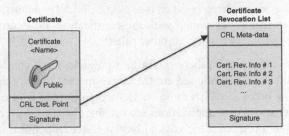

**Fig. 7.18** Complete Certificate Revocation List (CRL)

The simplest approach is always to provide a complete CRL containing revocation information of all revoked certificates in a trust domain like it is shown in Fig. 7.18. However, in some domain the size of the content of the CRL can get large by time and always downloading the full list could lead to unacceptable performance degradation regarding network resources. Another performance bottleneck can be the lifetime of a CRL. Each CRL has like any other certificate a specified time duration in which it is considered as valid and therefore trusted. Specifying a short duration implies an increase of the number of downloads of CRLs whereas a long duration leads to a higher risk of accepting a revoked certificate. Therefore, there are a number of concepts that can be applied in order to make a tradeoff between performance and security.

**Online Approach**

Besides the offline approach of certificate revocation there is also an approach using online mechanisms for retrieving revocation information about certificates. The online approach differ from the offline way in many aspects but the most important is that the EE (i.e., OPC UA user or application) needs to be online whenever a status of a certificate has to be validated. In the present context, online means that the user or the application has to have access to services allowing validating certificates which is provided by a relying third-party. One major standardized online mechanism is the Online Certificate Status Protocol (OCSP).

The OCSP is an online protocol specified by the PKIX group[12] of the IETF and is documented in [MAM+99]. OCSP is a simple request–response protocol that offers an EE to validate whether a number of certificates are revoked or not. Figure. 7.19 shows an example scenario of OCSP. Thereby the request contains information about the certificates that have to be validated like distinguished name of the issuers, hashes of the public keys, and the serial numbers of the certificates. A so-called OCSP responder receives and processes the request. The mentioned responder

---

[12]The PKIX working group was established in 1995 in order to develop Internet standards for PKIs based on X.509. More information about the working group can be found on their Web site (http://www.ietf.org/html.charters/pkix-charter.html).

checks for each certificate indicated in the request whether it is revoked by querying local data sources such as CRLs, revocation databases, or by consuming another OCSP responder. Once the states of all certificates are ascertained a response is sent back to the EE containing the revocation states of the requested certificates.

In order to help the EE to discover the appropriate OCSP responders, a special field of the certificate that has to be validated can be used which is indicated in Fig. 7.19. Typically URLs to the responders and a short description are provided. However, it is important that at least the responses returned by the OCSP responder are digitally signed in order to resist alteration during transit of the messages. This means that the certificate of the OCSP responder has to be obtained and trusted by the EE. But signing messages in general leads to a performance impact that has to be considered when using the protocol. In addition to that, the protocol only provides information about the revocation status which does not necessarily mean that the certificate is valid and can be trusted. Validation periods and proper context have to be validated with other mechanisms.

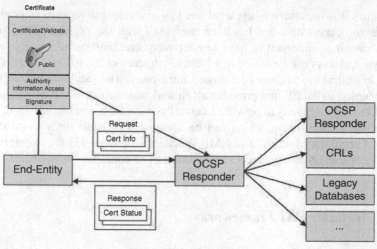

Fig. 7.19 OCSP example

### 7.7.3.6   Renew and Update Certificate

Certificates are created for a specific lifetime also called as validity period. When this lifetime expires then the certificate is considered as invalid since the correspondence of the data in the certificate with the contained public key cannot be ensured anymore. This means a new certificate has to be created at the latest when this lifetime has expired otherwise since the old one is not accepted by other parties anymore. Normally a new certificate is created some time before the old one expires in order to avoid service outages of the applications. In such a case, there are two possibilities to obtain a new certificate: renewing or updating an expired certificate.

Renewing an expired certificate means that the key pair is reused for the new certificate and the associated meta-data like subject name or key usage has not changed. Furthermore the strength of the key still meets the requirements of the environment. Similar to creating a new certificate the owner of the expired certificate requests a new certificate from the RA and provides the existing public key together with the same meta-data and receives a renewed certificate.

Updating an expired certificate means that a new key pair is created since the associated meta-data has changed or the strength of the key does not meet the requirements of the target environment anymore. Updating a certificate is very much like creating a new certificate in many cases since the meta-data will still be the same as in the expired certificate. A typical example of a case when a certificate has to be renewed is when the associated private key got lost.

### 7.7.3.7    Key Recovery

Sometimes it is necessary to use a private key associated to an expired certificate in order to decrypt data that has been encrypted with the expired public key. In such a case it is important to have key recovery mechanisms allowing to access old keys. The keys can be stored in a local key history of the EE and it can also be stored in central key archive of a trusted third-party. The local key history is directly coupled to the EE and provides a fast and easy access to old keys. The idea behind the key archive is to provide a central service for a number of EEs offering key recovery mechanisms which can be coupled with audit trails to satisfy the needs of regulatory bodies. The CMP specified in [AFK+05] for example considers key recovery as a protocol service that can be consumed by the EE.

## 7.7.4 Available PKI Frameworks

This section shows some commercial and noncommercial PKI products and briefly describes some typical examples of how these products can be deployed and used for OPC UA applications.

### 7.7.4.1    OpenSSL PKI

In the first example, OpenSSL [OSSL] is used for implementing a PKI. OpenSSL is an open source toolkit that implements Transport Layer Security (TLS) specified at [DR06] as well as a general purpose cryptographic library. OpenSSL is not intended as a full-featured PKI product for large environments but it provides the necessary functionality for smaller environments to be used as a PKI management tool. Figure 7.20 shows an example of how such a PKI can look like. An administrator acts as the RA and CA for representing the primary interface for all certificate-related

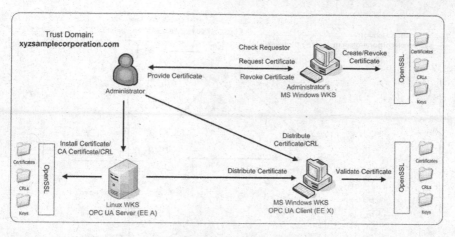

**Fig. 7.20** OpenSSL PKI example

issues. He creates, revokes, and deploys certificates manually with the OpenSSL tool installed on his computer. The OpenSSL tool uses a special directory structure for storing issued certificates, CRLs as well as the Administrator's Private Key. From security perspective it is important to protect these directories in a way that it can only be accessed by the administrator. The VA is represented by the OpenSSL cryptographic library and the OpenSSL PKI directory structure and therefore the OpenSSL toolkit has to be installed on every computer in the trust domain. In order to enable an automated validation of certificates the cryptographic library has to be integrated into the OPC UA application that has to be secured.

### 7.7.4.2    MS Windows Server 2003 PKI

Another example is the PKI [MS03] provided by Microsoft which is tightly integrated in the operating system Windows Server 2003. An example of a deployment scenario in which the MS Windows 2003 Server PKI is used is depicted in Fig. 7.21. The MS Certification Authority Server represents the CA that issues and revokes certificates of the PKI. The RA which registers and validates identities is partly represented by a MS ISS Web-server and by the ActiveDirectory. The pages presented by this Web-server are used for providing identity information which is verified by a Web-application using the ActiveDirectory which is the other part of the RA. The ActiveDirectory is used to validate users and computers submitting a certificate request. The VA used for validating received certificates is represented by a local database (namely the Windows Certificate Store) storing certificates and revocation information used for validating certificates and the Cryptographic Service Provider of the Windows Crypto Library integrated in OPC UA applications.

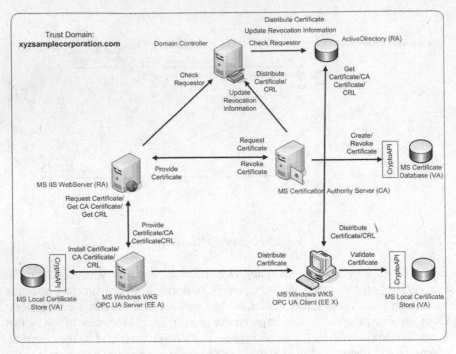

**Fig. 7.21** MS Windows 2003 PKI example

### 7.7.4.3    OpenXPKI

OpenXPKI [OXPKI] is an open source PKI provided by the OpenXPKI Foundation and is running under Apache-style license. The software is implemented in Perl and available for Debian, FreeBSD, and Suse Linux. Depending on its configuration the OpenXPKI software will act as a CA, RA, or EE. This means that on each node in the network the same software is installed and configured for its special role. Figure 7.22 shows an example deployment scenario in which the mentioned PKI is used. The OpenXPKI Server represents both RA and CA and uses MySQL database for storing certificates and revocation information as well as Private Keys. However, also other third-party databases can be used like Oracle, DB2, or Postgresql. An Apache Web-server represents the other part of the RA which provides Web pages allowing submitting certificate requests. Identity information is forwarded to the OpenXPKI Server which either uses internal mechanisms such as a central user database or uses external mechanisms like LDAP or Unix Pluggable Authentication Modules (PAM).[13] In this scenario, the VA is represented by the MySQL databases in conjunction with OpenSSL as the cryptographic toolkit used to validate the certificates. Based on the modular design of OpenXPKI also other cryptographic libraries can be used.

---

[13]PAM is a flexible mechanism for authenticating users in Unix environments.

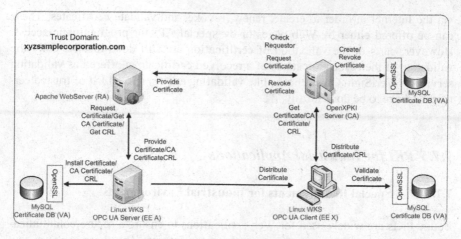

**Fig. 7.22** Linux OpenXPKI example

#### 7.7.4.4    VeriSign Managed PKI Services

The fourth example of a PKI product described in this document is the VeriSign Managed PKI Services.[14] This kind of PKI product differs from the others described before in a very fundamental aspect: the infrastructure is managed by a third party and is therefore a "blackbox" for users, computers, and applications which is shown in Fig. 7.23. They only need to consume special services from VeriSign

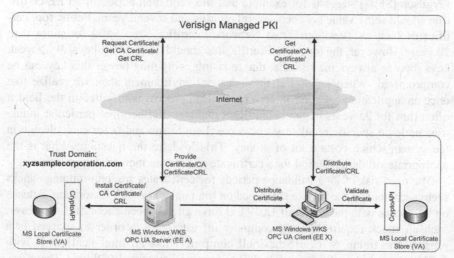

**Fig. 7.23** VeriSign managed PKI example

---

[14]The Web site of VeriSign providing more information about their Managed PKI Service can be found at [VMPKI].

via the Internet in order to create, renew, revoke, and validate certificates. These can be offered either by Web pages or by special API for programmatic access. However, parts of the validation of certification are still done locally. Only the validation of the revocation status of a received certificate is offered as validation service by VeriSign. Other checks like validating against a local list of trusted certificates have to be done locally.

## 7.7.5 PKI for Industrial Applications

### 7.7.5.1    Special Requirements for Industrial Environments

Today PKIs are widely used for Web applications to ensure a secure communication through unsecure environments such as the Internet. But there are very few cases in which PKIs have been used for industrial applications because they have partly different requirements. In the following, the specialties and the main issues are explained and hints for possible solutions are pointed out.

### 7.7.5.2    Certificate Expiration

Each certificate has a specified period of time in which it is considered as valid. If certificates are outside that period then the validation should fail. Schneier and Ferguson [SF03] suggests for example that the validation period of an EE certificate should some value between several months and several years. Public root certificates such as "VeriSign Trust Network" certificate are valid for more than 20 years. However, the long-lived certificates should have strong keys. With weak keys there is always the risk that due to rising computing power this key can be compromised. When looking at the industrial environment then we realize that once an application for controlling a production process is installed in the field it often runs for 25 years without significant changes. Furthermore particular industries underlie specific regulatory that force them to run audits for each change in the system which costs a lot of money. This leads to the question: What is the appropriate validation period for a certificate used by an industrial application?

The main risk of long validation periods for certificates are long-running attacks such as computing the private key based on the public key with factorizing. Attacks on RSA keys with the length of 1,039 bits have already been successful. However, such an attack requires a large computer infrastructure in order to succeed in a proper time frame. With off-the-shelf computers like an Intel Pentium D with 3 GHz it would take 95 years [Con07] to break a key with 1,039 bits! Therefore, one possible solution to the problems discussed earlier in this section is using certificates with strong keys (e.g., 2,048 bits or higher) together with a longer lifetime (e.g., 5–7 years) in order to reduce the number changes in the system. Some time before the existing certificate expires (e.g., 2–3 months) the administrator could be informed by a global OPC UA alarm generated by an OPC UA server. Thereby OPC UA clients subscribe for those special alarms published by an OPC UA server which is shown in Fig. 7.24. If for example the Application Instance Certificate of "OPC UA Client A" expires in 2 months the server generates a global alarm. Both the "Engineering Workplace" and the "Administration Workplace" receive the notification that the certificate will expire soon. The Administrator should now create and install the new certificate before the expiration date is reached.

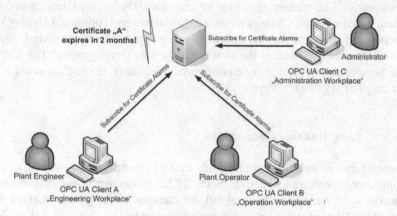

**Fig. 7.24** Certificate alarms

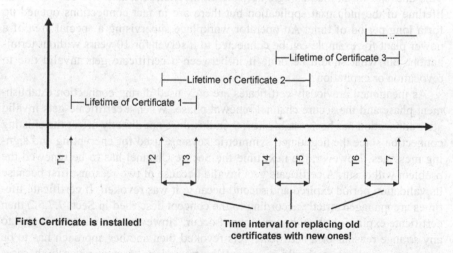

**Fig. 7.25** Managing certificate renewal

For doing that he can choose a proper point of time (e.g., when the plant is in maintenance mode or no production process is running) for installing the certificate and revoke the old one. As long as the old certificate is still in use, the administrator should be regularly reminded. Once the old certificate is replaced by the new one the alarm can be acknowledged. This procedure has to be repeated whenever a certificate is about to expire. This is illustrated in Fig. 7.25. In such a case a certificate has only to be renewed 4–5 times during the lifetime of a plant of 25 years (of course only if no certificate has been revoked meanwhile).

One could argue that using strong keys for signing, encrypting as well as for decrypting and signature verification extremely slows down the system's performance. However, in OPC UA certificates are only used during the connection establishment phase and during the secure channel renewal phase and not for the normal communication like reading or writing process data. During the connection establishment and the Secure Channel renewing symmetric encryption and signing keys are negotiated and thus the fast and efficient symmetric encrypting and signing operations are used instead of the slower Public Key Cryptography. The lifetime of the Secure Channel can also be configured adequately in order to avoid a frequent usage of asymmetric keys.

### 7.7.5.3 Long-Running Connections

A further issue of industrial applications that has to be addressed is how long-running connections are handled. In Sect. 7.7.5.2 it was mentioned that industrial applications are running without significant changes for 25 years, whereas most e-commerce Web applications have maximum connection duration below 24 h. This does not mean that a single network connection is established for the whole lifetime of the industrial application but there are in fact connections opened up for a long period of time. An operator workplace supervising a special area of a power plant for example can be connected to a server for 10 years without termination. But what should be done if in-between a certificate gets invalid due to revocation or expiration?

As mentioned previously certificates are only used during connection establishment phase and the secure channel renewal phase. When a certificate gets invalid after connection has been established, then this does not directly affect the existing connection since the negotiated symmetric keys are used for encrypting and signing messages. However, the next time the Secure Channel has to be renewed the problem will occur. A certificate gets invalid because of two reasons: first because its validation period expired and second because it was revoked. If certificate lifetimes are managed strictly according to the concept described in Sect. 7.7.5.2 then certificate expiration should normally not occur. However, if it still occurs due to any strange reasons or a certificate gets revoked then another approach has to be processed. Such cases should in general be treated as an error since both cases threat the system's security in terms of integrity and confidentiality. However, for some applications availability is more important then the other security goals like for the supervisory of a nuclear power plant and therefore fallback solutions are needed.

One possible solution is to use two Application Instance Certificates, one with a short lifetime and another one with long lifetime acts as a kind of default certificate. Whenever the establishment of a Secure Channel fails due to certificate validation the default certificate is used until a new certificate is available. Figure 7.26 shows how the lifetimes of these certificates are related to each other. As mentioned above the expiration of a certificate should be an exception and normally new certificate should be installed before the old one expires in order to prevent such situations.

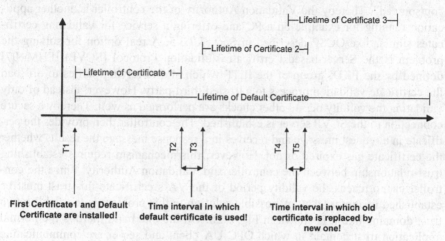

Fig. 7.26 Default Certificate

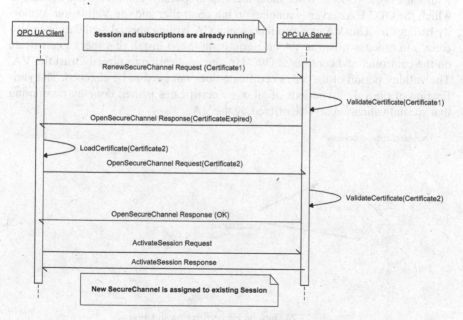

Fig. 7.27 Certificate expiration fallback solution

### 7.7.5.4   Devices Without an Internal Clock

As mentioned in earlier sections, validating certificates include the verification of the validation period. This process requires computer to have a clock in order to compare the dates and times. Obviously every common office PC has such an internal clock. But that is not true for every device or controller. How should the validation period be checked in such devices?

In such a case, the verification of the validity period of a certificate can also be "outsourced". Thereby the Validation Authority of the controller is another application running for example on a PC and offering a service for validating certificates similar like OCSP described in Sect. 7.7.3.5. A real option for solving the problem is the Server-based Certificate Validation Protocol (SCVP) [FHM+07] defined by the PKIX group of the IETF which allows relying parties to off-load the certificate validation process to a trusted third-party. However, instead of only validating the validity period other checks are performed as well. Thereby a secure connection to the SCVP server is established. The controller then provides the certificate in a request message and receives in a response message the results whether the certificate has expired or not. However, this mechanism requires establishing trust relationship between the controller and Validation Authority. Since the controller cannot check the validity period of the VA's certificate this trust must be established in another way. A possible solution to this problem is to establish two trust domains like it is shown in Fig. 7.28. On the one hand there is the normal application trust domain in which OPC UA client and server are communicating with each other. On the other hand there is a special validation trust domain in which the OPC UA server is running on the controller and the Validation Authority belongs to. This VA can also represent a CA issuing special "validation certificates". In order to trust the VA an administrator can install this special certificate on the controller and configures OPC UA the application to directly trust the VA. The validity period of the VA's certificate does not need to be checked. The verification of the validity periods of all other certificates is then done by consuming that special validation service offered by the VA.

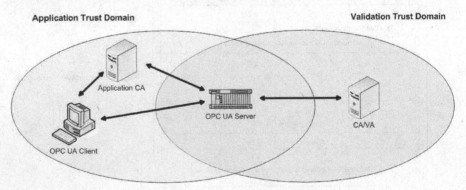

**Fig. 7.28** Outsourcing certificate validation

### 7.7.5.5    Validation Costs Time

If you find an interesting article in a Web shop and decide to buy it, would you wait 5–10 s until the Web server hosting the Web shop has validated your certificate? In most cases you would, since 5–10 s are not a very long time in order get a purchase confirmation. However, 5–10 s can be a very long time for industrial applications! Sometimes this is even far too long. Especially for applications in chemical or pharmaceutical industries waiting too long could lead to manufacturing poor products that cannot be sold. The question that has to be answered here is: How can the validation time of certificates be reduced?

In principle there are three parameters affecting the performance of certificate validation that can be influenced: the way how certificate revocation is checked, the length of the certification path of a certificate, and the extensions to be checked of a certificate. These parameters are discussed in the following.

For the first parameter, the way of checking certificate revocation, it is not easy to determine in general whether the offline or the online approach is faster since it depends on many factors. The offline approach uses CRLs for checking the revocation status. These are files containing the serial number of the revoked certificate and are stored locally on the device. This seems to be faster than checking the status with an online service. However, it must be considered that different CRLs can also be obtained from several locations and can get very large by time. Furthermore such a CRL must also be validated since it is signed by a certain publisher and a new CRL must be downloaded according to the "next update" date specified in the CRL. When using the online approach the performance of the validation depends on the communication protocol as well as on the service provider processing the validation. In a scenario in which the service provider resides in the same network segment or even on the same node the performance might be acceptable. However, there are also other scenarios in which the validation service has to be accessed over the Internet which is in the most cases not an option. This means the offline approach with a simple CRL might result in a better performance than using the online approach. But when CRL information has to be downloaded from multiple locations frequently you should think of introducing a central validation service in order to reduce the communication overhead.

The length of the certification path is represented by the number of CAs in the trust hierarchy up to the root CA of the trust domain. The validation of a certificate includes performing the same checks on each certificate in the trust hierarchy up to the root which has a significant impact on the performance of the system. In order to reduce the validation time it is desirable to restrict the number of intermediate CAs in an organization. The minimum validation time can be achieved by using self-signed certificates for each device since thereby only one certificate has to be validated. However, this may lead to a higher overhead when deploying and distributing certificates since every device has to have the certificate of every device it intends to communicate with in advance. In the most cases one common CA should be a proper tradeoff between performance and ease-of-use for industrial environments.

Finally, for X.509v3 certificates there are special extensions that can be checked during validation. Typical examples are KeyUsage, AlternativeNames for Issuer and Subject, or other policy definitions. In many cases these checks are optional and do not take too much time. Nevertheless the number of extensions that have to be checked should be restricted to minimum.

### 7.7.5.6    Certificate- and Key-Management for Controllers

OPC UA applications are intended to be run on controllers, but how do controllers manage certificates and keys when they have limited resources? Where are they stored? How are they loaded into the controllers?

In principle three types of artifacts have to be handled by controllers in order to be integrated in a PKI: trusted certificates, private keys, and CRLs if an offline validation approach is used. One approach is to store all artifacts on a memory card such as a CompactFlash which is supported by many controllers to extend their memory. There are even memory cards with password protection support like CompactFlash 4.0 so that the private key can be stored on it without being afraid that it can be used or manipulated by third-parties. But there is still the risk that the memory card could get lost or stolen. Another approach is to store the trusted certificates and CRLs on the memory card and load the private key and the associated certificate directly into the controller by using a secured protocol (like sFTP or proprietary protocols) supported by the controller. This has the advantage compared to the first approach that common memory cards can be used and the private key cannot be stolen that easy.

### 7.7.5.7    Self-Managed PKI vs. Managed by Third-Party

Finally, a last important topic is by whom the PKI should be managed. Section 7.7.4 shows different PKI examples including both self-managed PKIs and PKIs managed by a third-party. A self-managed PKI is under complete control of the organization also using the services. In the other scenario, a third-party provides the PKI services and the infrastructure which can be used by customers. A typical example for that scenario using VeriSign as the relying third-party is given in Sect. 7.7.4.4. Whereas both scenarios work quite well with organizations offering products in a Web shop such a decision can have crucial impacts for organization within industrial automation. What happens, for example, if the company offering PKI services and infrastructures goes bankrupt? Is it really so easy to move from one vendor to another if thousands of certificates are in use and already deployed?

In the following, the different advantages and disadvantages of both the self-managed and third-party managed PKI are discussed.

One advantage of self-managing a PKI is that the applying organization has the full control. If for example a certificate has expired and a new one is needed quickly, then the organization does not need to wait until a third-party verifies a certificate request. The same is true when intending to revoke a certificate which includes updating revocation information. Normally processing a revocation request and publishing revocation information is faster compared to "outsourcing" this task. Another advantage is that the organization has more flexibility. It is not dependent on the functionality and on the service the third-party provides. If for example the organization desires to change the way how certificates are validated against revocation from an offline approach (e.g., CRLs) to an online approach (e.g., OCSP) then it may be limited by the third-party since it only offers the offline version. Furthermore by self-managing a PKI an organization can adapt the PKI to its specific needs. Especially in the field of industrial automation this is an important aspect to consider. The applying organization knows its environments, the special requirements of their applications and of their domain whereas most third parties offering PKI services only consider common needs, requirement, and have limited domain knowledge (since they provide a generic product for range of different domains and industries). And a final advantage for self-managing PKIs is the independency. By signing a contract with a PKI provider an organization has also to be aware about risks and one major risk is thereby the PKI provider could go bankrupt. In such a case, no services are available anymore and applications of the organization may run into security problems. Obviously this will not happen that often and if it happens then the organization will be warned in advance. However, this will not always be the case and moving applications from one PKI provider to another is not a simple and cheap approach. All the certificates distributed have to be replaced by certificates issued by the new CA which can take while.

But there are also some disadvantages when self-managing PKIs which are mainly cost-related. First of all a proper technical infrastructure has to be established including software and hardware. Depending on the desired size and necessary complexity of the PKI the amount of infrastructure costs vary. In some cases existing workstations and servers can be used to host the PKI in other cases distributed trust domains have to be managed by sub-CAs which requires several servers which should deployed redundantly. Once the PKI is deployed and running it has to be maintained which means for example that software has to be updated or hardware has to be replaced. Besides the technical aspects there are also organizational issues that have to be addressed. One big topic here is the personnel that have to deal with the PKI which should in an ideal world be the administrator, not the end-user. However, even administrators have to be trained and introduced into the different PKI processes, policies, and applications. But training is not enough, the defined processes and policies have also to be followed accordingly. Another disadvantage that comes up compared to outsourcing PKI management is that many organizations do not have much experience in dealing with larger PKIs which either costs time for gaining experience or costs money for hiring experts in this area.

Finally, it can be concluded that the question whether managing a PKI on his own or outsourcing it to a third-party depends on many factors such as the size and the complexity of the PKI and costs. Simple and small PKI can be easily managed by most organizations without much effort, however, as soon as the several trust domains with different sub-CAs faces critical infrastructures some experts should at least be involved in the planning and deployment of the PKI.

### 7.7.5.8    PKI Example Scenario for OPC UA

After describing and discussing the abstract concepts of how certificates are to be managed we will give a simple and concrete example helping you getting started with this topic. Let us assume that we are acting as application vendors and want to develop a PKI concept for our OPC UA client and server.

First of all we have to think about which trust model (Sect. 7.7.2) our applications should support. We assume that the target environments in which these applications will run do not necessarily have an existing infrastructure for managing certificates. Therefore we decide that our applications should be able establishing trust without the need of a central Certification Authority. This can be achieved by applying a Direct Trust Model as described in Sect. 7.7.2 and is illustrated in Fig. 7.29. This model can be realized by using self-signed certificates for each application instance which is trusted by any other entity in our trust domain.

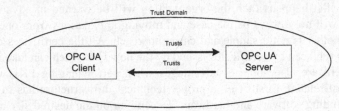

**Fig. 7.29** Example of a simple PKI trust model

Now we have to think about how such a trust model can be implemented. Thereby the technical and organizational infrastructure has to be established. The technical infrastructure includes applications and libraries for creating, deploying and validating certificates as described in Sect. 7.7.3. A proper selection is not always easy since there are lots of different PKI products available for managing environments of different sizes and complexities. Some of them are briefly introduced in Sect. 7.7.4. Since in our present example we consider only a small environment OpenSSL PKI is chosen for implementation. It contains powerful cryptographic libraries for creating and validating certificates as well as for storing certificates. Figure 7.30 shows how OpenSSL can be used for that purpose.

Thereby certificates are managed by three special directories with defined access restrictions. One of the directories organizes the trusted certificates as well as the certificates belonging to the owning application, another contains Certificate Revocation Lists (CRLs) and finally there is also a directory for Private Keys. All these entities are stored in a DER encoded format and are loaded by the applications with the OpenSSL library whenever they are needed (e.g., when encrypting or signing messages). But when and how are these entities actually created and deployed? Since certificates identify installed application instances they should be created when installing the application. Functions for creating certificates and the associated Private Keys are provided by the OpenSSL library which can be integrated in the application installer of both client and server. An installer could create self-signed certificates and Private Keys for the applications and automatically store them in the correct folders. In our scenario, OPC UA applications can only communicate with each other in a secure way when they directly trust each other. This means that if an application intends to communicate with another applications then each application has to store the certificate of the other application in its certificates folder. In our example, this can be done by an administrator manually installing them or by using special deployment tools (e.g., sFTP). In fact this shows also that an organizational infrastructure is needed for managing certificates. The main task besides installing and deploying certificates (which can also be automated) is maintaining the technical infrastructure. This includes renewing certificates and revoking certificates (i.e., putting a certificate that should not be trusted anymore in the CRL). Note that CRLs in the present example are used in the context of a certain OPC UA application. This means that each application has its own CRL since it acts as both Certification Authority and End-Entity. There is no common CRL provided by a central CA for all entities in the trust domain.

Once all certificate-related information on both sides is available in the store a secure communication between OPC UA client and server can be established.

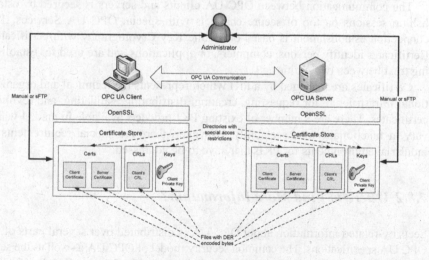

**Fig. 7.30** Example of a PKI deployment model

## 7.8    Summary

### 7.8.1 Key Messages

In today's industrial automation systems security is getting more important since control networks are not that isolated anymore and security incidents in such environments can have enormous financial and environmental impacts.

It is important to realize that security has a technical and an organizational notion. The most sophisticated security system with the strongest password encryption algorithm is useless if the password is written on a piece of paper lying on the desk of the administrator. Humans have to understand how important security is and how to deal with the topic. However, OPC UA is focusing on the technical perspective since it was not the goal of OPC UA addressing the organizational aspects since there are already detailed standards for that such as [ISA99].

It is not always clear how much security is necessary for certain environments. Furthermore, the level of security differs for each environment since they all have their special threats and requirements. This means that the proper level of security has to be investigated. An effective method for doing this is a security assessment which has a process-oriented approach. In order to determine proper security measures for OPC UA applications, the working group processed such an assessment and documented the results as a part of the specification.

OPC UA defines generic security architecture with different layers, each of them with certain responsibilities regarding security. Each layer can thereby be implemented by using different technologies specified in the mapping part of the OPC UA specification.

The communication between OPC UA clients and servers is secured by establishing sessions on top of secure channels with special OPC UA Services. The connection establishment is based on Public Key Cryptography with certificates. Certificates identify persons, computers, or applications and are used for establishing trust between two entities.

Certificates are managed by a PKI which represents the technical and organizational infrastructure for requesting, creating, distributing, validating, and revoking certificates. There are a number of existing PKI products available in market which vary in functionality and scalability. However, there are special requirements of industrial environments for PKIs that have to be addressed.

### 7.8.2 Where to Find More Information?

Security-related information about OPC UA is distributed over several parts of the OPC UA specifications. The common security model of OPC UA as well as the security assessment processed for OPC UA applications can be found in [UA Part 2]. The abstract definitions for security-related Services used for connection establishment and termination as well as for impersonation can be found in [UA Part 4]. Further discovery mechanisms are described in [UA Part 12]. [UA Part 6] defines the different technology mappings for the security layer of OPC UA applications. And finally [UA Part 7] describes the existing security profiles containing algorithms that should be supported by the applications which are used for deriving security policies.

In addition to OPC UA, a good source for addressing organizational aspect of security is [ISA99]. And finally a deep introduction into PKIs is given in [AL02].

### 7.8.3 What's Next?

The following chapter is about a generic application architecture for OPC UA. Thereby the different layers consisting of a stack, an SDK, and an application are described and the responsibilities are pointed out. Furthermore the OPC Foundation's standard deliverables for OPC UA are introduced.

# 8 Application Architecture

## 8.1 Introduction

This chapter describes an abstract architecture for OPC UA applications with different layers having defined responsibilities regarding OPC UA functionality. Afterward the deliverables of the OPC Foundation and their features are listed and it is pointed out how these are reflected in the abstract architecture.

## 8.2 Architectural Overview

When you intend to develop an application based on OPC UA you first have to think about what it should do by specifying the requirements and the functionality. Having that in mind you normally start designing the architecture of your application. Thereby certain design goals (e.g., portability, performance, or security) have to be agreed upon before first architectural concepts are developed. In this chapter, we will take a look at OPC UA from the design perspective and introduce a potential application scenario. We expect that this scenario will be applied by many application vendors. The main design goal thereby is the reuse of components and artifacts.

In this scenario, we assume that we have to develop an OPC UA client and a server. Both client and server will have application logic covering functionality tailored to concrete use cases. For example, the server has to access special data sources (e.g., data bases, devices, or other applications) or the client has to be integrated into another application (e.g., in a MES application). But they will also have application logic covering common functionality like managing connections, creating and processing OPC UA messages as well as securing them. Since we defined reuse as our main design goal it would make sense to separate use-case-specific and common functionality when designing the architecture. The common part can be further divided into two parts: the higher level functions like managing connections and processing Service messages and lower level functions like encoding, securing, and transmitting messages. The part providing the higher level functions can be considered as a Software Development Kit (SDK) and the part with the lower level functions can be represented by a protocol stack. The client and server applications are layered on top of the SDK. Based on these blocks we come to a very high level architecture shown in Fig. 8.1.

The above-described software layers are named as Application, SDK, and Stack and are described in more details in the following sections.

W. Mahnke et al., *OPC Unified Architecture*,
DOI: 10.1007/978-3-540-68899-0_8, © Springer-Verlag Berlin Heidelberg 2009

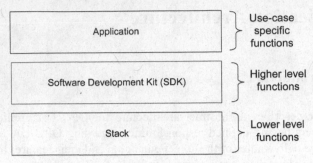

**Fig. 8.1** Architectural overview

## 8.3    Stack

As mentioned in Sect. 8.2, the Stack is a common part covering lower level func-tionality. In this section, we want to structure the Stack further into different parts leading to a more detailed architectural view like the one shown in Fig. 8.2.

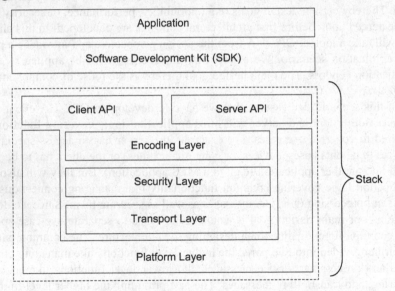

**Fig. 8.2** Stack overview

### 8.3.1  Interfaces

First of all, the layers above need somehow to access the Stack in order to send and receive messages. Both client and server can use the same stack since it pro-vides a lot of functionality that can be used for both sides such as encoding and securing messages. However, there are also functions specific to each side. For example the client is only sending requests and processing responses, whereas the server processes requests and sends responses. Therefore an access layer (i.e., interface) is needed for both the client- and the server-side (Client and Server API in the figure). They could, for example, offer methods for configuring the Stack, for managing the connection establishment, for sending OPC UA Service messages, and for notifying the layers above when messages are received.

## 8.3.2 Encoding Layer

The encoding and the decoding of messages are processed in the Encoding Layer. Once data structures representing Service messages are provided from the API layer they are serialized according to the special rules defined by OPC UA and passed to the layer beneath for further processing. Service messages received from the Security Layer are deserialized and passed as arguments of callback functions registered by the upper layer.

## 8.3.3 Security Layer

Encoded Service messages passed by the Encoding Layer to the Security Layer are then secured. Secured in this context means that depending on the configuration of the Secure Channel (Sect. 7.5.2.1) outgoing messages are signed and encrypted or only signed. In scenarios in which applications are running in isolated environments there must also be the possibility to disable message security by configuration. In addition, special security headers and footers are appended providing information for the receiver on how to decrypt the message and how to verify the signature of the message. The Security Layer of the receiver has to check the security headers and footers of incoming messages to know how they were secured. Depending on that messages are first decrypted and afterward the signature of the message is verified or only the signature is verified or none of these activities are done (in the case the message was not secured).

## 8.3.4 Transport Layer

The Transport Layer is responsible for transmitting and receiving messages as well as for dealing with errors at Network Layer. Before transmitting messages special transport headers are appended containing special information for example about the type and the length of the message. The Transport Layer of the receiver verifies whether it is well-formed meaning whether the type can be identified or whether the message is not too long[1] before forwarding it to the Security Layer.

---

[1] In UA TCP, the maximum message lengths are negotiated and verified at Transport Level.

### 8.3.5 Platform Layer

The reuse factor of the Stack can be increased by adding an additional layer to this model – the Platform Layer. The basic idea thereby is that all other layers of the Stack are developed in platform-neutral manner. Only the Platform Layer contains as name indicates platform-specific code like the integration of special libraries for managing sockets, threads, or cryptographic operations (e.g., encrypting and signing messages). This means that only the Platform Layer has to be changed in order to port the Stack to another platform, the other parts of the code can be reused.

## 8.4    Software Development Toolkit

On top of the Stack, the SDK Layer is located covering the higher level functionality. This layer can be in general composed of three parts which are illustrated in Fig. 8.3.

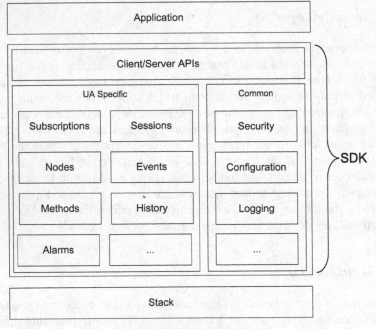

**Fig. 8.3** SDK overview

### 8.4.1 UA-Specific Functionality

The UA-specific part represents the implementation of the concepts and the Services specified in OPC UA. Note, that all the different aspects (like Sessions, Events, or Nodes) depicted in Fig. 8.3 have to be addressed by both the client and the server.

However, the semantic of these aspects for client and server is different (e.g., Client creates a Session request and server processes the client's Session request).

One important aspect is the management of OPC UA Sessions. As we learned the connection establishment of OPC UA includes creating a Secure Channel, establishing a Session, and activating the Session. The SecureChannel Services should be implemented in the Stack Layer to reduce the complexity in the SDK. Therefore, the Secure Channels should also be managed in that layer. The Session Services (i.e., CreateSession, ActivateSession, and CloseSession) are implemented in the present model in the SDK Layer. However, managing OPC UA Sessions does not only mean processing the Service requests and responses. There has also to be special logic behind like associating Sessions with the Secure Channel that secures the exchanged messages for that context. In addition, Sessions are run on behalf of users that have to be authenticated and authorized. Furthermore there are special Session parameters that have to be taken care of like the lifetime of the session or used locales. Such tasks are handled by a management class which can be called as a Session Manager.

Another important aspect is working with Nodes. Nodes are very essential to OPC UA and are used for organizing Address Spaces as well as for providing attribute values. Address Spaces in OPC UA reside on the server-side allowing clients to access and manipulate them via the NodeManagement and Attribute Service Sets. This means that on the server-side there has to be entities managing the Nodes (e.g., Node Manager) of the Address Space (i.e., Nodes and References) and the manipulation of the values contained in the Nodes (e.g., I/O Manager). Other concepts and Services like Subscriptions, Events, and History can be approached in a similar way.

OPC UA defines certain diagnostics information for Services and exposes it in the Address Space. It contains for example information about how often Services have been called. Managing this information is also a task for the SDK Layer since is also manages the Services of which the upper layer may not be aware of.

### 8.4.2  Common Functionality

The second part of the SDK Layer covers more general functionality that has to be implemented by clients and servers.

OPC UA exchanges certificates in order to establish secure connections. Before using them it has to be verified whether a received certificate can be trusted or not. OPC UA specifies what part of a certificate has to be validated to be trusted, however, it does not state how it has to be validated. Therefore common functionality has to be provided allowing the applications to validate certificates and accessing their associated certificate stores. An alternative to implementing that functionality in the SDK is using the Stack for that purpose. Since the Stack is a common component that should be used for large range of applications it is assumed that all applications use the same way of validating certificates. In heterogeneous environments, it sometimes can make more sense to implement that in SDK or even in the Application Layer when different sources for gathering certificates or certificate-related information (e.g., certificate revocation lists, private keys, or validation rules) have to be consumed.

Other important topics that belong to the common part are application configuration and logging.

### 8.4.3 Interfaces

The last part of the SDK discussed in this context represents the interfaces to the Application Layer. Client interfaces are needed for sending requests to the server and for receiving responses from it (i.e., callback interfaces). On the server side some interfaces for initializing and configuring the SDK should be provided as well as for integrating underlying systems acting as data providers.

## 8.5   Application

The Application Layer includes in principle two kinds of applications: clients and servers. The way how the architectures of these applications look like differs very much depending on the concrete scenario.

### 8.5.1 Client

One example for an OPC UA client application is a generic browser used for exploring and manipulating the Address Space provided by a server. The main tasks of the client is visualizing data provided by the SDK Layer and translating user interactions into calls to the SDK's API. The design of such an application from the functionality point of view can be quite simple which is shown in Fig. 8.4.

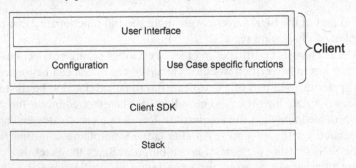

**Fig. 8.4** Example of a high-level client architecture

## 8.5.2 Server

In principle there are two kinds of server applications: one managing the whole address space in the main memory and another one accessing underlying systems for gathering Address Space information.

In the first case, the Address Space is stored in a special data source (e.g., database or XML file) and completely loaded into the main memory when the server starts up. This provides a fast access to information contained in the Address Space requested by clients.

In the second case, an OPC UA server facades an underlying system like a device, controller or DCS. In the last case, typically several sources are accessed, like a configuration database and several controllers. It is expected that many system vendors will first head such an approach in order to smoothly migrate existing applications to OPC UA. The main responsibilities of this layer are reading and writing data from the underlying system. A SDK could for example provide special callback interfaces for exchanging data in a simple way to reduce the complexity of the server implementation on top of the SDK. An example of that architecture is given in Fig. 8.5.

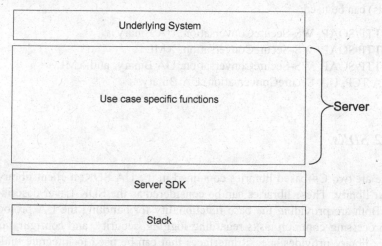

**Fig. 8.5** Example of a high-level server architecture

## 8.6    Deliverables Provided by the OPC Foundation

The OPC Foundation provides a set of deliverables that can make your life easier when developing OPC UA applications. Some of the deliverables follow the architecture described in Sect. 8.5. All of them are available in the so-called UA SDK. It contains thereby various Stacks, libraries, and sample applications.

## 8.6.1 Stacks

Both an ANSI-C-based and a C#-based Stack is provided with the UA SDK. A Java-based Stack was under development at the time when this book was written. It is recommended to use the UA stacks provided by the OPC Foundation in order to ensure interoperability between applications implemented in different development environments.

The ANSI-C Stack is implemented according to the architecture depicted in Fig. 8.2. It supports UA Binary encoding for the Encoding Layer, UA-Secure-Conversation for the Security Layer, and UA TCP for the Transport. For securing messages and validating certificates, the OpenSSL crypto library is applied and integrated in the platform-specific part of the Stack.

Alternatively there is also a .NET Stack written in C# which does not have a Platform Layer. Therefore the architecture is different to the one shown above. For the Encoding Layer it supports UA Binary and XML, UA-SecureConversation and WS-SecureConversation as Security Layer protocols, and the transport protocols UA TCP and SOAP/HTTP. However, only the following combinations of the protocols (also named as Stack profiles or mappings schemes; see Chap. 6 for more details) can be used:

- HTTP/SOAP, WS-SecureConversation, UA Binary
- HTTP/SOAP, WS-SecureConversation, XML
- HTTP/SOAP, WS-SecureConversation, UA Binary, and XML
- UA TCP, UA-SecureConversation, UA Binary.

## 8.6.2 SDKs

There are two C#-based libraries contained in the UA SDK: a client library and a server library. These libraries can be considered as the SDK Layer described earlier. Both are providing the base functionality for handling the UA protocol and for processing common tasks regarding logging, security, and configuration. The server library provides special interfaces that can be used to integrate underlying systems for example in order to read or write certain values. The client library implements a NodeCache for buffering Nodes and References. In addition to the client and server libraries, the SDK also provides a C#-based discovery server used by clients for identifying running endpoints of the server they can connect to.

C++-based UA SDKs for clients and servers were developed by a group of early adopter companies and are available as commercial libraries from Unified Automation. They are using the ANSI-C stack and are providing platform layers for different operating systems. Similar to the .NET UA SDK, the C++ SDKs are implementing common UA functionality to reduce the development effort for UA applications and are defining interfaces to integrate the application-specific information with the SDK.

## 8.6.3 Applications

The OPC Foundation's UA SDK provides both a sample client and server application written in C#. The client application is a generic OPC UA browser offering the base OPC UA functionality like browsing the Address Space, reading and writing Node attributes, subscribing for data changes and Events, and also more sophisticated concepts like calling Methods or using Views. Therefore, it is a powerful tool for learning and exploring the concepts of OPC UA. The server uses an in-memory Address Space including standard Nodes as well as an example describing a boiler and its components.

## 8.7    Summary

### 8.7.1 Key Messages

This chapter describes how the architecture of an OPC UA application typically looks like. The main design goal is thereby the reuse of artifacts (e.g., code and components). Therefore the following layers with certain responsibilities are defined: Application Layer, SDK Layer, and Stack Layer.

The Stack is responsible for the lower level functions like encoding and decoding messages, securing messages, as well as sending and receiving messages. In addition to that, it has a Platform Layer containing only platform-specific code whereas the other layers are written in platform neutral manner. This facilitates the portability of the Stack to other platforms.

The SDK contains higher level functionality covering UA-specific functions and common functions. The UA-specific part implements the OPC UA concepts and Services whereas the common part deals for example with configurations and logging. Additionally the server-side of the SDK provides interfaces in order to integrate other systems used as data providers.

The Application Layer covers the use-case-specific part of the functionality. Clients could, for example, process data received from the SDK in a special way in order expose it to the user. Servers could access underlying systems in order to expose its information via OPC UA to clients.

The OPC Foundation offers a set of OPC UA standard deliverables that system vendors can reuse. Some of the components already implement similar architecture as described in this chapter.

### 8.7.2 Where to Find More Information?

More information about the OPC UA standard deliverables can be found on the OPC Foundation Web site (http://www.opcfoundation.org/). More information about the C++ SDKs can be found at the Unified Automation Web site (http://www.unified-automation.com). Finally, the Web site of the OPC programmers' connection (http://www.opcconnect.com/) provides a section with SDKs that can a useful source when intending to implement OPC UA applications.

### 8.7.3 What's Next?

In Chap. 8 – System Architecture – different variants of OPC UA client–server concepts are introduced like chained or aggregating server. In addition, some related concepts regarding redundancy, discovery, and auditing are introduced.

# 9 System Architecture

## 9.1 System Environment

We mentioned several times in this book that OPC UA is designed in a generic manner and can therefore be applied in a diverse range of applications running at various locations within an organization's network. Figure 9.1 shows an example of an environment in which OPC UA is used in various ways. In this scenario, OPC UA servers are running on controllers of the Control Network, on Batch systems in the Operations Network, and are applied for MES application as a part of the production planning. Furthermore, an ERP system uses an OPC UA client as an interface for consuming services in the Corporate Network. In addition, there are not only different applications involved but also different platforms. The controllers require real-time operating systems, the Batch systems as well as the MES might be Windows-based and the ERP system might be deployed on UNIX platforms. Besides the possibility to run OPC UA on different platforms, it can also be used for applying different architectural concepts at system level. In our example, several architectural concepts can be identified such as redundancy (Batch servers), server-chaining (MES and Batch), or server aggregation (Batch and OPC UA servers running on the controllers).

The following sections describe how OPC UA can be used to apply these and other concepts at system level.

## 9.2 Basic Architecture Patterns

This section introduces different architectural patterns for OPC UA systems. Such patterns are either used for structuring systems and applications or used for solving certain design problems. In the following, four basic patterns, Client–Server, Chained Server, Server-to-Server Communication, and Aggregating Servers, are described that can be applied in different OPC UA-specific scenarios.

### 9.2.1 Client-Server

The first pattern–the Client–Server pattern – is the most common one and represents the basic OPC UA communication pattern (Fig. 9.2). There are two roles defined in this scenario: a server offering a service and a client consuming that service to fulfill certain tasks. The communication between them is defined by a contract they both agree upon. This means for the present context that an OPC UA client sends a well-formed request message to an OPC UA server, which answers to the request with an appropriate response message.

W. Mahnke et al., *OPC Unified Architecture*,
DOI: 10.1007/978-3-540-68899-0_9, © Springer-Verlag Berlin Heidelberg 2009

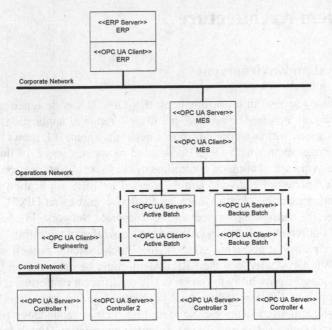

**Fig. 9.1** Example for an OPC UA system environment

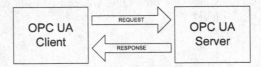

**Fig. 9.2** Client–Server pattern

## 9.2.2 *Chained Server*

In the Chained-Server pattern depicted in Fig. 9.3 three entities are involved: a common OPC UA client (OPC UA Client 1), an OPC UA server (OPC UA Server 1) with an embedded client (OPC UA Client 2), and a common OPC UA server (OPC UA Server 2). The OPC UA Client 1 exchanges messages with OPC UA Server 1 and the embedded OPC UA Client 2 communicates with OPC UA Server 2.

There are several use cases and scenarios in which the application of such a pattern is useful. One possible scenario could be to use the chaining server as a gateway. If, for example, OPC UA Client 1 only supports HTTP(s) as transport protocol and the server it intends to talk with resides in a network segment in which a firewall restricts the access to TCP combined with a special port, then a chaining server could act as a gateway in-between. Thereby, it translates HTTP(s) requests coming from the client to TCP and responses in TCP to HTTP(s) since it acts as client to OPC UA Server 2 and as a server to OPC UA Client 1.

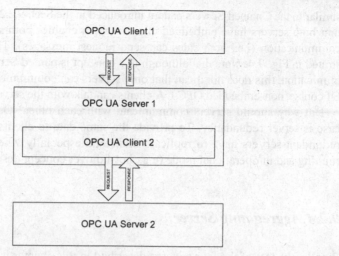

**Fig. 9.3** Chained Server pattern

## 9.2.3 Server-to-Server Communication

The term Server-to-Server communication sounds somewhat contradictory, since we know from the basic Client–Server pattern that a server provides services that are only consumed by clients. But how can servers communicate with each other? This can be achieved by embedding a client into a server. This concept is quite

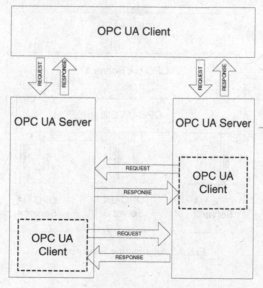

**Fig. 9.4** Server-to-Server pattern

similar to the Chained-Servers pattern introduced in the Sect. 9.2.2, with the exception that both servers have embedded clients, which enables both sides to initiate the communication (i.e., both sides can send request messages). This scenario is illustrated in Fig. 9.4. Note that although this concept is named Server-to-Server communication, this does not mean that only servers can communicate with each other. Of course, non-embedded OPC UA clients can talk with the servers as well.

But why should servers communicate with each other? One very typical use case is server redundancy. To provide the same data to clients in a failover case, redundant servers have to replicate their data especially when both servers are running and in operational mode (e.g., hot-failover concept described in Sect. 9.3).

## 9.2.4 Aggregating Server

Finally, the last of the four patterns described in this chapter is the concept of Aggregating Servers. This pattern is also similar to the Chaining-Server concept. In Fig. 9.5, an example for that concept is given. The common OPC UA Client talks with OPC UA Server 1 containing an embedded OPC UA Client. This embedded client accesses data provided by multiple other OPC UA servers. The data retrieved from these servers is prepared or processed in a special way by the intermediate server before a response is sent back to the common client.

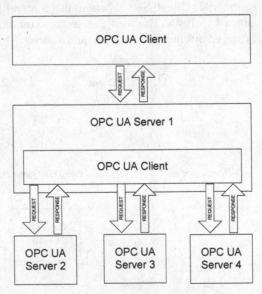

**Fig. 9.5** Aggregating Server pattern

Such a pattern can, for example, be applied in the field of MES. In such a scenario, the common OPC UA client can be used for executing and supervising production requests. A production request contains among others information about the type and the quantity of the product that has to be manufactured. OPC UA Server 1 processes the request and distributes subtasks to the underlying servers. Each of the aggregated servers is thereby responsible for a defined part of the production process. Once they have completed their tasks, they return the results to OPC UA Server 1, which composes a response for the common client. Before sending the response to the common client, the data obtained from the aggregated servers can be prepared in a special way for the client. For example, the overall status of the request or some statistical data like number of occurred errors can be returned.

The main difference between an aggregating server and a chaining server is that the chaining server just passes the data of the underlying server(s), while an aggregating server typically concentrates the information of the underlying server(s).

## 9.3 Redundancy

Redundancy in general is the existence of multiple critical components of a system in order to increase the reliability. If an error occurs in one of the components, then another one is used instead.

In OPC UA, redundancy is based on the existence of duplicate client or server applications and can be achieved by using special data structures and services of OPC UA. In the following, we distinguish between client and server redundancy.

### 9.3.1 Client Redundancy

Client redundancy is needed in environments in which, for example, a continuous supervisory of a production process is needed. Another example is when an OPC UA server aggregates data from underlying servers to perform special calculations (Sect. 9.2.4). OPC UA supports these types of redundancy by applying the TransferSubscriptions Service in combination with monitoring client information residing in the server's Address Space.

Figure 9.6 illustrates an example of how this can work. Let us assume that we have an active OPC UA client with running data subscriptions and a backup client. This backup client monitors the session information of the active client in the server address space in the same way any other data is monitored in OPC UA. Once the active client fails and the status of the session changes in the address space, the backup client uses the service TransferSubscriptions to get all running subscriptions from the active client. Subscriptions can survive sessions since their lifetime is independent from the session lifetime. The server must thereby buffer data to be sent to the client during this failover process to avoid loosing data. This mechanism requires the backup client to have knowledge about the SessionId for monitoring the session and in addition the SubscriptionId for transferring the subscriptions of the active client. However, there is no standard way specified by OPC UA for exchanging this information between those clients.

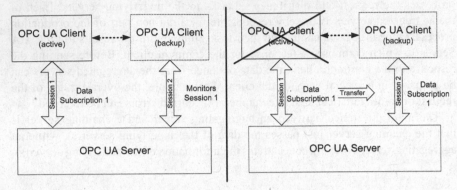

**Fig. 9.6** Example of client redundancy

## 9.3.2 Server Redundancy

Server redundancy can be further differentiated in transparent server redundancy and nontransparent server redundancy.

### 9.3.2.1  Transparent Server Redundancy

In the first approach, server redundancy is handled transparently to the client. This means that in a failover case the client does not realize that an error occurred and

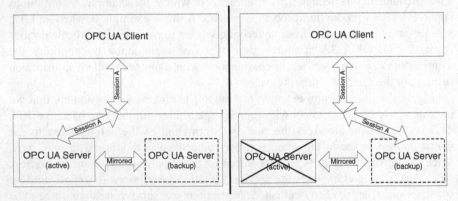

**Fig. 9.7** Transparent server redundancy

it does not need to do anything to continue performing its tasks. However, the server has the full responsibility to ensure that the client can access its required data. This means that the redundant servers have to be mirrored. They have to have exactly the same data and session information. Figure 9.7 shows an example of how this can look like in the context of OPC UA. If the active server is not available anymore, further requests are redirected to the identical backup server.

Although clients do not have to do anything special accessing a redundant server, the information that they are accessing a redundant server can be found in the Address Space. To achieve requirements from FDA,[1] the server also exposes an Id that uniquely identifies the server in the redundant set of servers.

### 9.3.2.2  Nontransparent Server Redundancy

In contrast to the above described transparent server redundancy concept, the nontransparent server redundancy requires some actions of the client to continue its work in the case when the server fails. For this type of redundancy, OPC UA specifies several failover modes defining for each case the role of the backup server. Depending on the selected failover mode at the client side, different actions to support redundancy have to be performed. Table 9.1 describes each mode and the roles of the backup server as well as the required actions for the client side.

### 9.3.2.3  Nontransparent Server Redundancy Approaches

To perform the failover, the client has to create a new session to a backup server and transfer the subscription data of the previous session to the new session. For doing that, OPC UA proposes two approaches: by duplicating subscriptions or by using the TransferSubscriptions Service. Both ways are described later. Since this mechanism can be reused by any type of OPC UA client, it makes sense to encapsulate this functionality into a separated component (Failover Proxy).

The first approach (Fig. 9.8) requires only actions of the Failover Proxy residing on the client side. In this case, it acts as proxy and creates a connection on both active and backup server. Furthermore, all subscriptions created on the active server are created on the backup as well while sampling or reporting is only enabled on the active one. Other service requests such as Read or Write are only forwarded. If, in a failover case, the active server is not accessible, then the proxy component enables sampling or reporting on the backup server.

---

[1] The U.S. Food and Drug Administration (FDA) define requirements for companies developing applications for the consumer industry in the United States

**Table 9.1** Failover modes and client side actions

| Failover mode | Role of the backup server | Client side actions |
|---|---|---|
| Cold | Backup server is running but not active. Once the active server fails the backup is activated. | **On initial connection:**<br><br>1. Nothing to do<br><br>**At Failover:**<br><br>1. Connect to backup server<br>2. Create subscriptions and add monitored items<br>3. Activate sampling on the subscriptions<br>4. Activate reporting of notifications |
| Warm | Backup server is running and active but it cannot connect to actual data points. This is applied in scenarios in which the number of connections to the underlying devices is limited. Therefore, the backup server only connects to the device in the case of a failover. | **On initial connection:**<br><br>1. Connect to both active and backup<br>2. Create subscriptions and add monitored items (enable subscription on active server and disable on backup server)<br><br>**At Failover:**<br><br>1. Activate sampling on the subscriptions<br>2. Activate reporting of notifications |
| Hot | Backup server is like the active server full operational and can be used for accessing data. When the active server breaks, then the backup server is running with a higher load since all clients previously connected to the active server move to the backup server. | **On initial connection:**<br><br>1. Connect to both active and backup<br>2. Create subscriptions and add monitored items<br>3. Activate sampling on the subscriptions<br><br>**At Failover:**<br><br>1. Activate reporting of notifications |

The second approach requires actions of the Failover Proxy component on the client side and additional actions on the server side. The proxy on the client side only creates subscriptions on the active server. The active server mirrors all created subscriptions to the backup server. Once the active server fails, the proxy creates a new session on the backup server and uses the TransferSubscriptions Service for getting the subscriptions of the previous session. This is exemplified in Fig. 9.9.

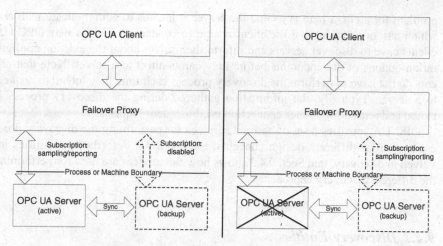

**Fig. 9.8** Nontransparent server redundancy – approach 1

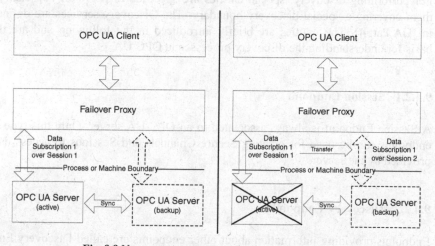

**Fig. 9.9** Nontransparent server redundancy –approach 2

## 9.4    Discovery

### 9.4.1  Why Discovery?

In large OPC UA environments, there might be scenarios in which many OPC UA servers with different endpoints are provided. Each endpoint can have different configurations regarding communication, encoding, or security as well. In addition, the servers can run at different locations (e.g., network segments or sites). The problem for a client here is to find the server it intends to communicate with and which has an endpoint that the client is able to connect to. This is why OPC UA clients have to discover servers and inform themselves about the existing configuration options of the endpoints before they can connect to a server. Note that clients do not have to perform the discovery process each time they intend to connect to a server. Typically, the information gathered during the discovery process is stored and reused for further connection establishment requests.

OPC UA specifies a set of abstract services for performing the discovery process as well as different design concepts. Section 9.4.2 describes the entities involved in discovery, and Sect. 9.4.3 shows how the services are used for performing the different discovery approaches.

## 9.4.2 Discovery Entities

For performing discovery, special entities are specified in [UA Part 12], each of them covering a special discovery boundary. The Discovery services are defined in [UA Part 4]. The entities are briefly introduced in the following and are the basis for understanding the discovery processes in OPC UA.

### 9.4.2.1  Session Endpoint

A Session Endpoint is always associated to an OPC UA server. Only this type of endpoints can be used for creating Secure Channels and Sessions to access data provided by the server.

### 9.4.2.2  Discovery Endpoint

Endpoints providing information about other endpoints are called Discovery Endpoints. This type of endpoint is either created by an OPC UA server providing data to clients or created by a Local or Global Discovery Server.

### 9.4.2.3  Local Discovery Server

If a discovery server resides on the same machine as the OPC UA servers of which it provides the Discovery Endpoints, then it is named as the Local Discovery Server. Multiple servers running on a single machine can share the same Local Discovery Server.

### 9.4.2.4   Global Discovery Server

This discovery server maintains information about existing servers in a network and is accessible at a well-known address such as an URL or simply an IP address together with a port. More precisely, it provides the available Discovery Endpoints to which clients can connect to in order to get information about the Session Endpoints.

## 9.4.3 Discovery Process

Before clients can start the discovery process the installed servers (i.e. the endpoints) have to be registered in the discovery servers by using the RegisterServer Services defined in [UA Part 4]. Thereby a description and the discovery URL has to be provided.

The discovery process itself is performed by exchanging discovery messages among the above defined entities. There are a number of ways of how this process can be performed. The basic approaches are described in the following.

### 9.4.3.1   Simple Discovery

In the case that a client already has the address of the OPC UA server (e.g., by configuration), it only sends a GetEndpoints request to the server to get the descriptions of the available Session Endpoints. Once the client received the response from the Discovery Endpoints, it selects an appropriate Session Endpoint and establishes a connection to the selected endpoint starting with an OpenSecure-Channel request. This is illustrated in Fig. 9.10.

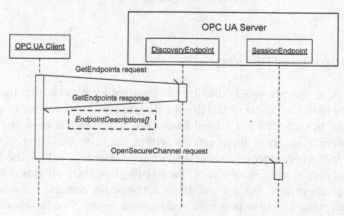

**Fig. 9.10** Simple discovery

### 9.4.3.2  Normal Discovery

There will also be scenarios in which multiple OPC UA servers are running on a single machine. In such a case, the client asks the Local Discovery Server for the existing servers by sending a FindServers request. The address at which a client can access the Local Discovery Server is either well-known[2] or preconfigured in the client by the administrator. If the desired server is listed in the ServerDescriptions returned by the Local Discovery Server, the client extracts the DiscoveryURL and connects to the Discovery Endpoint of the server and proceeds like described in the Simple Discovery case. In Fig. 9.11, it is shown how Normal Discovery is performed.

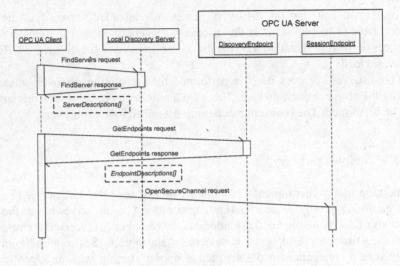

**Fig. 9.11** Normal discovery

### 9.4.3.3  Hierarchical Discovery

If OPC UA servers are widely distributed at several locations within the network, it might be hard for a client to identify the desired server or even the machine it is running on. In such a case, a Global Discovery Server should be introduced providing information about these servers within the network. Thereby the client sends a FindServers request to a well-known (or preconfigured) Global Discovery Server and obtains the descriptions of the existing machines offering a Local Discovery Servers or OPC UA servers. If the returned list contains the desired OPC UA server, then the client proceeds as described in the Simple Discovery case,

---

[2]Port 4840.

otherwise it selects an appropriate Local Discovery Server running on a certain machine (e.g., the description may give hints that facilitates the decision which one to select) and proceeds like in the Normal Discovery described earlier. The complete message exchange for hierarchical discovery is depicted in Fig. 9.12.

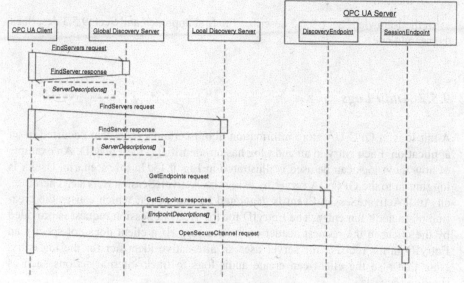

**Fig. 9.12** Hierarchical discovery

## 9.5   Auditing

### 9.5.1 Overview

Auditing in the context of OPC UA means the tracking of activities of OPC UA applications, including normal and abnormal behaviors. It ensures thereby the traceability of the system for several purposes. One example is debugging applications on errors by extracting information from audit logs. Another example is forensic[3] activities after a security incident occurred. And in some special industries (e.g., consumer industries), it is even a hard requirement defined by regulatory bodies.

Auditing can be accomplished by one of the following approaches or by applying both of them:

---

[3]Forensic in the context of security means gathering information that help to identify the reason why a certain security incident occurred (e.g., a hacker that intruded into a system). A typical activity is thereby exploring different log files to detect strange behaviors or anomalies.

- OPC UA applications generate audit events and store the audit information in logfiles or databases.
- OPC UA applications generate audit events and publish the audit event to which clients can subscribe. Thereby, clients can store audit information to special locations.

In the following, Sect. 9.5.2 describes the first approach and Sect. 9.5.3 describes the second one.

## 9.5.2 Audit Logs

Audit logs in OPC UA store information about certain events that occurred in an application. Each entry in an audit log has an identifier – the EntryID. An example of how audit logs can be used is illustrated in Fig. 9.13. In this scenario, UserA is logging in to the OPC UA server by using the ActivateSession Service. Therefore, an AuditActivateSessionEvent is generated by the server, which causes the creation of an audit log entry. The EntryID for the ActivateSession request is provided by the client in the request header of the message. If a client does not specify an EntryID in his request, the server uses an alternative identifier for the log entry. Note that also the client can create audit logs to track internal actions such as sending requests.

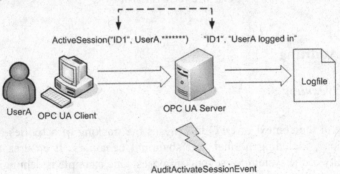

**Fig. 9.13** Example of how audit logs can be used

## 9.5.3 Audit Events

Audit events are different kinds of events occurring in a system for which a system should generate an audit log entry. OPC UA specifies a wide range of different audit event types that can be used directly or for subtyping a more specialized type. Clients can subscribe for audit events in the same way they subscribe for other events. An example is given in Fig. 9.14. In this example, during a Secure

Channel establishment it turns out that a certificate has expired. Therefore, an AuditCertificateExpiredEvent is created. Since the Admin workstation has also an OPC UA client, which subscribes for audit events of this type, it gets notified by the server. Now the administrator knows that certain clients identified with the EntryID need new certificates.

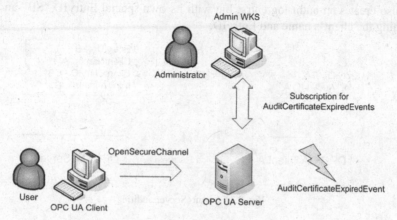

**Fig. 9.14** Example of how audit events can be used

## 9.5.4 Service Auditing

For each of the Service Sets defined in [UA Part 4] certain event types for auditing are defined and also how to deal with the events. For example, for the Secure-Channel Service Set the following special Event Types should be used:

- AuditOpenSecureChannelEventType for OpenSecureChannel Service
- AuditCloseSecureChannelEventType for CloseSecureChannel Service
- Subtypes of AuditCertificateEventType for certificate errors.

If the granularity of the types is not sufficient, they can easily be subtyped and additional ones can be defined. These EventTypes are used in both cases, when a service call fails and succeeds. For some services like for the services of the Discovery Service Set, no special EventTypes are defined. In this case, the base type AuditEventType can be used or a custom subtype if it.

A specific Profile is defining whether a server supports auditing by generating audit events.

## 9.5.5 Use Cases

This section describes how to handle audit logs and how they look like in certain system architectures (Sect. 9.2).

### 9.5.5.1    Client and Server Auditing

The first scenario describes the common client–server architecture shown in Fig. 9.15. When a client sends a request message to the server, then the client creates an audit log entry with the EntryID "CA". When the server receives the message, it also creates an audit log entry, but with its own special EntryID "SB" and containing the client's name and EntryID.

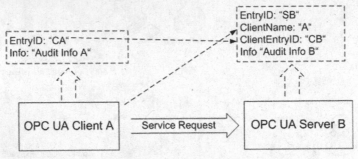

**Fig. 9.15** Client–Server auditing

### 9.5.5.2    Aggregating Server

When considering a scenario in which an aggregated server is used as illustrated in Fig. 9.16. The first step is similar to the normal client–server approach described earlier. In the second step, the aggregating server sends a request to OPC UA Server C. When this server receives the message, it creates an audit log entry with the EntryID "SC" and the ClientName is thereby the name of the aggregating server "B" its EntryID "SB".

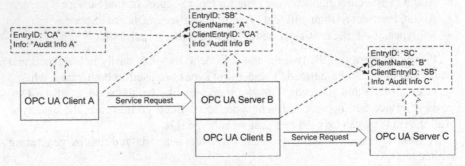

**Fig. 9.16** Aggregating server auditing

### 9.5.5.3    Aggregation through a nonauditing server

The last use case considered in this section describes auditing in a scenario in which an aggregating server is used that does not support auditing. However, the server it connects to does. Figure 9.17 depicts such a case. OPC UA Client A creates an audit log when it sends a request to the OPC UA Server B, which does not create an audit event but includes the EntryID in the request message it sends to Server C. When Server C receives the request from B, it creates an audit log entry with ClientName of "B" and the EntryID "CA" belonging to client A.

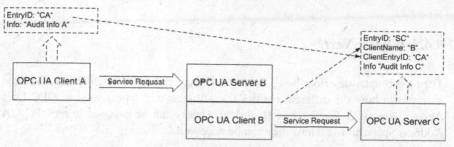

Fig. 9.17 Aggregation through a nonauditing server

## 9.6    Summary

### 9.6.1 Key Messages

Applications based on OPC UA can be run at different levels in an automation network and is therefore applied for a diverse range of scenarios. However, there is a number of generic architectural patterns representing typical use cases or solving certain design problems. One problem domain in which some of the patterns can be applied is redundancy. OPC UA provides information about dealing with both client- and server-redundancy. On the server side, it is distinguished between transparent and nontransparent redundancy. Another important topic regarding the system architecture is discovery. Before an OPC UA client connects to a server, it first has to get information about how it can establish the connection. There are different possible configurations regarding communications protocols, encoding, and security. OPC UA specifies different ways of how discovery can be performed. When considering installing OPC UA applications in a concrete environment, it has to be taken care of how to configure and deploy those applications regarding discovery. Auditing is important also required for a number of reasons like for detecting errors or for accountability requirements defined by regulatory bodies. Therefore, OPC UA specifies how auditing is done with services and events.

### 9.6.2 Where to Find More Information?

The different concepts regarding redundancy in OPC UA are defined in [UA Part 4] as well as how services and events are audited. Some more general information about auditing can also be found in [UA Part 2]. Special EventTypes for audit events are provided in [UA Part 3] and [UA Part 5]. There are two sources describing the discovery mechanisms of OPC UA: [UA Part 4] defines common services whereas [UA Part 12] comes up with different concepts of how the discovery process can be performed.

## 9.6.3 What's Next?

The next chapter describes how Classic OPC can be mapped to OPC UA. Thereby, it is shown how the different entities (i.e., objects and types) used in OPC Data Access, Alarms & Events, and Historical Access can be exposed in an OPC UA Address Space and also how they can be accessed.

# 10 Mapping of COM OPC to OPC UA

## 10.1 Overview

The Classic OPC standard, especially the OPC DA interface, is very successful. It is implemented in more than 15,000 products and used in a huge installed base. This makes the mapping of COM based OPC interfaces to OPC UA an important task, allowing the installed base to profit from the advantages of OPC UA and to provide OPC vendors an easy migration strategy.

OPC UA keeps the successful concepts of Classic OPC. This was an important design goal of OPC UA. It allows the mapping between OPC UA and existing standards. Classic OPC can be mapped to OPC UA without loosing information. Mapping from OPC UA to Classic OPC is possible but may lead to loss of information.

The mapping is the base for proxies and wrappers (see chap. 11) used to translate the different standards from and to OPC UA. A proxy allows Classic OPC clients to access UA server and a wrapper allows UA clients to access Classic OPC servers. But the mapping is also important for the migration of existing OPC products to OPC UA. It enables existing OPC information to be exposed with OPC UA to use the advantages of the reliable and secure communication features of OPC UA without the need to support new features. They can be added over time in an iterative development and improvement process.

Based on the experience from several projects to integrate OPC UA in existing OPC products, it is much more efficient and from a product point of view less error-prone to integrate OPC UA directly into an existing product, since the OPC DA interface hides normally information that is useful to implement OPC UA.

The use of wrappers and proxies should be limited to the integration of the installed base into OPC UA communication and to add OPC UA support to legacy products, which are not longer updated.

This chapter provides mapping tables between Classic OPC terms and constructs and OPC UA. It does not explain the Classic OPC terms. The OPC UA terms are explained in the Chaps. 2 and 5 of this book. Therefore, this chapter requires knowledge about Classic OPC terms to understand the mapping.

## 10.2 OPC Data Access 2.05A and 3.0

Most of the OPC UA facets needed to implement the complete OPC Data Access functionality are contained in the base specifications of OPC UA. Only some process automation specific VariableTypes are defined in [UA Part 8].

W. Mahnke et al., *OPC Unified Architecture*,
DOI: 10.1007/978-3-540-68899-0_10, © Springer-Verlag Berlin Heidelberg 2009

The standard server profile described in Chap. 12 contains the OPC UA features necessary to replace an OPC Data Access server.

## 10.2.1 Address Space

Only a very small set of the OPC UA modeling capabilities is used to expose an OPC Data Access Address Space with OPC UA. The main components are Folder Object, Data Variables, Organizes, and HasComponent References. Table 10.1 describes the complete mapping more detailed.

**Table 10.1** Mapping address space OPC DA to UA

| OPC DA | OPC UA |
|---|---|
| Nodes in the Address Space | |
| Branches are used to structure the hierarchical Address Space | Branches can be represented with Folder Objects. The hierarchy is spanned with Organizes References. The root in OPC DA is the Objects Folder in OPC UA |
| OPC Items are used to represent data in the Address Space. They are the leafs of Branches | Data Variables are used to represent OPC Items. The Data Variables are structured using Folder Objects and HasComponent References |
| Variable Types | |
| OPC Item with no EUType | VariableType is BaseDataVariableType |
| OPC Item with EUType Analog | VariableType is AnalogItemType |
| OPC Item with EUType Enumerated | VariableType is TwoStateDiscreteType or MultiStateDiscreteType |
| Properties and Attributes | |
| ItemID A string uniquely identifying an item in the server Address Space | NodeId Numeric, string, GUID, or opaque identifier including a namespace used to uniquely identify a Node in the server Address Space. The ItemID can be mapped to the string identifier |
| Property Item Canonical Data Type | Attributes DataType, ValueRank, and ArrayDimensions |
| Properties Item Value, Item Quality, and Item Timestamp | Attribute Value containing the Value, status, and timestamps. The DA timestamp is mapped to the UA server timestamp |
| Property Item Access Rights | Attributes AccessLevel and User AccessLevel |

(*Continued*)

| Property Server Scan Rate | Attribute MinimumSamplingInterval |
|---|---|
| Property EU Units | Property EngineeringUnits |
| Property Item Description | Attribute Description |
| Properties High EU and Low EU | Property EURange |
| Properties High Instrument Range and Low Instrument Range | Property InstrumentRange |

## 10.2.2 Access Information

The context created for the communication, the methods for creating the context, and the methods to access information have different names, but they can easily be mapped from OPC DA to OPC UA. Table 10.2 lists the mapping necessary to provide the same level of access to OPC DA information in OPC UA.

**Table 10.2** Mapping information access from OPC DA to UA

| OPC DA | OPC UA |
|---|---|
| Context | |
| COM Object OPCServer | OPC UA Session |
| COM Object OPCGroup | OPC UA Subscription |
| OPCItem in a Group | Data Monitored Item in a Subscription |
| Creating Context | |
| CoInitializeEx<br>CoInitializeSecurity<br>CoCreateInstanceEx creates OPCServer | OpenSecureChannel<br>CreateSession<br>ActivateSession |
| AddGroup<br>IOPCGroupStateMgt::SetState<br>RemoveGroup | CreateSubscription<br>ModifySubscription<br>DeleteSubscriptions |
| AddItems<br>RemoveItems | CreateMonitoredItems<br>DeleteMonitoredItems |
| Accessing Information | |
| ChangeBrowsePosition<br>BrowseOPCItemIDs<br>GetItemID<br>QueryAvailableProperties | Browse |
| IOPCItemIO::Read<br>IOPCSyncIO::Read<br>IOPCSyncIO2::ReadMaxAge<br>IOPCAsyncIO2::Read<br>IOPCAsyncIO3::ReadMaxAge<br>IOPCItemProperties::GetItemProperties | Read |

(*Continued*)

| IOPCItemIO::WriteVQT<br>IOPCSyncIO::Write<br>IOPCSyncIO2::WriteVQT<br>IOPCAsyncIO2::Write<br>IOPCAsyncIO3::WriteVQT | Write |
|---|---|
| OnDataChange | Publish |
| GetStatus<br>ShutdownEvent | Read or monitoring of ServerState and ServerStatus Variables |

## *10.2.3 OPC XML-DA 1.01*

OPC XML-DA was already reduced to the core functionality necessary for Data Access; therefore, it is even easier to map OPC XML-DA to OPC UA. OPC XML-DA uses the same Address Space concept like COM-based OPC DA. Therefore, the mapping described in Table 10.1 applies. Table 10.3 describes the mapping of the information access part of OPC XML-DA to OPC UA.

**Table 10.3** Mapping information access from OPC XML-DA to UA

| OPC XML-DA | OPC UA |
|---|---|
| Browse | Browse |
| Read<br>GetProperties | Read |
| Write | Write |
| Subscribe<br>SubscriptionPolledRefresh<br>SubscriptionCancel | CreateSubscription<br>Publish<br>DeleteSubscriptions |
| GetStatus | Read or monitoring of ServerState Variable |

## 10.3   OPC Alarm and Events 1.1

The mapping of OPC Alarm & Events to OPC UA is not as straightforward as the mapping of OPC DA. OPC A&E provided already an Information Model for Events and Process Alarms. But the model is very static and limited compared to the generic and extensible model provided by OPC UA. This makes the mapping more complex than for DA.

The simple and tracking Events defined in OPC A&E can be implemented with OPC UA by just using the base specifications of OPC UA, since monitoring Events and defining EventTypes is already defined there. For the mapping of condition

Events, the OPC UA Alarms & Conditions Information Model [UA Part 9] is needed. This Information Model is described in Sect. 4.9.

## 10.3.1 Address Space

There are three main groups of mappings that need to be addressed. The first group is the Areas and Event sources used to structuré sources for Events in a hierarchy. The second group is the Event type used to classify the Events and the third group is the conditions used to represent process alarms. Table 10.4 describes the mapping more detailed.

**Table 10.4** Mapping address space OPC A&E to UA

| OPC A&E | OPC UA |
|---------|--------|
| Nodes in the Address Space | |
| Areas are used to structure the hierarchical Address Space | Areas can be represented with Folder Objects. The hierarchy is spanned with HasNotifier References. The root in OPC A&E should be the Server Object in OPC UA |
| Sources are the event sources in the Address Space | Sources could be represented by Object or by Variables depending on the type of Source. The Sources are referenced with the HasEventSource Reference from the Folder Objects |
| Event Types | |
| Simple Event | BaseEventType |
| Tracking Event | AuditEventType |
| Condition Event | AlarmConditionType |
| EventCategories define a list of server specific Event Types for each base Event Type | Mapped to a derived Event Type of BaseEventType, AuditEventType, or AlarmConditionType |
| Event Fields | |
| dwEventType / dwEventCategory | EventType |
| szSource | SourceName |
| ftTime | Time |
| szMessage | Message |
| dwSeverity | Severity |
| Conditions | |
| Enabled state | Condition State Machine |
| Active state | Alarm Active State Machine |
| Acked state | Acknowledge State Machine |

## 10.3.2 Access Information

As mentioned earlier in this chapter, the mapping of the Address Space information is not straightforward. But also the access to the information is different and more generic in OPC UA.

One difference is that OPC A&E provides only one filter per Subscription, and in OPC UA, the Subscription can have a list of MonitoredItems, each of them defining an Event filter and it can also contain a mix of data change Monitored Items and Event Monitored Items. Another difference is the selection of Event Fields and the possible filters. In OPC A&E, the provided Event attributes are defined by the base Event Type[1] and additional attributes can be requested and the filter is limited to a small and fixed list of filter criteria. In OPC UA, there is no default Event field that is delivered to the client. The client is able to select only the fields he is interested in. The filter criteria in OPC UA are much more flexible by allowing filtering on all Event fields. Figure 10.1 shows the main differences between OPC A&E and OPC UA.

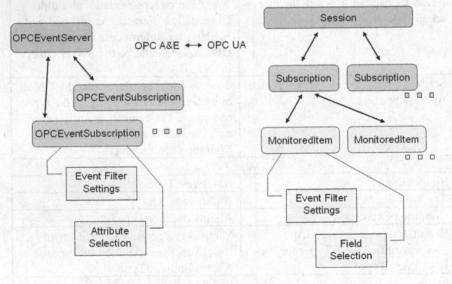

**Fig. 10.1** Communication context in OPC A&E and OPC UA

Table 10.5 contains more details for the mapping of information access between OPC A&E and OPC UA.

---

[1]Simple, Tracking of Condition Event.

**Table 10.5** Mapping information access from OPC A&E to UA

| OPC A&E | OPC UA |
|---|---|
| Context | |
| COM Object OPCEventServer | OPC UA Session |
| COM Object OPCEventSubscription | OPC UA Subscription |
| | Event Monitored Item |
| Creating Context | |
| CoInitializeEx | OpenSecureChannel |
| CoInitializeSecurity | CreateSession |
| CoCreateInstanceEx creates Server | ActivateSession |
| CreateEventSubscription | CreateSubscription |
| SetFilter | CreateMonitoredItems |
| Accessing Information | |
| ChangeBrowsePosition | Browse |
| BrowseOPCAreas | Read |
| QueryEventCategories | |
| QueryConditionNames | |
| QuerySubConditionNames | |
| QuerySourceConditions | |
| QueryEventAttributes | |
| GetConditionState | Read |
| EnableConditionByArea | Methods on Condition State Ma- |
| EnableConditionBySource | chines called with the Call Service |
| DisableConditionByArea | |
| DisableConditionBySource | |
| OnEvent | Publish |
| GetStatus | Read or monitoring of ServerState |
| ShutdownRequest | and ServerStatus Variables |

## 10.4   OPC Historical Data Access

The OPC UA Historical Access functionality is defined in [UA Part 11], and the Aggregates to retrieve calculated Values from the raw Values in the history database are defined in [UA Part 13]. This book provides Historical Access specific information in Sects. 4.6 and 5.9.

The main difference between OPC Historical Data Access and the History Access functionality in OPC UA is the additional support of Event History not included in Classic OPC.

## 10.4.1 Address Space

Only a very small set of the OPC UA modeling capabilities is used to expose an OPC Historical Data Access Address Space with OPC UA. The main components are Folder Object, Data Variables, Organizes, and HasComponent References. Table 10.6 describes the mapping more detailed.

Table 10.6 Mapping address space OPC HDA to UA

| OPC HDA | OPC UA |
|---------|--------|
| Nodes in the Address Space | |
| Branches are used to structure the hierarchical Address Space | Branches can be represented with Folder Objects. The hierarchy is spanned with Organizes References. The root in OPC HDA is mapped to the Objects Folder in OPC UA |
| OPC Items are used to represent data in the Address Space. They are the leafs of Branches | Data Variables with the HistoryRead flag set in the AccessLevel are used to represent OPC Items. The Data Variables are references with the HasComponent Reference from the Folder Objects |
| HDA Item Attributes mapped to UA Attributes and Properties | |
| OPCHDA_ITEMID<br>A string uniquely identifying a item in the server Address Space | NodeId<br>Numeric, string, GUID or opaque identifier including a namespace used to uniquely identify a Node in the server Address Space |
| OPCHDA_DATA_TYPE | Attributes DataType, ValueRank and ArrayDimensions |
| OPCHDA_ARCHIVING | Attribute Archiving |
| OPCHDA_DESCRIPTION | Attribute Description |
| OPCHDA_ENG_UNITS | Property EngineeringUnits |
| OPCHDA_STEPPED and Attributes which affect how the data is historized | Historical configuration object. |

## 10.4.2 Access Information

The context created for the communication, the methods for creating the context, and the methods to access information have different names but they can easily be mapped from OPC HDA to OPC UA. Table 10.7 lists the mapping necessary to provide the same level of access to OPC HDA information in OPC UA.

**Table 10.7** Mapping information access from OPC HDA to UA

| OPC HDA | OPC UA |
|---|---|
| Context | |
| COM Object OPCHDAServer | OPC UA Session |
| COM Object OPCHDABrowser | OPC UA Session |
| Creating Context | |
| CoInitializeEx<br>CoInitializeSecurity<br>CoCreateInstanceEx creates OPCHDAServer | OpenSecureChannel<br>CreateSession<br>ActivateSession |
| GetItemHandles<br>ReleaseItemHandles | RegisterNodes<br>UnregisterNodes |
| Accessing Information | |
| ChangeBrowsePosition<br>GetEnum<br>GetItemID | Browse |
| GetItemAttributes | Read |
| IOPCHDA_SyncRead::ReadRaw<br>IOPCHDA_AsyncRead::ReadRaw<br>IOPCHDA_SyncRead::ReadModified<br>IOPCHDA_AsyncRead::ReadModified | HistoryRead with read detail<br>ReadRawModified |
| IOPCHDA_SyncRead::ReadProcessed<br>IOPCHDA_AsyncRead::ReadProcessed | HistoryRead with read detail<br>ReadProcessed |
| IOPCHDA_SyncRead::ReadAtTime<br>IOPCHDA_AsyncRead::ReadAtTime | HistoryRead with read detail<br>ReadAtTime |
| IOPCHDA_SyncUpdate::Insert, Replace<br>and InsertReplace<br>IOPCHDA_AsyncUpdate::Insert, Replace<br>and InsertReplace | HistoryUpdate with update detail<br>UpdateData |
| IOPCHDA_SyncUpdate::DeleteRaw<br>IOPCHDA_AsyncUpdate::DeleteRaw | HistoryUpdate with update detail<br>DeleteRawModified |
| IOPCHDA_SyncUpdate::DeleteAtTime<br>IOPCHDA_AsyncUpdate::DeleteAtTime | HistoryUpdate with update detail<br>DeleteAtTime |
| IOPCHDA_AsyncRead:: AdviseRaw<br>IOPCHDA_AsyncRead::AdviseProcessed | Subscription with Data or Aggregate Monitored Item |
| GetAggregates | Browse and Read starting from Object HistoryAggregates |
| QueryCapabilities | Browse and Read HistoryServer-Capabilities Object. |
| GetHistorianStatus | Read or monitoring of ServerState and ServerStatus Variables |

## 10.5    Summary

### 10.5.1  Key Messages

Most of the Classic OPC features can be mapped straightforward to OPC UA, since OPC UA adopted a lot of the concepts and similar functionality has just different names in OPC UA. The main reason for different names is the much wider approach of OPC UA, where defined terms need to cover more functionality than in Classic OPC. For example, an OPCGroup in OPC DA and an OPCEventSubscription in OPC A&E and a Subscription in OPC XML-DA became a Subscription in OPC UA covering both DA and A&E.

Just by looking through the mapping tables, it can be seen that OPC UA is much more generic than Classic OPC. A long list of different interface methods used to access information in Classic OPC is replaced with a few generic OPC UA Services. Different concepts to represent information in the Address Space are replaced with one generic and extensible instance and type model in OPC UA.

### 10.5.2  Where to Find More Information?

The mapping tables in this chapter just give a hint how to map different terms, concepts, and features from Classic OPC to OPC UA. They are a starting point to find the details in the different OPC specifications for Classic OPC and OPC UA. These specifications are the main source for additional information to implement the mappings. SDK documentations and the documentations for the wrappers and proxies provided by the OPC Foundation may give additional hints.

### 10.5.3  What's Next?

The mapping from Classic OPC to OPC UA described in this chapter is used in the implementation of wrapper and proxy components or for the integration of OPC UA into existing OPC products. These migration strategies are described in the next chapter.

# 11 Migration

## 11.1 Overview

OPC UA provides migration strategies for different requirements and levels of OPC UA adoption. The first level does not require changes in existing products. Wrappers and proxies provided by the OPC Foundation are able to translate the different Classic OPC interfaces to OPC UA and vice-versa. This level is appropriate for integrating the installed base of OPC products and legacy products into OPC UA communication networks. This migration strategy is explained more detailed in the next sections.

For OPC product vendors, the other levels of migration are more important. The second level uses the mappings described in the previous chapter to expose the same features as in the existing products with OPC UA. This does not require any changes on internal interfaces to access information of a system exposed with Classic OPC today. The advantage over the use of wrappers is a higher performance, fewer limitations, and less maintenance efforts by avoiding an additional wrapper software layer. From a product point of view,[1] this is not much more effort than using the integration of the wrappers. This level allows OPC products already to profit from all enhancements regarding the reliable and secure communication between distributed systems.

In an iterative development and improvement process, it is easy to add additional features supported by OPC UA. A good example is the support of the new feature Methods. For adding this feature to an OPC UA Data Access server, it is only necessary to support the Method NodeClass with the Properties to describe the input and output arguments of a Method and the Call Service to enable a client to call the provided Methods. Since OPC UA is flexible and extensible, more and more features can be added over time.

## 11.2 Wrappers: Access COM Server from UA Client

OPC UA Wrappers are used to allow OPC UA clients to access Classic OPC servers. Such a wrapper component is an OPC client for one of the Classic OPC standards accessing a server and at the same time the wrapper is an OPC UA server allowing UA clients to talk to the wrapped server.

Figure 11.1 shows the components of a UA wrapper providing access to an OPC Data Access server for UA clients.

---

[1] The development effort is only a small part of the product costs. Testing, documentation, and long-term support needs to be provided also for the wrappers.

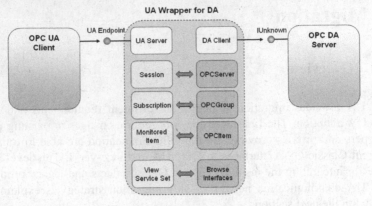

Fig. 11.1 UA wrapper providing access to OPC DA servers

The UA DA wrapper implements a UA server exposing UA Endpoints, allowing UA clients to access the data from any server providing an OPC Data Access compliant interface. A Session created by a UA client results in the creation of an OPCServer object in the OPC DA server and a Subscription with Monitored Items is mapped to an OPCGroup with OPCItems. The View Service Set implemented in the wrapper uses the mapping described in Sect. 10.2.1 and the browse and property access interfaces defined for OPC DA.

Figure 11.2 shows the components of a UA wrapper providing access to an OPC Alarm & Events server for UA clients.

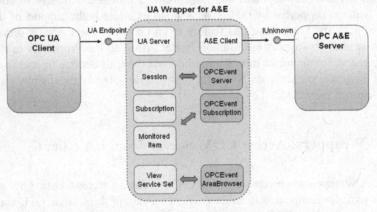

Fig. 11.2 UA wrapper providing access to OPC A&E servers

The UA A&E wrapper implements a UA server exposing UA Endpoints, allowing UA clients to receive Events from any server providing an OPC Alarm & Events compliant interface. A Session created by a UA client results in the creation of an OPCEventServer object in the OPC A&E server and a Monitored Item created in a Subscription is mapped to an OPCEventSubscription. The View Service Set implemented in the wrapper uses the mapping described in Sect. 10.3.1 and the browse and event type access methods defined for OPC A&E.

## 11.3 Proxies: Access UA Server from COM Client

OPC UA Proxies are used to allow Classic OPC clients to access OPC UA servers. Such a proxy component is an OPC UA client accessing a UA server and at the same time the proxy is a Classic OPC server exposing a COM interface, allowing clients using one of the Classic OPC standards to access OPC UA servers.

Figure 11.3 shows the components of a proxy providing access to an OPC UA server for OPC DA clients. The proxy implements the mapping described in Sect. 10.2.1.

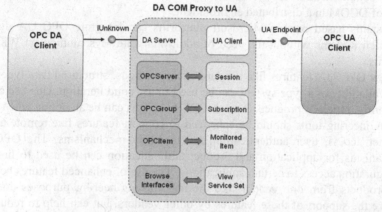

**Fig. 11.3** DA COM proxy providing access to OPC UA server

Figure 11.4 shows the components of a proxy providing access to an OPC UA server for OPC A&E clients. The proxy implements the mapping described in Sect. 10.3.1.

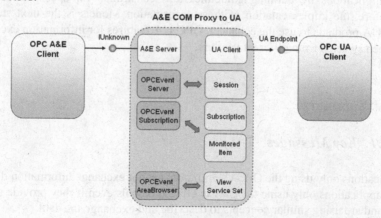

**Fig. 11.4** A&E COM proxy providing access to OPC UA server

## 11.4    Native Development

The Wrappers and Proxies are used to integrate OPC UA applications with existing applications based on Classic OPC. Their use should be restricted to legacy products and existing installations, since the additional software layer creates performance overheads and adds additional configuration and maintenance effort.

SDKs and UA Stacks for different programming languages and development environments make the native integration of OPC UA into a product a manageable task. Existing OPC functionality can be exposed with OPC UA in a first iteration step. This allows using Classic OPC and OPC UA in parallel. The advantages of this first step are the integration of existing OPC features like DA, HAD, and A&E into one address space and the use of the reliable, secure, and easy to configure communication features of OPC UA. This first step overcomes the limitations of DCOM in a distributed environment.

Systems based on non-Microsoft platforms can integrate OPC UA directly into their systems without the need of additional gateways running on Windows systems.

New OPC UA features like the support of methods, structured data types, and the availability of a type system can be used in a second iteration. One use case is the configuration of products through OPC UA. This can be an option when existing engineering tools should be enhanced to support features like remote access, internet access, user authentication, and security mechanisms. The OPC UA mechanisms for application and product authentication can be used to limit the configuration access to certain applications. The use of enhanced features between the products from one vendor like the use for engineering purposes does not require the support of these features by other vendors, but can help to reduce the design and development efforts when features supported by OPC UA are needed in a product.

Domain-specific Information Models will make use of the new features and capabilities of OPC UA. This enhances the usability and interoperability of OPC UA applications by defining guidelines and constraints for special use cases. Therefore, the implementation of these Information Models is the next step for OPC UA products to use the enhanced OPC UA features for information exchange between systems from different vendors.

## 11.5    Summary

### 11.5.1    Key Messages

Applications only using the OPC UA protocol cannot exchange information directly with applications only using the Classic OPC protocols even if they provide similar data and are using similar concepts to describe and exchange the data.

The mapping between such applications is provided by wrapper and proxy components developed by the OPC Foundation. These components can be used to integrate OPC UA applications into existing OPC installations or to use legacy OPC products in OPC UA communication environments.

The wrappers and proxies are not adding any new OPC UA features. They are only translating the Classic OPC functionality to OPC UA. These components are implementing the mapping described in Chap.10 but they can be used together with any OPC compliant product to translate OPC UA to Classic OPC and vice-versa. The main used case for these components is the integration with the installed base and legacy OPC products.

This covers the important design goal of OPC UA to allow easy migration from Classic OPC to OPC UA to protect investments in OPC and to use the large installed OPC base for OPC UA.

Another aspect is the reuse of successful OPC concepts and the integration of all existing OPC standards in one generic model. This allows existing OPC products to migrate to OPC UA by following the mappings described in Chap. 10. These products can provide or use OPC UA and Classic OPC in parallel in one product without loosing already provided functionality. New OPC UA features can be added over time.

## 11.5.2  Where to Find More Information?

The wrapper and proxy components can be downloaded from the OPC Foundation web site.

## 11.5.3  What's Next?

The next chapter introduces Profiles. They are used to declare what features an OPC UA product ensures to support. Applications exchange these profiles to know what they can expect from the application they want to exchange data with.

# 12 Profiles

## 12.1 Motivation

OPC UA combines the functionality of OPC DA, OPC HDA, and OPC A&E, and introduces additional features like historical Events and Methods. Not every OPC UA application will support all the functionality of OPC UA. For example, a server running on an embedded device may not provide any historical information or may even not be able to support subscriptions. Some servers are able to track changes in their Address Space, others not. The same is true for clients. For example, some clients will only deal with current data, others will only subscribe to Events. To handle OPC UA applications with different functionalities, OPC UA introduces Profiles.

Profiles define the functionality of an OPC UA application. A Profile can be used by vendors for marketing ("my product supports these features") and as decision support for customers ("I need a product supporting these features"). To verify that an application really supports a Profile there are test cases defined for the features of a Profile. Independent testing authorities will test the applications and create signed Software Certificates for the application. Those Certificates contain information about the supported Profiles.

Profiles are not only used as human-readable announcement, but information about the supported Profiles is also exchanged between OPC UA applications. This allows applications to reject connections when their counterpart does not support required Profiles. It also illustrates the features supported by an application and allows other applications to only use those features and not try to use features that are not supported.

In the following section we will introduce the different building-blocks for Profiles and explain the different kinds of Profiles. Afterwards we will look at client- and server-related Profiles as well as transport- and security-related Profiles. Finally we will describe the certification process of how you can get signed Software Certificates.

## 12.2 Profiles, Conformance Units, and Test Cases

An OPC UA application can support several Profiles and each Profile can contain other Profiles. There are different categories of Profiles: server-related, client-related, security-related, or transport-related. A Profile is typically composed of several Conformance Units. A Conformance Unit is a testable unit. An example of a Conformance Unit is the Call Service. Each Conformance Unit has Test Cases. Test Cases for the Call Service are, for example, calling one Method in a Service invocation or calling several Methods. The Profiles and Conformance Units are defined in [UA Part 7], whereas the Test Cases are defined in the separated test specifications [OPCTL Part 8], and [OPCTL Part 9]. The relations from Profiles to from Profiles to Conformance Units and Test Cases are summarized in Figure 12.1.

W. Mahnke et al., *OPC Unified Architecture*,
DOI: 10.1007/978-3-540-68899-0_12, © Springer-Verlag Berlin Heidelberg 2009

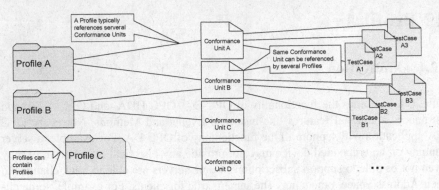

**Fig. 12.1** Profiles, Conformance Units, and Test Cases

## 12.3 Profiles for Server Applications

There are two kinds of server-related Profiles: facets and full-featured. Full-featured Profiles define a set of Conformance Units that are expected to be supported by a large amount of applications. A UA server needs to support at least one full-featured Profile. Facets define certain facets of the server like supporting event subscriptions. Full-featured Profiles already contain some facets, but additional facets can be added to a server, extending the functionality supplied by the server.

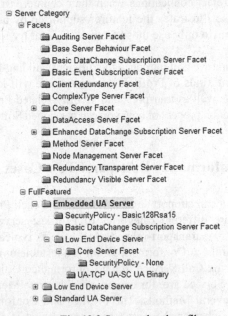

**Fig. 12.2** Server-related profiles

In Figure 12.2, the list of facets and full-featured server-related Profiles is shown. As an example, the Embedded UA Server is expanded. You can see that it contains facets and another full-featured Profile. It does not only reference server-related Profiles but also transport- and security-related Profiles. Please be aware that the list of Profiles can always be extended and Fig. 12.2 contains only facets regarding Part 1–8 of the specification. There will be additional Profiles, for example, for Historical Access.

## 12.4   Profiles for Client Applications

Unlike server-related Profiles, client-related Profiles define only facets of a client. It is not expected that there will be a large set of clients supporting the same group of facets and therefore there is no need for full-featured client-related profiles. Clients will pick and choose the facets they are supporting.

## 12.5   Transport Profiles

The transport-related Profiles define the supported communication protocols of an OPC UA application. Thus they define only a facet. Currently there are five Profiles, one for each reasonable combination of security protocol, transport protocol and encoding, and one combining two encodings. This is summarized in Fig. 12.3.

It is expected that servers will support as many of the transport-related Profiles as possible to allow for as great a range of interoperability. Clients would support all transports that they could reasonably expect in their domain, for example, an ERP system may never expect anything but SOAP-HTTP and thus would only support SOAP-HTTP transports.

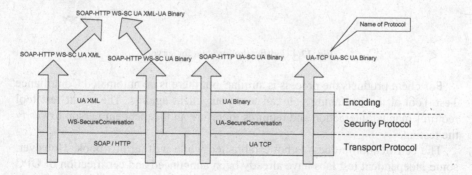

**Fig. 12.3** Transport-related profiles

## 12.6    Security Profiles

The security-related Profiles define the security algorithms and key length used to sign and encrypt messages and whether certificates are validated. Security-related Profiles always only define a facet. Currently there are three security-related Profiles defined: Basic128Rsa15, Basic256, and None. Since encryption algorithms get compromised over time due to increasing computing power, it is expected that additional security-related Profiles will be defined over time either increasing the required key length or exchanging the security algorithms.

## 12.7    Certification Process

The OPC Foundation will serve as authority signing Software Certificates that contain certain Profiles. To get your Software Certificate signed, you have two choices. In Fig. 12.4, the process regarding server products is shown. First you have to run the Compliance Test Tool testing your server. Then you can either go to an Interoperability Workshop to receive a self-tested compliance logo (which you can use for marketing) and the signed Software Certificate. Or you can use an independent test-lab testing your server product. In that case you get the golden certified compliance logo and the signed Software Certificate.

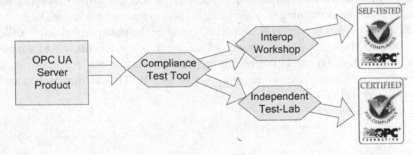

Fig. 12.4 Certification process for servers

For client products the process is similar, but there is no automated Compliance Test Tool at the beginning you can test your client against. The client test tool requires manual interaction and requires therefore an independent person to verify the testing.

The certification process is not established while writing this book. However, some independent test labs have already been announced and certification of OPC UA products will be available soon after the release of first products.

The certification process only reflects Profiles provided by the OPC Foundation. It is possible for other organizations, for example, those defining domain-specific Information Models, to define their own Profiles. These Profiles can reference

Conformance Units and Profiles of the OPC Foundation. It is also allowed creating additional Conformance Units. Those domain-specific Profiles are not tested by the OPC Foundation and the certification of Software Certificates referencing those Profiles must be managed by the organizations defining the Profiles.

## 12.8   Summary

### 12.8.1  Key Messages

Profiles are the mechanism for scaling OPC UA applications. There are full-featured server-related Profiles defining low-end device servers, embedded servers, and standard servers. Additional full-featured servers may be defined as in the future. For client applications only facets are defined, that is, each client will choose which client-related Profiles it supports. Transport- and security-related Profiles define the supported transport and security mechanisms and can be applied on client and server applications.

The certification process provides trust that an application claiming to support a Profile is tested and true supported the claimed Profile. The Profile mechanism of OPC UA is open, that is, other organizations may define additional Profiles for their domains and can set up their own certification environment.

### 12.8.2  Where to Find More Information?

Profiles and Conformance Units are defined in [UA Part 7]. The Test Cases are defined in [OPCTL Part 8], and [OPCTL Part 9]. However, to get an overview over the available Profiles, we suggest using the Profiles web page of the OPC Foundation (http://www.opcfoundation.org/UAProfiles), where you can browse the Profiles and see the dependencies to other Profiles and the Conformance Units.

### 12.8.3  What's Next?

In the next chapter we will finally take a look at the performance of OPC UA. There you will see how the chosen transport and security settings will affect the performance, but especially how the chosen encoding can slow down or boost your performance.

# 13 Performance

## 13.1 Overview

One of the requirements for OPC UA was to maintain or even enhance the performance of Classic OPC. Performance in this context does not only mean speed of communication, it also means less load and resource requirements on the target system. It was an important lesson learned with the adoption of OPC XML-DA in embedded systems where processing XML messages was a problem for those not optimized for string handling.

OPC UA must scale from small embedded systems up to enterprise systems with different requirements regarding speed and type of transferred data. In embedded systems, where smaller pieces of data must be transferred in short time intervals, the performance and minimal system load is the most important requirement. In enterprise systems, where structured data must be processed in a transaction- and event-based manner, the efficient handling of structured data is more important than the absolute speed of data transfer. OPC UA uses different transport technologies to cover all these requirements and to ensure the scalability of OPC UA.[1] For embedded systems and UA products used in an automation environment, the preferred transport mechanism will be the optimized UA TCP protocol with binary encoding. For enterprise systems, the preferred mechanism may be Web Services using binary or XML encoding.

There are more performance relevant aspects than only the different transport and encoding mechanisms implemented by the UA Stacks. The application layer, the integration of the application with the UA Stacks, and the way how the application layer can access the provided data has much more impact to the performance than the UA Stacks. If the data source is in a device connected via a serial link to a PC running the OPC UA server, the performance bottleneck will be always the serial connection and not the OPC UA communication.

For these reasons it is impossible to provide general performance numbers for OPC UA products. This chapter provides numbers for the UA Stack layer performance compared with COM and with the different possible transport and encoding mechanisms. These numbers give a hint for the best possible performance. Very efficient UA applications having direct access to the data may reach these numbers but typical UA applications, for example, a UA server talking to a device will cause overheads in the communication, which can be much higher than the numbers provided in this chapter. In this case the numbers give a hint about the expected load created by the OPC UA part of the application.

---

[1] There are also other requirements for having two protocol versions like communication through firewalls and internet access.

W. Mahnke et al., *OPC Unified Architecture*,
DOI: 10.1007/978-3-540-68899-0_13, © Springer-Verlag Berlin Heidelberg 2009

## 13.2    Performance Numbers

The environment used to measure the absolute numbers to compare OPC UA with OPC Data Access was based on two Pentium 4 PCs with 2.4 GHz and a 100 MBit network. The performance measurement covers the roundtrips necessary for a typical Read method call depending on the number of Variables included in the bulk operation. The method called for OPC DA was IOPCSyncIO::Read, and for OPC UA the Read service was called using numeric NodeIds from registered Variable Nodes. The measurement was executed with special server applications without application logic just creating return parameters with valid values. Figure 13.1 shows the applications used to measure the performance numbers.

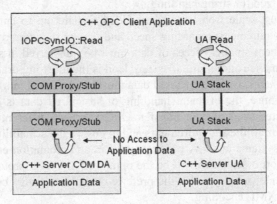

Fig. 13.1 Application setup used for measurement

All applications in the measurements used to compare COM with OPC UA are C++ based applications. The data type used in the Read methods was a four byte integer value.

The methods were called in a loop for different configurations.

- OPC DA using
  - remote communication with DCOM
  - local COM communication.
- OPC UA with UA TCP and binary encoding
  - remote communication without security
  - remote communication using the security profile Basic128RSA15 with security mode sign&encrypt
  - local communication without security.

Table 13.1 shows the absolute numbers for a Read roundtrip in milliseconds for remote UA communication without security.

**Table 13.1** Call time in milliseconds for read using remote communication

| Number of variables in one read call | UA without security |
|---|---|
| 1 | 0.28 ms |
| 10 | 0.35 ms |
| 100 | 0.93 ms |
| 1000 | 5.26 ms |

Figure 13.2 shows the factor comparing the remote OPC DA Read using DCOM and the remote OPC UA Read with and without security. The baseline is the numbers for the OPC UA Read without security.

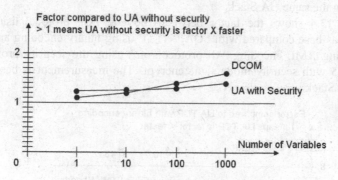

**Fig. 13.2** Factor comparing UA with DCOM

The remote numbers are indicating that the OPC UA communication is more efficient than the DCOM communication where the factor of performance improvement over DCOM is between 1.1 for small messages and factor 1.6 for Read calls with 1,000 Variables. When adding the high level of security provided by OPC UA, which was not available for DCOM, the OPC UA communication is still providing the same performance like Classic OPC.

Figure 13.3 shows the factor comparing the local OPC DA Read using COM and the local OPC UA Read without security.

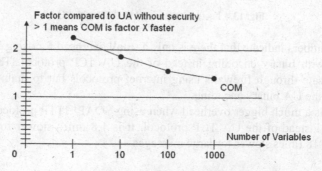

**Fig. 13.3** Factor comparing UA with COM

The local measurement indicates that the local COM communication used with Classic OPC is a little bit faster than the OPC UA communication, where the difference is a factor of 2.3 for small messages and a factor of 1.4 for a Read with 1,000 Variables. The OPC UA stack at the moment does not have any optimization for the local communication using the same mechanisms like for the remote communication. Improvements for the local use case can reduce the difference in the future. Measurements with instrumented UA Stacks are indicating that the overhead for the TCP communication can be minimized by using a local data exchange mechanism like named pipes for small messages. For larger messages most of the time is used by the serializers used to encode and decode the Service calls. This time can be reduced by eliminating the serialization between applications using the same UA Stack.

Figure 13.4 shows the factor between the UA TCP protocol using binary encoding as base compared with SOAP/HTTP using binary encoding and SOAP/HTTP using XML encoding. All protocols are using the security profile Basic 128RSA15 with security mode sign&encrypt. The measurement is based on the .NET UA Stack.

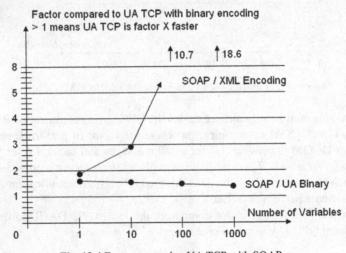

**Fig. 13.4** Factor comparing UA TCP with SOAP

The numbers indicate that there is only a small overhead for using SOAP/HTTP protocol with binary encoding instead of the UA TCP protocol. This allows to communicate through firewalls using internet protocols but to maintain the efficiency of the UA binary encoding.

There is a much bigger overhead when using SOAP/HTTP protocol with XML encoding instead of the UA TCP protocol. It is 1.8 times slower for small messages and 18 times slower for large messages.

## 13.3  Summary

### 13.3.1 Key Messages

OPC UA maintains the performance of Classic OPC with the optimized UA protocol but adds security and reliability for communication between distributed systems. By integrating OPC UA directly into embedded system, an additional communication layer can be removed and the performance and flexibility can be improved.

Like for Classic OPC, the performance of OPC UA products does normally depend more on the efficiency of the application and the internal performance of the system accessing the data provided by the system than on the OPC communication.

The Web Service base UA communication has impact on the performance. Especially, the XML-encoded Web Services create much more overhead but they provide flexibility in use cases where performance is not the most important requirement.

### 13.3.2 Where to Find More Information?

Concrete performance numbers of OPC UA products may be available in the documentation of those products.

On the OPC Foundation web site, you can find presentations of developer conferences containing additional performance measurements, including the comparison of different data types.

### 13.3.3 What's Next?

In the next chapter – the last one of this book – we will summarize OPC UA and discuss the complexity of OPC UA, pointing out that it is simple in most cases and explain why some parts must have some complexity. We also provide an outlook of what we expect to happen in the near future regarding OPC UA.

# 14 Conclusion and Outlook

## 14.1 OPC UA in a Nutshell

OPC Unified Architecture (OPC UA) is the new standard for data communication in process automation and beyond, provided by the OPC Foundation. It is expected that OPC UA will replace the very successful Microsoft-DCOM-based specifications of the OPC Foundation (DA, HDA, and A&E) over the next few years as OPC UA unifies all the functions provided by those specifications. Because of its platform-independence and use of state-of-the-art Web service technology (see Chap. 6) it is expected that OPC UA will be applied in an even wider range of industries and applications, compared to Classic OPC. It can be deployed on devices, DCS, MES and ERP systems. The small set of easy-to-use services (see Chap. 5) allows accessing the unified address space in a reliable and secure manner (see Chap. 7). By using binary encoding on the wire OPC UA is a high-performance solution, significantly faster than XML data exchange (see Chap. 13).

OPC UA not only addresses data communication but also information modeling (see Chap. 2). With its rich address space model, it allows high-value metadata exposure and thus provides significantly more information than before. For this purpose, OPC UA uses object-oriented concepts and allows a full-meshed network of nodes related by multiple types of references. There is a high interest in these capabilities in many domains and there are already projects to standardize information models based on OPC UA. Examples of such activities are FDI where a common field device description is targeted and common activities with PLCopen (Industrial Control), MIMOSA (Maintenance Information – ERP and above), and S95 (Production Information – MES) (see Chap. 4).

With its profiles (see Chap. 12) OPC UA scales well from small servers to highly sophisticated systems. Small servers only providing simple functionality are able to run on limited hardware, exposing only a small set of simple data. Highly sophisticated servers are able to expose a large amount of complex information and to support complex functionality like querying the address space (see Chap. 9).

Nevertheless, some people are complaining that "Everything is so complicated" in OPC UA. Therefore, in the next section we will take a look at this objection against OPC UA. Finally, there is an outlook examining how OPC UA may be applied in the market and what is missing in it, to improve it even further.

## 14.2 Is OPC UA Complicated?

Over the last couple of years we had several discussions about OPC UA with people from different domains, backgrounds and, of course, different companies. Most of

W. Mahnke et al., *OPC Unified Architecture*,
DOI: 10.1007/978-3-540-68899-0_14, © Springer-Verlag Berlin Heidelberg 2009

them were excited about the power and possibilities that OPC UA offers. However, there were a few people complaining about the complexity of OPC UA. A quick and simple answer is that OPC UA is very simple for users of base functionality. For users of advanced features, it is not complex but as simple and generic as possible, and still very powerful. Of course this answer does not really help to convince people. Thus, in the following sections, we explain the features involved in several different places in OPC UA, why it is designed in the way it is, and what this means for people actually using OPC UA. The management summary is given in Sect. 14.2.6.

## 14.2.1 Are OPC UA Services Difficult to Handle?

Looking at the OPC UA Services, you can see that actually the number of Services is very small. OPC UA has only 37 Services, of which three Services deal with discovery and six with connection handling. That leaves 28 Services to actually access OPC UA data. Let us compare that with the old and very successful OPC DA specification. This specification deals only with current data, not events, history or a rich information model and thus deals only with a subset of functionality provided by the OPC UA specification. Nevertheless, the old OPC DA specification had nearly 70 methods.[1] That shows that the OPC UA Service framework is designed for simplicity. The intention was not to provide two Services offering the same functionality in a different manner.[2] Thus OPC UA does not offer several Services with browsing functionality but one Browse Service that allows the setting of filters on References, NodeClasses, etc. and specifying what information should be returned, such as the name or the type of information of the referenced node.

OPC UA Services are designed in a service-oriented manner, always providing bulk operations. For example the Call Service does not call a single method but allows calling a set of methods with one Service call. That design principle reduces the number of roundtrips for a set of operations and is a common feature in service-oriented architecture. It is also used in object-oriented APIs like the OPC DA specification and a reasonable compromise between simplicity and performance.

There are three concepts in the OPC UA Service framework that can be considered to be complex: First of all the query capabilities of OPC UA, second the publish mechanism of OPC UA, and third the connection establishment.

---

[1]The OPC DA specification does not use a pure object-oriented design but supports bulk operations instead of simple methods and thus the numbers are comparable.

[2]There are some minor exceptions from that rule. For example, the Read service and the subscription mechanisms both provide access to actual data. However, the use cases are very different and thus the simple Read only reading a value once and the subscription requiring some setup first and then getting changes of the value are both supported.

In the first case the complexity is inherent to the provided functionality. Complex queries are complex in SQL [ISO08a] or OQL [CBB+00] as well. Queries are an optional feature in OPC UA and many servers will not support it and it does not even make sense to support it in many scenarios where the amount of data in the server is small and browsing the address space is the best way to deal with the data. However, there will be OPC UA servers having a huge address space with millions of nodes and in that scenario the querying capabilities become a requirement to efficiently find data in the server. But a complex problem cannot be solved without any complexity.

The second complex concept of OPC UA is the publish mechanism. The publish mechanism allows the logical callback to asynchronously send notification messages to a client containing data changes or event data without establishing a real backward channel from the server to the client. The main reason for designing the publish mechanism in that way was that OPC UA potentially runs in a Web Service environment, connecting clients and servers over the Internet or intranet, having firewalls between them. In that environment, it is easy to "talk" from a client to a server but often impossible to "talk" from the server to the client (that would require the server to be a client and more important the client to become a server). Introduced as a second method to do callbacks, the OPC UA working group found that the publish mechanism is always as good as a real callback mechanism, considering the additional requirement of sending keep-alive messages and sequence numbers to have a reliable communication in an unreliable environment. Thus the callback approach was discarded and only the publish mechanism is part of the OPC UA specification as it provides the same functionality as a real callback. In addition, the callback mechanism would highly increase the complexity regarding security mechanisms, as another secure connection has to be established from the OPC UA server to the client. Here again the simplicity of the OPC UA Service framework can be seen: only one method is available for one purpose. However, it requires some time to truly understand the publish mechanism. The good news is that only a very small number of people really have to understand the mechanism. Most people will use a server or client SDK that deals with the mechanism and provides real callbacks internally.

The third complex concept in OPC UA is connection establishment. This step requires establishing a secure channel. On top of the secure channel a session has to be created. The secure channel provides security on the transport level, which means that messages can be encrypted and signed.[3] OPC UA uses WS-SecureConversation as part of the WS-* standard [OASIS07] for its secure channel when SOAP messages are exchanged in the Web Service world and adapts this specification to UA-SecureConversation when the high performance UA TCP is used. Details of the technologies used for secure channels are given in Chap. 7, including why no

---

[3]Security has to be implemented in certified OPC UA products (see Chaps. 7 and 12). Whether security is enabled in a concrete installation depends on the configuration based on the security requirements of the installation.

standard protocols like TLS/SSL can be used, based on requirements for OPC UA, such as having long-running connections, etc. On top of such a secure channel, multiple sessions can be created, decoupling the secure communication from the session management on the application level. The described steps are very common and a good security design in various ways. Therefore they are necessary for ensuring a secure and reliable communication between clients and servers. The good news is that again only a few people really have to deal with it, as an OPC UA SDK will provide a connect method that hides the handshaking to establish a connection.

To summarize the discussion:

1. The OPC UA Service framework (measured by the number of Services) is very simple.
2. OPC UA Services are designed for bulk operations to avoid roundtrips. This increases the complexity of the Services but greatly improves the performance. Also, Classic OPC has been designed in a similar way for most methods. Handling of bulk operations is commonly used and thus it is not "too complex to be used."
3. OPC UA queries are complex; however this is part of the addressed problem. OPC UA queries are an optional feature, useful only for large address spaces.
4. The publish mechanism of OPC UA is required in environments where the OPC UA client cannot act as a server (firewall). Using only this mechanism reduces the complexity of OPC UA (compared to adding a real callback, especially if security is considered). OPC UA SDKs will hide the mechanism and provide real callbacks anyway.
5. The connection establishment in OPC UA uses proven security mechanisms and adapts them to the needs of OPC UA. Thus some messages have to be exchanged, but this complexity will be hidden by an OPC UA SDK offering only a connect method.

Thus OPC UA Services are not complex but very simple with regard to the provided functionality and the addressed non-functional requirements such as security and reliability. Using an SDK will further hide the complexity in the Services, for example, by hiding the connection establishment and the publish mechanism.

## 14.2.2  Is Information Modeling a Pain?

OPC UA does not only standardize the data communication but also provides a meta model allowing standardized information models built on top of it. The old OPC DA specification provided a very simple but limited way to expose data items in a hierarchy. OPC UA supports the same simple approach to build a hierarchy of data variables but it also allows exposing rich models.

There are other specifications like DSSP [MS07] or DPWS [MS06] that only standardize the data exchange without specifying a model. They may define a fixed or extendable set of operations that a server provides and a client can call. The client can ask for the metadata of the operation, i.e., what data the operation will provide. However, there is no fixed syntax[4] and semantic for the data exchanged. Obviously those specifications look less complicated at first glance as they exclude the modeling capabilities. But let us take a look at Figs. 14.1 and 14.2 to see the implications of those different approaches. With a standardized protocol for data communication, there is interoperability between applications on the communication level (right side of Fig. 14.1). Here, no point-to-point integration is needed as in the left side of Fig. 14.1.

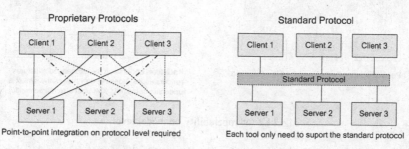

**Fig. 14.1** Interoperability on protocol level

But if no meta model is provided and the structure of the exchanged data depends on a concrete application,[5] there is no interoperability on what data are exchanged, and therefore no interoperability at the model level (left side of Fig. 14.2). Clients cannot generically interpret the data provided by the server and cannot generically provide data to the server.

OPC UA offers a solution shown in the right side of Fig. 14.2. It provides the data in a way that generic OPC UA clients are able to deal with all the data (subscribe to data, browse the address space, etc.). However, OPC UA still allows servers to define their domain and vendor-specific model, based on the standardized meta model. The Services are all based on the meta model and thus a generic client can deal with all the data. But not all semantic of the concrete model is directly captured in the meta model since it is an extensible model and not a concrete model tailored to one specific domain.[6] However, the meta model provides all information about the extensions and thus a generic client can easily display all semantic information, but some of them have to be interpreted by a user. Clients can be implemented with built-in knowledge of concrete OPC UA Information Model Standards and thus no additional interpretation by the user is needed.

---

[4]Other then XML without an XML-Schema.

[5]And of course a client also has to send data to the server in a format the server expects.

[6]The OPC UA meta model is tailored to the broad domain of exchanging real-time related data, including events and history, but not to a concrete domain like drilling or pulp and paper.

Standard Protocol and Proprietary Model            Standard Protocol and Standard Meta Model

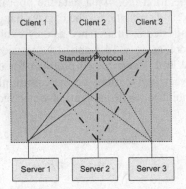
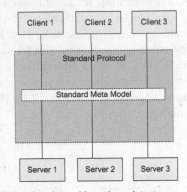

Point-to-point integration on model level required    Each tools understand the exchanged structures
                                                       (understanding does not only means the syntax is
                                                       understandable (e.g. XML) but also the semantic)

**Fig. 14.2** Interoperability on model level

Let us take a quick look at the implications for client and server developers, whether a meta model is provided or not. Obviously, having a common model makes life much easier for client developers as they can implement their clients with knowledge of one model supported by all servers. Otherwise they would have to deal with several servers providing different data structures. However, leaving the data structures undefined seems like a great opportunity for server developers. They have complete freedom to do whatever they want to do. But they also have all the work to do. It took the OPC UA working group several years to develop the meta model that is able to access and change real-time related data, alarms and events, and the history of both. Of course a specific server does not have to provide a generic meta model as OPC UA has to do, but there is still a lot of work to do and many pitfalls to avoid. And after creating their own model they have to document it, so that clients are able to get access to the data and users understand at least a basic semantic so they are able to deal with the provided data and the ways to access them. Looking at all those tasks, mapping the data to a well-defined meta model and enriching the server to a concrete model using the extension mechanisms does not seem so complicated anymore.

After explaining the need for a meta model in OPC UA there is still the question of its complexity. The Classic OPC specifications, for example, only provided one[7] concrete and very simple model. The reason for having the more powerful and more complex model in OPC UA is that it allows exposing much more semantic and thus much more information. Since OPC UA does not target one concrete domain, it allows defining information models for concrete models tailored to specific domains. Therefore we have typed objects and references, etc. To

---

[7]Actually one per specification.

expose more information in a usable way more concepts have to be introduced and this increases the complexity. However, the complexity is found in the information provided additionally. If no additional information needs to be provided, the OPC UA model becomes very simple. For example, the OPC DA wrapper of the OPC Foundation wraps any OPC DA server. Since the OPC DA server does not provide complex information, the OPC UA model of the wrapper is very simple (see Chap. 10). It contains only one hierarchy with OPC UA Folder Objects for the OPC DA Branches and OPC UA Variables for the OPC DA Items. OPC DA properties are provided as OPC UA Properties. No detailed type information (all Objects are of the same type), no additional ReferenceTypes, no ModelChangeEvents tracking changes on the model, no other fancy stuff is to be found. It is optional to use those features and it does not make sense to use them in many cases. However, if you need to provide more information, it is very useful to have those concepts in place so you can use them appropriately. As it is the choice of the server to use features regarding the modeling, it is the choice of the client to decide what features it wants to use. Programming against types is a very powerful feature and very helpful when creating process graphics or other user interfaces specific for certain OPC UA types. However, a simple client providing only browsing capabilities will never use this feature.

Information modeling can be done very easily, keeping everything very simple. Then little effort is required and using some very basic OPC UA modeling concepts keeps everything very simple. The OPC DA wrapper is a good example of that approach. But if more information must be provided OPC UA is equipped with the necessary concepts to allow it. The complexity is based on the information to be modeled, not in OPC UA itself.

### 14.2.3 Transport Protocols and Encodings: Why So Many?

OPC UA defines an abstract set of Services that is mapped to different technologies. Currently there are two protocol mappings and two encodings supported. The reason for having abstract Services is that, if a new technology for data communication enters the stage, OPC UA can be adapted to that technology just by defining another mapping. But why does OPC UA support two protocols and two encodings from the beginning? The reason is that OPC UA will be applied in different application domains with different requirements. Supporting HTTP and UA TCP (see Chap. 6) allow it to run Internet applications crossing firewalls with HTTP as well as running optimized applications with limited resources via the UA TCP protocol, which is optimized for the wire (no overhead) and the needed resources (no HTTP stack needed). But the main optimization on the wire is not UA TCP versus HTTP but exchanging binary encoded data versus XML encoded data. Unlike other protocols, OPC UA does not require the data to be first converted to XML and then binary encoded; the data is directly binary encoded and is thus very efficient. However, there are applications that do not need high performance but data provided in a generic way (which nowadays means in XML) to be able to handle them easily. Those applications are typically placed not on the bottom, but the top of the automation pyramid. Therefore OPC UA supports XML encoding as well. Figure 14.3 summarizes the use of different protocol options in a simplified form.

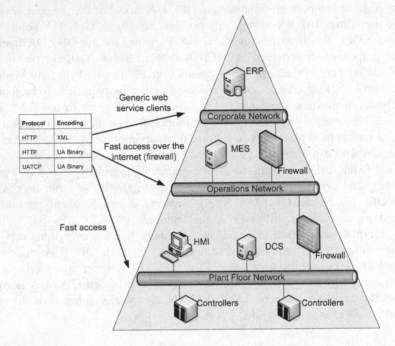

**Fig. 14.3** Simplified view of OPC UA transport protocols and encodings

After understanding why OPC UA supports different technology mappings, we will discuss how this affects people dealing with OPC UA. The good news is that anybody using an OPC UA SDK or even only an OPC UA stack provided by the OPC Foundation could not care less about that. The OPC UA Services stay the same and thus the server or client implementation stays the same, no matter what the stack uses to communicate with another stack (see Chap. 8 for details). Only those people developing stacks or using generic toolkits, for example, to generate clients talking to Web Services (e.g., by a WSDL) are affected by supporting different protocols and encodings. It is the job of stack developers, so we will not argue about that. Generic toolkit users bound to a technology like Web Services are bound to the technology provided by the toolkit. But those users choose to use that generic toolkit (which is of course reasonable in some scenarios) and therefore they are intentionally bound to that technology. This leads to potential interoperability problems between OPC UA servers and OPC UA clients supporting different technologies. But here again OPC UA profiles are a good mechanism to avoid that and new technologies are not provided so often that one must fear an explosion on OPC UA technology mappings.

## 14.2.4  Implementation Issues

A few people have complained about the lack of comfort of OPC UA SDKs. This is of course something we cannot answer in general but it depends on the used SDK. As a general statement, people have to be aware that OPC UA is a new specification and thus people are dealing more with developing initial products than with providing a perfect SDK. The comfort of OPC UA SDKs will increase in future.[8] However, the SDKs we are aware of already support the developer quite well by implementing all the housekeeping functions of the OPC UA Service framework.

Let us take a look at server-side development. You do not have to deal with subscriptions; you only have to provide the data that are to be published. You do not have to deal with queue management, republishing, or packing of data. There is infrastructure to manage OPC UA nodes in the server. Thus you only have to configure the Address Space of your server. This can be done by an XML configuration where most of the code is generated.

On the client-side, you get real callbacks, you can connect by one call, etc. So there is already a lot of comfort in the SDKs we are aware of. However, there is still room for improvements, e.g., fancy wizards, graphical modeling tools, etc.

## 14.2.5  Migration of Existing Code

For somebody with Classic OPC servers and clients it might seem like a large amount of work migrating to OPC UA. Since the OPC Foundation provides wrappers for the Classic OPC servers as well as proxies for the Classic OPC clients, this is obviously not true if you do not want to change your existing code. You simply deploy the provided proxies or wrappers with your existing product and you are ready for OPC UA. However, let us take a quick look at what you need to do for native OPC UA support in existing products. As OPC DA is the most popular Classic OPC specification, we will examine what to do in that case.

In the case of an OPC DA client, it is easy to replace the existing code for reading, writing, and adding groups and items to receive data changes with similar concepts from UA, such as subscriptions and monitored items. UA client SDKs will provide data change callbacks on top of a subscription hiding the publish

---

[8]This is a general statement true for all SDKs in all domains. The comfort and quality of an SDK always increases from very early versions (1.0 or even less) to higher and more stable versions.

mechanism. The biggest change is the handling of NodeIds instead of pure string based ItemIDs in old OPC DA. For the configuration part the browsing and property access methods from OPC DA can be replaced with the UA Browse Service calls. This is all the functionality most OPC DA clients use today.

In the case of an OPC DA server, there are only a few Services that need to be implemented like Read, Write, Browse, and the delivery of data changes to a UA SDK. All other Services are implemented by a UA SDK or are not needed for supporting DA functionality. Providing the required data model is also very simple as exposing a pure DA address space with no type system uses only a small number of predefined types of OPC UA.

As the OPC UA design is generic and extensible, it is easy to choose an iterative development approach to add UA features over time to a product, starting with a pure DA implementation. For example, to add OPC UA Method support, a product must implement one more UA Service and one more NodeClass to expose the Methods in the Address Space.

Let us assume you plan to migrate your products to a higher-level programming language like JAVA or .NET. Using Classic OPC requires you to deal with the interop from COM to the modern programming language. This can become a real problem when you deal with multiple threads, the life-cycle of COM objects, etc. [Ge03]. Instead you can directly target OPC UA as communication interface. Here, your product can use UA SDKs and stacks natively developed for those programming languages. Thus, the new code is separated from any COM-based code. To connect to Classic OPC products, you can use the wrappers and proxies provided by the OPC Foundation. This is exemplified in Fig. 14.4, where a C++-based OPC DA client is migrated to .NET and uses OPC UA as the new communication infrastructure.

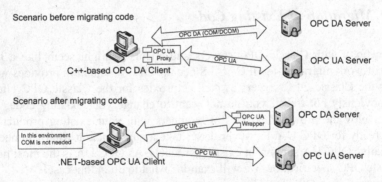

**Fig. 14.4** Migrating Classic OPC applications to modern programming languages using OPC UA

To summarize this section, OPC UA gives you a reasonable migration strategy to move a Classic OPC environment to OPC UA in different levels. The lowest level is to use the proxies and wrappers; the next level is to expose the same level of information you expose today with UA and the next level is to add additional UA features like Methods or a type system over time. If you want to migrate your code to a modern programming language, using OPC UA provides you a solution that does not require you to deal with all the COM interop problems and allows separating your new code from COM.

## 14.2.6 Management Summary

OPC UA is just as complex as it has to be, to fulfill the requirements of a secure and reliable communication, able to run in different environments including different networks separated by firewalls. The binary encoding provides high performance data exchange. Unlike other protocols OPC UA defines a meta model and thus not only provides interoperability regarding the protocol but also regarding the exchanged data. By defining an extensible base model with all the information necessary to know what data have to be exchanged but still allowing refinements and extensions to the model OPC UA is a well-suited compromise for a specification applied in various domains. Information model standards based on OPC UA define a more specific model tailored to the domain that is extended by vendor specific information. Generic OPC UA clients can easily access all this information. OPC UA profiles allow servers to be scaled from small servers with limited functionality able to run on limited resources to highly sophisticated servers providing a large amount of complex data with the full power of OPC UA.

## 14.3   Outlook

A first release of Part 1–5, 8, 10, and 11 of the OPC UA specification has been released from July 2006 to January 2007. Those specifications did not contain the release of technology mapping and therefore could not be applied in products.

While writing this section the technical advisory counsel of the OPC Foundation has already voted and agreed to release updated versions of Part 1–8 of the specification. Those specifications include the technology mapping and so we finally have a specification that can be used to build products. However, some last comments still need to be integrated into the final documents. The final release has not been done will we write this last section, but we expect that the specification is released when you can read the book beginning of 2009.

Even more important than having a released specification is that all building blocks provided by the OPC Foundation, namely the stack, are available and working. The early adopters of OPC UA have first products ready and already released when you can read this book.

We have experienced such a big interest in OPC UA that we expect a wide adoption even in areas where Classic OPC is not used today. OPC UA can be applied on devices, controllers, DCS up to MES and ERP systems and thus has a brighter scope then Classic OPC. This does not imply that OPC UA will replace all products supporting Classic OPC in the near future. The wrappers and proxies provided by the OPC Foundation are a good strategy dealing with those legacy products that will run probably for the next decade or longer. In the first step of adoption we expect that existing OPC products will be migrated to OPC UA supporting both Classic OPC and UA. The second area of early adoption will be on embedded and non Microsoft systems where OPC is needed but can not be used today. Both groups of products will mainly profit from the platform independent and reliable communication features.

A big opportunity provided by OPC UA is defining standard Information Models using OPC UA. Here, the access to domain-specific information is standardized and the secure, reliable, interoperable and platform-independent communication mechanism of OPC UA can be used. In Sect. 4.10, some of currently ongoing activities are listed. We expect that other initiatives will follow as soon as OPC UA is applied in the marked.

Finally let us take a look at OPC UA from the technical perspective. Is every feature that should be integrated into OPC UA built into it? We had a list of improvements for the version released in 2006, for example bulk browse operations. But they are already integrated in the updated version. Some of the features we can see for the future are standardized rules for cardinality restrictions and the support for transactions. Both can easily be built on top of OPC UA by defining standardized ModellingRules or standardized Methods creating a transaction context. Thus neither the Service definitions must be changed or extended nor must the stack implementation be adapted to include those features. This shows again flexibility of OPC UA. We hope this book helped you understanding OPC UA and you are now ready to apply OPC UA in your environment.

# 15 Literature

[AFK+05] C. Adams, S. Farrell, T. Kause, T. Mononen: Internet X.509 Public Key Infrastructure Certificate Management Protocol, RFC 4210, 2005

[Al01] H. Alvestrand: Tags for the Identification of Languages, RFC 3066, 2001

[AL02] C. Adams, S. Lloyd: Understanding PKI, Second Edition, Addison-Wesley, 2002, ISBN 0-672-32391-5

[CBB+00] R.G.G. Cattell, D.K. Barry, M. Berler, J. Eastman, D. Jordan, C. Russell, O. Schadow, T. Stanienda, F. Velez: The Object Data Management Standard: ODMG 3.0, Morgan Kaufmann, 2000, ISBN 1-55860-647-5

[Con07] S. Contini, Factorization Records, 2007, http://www.crypto-world.com/announcements/m1039.txt

[DR06] T. Dierks, E. Rescorla: The Transport Layer Security (TLS) Protocol Version 1.2. RFC 4346, 2006

[ECT06] EDDL Cooperation Team: Tutorial for EDDL Phase 2 UA Information Model, 2006

[FDT08] FDT Group: OPC UA Information Model Specification for FDT, Version draft 0.11, 2008

[FHM+07] T. Freeman, R. Housley, A. Malpani, D. Cooper, W. Polk: Server-based Certificate Validation Protocol (SCVP), RFC 5055, 2007

[Ge03] S. Gentile: COM Interop Not Fundamentally Flawed But Hard, Sam Gentile's Weblog, 2003, http://radio.weblogs.com/0105852/stories/2002/12/21/comInteropNotFundamentally-FlawedButHard.html

[HPF+02] R. Housley, W. Polk, W. Ford, D. Solo: Internet X.509 Public Key Infrastructure Certificate and Certificate Revocation List (CRL) Profile, RFC 3280, 2002

[IL06] F. Iwanitz, J. Lange: OPC: Fundamentals, Implementation, and Application, Hüthig, 2006, ISBN 3-77852-904-8

[ISA88] ANSI/ISA-88.01-1995 Batch Control Part 1 Models and Terminology, 1995, ISBN: 1-55617-562-0

[ISA95] ANSI/ISA-95.00.01-2000 Enterprise-Control System Integration Part I: Models and Terminology, 2000, ISBN: 1-55617-727-5

[ISA99] ANSI/ISA-99.00.01-2007 Security for Industrial Automation and Control Systems: Concepts, Terminology and Models, 2007

[ISO08a] ISO/IEC 9075-2: 2008: Information technology – Database languages – SQL – Part 2: Foundation (SQL/Foundation), 2008

[ISO08b] ISO/IEC 9075-11: 2008: Information technology – Database languages – SQL – Part 11: Information and Definition Schemas (SQL/Schemata), 2008

[LH05] S. Lipner, M. Howard: The Trustworthy Computing Security Development Lifecycle, 2005, http://msdn.microsoft.com/en-us/library/ms995349.aspx

[MAM+99] M. Myers, R. Ankney, A. Malpani, S. Galperin, C. Adams: Internet Public Key Infrastructure Online Certificate Status Protocol – OCSP, RFC 2560, 1999

[MAS+99] M. Myers, C. Adams, D. Solo, D. Kemp: Internet X.509 Certificate Request Message Format, RFC 2511, 1999

[MS03] Public Key Infrastructure for Windows Server 2003, https://www.microsoft.com/windowsserver2003/technologies/pki/default.mspx

[MS06] Microsoft: Devices Profile for Web Services (DPWS), February 2006, http://schemas.xmlsoap.org/ws/2006/02/devprof

[MS07] Microsoft: Decentralized Software Services Protocol – DSSP/1.0, July 2007, http://www.microsoft.com/robotics

[OASIS04] OASIS: WS-Security 1.0, OASIS Standard, March 2004, http://docs.oasis-open.org/wss/2004/01/oasis-200401-wss-soap-message-security-1.0.pdf

[OASIS07] OASIS: WS-SecureConversation 1.3, OASIS Standard, March 2007, http://docs.oasis-open.org/ws-sx/ws-secureconversation/v1.3/ws-secureconversation.html

[OASIS07a] OASIS: WS-SecurityPolicy 1.2, OASIS Standard, July 2007, http://docs.oasis-open.org/ws-sx/ws-securitypolicy/200702/ws-securitypolicy-1.2-spec-os.html

[OASIS07b] OASIS: WS-Trust 1.3, OASIS Standard, March 2007, http://docs.oasis-open.org/ws-sx/ws-trust/200512/ws-trust-1.3-os.html

[OMG08] Object Management Group: UML Resource Page, 2008, http://www.uml.org/

[OSSL] OpenSSL project, 2008, http://www.openssl.org/

[OXPKI] OpenXPKI Foundation, OpenXPKI Framework, 2008, http://www.openxpki.org/

[OPCTL Part 8] OPC Foundation: Test Lab Part 8: UA Server, Draft 0.92

[OPCTL Part 9] OPC Foundation: Test Lab Part 9: UA Client, Draft 0.1

[Pet08] D. Peterson: OPC UA Security Assessment, 2008, http://www.digitalbond.com/index.php/2008/08/14/opc-ua-assessment-series-part-1/

[PKCS#7] RSA Labs, PKCS #7: Cryptographic Message Syntax Standard, 1993, http://rsa.com/rsalabs/node.asp?id=2129

[PKCS#10] RSA Labs, PKCS #10: Certification Request Syntax Standard, 2000, http://rsa.com/rsalabs/node.asp?id=2132

[SF03] B. Schneier, N. Ferguson: Practical Cryptography, Wiley, 2003, ISBN 0-471-22357-3

[UA Analyzer] OPC UA Specification: Part XIII: Analyzer Devices, Draft Version 0.30.00, December 2008, OPC Foundation

[UA Part 1] OPC UA Specification: Part 1 – Concepts, Release Candidate Version 1.01.04, August 2008, OPC Foundation, http://www.opcfoundation.org/UA/Part1

[UA Part 2] OPC UA Specification: Part 2 – Security Model, Release Candidate Version 1.01.53, October 2008, OPC Foundation, http://www.opcfoundation.org/UA/Part2

[UA Part 3] OPC UA Specification: Part 3 – Address Space Model, Release Candidate Version 1.01.19, January 2009, OPC Foundation, http://www.opcfoundation.org/UA/Part3

[UA Part 4] OPC UA Specification: Part 4 – Services, Release Candidate Version 1.01.36, January 2009, OPC Foundation, http://www.opcfoundation.org/UA/Part4

[UA Part 5] OPC UA Specification: Part 5 – Information Model, Release Candidate Version 1.01.21, January 2009, OPC Foundation, http://www.opcfoundation.org/UA/Part5

[UA Part 6] OPC UA Specification: Part 6 – Concepts, Release Candidate Version 1.00.10, October 2008, OPC Foundation, http://www.opcfoundation.org/UA/Part6

[UA Part 7] OPC UA Specification: Part 7 – Profiles, Release Candidate Version 1.00.04, January 2009, OPC Foundation, http://www.opcfoundation.org/UA/Part7

[UA Part 8] OPC UA Specification: Part 8 – Data Access, Release Candidate Version 1.01.12, August 2009, OPC Foundation, http://www.opcfoundation.org/UA/Part8

[UA Part 9] OPC UA Specification: Part 9 – Alarms and Conditions, DRAFT Version 0.93q, November 2007, OPC Foundation, http://www.opcfoundation.org/UA/Part9

[UA Part 10] OPC UA Specification: Part 10 – Programs, Version 1.00, January 2007, OPC Foundation, http://www.opcfoundation.org/UA/Part10

[UA Part 11] OPC UA Specification: Part 11 – Historical Access, Version 1.00, January 2007, OPC Foundation, http://www.opcfoundation.org/UA/Part11

[UA Part 11Draft] OPC UA Specification: Part 11 – Historical Access, DRAFT Version 1.01, July 2008, OPC Foundation

[UA Part 12] OPC UA Specification: Part 12 – Discovery, DRAFT Version 1.00.03, November 2007, OPC Foundation, http://www.opcfoundation.org/UA/Part12

[UA Part 13] OPC UA Specification: Part 13 – Aggregates, Release Candidate Version 1.0, July 2008, OPC Foundation, http://www.opcfoundation.org/UA/Part13

[UA Devices] Devices, DRAFT Version 0.75, December 2008, OPC Foundation

[VMPKI] Verisign: Managed PKI Service, 2008, http://www.verisign.com/authentication/enterprise-authentication/managed-pki/index.html

[W3C02] W3C: XML Encryption Syntax and Processing, W3C Recommendation, December 2002, http://www.w3.org/TR/xmlenc-core/

[W3C04a] W3C: XML Schema Part 1: Structures, Second Edition, W3C Recommendation, October 2004, http://www.w3.org/TR/xmlschema-1/

[W3C04b] W3C: XML Schema Part 2: Datatypes, Second Edition, W3C Recommendation, October 2004, http://www.w3.org/TR/xmlschema-2/

[W3C04c] W3C: Web Services Addressing (WS-Addressing), W3C Recommendation, August 2004, http://www.w3.org/Submission/ws-addressing/

[W3C07a] W3C: SOAP Version 1.2 Part 1: Messaging Framework, Second Edition, W3C Recommendation, April 2007, http://www.w3.org/TR/soap12-part1/

[W3C07b] W3C: SOAP Version 1.2 Part 2: Messaging Framework, Second Edition, W3C Recommendation, April 2007, http://www.w3.org/TR/soap12-part2/

[W3C08] W3C: XML Signature Syntax and Processing, Second Edition, W3C Recommendation, June 2008, http://www.w3.org/TR/xmldsig-core/

# Appendix A: Graphical Notation

## Motivation and Relation to UML

OPC UA defines a graphical notation for an OPC UA Address Space [UA Part 3]. It defines graphical symbols for all NodeClasses and how References of different types can be visualized. It is used to show you a view on the Address Space by browsing it and reading current values. Thus it does not consider historical data or events that are not visible in the Address Space. This notation is already used in several parts of the specification and we use it in this book as well.

It is obvious that having a graphical notation to visualize OPC UA data is desirable. Most people who want to define an Information Model need that possibility. This is needed independent of whether they define a standard Information Model, a vendor-specific or even product- or server-specific one. By standardizing the visualization, people can easily exchange their diagrams and understand each other without the need to translate different notations.

However, there is already a very popular standard notation broadly used in various phases of software development called UML [OMG08]. An obvious question is why not to use this notation so that nobody familiar with UML has to learn a new one? For those not familiar with UML, you can skip the rest of this section and take the simple answer that in the end the OPC UA notation is actually stereotyped UML. For those familiar with UML, we go a little bit more into details.

Actually the OPC UA specification has already an informative Appendix defining the OPC UA meta model in UML [UA Part 3]. Since instances are part of the model like the base ReferenceTypes, the UML model has to deal with instances and classes. Looking at this model you can also see some difficulties. For example, there is a UML-Class called ObjectType. Thus, OPC UA ObjectTypes become instances of that UML-Class. But OPC UA also deals with Objects. They are instances of the UML-Class Object but of course also instances of the Object-Types. UML is not perfectly designed to support these different levels with its base concepts. But UML allows defining stereotypes for special instances. This concept is already used in the UML model defined by the OPC UA specification. But UML also allows defining specific graphical representations for stereotyped model elements. Although this was not done in the UML model defined in the OPC UA specification, the graphical notation defined by the OPC UA specification is in the end nothing but stereotyped UML using specific graphical elements for the different NodeClasses of OPC UA.

Thus, in the end it should be very simple for everybody familiar with UML to understand the OPC UA notation. The only thing to consider is that all Nodes you see in the diagrams would be mapped to instances in UML, thus you are only looking at UML object diagrams. The OPC UA NodeClasses would be mapped to UML-Classes.

## Notation

The graphical notation defined by OPC UA gives you a view on an OPC UA Address Space. The granularity of details can vary, and you can, for example, visualize the Attributes of a Node, but you do not have to. You can also combine this by only exposing some Attributes of a Node that are important for the diagram. The same is true for References of a Node; you can expose a few and do not expose other.

Each NodeClass has its own graphical element as shown in Table A.1. The DisplayName of the Node is shown as text inside the Node. NodeClasses representing types always have a shadow beneath it; otherwise they have the same graphical representation as there instances (only applicable for Objects and variables since DataType instances and ReferenceType instances are not represented as Nodes). Unlike defined by OPC UA, we use italic font style to expose that a type is abstract, and concrete types do not use italic. In the OPC UA specification, all types use italic, independent if they are abstract or not. The UML way of dealing with this seems more suitable for us.

References between Nodes are represented by lines between them. Arrows expose the direction. There are some special forms for specific base ReferenceTypes, as exposed in Table A.2. All other ReferenceTypes must put in the ReferenceType

**Table A.1** Notation of NodeClasses

| NodeClass | Graphical Representation | Comment |
|---|---|---|
| Object | Object | Can contain the TypeDefinition separated by "::", e.g., "Object1::Type1" |
| ObjectType | *ObjectType* | Abstract types use italic, concrete types not |
| Variable | Variable | Can contain the TypeDefinition separated by "::", e.g., "Variable1::Type1" |
| VariableType | *VariableType* | Abstract types use italic, concrete types not |
| DataType | *DataType* | Abstract types use italic, concrete types not |
| ReferenceType | *ReferenceType* | Abstract types use italic, concrete types not |
| Method | Method | – |
| View | View | – |

name on the line and use the notation of a symmetric, asymmetric, or hierarchical ReferenceType exposed in Table A.2.[1] Please note that the HasSubtype Reference points with the arrow in the inverse direction to point from the subtype to the supertype like in all other graphical notations known to the authors.

**Table A.2** Notation of References based on ReferenceTypes

| ReferenceType | Graphical Representation |
|---|---|
| Any symmetric ReferenceType | ◄——— ReferenceType ——► |
| Any asymmetric ReferenceType | ——— ReferenceType ——► |
| Any hierarchical ReferenceType | ——— ReferenceType ——▷ |
| HasComponent | ——————————┼ |
| HasProperty | ——————————╫ |
| HasTypeDefinition | ——————————►► |
| HasSubtype | ◁◁——————— |
| HasEventSource | ——————————▷ |

The Attributes of a Node can be put inside the graphical element representing the Node. This is exemplified using an Object in Fig. A.1, but it can be applied on any NodeClass. As shown in Fig. A.1, you can either provide all Attributes (A) or only some Attributes (B). Since this makes it ambiguous for optional Attributes whether they are provided, you can make this explicit by striking that Attribute out, as shown in (C).

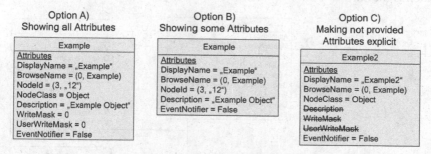

**Fig. A.1** Attributes included in Node

There are some built-in DataTypes having internally a structure that are often used in OPC UA diagrams like LocalizedText (e.g., in the DisplayName) or QualifiedName (in the BrowseName). For those it is not needed to provide the whole

---

[1] Please be aware that each Reference connects two concrete Nodes, thus you do not have any cardinality restrictions or role names on them like you would have in UML class diagrams. We are on the level of UML object diagrams where you do not have those things either.

information. For the LocalizedText and the QualifiedName, it is enough to provide the string-part as done in all diagrams of this book. However, the LocaleId respectively the NamespaceIndex can be exposed by prefixing them, separated by a ":".

To avoid a large amount of Nodes in a diagram, it is allowed to handle Properties similar to Attributes exposing them inside the Node. This is shown in Fig. A.2. Of course, this is a limited representation and here you cannot reference the Properties since they are not shown as Nodes.

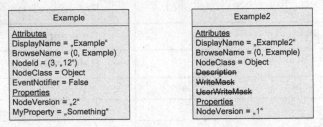

**Fig. A.2** Properties and Attributes included in Node

## Example

We will take a look at a small example to point out the different possibilities using the graphical notation of OPC UA. In Fig. A.3, you can see the Device1 Object having a DataVariable and two Properties. In addition, the reference to its TypeDefinition is shown.

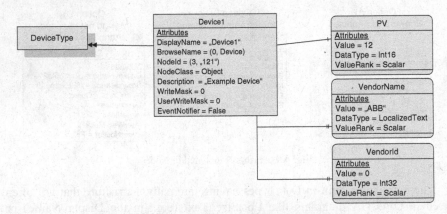

**Fig. A.3** Example of a Device Object exposing References

In Fig. A.4, the same information is provided (except for the data types of the Properties). Here, the Properties are included in the Node as well as the TypeDefinition name and thus only the Data Variable is exposed as additional Node. Please be aware that this simplified notation has some drawbacks. For example,

Example 331

the DisplayName of the ObjectType does not have to be unique. In Fig. A.3, you could expose the NodeId of the TypeDefinition Node as well (which must be unique), this is not possible in Fig. A.4.

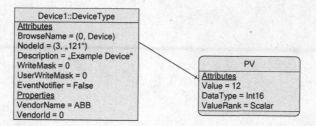

**Fig. A.4** Example of a Device Object including TypeDefinition and Properties

# Appendix B: NodeClasses and Attributes

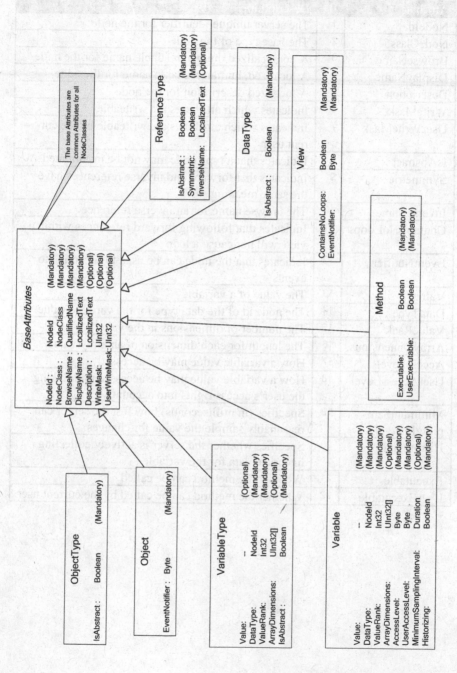

**Table B.1** List of Attributes

| Attribute | ID | Description |
|---|---|---|
| NodeId | 1 | The server unique identifier for the node |
| NodeClass | 2 | The base type of the node |
| BrowseName | 3 | A nonlocalized, human readable name for the node |
| DisplayName | 4 | A localized, human readable name for the node |
| Description | 5 | A localized description for the node |
| WriteMask | 6 | Indicates which attributes are writeable |
| UserWriteMask | 7 | Indicates which attributes are writeable by the current user |
| IsAbstract | 8 | Indicates that a type node may not be instantiated |
| Symmetric | 9 | Indicates that forward and inverse references have the same meaning |
| InverseName | 10 | The browse name for an inverse reference |
| ContainsNoLoops | 11 | Indicates that following forward references within a view will not cause a loop |
| EventNotifier | 12 | Indicates that the node can be used to subscribe to events |
| Value | 13 | The value of a variable |
| DataType | 14 | The node id of the data type for the variable value |
| ValueRank | 15 | The number of dimensions in the value |
| ArrayDimensions | 16 | The length for each dimension of an array value |
| AccessLevel | 17 | How a variable value may be accessed |
| UserAccessLevel | 18 | How a variable value may be accessed after taking the user's access rights into account |
| MinimumSamplingInterval | 19 | Specifies (in milliseconds) how fast the server can reasonably sample the value for changes |
| Historizing | 20 | Specifies whether the server is actively collecting historical data for the variable |
| Executable | 21 | Whether the method can be called |
| UserExecutable | 22 | Whether the method can be called by the current user |

# Appendix C: Base Information Model Reference

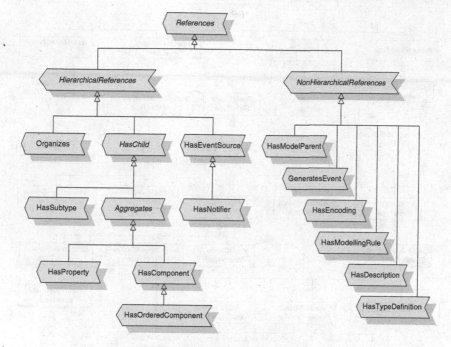

**Fig. C.1** ReferenceType Hierarchy

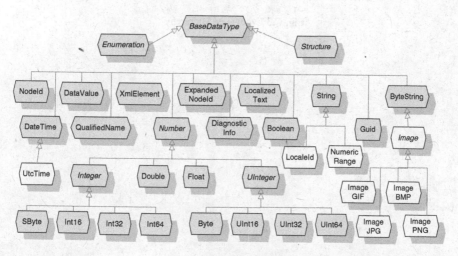

**Fig. C.2** DataType Hierarchy

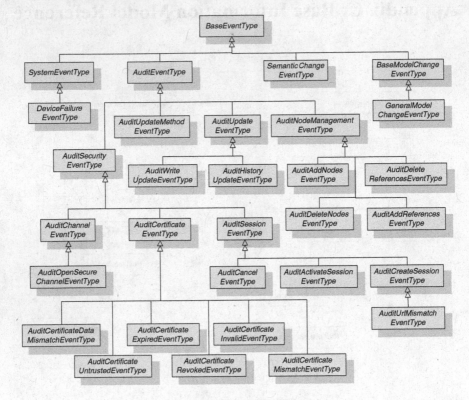

**Fig. C.3** EventType Hierarchy

# Index